Information Technology Law in the Czech Republic

Information Technology Law in the Czech Republic

Radim Polčák
Jakub Harašta
Pavel Koukal
Tereza Kyselovská
Pavel Loutocký
Matěj Myška
Michal Petr
Tomáš Gřivna
Josef Donát
Tomáš Ščerba
Miroslav Uřičař

This book was originally published as a monograph in the International Encyclopaedia of Laws/Privacy and Technology Law.

Founding Editor: Roger Blanpain
General Editor: Frank Hendrickx
Volume Editors: Jos Dumortier, Pieter Gryffroy, Ruben Roex & Yung Shin Van Der Sype

Wolters Kluwer

Published by:
Kluwer Law International B.V.
PO Box 316
2400 AH Alphen aan den Rijn
The Netherlands
E-mail: lrs-sales@wolterskluwer.com
Website: www.wolterskluwer.com/en/solutions/kluwerlawinternational

Sold and distributed by:
Wolters Kluwer Legal & Regulatory U.S.
920 Links Avenue
Landisville, PA 17538
United States of America
E-mail: customer.service@wolterskluwer.com

ISBN 978-94-035-0817-7

e-Book: ISBN 978-94-035-0827-6
web-PDF: ISBN 978-94-035-0837-5

The Authors

Prof. JUDr Radim Polčák, Ph.D. is the vice-rector of Masaryk University (muni.cz) and the Head of the Institute of Law and Technology at the Faculty of Law, Masaryk University (cyber.law.muni.cz). He is a founding fellow of the European Law Institute and the European Academy of Law and Information and Communication Technology (ICT), a panellist at the ADR.eu and a member of academic institutions and scientific consortia around the EU. He is the general chair of the Cyberspace conference (cyberspace.muni.cz), the founder of the *Masaryk University Journal of Law and Technology* (mujlt.law.muni.cz) and the *Review of Law and Technology* (in Czech – revue.law.muni.cz). He also served as the Special Adviser for Robotics and Data Protection Policy to the European Commission and as the head of expert committee that developed the Czech Cybersecurity Act. Currently, Doc. Polčák serves as the national expert for the Czech Republic at the Global Partnership for Artificial Intelligence (GPAI), as a member of the Czech Digital Team (advisory board of the Deputy Prime Minister for digitization), of the Legislative Council of the Czech Government and of the Appellate Committee of NCISA. Doc. Polčák authored or co-authored over 150 scientific papers, books and articles namely on topics related to cyberlaw and legal philosophy.

JUDr Josef Donát, LLM, is a Czech lawyer, partner of ROWAN LEGAL, arbitrator and registered mediator, and holder of several prestigious domestic and foreign awards in the field of ICT law (Lawyer of the Year, Legal 500, Chambers & Partners Europe). In his practice, he has long been involved in large-scale projects on digitalization, electronic identification, cloud computing, cybersecurity, and delivery of information systems. He is the principal author of the unique publication *Law on the Net: a guide to law on the internet* (2016), he also contributed to various other publications such as *Law on the Right to Digital Acts* (2021), *Cyber Law in the Czech Republic* (2020), and the *Personal Data Processing Act* (2019). He regularly lectures at universities and international conferences.

The Authors

Prof. JUDr Tomáš Gřivna, Ph.D. is the Head of the Department of Criminal Law at the Law Faculty of Charles University. He teaches and publishes in criminal law and cybercrime. He is a member of editorial boards of various criminal law-focused legal journals in the Czech Republic (e.g., *Criminal law* published by Wolters Kluwer Czech Republic, *Criminal Law Review* published by C. H. Beck). He is also a practising lawyer, a member of the Czech Bar Association, vice-president of the Defence Union of the Czech Republic and expert advisor to various business and public bodies. Doc Gřivna is author or co-author of over 180 scientific papers, books, commentaries and articles namely on topics related to criminal law.

JUDr Jakub Harašta, Ph.D. is an assistant professor at the Institute of Law and Technology, the Faculty of Law, Masaryk University. He earned Master's degrees in Law (2013) and Security Studies (2020), and a Ph.D. in Law (2018) at Masaryk University. He is editor-in-chief of *Masaryk University Journal of Law and Technology*, former guest research fellow at Minerva Centre for the Rule of Law under Extreme Conditions, University of Haifa (2015) and former post-doctoral fellow at Centre for Cyber Law and Policy (2018). Dr Harašta is actively engaged in research in cyber security, electronic evidence and legal informatics.

Doc. JUDr Pavel Koukal, Ph.D. is an associate professor within the Department of Civil law and also the Institute of Law and Technology, Faculty of Law, Masaryk University. He is an expert in the area of the intellectual property protection, but he has also authored various publications in the area of the civil law and private international law as well. Doc. Koukal has been involved as the national expert in the study on the industrial designs protection and national rapporteur in several comparative studies of the World Association of Comparative Law. He also collaborates with the University of Krems, the University of Göttingen and Kazimieras Simonavicius University in the framework of the DDM4SME project. Doc. Koukal is the main co-author of the Czech Commentary to the Trademarks Act, the Industrial Designs Protection Act and co-author of the Commentary to the Czech Civil Code. His 2019 habilitation thesis focused on the public domain in copyright law and its human rights foundations.

JUDr Tereza Kyselovská, Ph.D. is an assistant professor at the Department of International and European Law at the Faculty of Law, Masaryk University. She is a member of the Editorial Board of the *Journal of Jurisprudence and Legal Practice* and member of the Academic Senate of the Faculty of law. In her pedagogical and scientific work, she mainly focuses on the issues of private international law, intellectual property rights and the influence of Internet and electronization.

JUDr Pavel Loutocký, Ph.D. is a post-doctorate researcher and lecturer at the Institute of Law and Technology, Faculty of Law, Masaryk University. He is also a post-doctorate researcher and head of the section at the Centre for Education, Research and Innovation in Information and Communication Technologies, Faculty of Informatics, Masaryk University. He is an external lecturer at the Queen Mary University of London and Georg-August-Universität Göttingen. He has completed a year of studies at the University of Abertay, Dundee, Scotland (2010) and a Ph.D. at the Institute of Law and Technology (2019), Masaryk University, Faculty of Law. Since 2012, he has been a regular member of selected working groups within the United Nations Commission on International Trade Law (UNCITRAL). Dr Loutocký is actively engaged in research and teaching in the area of electronic documents and contracting, cybersecurity, online consumer protection, Online Dispute Resolution (ODR) or eGovernment.

Doc. JUDr Matěj Myška, Ph.D. is an associate professor and Deputy Head of the Institute of Law and Technology, Faculty of Law, Masaryk University (cyber.law.muni.cz). He serves as the Guarantor of the LLM programme in ICT Law (llm.law.muni.cz) and coordinator of English-taught Ph.D. programmes at the Faculty of Law (phd.law.muni.cz). He is the General Chair of the national conference *České arvo a informační technologie* (cpit.law.muni.cz) and member of the organizing committee of the international conference Cyberspace (cyberspace.muni.cz). He also assists the Technology Transfer Office of Masaryk University (ctt.muni.cz) as a lawyer. He is an external lecturer at the University of Göttingen. His professional focus lies in ICT law and intellectual property, particularly digital copyright. In his latest book, he dealt with the exceptions and limitations in the digital environment (Wolters Kluwer, 2020).

The Authors

Doc. JUDr Michal Petr, Ph.D. is the Head of the Department of International and European Law at the Faculty of Law of the Palacky University in Olomouc, Czech Republic. He works there as a senior researcher focusing on economic aspects of EU integration, in particular competition law, state aid, public procurement and regulation of network industries. He gained his experience while working for the Organisation for Economic Co-operation and Development (OECD) in 2011 and 2012 and especially at the Czech Competition Authority (CCA), where he was working since 2003, in 2010–2015 as its Vice-Chairman responsible for completion law and policy. He authored numerous publications concerning EU law, regulation of network industries and due process. He is a member of the advisory appellate committee of the CCA and the Czech National Bank (CNB).

JUDr Tomáš Ščerba, Ph.D. is an attorney-at-law admitted to the Bar in the Czech Republic and Local Partner at the Prague office of leading international law firm White & Case, with twelve years of experience as a practising attorney under his belt. He studied at the law faculty of Ghent University and graduated from Masaryk University in Brno where he was awarded his JD and PhD for work on the legal aspects of electronic contracts. Dr Ščerba regularly lectures at Czech and foreign universities and at the Institute of Law and State of the Czech Academy of Science, and is a sought-after speaker at various expert conferences. His primary focus is on information and telecommunications technology law with particular emphasis on cyber security, electronic documents, digital disruption projects, AI, regulatory compliance, data processing and IT/IP transactions. He is a member of the Editorial Board of *Masaryk University Journal of Law and Technology* as well as other prestigious periodicals.

JUDr Miroslav Uřičař is a partner and attorney-at-law at LEGALITÉ advokátní kancelář s.r.o. (LEGALITÉ Lawyers). In his practice, Miroslav specializes mainly in privacy and personal data protection, regulatory issues related to network industries, especially the electronic communications and other network industries, compliance, ICT law, and litigation. He draws on his practical experience and knowledge of the electronic communications sector and related areas (TV broadcasting, payment transactions regulation and others) and also from his eighteen-year tenure in top-managerial positions with a leading provider of electronic communications services, T-Mobile Czech Republic – as General Counsel, he was responsible for the legal department and departments of regulation, external relations, corporate security and compliance. Dr Uřičař is also an arbitrator of the Arbitration Court attached to the Economic Chamber of the Czech

Republic and the Agricultural Chamber of the Ceska Republika (Czech Republic) (CR), member of the Commission for Administrative Law of the Legislative Council of the Government of the CR, member of the Remonstrance Commission of the Energy Regulatory Office as well as a cooperating legal expert of the professional peer-reviewed scholarly magazine on information systems security, administration and risk management – Data Security Management.

The authorships of various sections in this monograph are as follows:

- Radim Polčák – General Introduction (Chapters 1–5), Part V, Chapters 1, 2, 4.
- Josef Donát – Part I, Chapter 7, Part III, Chapters 4, 7.
- Tomáš Gřivna – Part VI.
- Jakub Harašta – Part I, Chapter 8, Part II, Part V, Chapter 3.
- Pavel Koukal – Part III, Chapter 6, Part IV, Chapters 1, 2, 3, 6, 8.
- Tereza Kyselovská – Part I, Chapter 3.
- Pavel Loutocký – Part III, Chapters 1, 2, 3, 5.
- Matěj Myška – Part IV, Chapters 4, 5, 7.
- Michal Petr – Part I, Chapter 4.
- Tomáš Ščerba – Part I, Chapters 1, 2.
- Miroslav Uřičař – Part I, Chapters 5, 6.

The Authors

Table of Contents

List of Abbreviations

ADR	Alternative Dispute Resolution
ACISS	Act on Certain Information Society Services
AEC	Certain Related Acts
API	Application Programming Interface
B2B	Business-to-Business
B2C	Business-to-Consumer
CAD	Computer-Aided Design
ccTLD	Country-Code Top Level Domain
CCA	Czech Competition Authority
CERT	Community Emergency Response Team
CSU	Český Statistický Úřad (Czech Statistical Office)
CTO	Czech Telecommunications Office
CJEU	Court of Justice of the European Communities
CNB	Czech National Bank
CZ.NIC, z.s.p.o.	Czech National Domain Authority for.cz domain registry
CLA	Collection of Laws and International Treaties
CMO	Collective Management Organization
CR	Česká Republika (Czech Republic)
CSIRT	Computer Security Incident Response Team
CZK	Česká koruna (Czech Crown)
DLT	Distributed Ledger Technology
DSM	Digital Single Market
EC	European Communities
ECSPR	European Crowdfunding Service Provider Regulation
EEA	European Economic Area
EU	European Union
ENISA	European Union Agency for Cybersecurity
GTC	General Terms and Conditions
GUI	Graphical User Interface

List of Abbreviations

IDI	Integrated Data Interface
IHIS	Institute of Health Information and Statistics of the Czech Republic
ICT	Information and Communication Technology
ISA	Information Systems of Public Administration
ISBR	Information System of Basic Registers
ISSP	Information Society Service Provider
ISO	International Organization for Standardization
IZIP	Internetová Zdravotní Knížka Pacienta (Internet Health Book of a Patient)
NATO	North Atlantic Treaty Organisation
NBU	Národní Bezpečnostní Uřad (National Security Authority)
NCISA	National Office for Cyber and Information Security
OECD	Organisation for Economic Cooperation and Development
PILA	Private International Law Act
PRS	Public Regulated Service
RRTV	Radio and Television Broadcasting Council
Sb.	Sbírka zákonů (Collection of Laws of the Czech Republic)
SMS	Short Message Service
SPT	Správa Pošt a Telekomunikací (Post and Telecommunications Administration)
UGC	User-generated Content
UK	United Kingdom
US	Ústavní Soud (Constitutional Court of the Czech Republic)
UNCTAD	United Nations Conference on Trade and Development
UOHS	Office for the Protection of Competition
UOOU	Office for the Protection of Personal Data
WIPO	World Intellectual Property Organization

General Introduction

Chapter 1. General Background of the Country

§1. General Information

1. The Czech Republic [*Česká republika*] is a typical example of a continental European parliamentary democracy. It was established on 1 January 1993 as a successor to the former Czechoslovakia when the former federation was split into two new countries, the Czech Republic and the Slovak Republic (Slovakia).

2. The Czech Republic is a landlocked country having a total area of 78,866 km^2 – which consists mostly of arable land and forests. It is situated in the middle of central Europe and has borders with Austria, Germany, Poland and Slovakia. The total population of the country slightly exceeds 10 million. The local currency is the Czech Crown (CZK) [Koruna] having a current exchange rate with the euro at approximately CZK 25 CZK/ EUR 1. The gross national product per capita in 2021 was U.S. dollar (USD) 24,430 and the Czech economy is currently rated at above 90% of the EU average on the Purchasing Power Standards scale.[1]

§2. Government

3. The system of government is based on the model of division of powers. The supreme lawmaking body is the Parliament, which consists of two chambers – the Chamber of Deputies [*Poslanecká sněmovna*] and the Senate [*Senát*]. Most bills (with exceptions) must be passed by both the chambers; however, a refusal by the Senate might be overruled by the Chamber of Deputies similarly as a presidential veto.

4. Despite the fact that the Czech Republic is a unitary country, there also exist territorial self-governing units with some decentralized lawmaking and executive powers, namely municipalities (ground level of territorial self-governance) and regions (higher level of territorial self-governance). Their powers, however, only include particular matters of local interest.

1. *See* the Purchasing power adjusted GDP per capita report by Eurostat at ec.europa.eu/eurostat, code: sdg_10_10.

5. Executive powers are, in general, divided between the government, ministries and supreme State authorities. The government is responsible to the Chamber of Deputies and the ministries respond to the government. Other supreme State offices are either independent (like in the case of the Czech National Bank (CNB) or the Supreme Audit Office) or subordinate to the government or the Parliament. The structure of the ministries is as follows:

- Ministry for Regional Development.
- Ministry of the Environment.
- Ministry of Labour and Social Affairs.
- Ministry of Interior.
- Ministry of Foreign Affairs.
- Ministry of Defence.
- Ministry of Industry and Trade.
- Ministry of Health.
- Ministry of Justice.
- Ministry of Finance.
- Ministry of Education, Youth and Sports.
- Ministry of Transport.
- Ministry of Agriculture.
- Ministry of Culture.

6. In 2007, there was a change made in the organization of ministries that was relevant to the Information and Communications Technology (ICT) sector, when the Ministry of Informatics was dissolved and its powers were attributed to other ministries.

§3. Judiciary

7. Judicial powers are exercised by independent courts, which form a unified hierarchy within the following structure:

(1) District courts [*okresní soud*] – in Brno, named as the municipal courts [*městský soud*]; in Prague, named as circuit courts [*obvodní soud*].
(2) Regional courts [*krajský soud*] – in Prague, named as the municipal courts [*městský soud*].
(3) Higher courts [*vrchní soud*].
(4) Supreme Courts, in particular the Supreme Court [*Nejvyšší Soud (NS)*] and the Supreme Administrative Court [*Nejvyšší správní soud (NSS)*].

8. There are, in general, three types of litigation, that is, civil, criminal and administrative. While the system of courts is unified (with an exception at the level of Supreme Courts), there are no special courts, but specialized chambers and divisions within the general courts. Most procedures, depending on the merits, commence at the level of district or regional courts. The particular rules for delimitation of jurisdictions are set in the procedural codes:

- Act No. 141/1961 Sbirka zakonu (Sb.), Code of Criminal Procedure.
- Act No. 99/1963 Sb., Code of Civil Procedure (currently being reviewed).
- Act No. 150/2002 Sb., Code of Administrative Procedure.

9. In civil or criminal procedure, the line of instances is usually set as follows (depending on the merits of the case):

District Court (first instance) – Regional Court (appeal) – Supreme Court (cassation)
or
Regional Court (first instance) – Higher Court (appeal) – Supreme Court (cassation).

10. All decisions of the State administration are, with minor exceptions, reviewable by independent courts within the regime of administrative justice. In administrative procedure, there are only two instances,[2] that is:

Regional Court (First Instance) – Supreme Administrative Court (Cassation).

11. While the main aim of the general courts is to protect legality at the level of statutory law (*see* below), the protection of constitutionality and basic rights falls within the scope of the jurisdiction of the Constitutional Court [*Ústavní soud*]. Not being a part of the system of regular courts, the Constitutional Court might quash any decision or piece of legislation of any Czech institution in cases when it is contrary to the Constitutional Order. Therefore, the Constitutional Court plays an important role both in lawmaking and the judiciary.

§4. Sources of Law

12. Sources of black-letter law are divided according to their legal importance into three major groups:

- Constitutional Order [*Ústavní pořádek*], which consists of the Constitution [*Ústava*], the Charter of Fundamental Rights and Basic Freedoms [*Listina základních práv a svobod*] and other constitutional Acts [*ústavní zákony*].
- Statutory law, which consists of Acts of Parliament [*zákony*] and legal measures of the Senate[3] [*zákonná opatření Senátu*].
- Under-statutory law (by-laws), which consists of governmental decrees [*nařízení vlády*], ministerial decrees [*vyhlášky ministerstev*], decrees of supreme State authorities [*vyhlášky ústředních orgánů státní správy*], decrees of municipalities

2. It is to be noted that, in administrative procedures, the courts decide only on disputes that have arisen from administrative proceedings and where regular revision instruments were already unsuccessfully used by the claimant.
3. When the Chamber of Deputies is dissolved, the Senate may pass legal measures that substitute Acts of the Parliament. After re-assembly of the Chamber of Deputies, the measures then have to be approved – or they are automatically derogated.

[*nařízení obcí*], decrees of regions [*nařízení krajů*], ordinances of municipalities [*obecně závazné vyhlášky obcí*] and ordinances of regions [*obecnězávazné vyhlášky krajů*].

13. The Czech Republic inherited the legal system of former socialist Czechoslovakia. Since the political changes in 1989, many parts of statutory law have been newly created or substantially amended. However, some core codifications, namely the Code of Civil Procedure, Code of Criminal Procedure and others, were only marginally amended and still wait for recodification.

14. Statutory laws and by-laws that apply on the entire territory of the country are published in the Collection of Laws (*Sbírka zákonů* – further referred to as 'Sb.'). The official version of the Sbírka zákonů is still published in print, while only informative offprints are made available online.[4] The government had repeatedly announced a digital promulgation system, named eSbírka, that should provide for official or at least informative versions of full texts of applicable Czech laws. However, this system has still not been launched with the planned rollout currently expected at the beginning of 2022.

15. Unfortunately, there is no general translation service for Czech legislation, so only a few particular Acts and codes are freely available in English or other language versions, mostly on the websites of ministries and other supreme authorities. Particular translations are made mostly on a commercial basis – and normally are not freely accessible.

16. Unlike Sbírka zákonů, there is online publication platform for local by-laws called Sbírka právních předpisů (Collection of Legal Regulations). It was launched in January 2022 and the law[5] requires all regions and municipalities, under the sanction if inapplicability, to upload their complete set of by-laws before January 2025.

17. Besides statutes, there is a growing importance of case law of the Higher and Supreme Courts. The still ongoing debate about the relevance of case law was clarified by jurisprudence of the Constitutional Court in favour of the binding effect of established case law. Thus, we can state that the case law of the Supreme Courts represents one of the sources of Czech law.

In this respect, the Constitutional Court held in III. US 252/04 that:

> the settled court interpretation shall act (-) as the basis for deciding similar future cases in order to preserve the principles of legal certainty, foreseeability of law, protection of justified legal expectations and formal justice (equality).

4. The Internet version of the Sbírka zákonů containing the offprints of printed official texts is available on the Internet at: http://aplikace.mvcr.cz/sbirka-zakonu/.
5. *See* Act No. 35/2021 Sb.

18. Case law of the Supreme Courts and the Constitutional Court is now published on the Internet.[6] The databases are freely accessible and are continuously being updated by older decisions. There are also issued official collections of the decisions of the Supreme Court, the Supreme Administrative Court and the Constitutional Court[7] – these publications include the most important decisions as selected by special publication chambers.

19. Case law of lower courts is not generally available online. Anonymized texts of decisions of lower courts are only available upon individual requests under the Freedom of Information Act (Act. No. 106/1999 Sb.). Selected decisions of lower courts are also seldom chosen for publication in collections of decision of the Supreme Court or Supreme Administrative Court.

§5. International and European Law

20. The Czech Republic is a monist country, which means that sources of international public law, namely international treaties, are directly enforceable. The grounds for direct applicability of international treaties are laid down in Article 10 of the Constitution, which reads as follows:

> **Art. 10**
>
> Promulgated international agreements, the ratification of which has been approved by the Parliament and which are binding on the Czech Republic, shall constitute a part of the legal order; should an international agreement make provision contrary to a law, the international agreement shall be applied.

21. International treaties have a priority in application over local statutory laws. The possible conflict between directly enforceable international agreements and the Constitutional Order is prevented by Article 87/2, which lays down the procedure of control of constitutional conformity of international agreements by the Constitutional Court prior to their ratification. This provision reads as follows:

> (2) The Constitutional Court shall also decide on the conformity of international agreements under Art. 10a and Art. 49 with the constitutional order prior to their ratification. Until a ruling of the Constitutional Court is delivered, an agreement cannot be ratified.

22. The Czech Republic became a Member State of the European Union (EU) on 1 May 2004; directly applicable EU laws, namely the EU regulations, now have *de iure* the position of international agreements. Therefore, they have the priority in application over local statutory laws.

---

6. The database of the Supreme Court is at: www.nsoud.cz; the database of the Supreme Administrative Court is at: www.nssoud.cz and the database of the Constitutional Court is at: nalus.usoud.cz.
7. The Constitutional Court also issues a special collection of selected decisions translated into English.

23. The Czech Republic is also a member of the Council of Europe and is subject to the jurisdiction of the European Court of Human Rights. Besides this, the Czech Republic is also a member of more than four hundred bilateral and over three hundred multilateral international agreements.

Chapter 2. Telecommunications Infrastructure

§1. Introductory Note to Statistical Figures

24. As the Czech Republic has a centralized statistical service, most of the below data can be taken from the Czech Statistical Office [*Český statistický úřad (CSU)*], also, since most of the below data was collected and processed according to Regulation (EC) No. 808/2004, concerning Community statistics on the information society, it may also be directly compared with similar data from the other EU Member States.

25. The structure of this chapter follows the structure of statistical research focusing separately on landlines, mobile services and Internet access. There might occur slight differences between the below results and figures published by the European Statistical Office (EUROSTAT) caused by the fact that the Czech Statistical Office gathers data for all individuals above 16 years of age (EUROSTAT publishes data for individuals between 16 and 74 years of age) and for all households (EUROSTAT publishes data only for households with at least one member with age between 16 and 74 years).

§2. Landlines

26. Landlines for voice communications were, until 2000, provided by the State-owned (later privatized) telecommunications company, Správa Pošt a Telekomunikací (SPT) Telecom. The largest growth of the landline infrastructure occurred around 1995–2000, when landlines became highly demanded by households as well as by business units. The end of the monopoly on mobile voice services, the development of mobile networks and the consequent decrease in prices for mobile services led to a decline in this growth and, later, even to a decline in the absolute numbers of landlines. Consequently, the recent number of landlines is getting close to numbers at the beginning of the 1990s. Table 1 demonstrates development in the number of landlines showing changes after the political transition in the 1990s and the recent decline due to growth in mobile voice and data services (data in the number of landlines × 1000).

Table 1 Number of Landlines in the Czech Republic

	1989	*1995*	*2000*	*2005*	*2010*	*2015*	*2020*
Landlines	1557	2395	3676	3210	2351	1896	1334

Source: Data taken from the Czech Statistical Office Report No. 061004-22, Table A.2.

§3. Mobile Networks

27. The growth in commercial mobile networks was, from the beginning of the 1990s, burdened by the persisting monopoly of SPT Telecom and of its branch, Eurotel. Substantial growth in the penetration of Czech household and commercial sectors by mobile network services came first with the introduction of the GSM standard (earlier commercial services used the NMT standard) – together with partial de-monopolization of the Czech market. Table 2 shows the growth in the number of activated Subscriber Identity Module (SIM) cards from 1995 onwards. Figures from past several years clearly indicate that the mobile market has been saturated and that further growth in absolute figures is not very likely to occur (data in the number of active SIM cards × 1,000).

Table 2 Number of Active SIM Cards in the Czech Republic

	1995	*2000*	*2005*	*2010*	*2015*	*2020*
Active SIMs	456	4338	11,450	12,992	14,017	14,600

Source: Data taken from the Czech Statistical Office Report No. 061004-22, Table A.3.

28. The structure of mobile services that are being used among the Czech population still corresponds with remaining relatively high prices, namely of data services, and a relatively low level of broadband mobile coverage compared to other EU Member States. Therefore, the most frequently used are voice services and Short Message Service (SMS). The use of mobile broadband Internet grew dramatically between 2012 and 2021 from 8.3% to 87.2%,[8] whereas the major increase in past two years was probably also driven by the COVID-19 pandemic and consequent increase in the use of information society services. Despite statistical figures showing that broadband wireless Internet access is available to 100% of users of mobile networks,[9] the actual coverage of broadband services is still limited namely in less populated areas, including a significant part of the railway connection between two biggest cities in the Czech Republic, Praha and Brno.

29. Given the above figures, it is a bit paradoxical that the mobile telecommunications market is divided only between three dominant operators. This lack of competition then results in numerous technological and economic effects, including the general price level of mobile services. In a large comparative study carried out by the European Commission in 2017 and published in 2018, the Czech Republic was listed among the EU-members with the most expensive mobile rates (together with Hungary, Cyprus and Greece).[10]

8. Data taken from Czech Statistical Office Report – IT in Households and among Individuals, Table 3.
9. *See* Czech Statistical Office Report ICT Infrastructure, Table A.11.
10. *See* the Mobile Broadband Prices in Europe 2017 (Final Report and Executive Summary), p. 6.

§4. INTERNET ACCESS

30. Unlike in cases of some of the other new EU Member States, the Czech Republic has relatively good predispositions for easy coverage of a relatively high proportion of its population by broadband Internet connectivity. Consequently, the demand for broadband Internet access in the business sector as well as among households can be satisfied without a need for any massive or extraordinary investments countering geographical or other natural constraints.

31. The main statistical criterion of the development of Internet infrastructure is the penetration of the Czech population with Internet access (*see* below). Table 3 demonstrates the use of Internet among various groups of the Czech population (data in % of Internet users). The only significant change in past years can be observed in higher age groups and among the population with basic education.

Table 3 Internet Users in the Czech Republic.

Group	*2005*	*2010*	*2015*	*2021*
Age 16–24	63.7	92.3	97.0	99.3
Age 25–34	40.5	83.1	95.4	98.6
Age 35–44	41.1	79.7	93.9	97.9
Age 45–56	29.3	65.8	86.7	96.5
Age 55–64	15.3	42.1	68.0	84.0
Age 65+	2.2	13.2	28.4	42.7
Basic education	2.1	15.3	49.2	76.8
Higher education	41.7	73.5	95.0	98.2
University education	72.1	87.9	99.4	99.6

Source: Data taken from Czech Statistical Office Report No. 061004-22, Table C2.

32. The proportion of broadband versus low bandwidth Internet connection is not a relevant criterion in the Czech Republic, as broadband represents a standard type of Internet connection. Fixed Internet connection was in 2020 mostly through xDSL (41.7%), cable TV (26.8%) and fibre optics (31.5%). The development from xDSL towards greater proportion of faster fibre optics is relatively slow – from 24.5% in 2015.[11]

33. Internet users access information society services mostly through PCs (49.5%), laptops (79.6%) and mobile phones (72.1%). There is also steadily

11. *See* Czech Statistical Office report ICT Infrastructure, part Internet Infrastructure, Table A.1.

growing percentage of Internet users who access these services with tablets (304%), smart TVs (44.8%) and other small devices such as e-book readers, smart watches etc. (23.4%).[12]

34. Major Czech Internet access providers are organized in Neutral Internet X-change.[13] Its role is to coordinate interconnectivity and technology standardization among its members. The recent capacity that is being administered by its members is approximately 12,000 Gbps. Another major association that provides Internet connectivity to academic institutions is the CESNET.[14]

12. *See* Czech Statistical Office report No. 062004-21, Table 4.2.
13. *See* nix.cz.
14. *See* cesnet.cz.

Chapter 3. The Information and Communications Technology Market

§1. Structure and Size of the ICT Market

35. The Czech ICT market is described here using the United Nations Conference on Trade and Development (UNCTAD) methodology that makes a distinction on the supply side of the ICT market to manufacturing, wholesale, telecommunications and computer-related services. Relevant factors for evaluating shape and performance of ICT market according to this methodology include sector size, business performance, investment, employment and innovation, research & development.[15]

36. The ICT sector does not represent overly significant segment of the Czech economy. Sales in all above ICT industries in the Czech Republic amounted in 2020 at roughly 6.5% of total sales generated in the Czech economy. The significance of the ICT market to the Czech economy has not even evolved throughout the past two decades. In 2010, the percentual share of sales in ICT industries was 6.1%. It then declined around 2013 to 5.6% but got back to 6.5% by 2020.[16]

37. Despite significant public support going to technology start-ups, small business units from ICT industries generate only 0.2% of sales generated in the Czech Republic by units with up to 49 employees. To the contrary, the share of large ICT enterprises (more than 250 employees) on overall sales in the Czech economy in this segment represents 7.8%.[17]

§2. Performance and Added Value

38. Overall sales in ICT seem not overly significant to the Czech economy, but other statistical figures show that the Czech ICT sector consists of industries that provide for relatively high added value.

39. Statistical reports mostly deduct added value from profitability. In that respect, it is of note that ICT industries generated 8.3% of overall profit of Czech businesses,[18] while being only at 6.5% of annual turnover (*see* above). Despite the biggest increase in profitability of ICT industries came in 2020 and might have been linked with the COVID-19 pandemic, there was a steady increase of profitability across the ICT sector since 2010.

15. *See* the UNCTAD Manual for the Production of Statistics on the Information Economy [2009 Revised edition], document No. UNCTAD/SDTE/ECB/2007/2/REV.1, available at unctad.org, p. 13.
16. *See* Czech Statistical Office Report Sectors of Information Economy, Table 7, available at czso.cz.
17. *See ibid.*
18. *See* Czech Statistical Office Report Sectors of Information Economy, Table 16, available at czso.cz.

40. Besides profitability, there might be also other ways of looking at added value and respective indicators thereof. One of possible indicators of added value might be also research & development costs and especially the costs of research staff.

41. The overall contribution of the Czech ICT sector to research & development personnel costs incurred by business units in the Czech Republic is steadily above 20% since 2005 and reached 31.4% in 2020.[19] That is relatively very high number, considering the above contribution of Czech ICT sector on overall turnover if Czech business units.

42. In that respect, it is also of note that nearly zero research and development costs are incurred in the Czech Republic by wholesale and telecommunications businesses. As only slightly above 1% of Czech research and development personnel costs are incurred by ICT manufacturing business, it means that more than 29% of personnel costs that are invested by Czech business units into research and development go to ICT services.[20]

43. The above figures demonstrate that ICT manufacture, yet significantly contributing on overall sales in Czech ICT and on the overall Czech exports, is not based on local research. Similarly, telecommunications that are steadily proving a highly profitable industry in the Czech Republic, show nearly no investment in research & development which means that these high-margin sales are based on results of research done outside the Czech Republic.

§3. Labour Market in ICT

44. The size of the ICT sector in the Czech Republic steadily corresponds to employment data. In 2020, ICT industries employed 4.3% of Czech employees which represents a steady increase from 3% in 2005.[21] As positions in ICT regularly require relatively higher qualifications and especially ICT services normally operate with higher added value, it is no wonder that wages are above the average of the Czech private sector. Statistics show that employees in ICT industries earned 169% of average wages in Czech private sector with lowest rate in ICT manufacture (101.2%) and highest in ICT services (191.1%).

45. The percentage of Czech population employed in ICT was in the past years oscillating around the average of EU27. However, Czech ICT sector has the worst gender balance in the EU with below 20% of women overall employed in ICT and

19. *See* Czech Statistical Office Report Sectors of Information Economy, Table 12, available at czso.cz.
20. *See ibid.*
21. *See* Czech Statistical Office Report Sectors of Information Economy, Table 2, available at czso.cz.

below 12% in managerial positions.[22] Gender balance is no better in higher education where numbers from 2019 indicated only 16% of women among university students in ICT and 18% among graduates – both being below the EU27 average.[23] Several public and private initiatives aim at improving this situation by gender-oriented promoting of ICT education and employment opportunities.[24]

---

22. *See* Czech Statistical Office publication Digital Economy in Numbers (2021), p. 12, available at czso.cz.
23. *See* Czech Statistical Office Report ICT Experts, Students and Graduates, Table B5, available at czso.cz.
24. *See* for example czechitas.cz.

Chapter 4. E-commerce: Facts and Figures

§1. Introductory Note to E-commerce and Statistical Figures

46. E-commerce historically fell under the jurisdiction of the Ministry of Informatics.[25] After its dissolution in 2007 and the split of its powers into other ministries and central offices, there has been no central State authority for the development of the information society and digital economy. The Government of the Czech Republic established in 2015 the Governmental Council for the Information Society [*Rada vlády pro informační společnost*] in order to replace the policy-making role of the dissolved ministry. The Council was not active since its establishment and it started frequently meeting only in 2021. At the beginning of 2022, the Government presented a draft update of its Statute that should more clearly define its role namely in Digital Czechia programme[26] in policymaking regarding the Digital Czechia strategy. However, the role of the Council is primarily envisaged in e-government initiatives. Consequently, the governmental roles in various agendas of digital economy, incl. executive and regulatory powers representing the Czech Republic at EU bodies and institutions, legislative drafting etc. remain split mostly between the Ministry of Industry and Trade, Czech Telecommunications Office (CTO), Ministry of Regional Development and the Office of the Government. Minor roles in particular segments of the digital economy are also played by other ministries such as the Ministry of Transportation, Ministry of Finance and others.

47. Representative large-scale statistical research in the sector of information society services, including digital economy, is periodically conducted by the Czech Statistical Office [CSU], having its results freely available on the webpage of the Office at: www.czso.cz – in Czech and English.

48. Growth in both Business-to-Business (B2B) and Business-to-Consumer (B2C) e-commerce is driven by the growing penetration of information society services. This tendency can be illustrated in Table 5 by the comparison of percentage of households that have an Internet connection. The statistics is broken down to five groups of households according to income levels. While the availability of Internet connection is currently nearly total in the highest three quintiles, it is still only over a half in the 20% (1st quintile) of the lowest-income households with no significant increase from 2016. The statistics only shows significant growth between 2016 and 2021 in the middle-income segment (3rd quintile).

---

25. The main political document produced by the Ministry of Informatics in order to outline the priority areas of the development of e-commerce was the White Book on Electronic Commerce [*Bílá kniha o elektronickém obchodu*]. It is available only in Czech at archived webpages of the dissolved ministry at: http://www.komora.cz/Files/Soubory/White-paper.doc.
26. Digital Czechia is a coordinated set of projects and strategies that aims at the development of the Czech information society- *see* digitalnicesko.cz (only available in Czech).

Table 5 Percentage of Households That Have an Internet Connection

Household income	*% of households with internet*		
	2016	*2019*	*2021*
1st quintile	47.5	50.7	53.4
2nd quintile	66.7	68.9	74.4
3rd quintile	75.2	89.6	90.2
4th quintile	92.6	97	97.5
5th quintile	97.5	99.3	99.6

Source: Data taken from Czech Statistical Office Report – IT in Households, Table 4.

49. Compared to other European countries, the general penetration of households by Internet connection is still relatively low.[27] This is caused primarily by market development and by the relative lack of competition in the last-mile sector. Consequently, the prices for household connections decline slower than in other comparable countries and that still puts a major constraint on faster development in this field.

50. The Internet service accessibility among business units of all kinds is relatively high. Since 2015, business units of all sizes steadily report above 95% connectivity with current (2021) figures oscillating around 99% and speeds above 30 Mb/s.[28]

§2. E-COMMERCE: BUSINESS PERSPECTIVE

51. Table 6 demonstrates the percentage of business units using Internet for sales or purchases in 2020. These figures combine web-based transactions and transactions conducted by exchange of electronic documents. The percentage of business units that use Internet for purchasing grew substantially in the past decade. Data from 2010 show the percentage of business units purchasing on the Internet between 39% and 61% while figures from 2021 are between 60% and nearly 80%. In comparison, data from 2001 demonstrate only 12% to 30% business units purchasing over the Internet. The percentage of businesses that sell over Internet is relatively low totalling at 23%–52% and the statistics show almost no change in the past five years. The only significant growth was from 48% in 2015 to 52% in 2020 among large enterprises (more than 250 employees).

27. *See* Eurostat data on Level of internet access – households, online data code: TIN00134, available at ec.europa.eu/eurostat/.
28. Data taken from Czech Statistical Office Report Use of ICT in business units, Tables 2a and 2d.

Table 6 Percentage of Business Units Using Internet for Sales or Purchases in 2020

Size of Enterprise	*% of Businesses Purchasing Over Internet*	*% of Businesses Selling Over Internet*
Small	60.3	23.0
Medium	71.7	30.7
Large	79.7	52.3

Source: Data taken from Czech Statistical Office Report ICT in Business, Tables 6a and 6g.

52. These figures still substantially differ in most sectors according to the size of the enterprise. While smaller enterprises report relatively lower percentages, bigger enterprises use e-commerce methods much more frequently for purchasing as well as for sales.

53. Compared to a relatively low proportion of turnover performed using ICT in the past, relatively many enterprises traditionally used ICT for communicating with clients or for disseminating information via websites. Overall nearly 75% of business units (more than 90% of large enterprises) have been using corporate websites from 2010. Table 7 demonstrates the percentage of business units using corporate websites and social media accounts as of 2021.

Table 7 Business Units Using Websites and Social Media

Industry	*Using Own Website (%)*	*Using Own Social Media Account(%)*
Manufacture	85.3	45.0
Energy, waste	87.4	34.3
Construction	80.8	27.8
Retail	67.8	61.8
Accommodation	94.5	89.8
Transportation	67.4	41.4
Real Estate	75.3	35.3
ICT	94.0	83.7

Source: Data taken from Czech Statistical Office Report ICT in Business, Tables 4 and 7.

54. From the above figures, we can deduce that almost all business units have access to the Internet and actively use ICT, but still a relatively small percentage of transactions are concluded using methods of e-commerce. Thus, there is still substantial trade potential in the sector of solutions for effective e-commerce and specifically m-commerce.

55. The only sector where electronic transactions are performed in substantial proportions is in electronic banking and financial services. Here, massive development took place between 2001 and 2007, as shown in Table 8 describing the proportion of business units using e-banking. Since 2015, the number of business units that do not use e-banking became statistically irrelevant.

Table 8 Percentage of Business Units Using e-Banking

Employees	*2001 (%)*	*2007 (%)*	*2015 (%)*
10–49	42.8	85.5	92.1
50–249	61.4	93.5	95.4
250+	65.1	94.3	97.4

Source: Data taken from the Czech Statistical Office Report ICT in Enterprises, 2021, Table 2.

§3. E-COMMERCE: CONSUMER PERSPECTIVE

56. Digital skills of consumers and their motivation to use information society services represent a necessary precondition for the development of e-commerce. Table 9 shows the percentage of Internet users who used e-shops, e-banking and e-health services in 2021. Relatively low percentage of e-banking users among the age group of 16–24 years old population is caused mostly by the age limit for full legal capacity (incl. the capacity to own and independently operate a bank account) that is set in the Czech Republic at eighteen years. It is of note that the percentage of users of e-health services remained below 50% in all age groups despite these services were used also for various booking or filing procedures during the COVID-19 pandemic.

Table 9 Percentage of Internet Users Who Used E-shops, E-banking and E-health Services in 2021

Age	*e-banking*	*e-shops*	*e-health*
16–24	68.5	87.0	25.8
25–34	91.8	94.7	34.5
35–44	88.5	90.8	39.7
45–54	84.3	85.3	39.3
55–64	79.3	73.9	45.4

Age	*e-banking*	*e-shops*	*e-health*
65-74	64.0	59.1	40.1
75+	40.8	38.6	33.3

Source: Data taken from the Czech Statistical Office report Digital Skills, Table 3 and Report No. 062004-21, Table 13.1.

57. The Czech Statistical Office also processes data on some advanced digital skills such as picture or video editing, adjustment of settings of user software or programming. These skills are for nearly three decades well established as parts of curricula at Czech basic and secondary educational institutions. However, photo editing skills were reported in 2021 by less than 50% of Internet users in all age groups above 25 years. Programming skills were reported in 2021 only by approximately 10% of Internet users between 15 and 34 years, whereas the percentage in higher age groups is not statistically significant.[29]

58. The overall percentage of Czech Internet users who shopped online in 2021 exceeded 80% which makes nearly 70% of the Czech population of age above 16 years. Table 10 provides for the breakdown to particular categories of consumer goods and services in 2020. Some categories, such as clothing or consumer electronics, are steadily growing, while others, such as food and meals, have been boosted in 2020 and 2021 by the change of consumer behaviour due to the pandemic of COVID-19.

Table 10 Percentage of Czech Internet Users Aged 16+ Who Shopped Online for Consumer Goods in 2020

Consumer Goods	*Consumers (%)*
Food, drinks, pet feed	25.2
Meals – restaurants, fast food	35.4
Drugs, medicinal products	18.2
Clothing, shoes	67.8
Consumer electronics, IT	22.9
Toys	17.5
Utilities (online contracting for energy, waste etc.)	2.0
Electronic communications (online contracting for mobile phone services, internet access etc.)	7.7

Source: Data taken from the Czech Statistical Office Report No. 062004-21, Tables 14.1, 14.3, 14.12 and 14.5.

29. Data taken from the Czech Statistical Office Report Digital Skills, Table 1.

59. It is of note that despite shopping for various types of goods became relatively normal for Czech Internet users in past years, the percentage of Czech Internet users who online conclude contracts for regular consumer services is still very low. The percentage of electronic contracting for services of electronic communications is in the Czech Republic at approx. a half of the average of EU27 and the percentage of users who online concluded a contract for energy or other utilities is only at a fifth of the average of EU27.

60. Relatively low is also the percentage of Czech Internet users who engage, actively or passively, in consumer-to-consumer shared economy. Table 11 shows proportions of Internet users who sold or bought goods at some of C2C marketplaces or used some of shared accommodation or transportation services in 2021.

Table 11 Percentage of Internet Users Who Used Shared Economy Services in 2021

Age	*Sold Goods at Internet Marketplace (%)*	*Bought Goods at Internet Marketplace (%)*	*Used Shared Accommodation or Transportation Service (%)*
16–24	14.5	27.5	4,3
25–34	19.6	39.9	5,7
35–44	14.4	32.0	5,0
45–54	8.8	23.0	2,6
55–64	5.2	21.9	1,5
65-74	3.8	14.0	1,8
75+	0.8	6.9	0,4

Source: Data taken from the Czech Statistical Office Report No. 062004-21, Table 14.11.

61. The above low figures regarding the use of shared transportation services may be caused by relatively complex regulatory situation in the Czech Republic that does not allow for truly shared (i.e., unlicensed and unprofessional) services, such as Uber, to operate on the Czech market. C2C sales using contracting platforms are, to the contrary, relatively very popular. In that respect, it might be of note that the Czech market is not dominated by international online marketplaces such as eBay, but it is controlled by local service providers, such as aukro.cz. The overall sentiment of the Czech consumers towards local services can be also demonstrated on the example of search engines. In 2015, the market share of the Czech local search engine, seznam.cz, was nearly on par with Google. That, however, developed over the past years into the current situation of Google holding above 80% market share and seznam.cz being at approximately 12%.[30]

30. *See* Browser Market Share Worldwide statistics at Statcounter Globalstats – gs.statcounter.com.

Chapter 5. E-government Initiatives

§1. Shape and Performance of the Czech E-government

62. E-Government and digitization of public sector represent a permanent topic of the Czech politics. Practically all governments during the past decades included the development of e-Government and e-Justice among their priorities. However, poor coordination and project management as well as frequent procurement issues (lock-ins, high prices or even systemic corruption)[31] led to the situation that is far from perfect. In the eGovernment Benchmark 2021, the Czech e-Government services scored overall 63% which is even 5% below the EU27 average.

63. One of key reasons for sub-par performance of the Czech e-government is the absence of a centralized strategy and architecture of e-government services. Originally, there used to exist the Ministry of Informatics that was supposed to cover also the digitization of public sector, but it never actually coordinated the procurement of systems and services across the Czech public sector. Currently, there is the Office of the Main Architect of e-Government that recently (2022) moved from the Ministry of Interior to the Office of the Government, but its scope and competences are relatively limited, as it only tries to coordinate development activities that take place at various ministries and other central state bodies. There are also various state-owned IT corporations that relatively independently cater the needs of particular ministries such as NAKIT (for the Ministry of Interior), Státní pokladna Centrum sdílených služeb (SPCSS – for the Ministry of Finance) or Cendis (for the Ministry of Transport).

64. One of the aims of the current government is to better coordinate the development of public information systems and, besides moving the Office of the Main Architect of e-Government under the central Office of the Government, it also plans to integrate parts of some state corporations into two state agencies that are planned to act as delivery units for most of large e-Government initiatives. This plan, however, seems outstandingly ambitious, given the past experience with similar integration efforts.

65. Besides lack of clear visions and coordinated development, the biggest problem of the Czech e-Government remains the existing vendor lock-ins. It was quite regular in the nineties that public sector bodies started completely outsourcing their information systems to private vendors. This process was often happening under dubious circumstances and some of such procurements later turned out as major corruption scandals. In result, respective ministries and other public bodies were often left not only with information systems of rather poor quality but also without technical capabilities and even intellectual property rights necessary for their development.

---

31. *See* Ivan Langr, *Public Procurement in the Systemic Corruption Environment: Evidence from the Czech Republic*, NISPAcee Journal of Public Administration and Policy. 11. 53–79 (2018). 10.2478/nispa-2018-0013.

66. This rather wild outsourcing often led to a situation when IT staff at public bodies was limited to personnel whose role was primarily to process invoices from the vendors. Consequent loss of control and fundamental know-how over respective systems and processes is still evident. To the contrary, public sector bodies that either chose for insourcing of their information systems or at least maintained control over its know-how and process 'ownership' turned out being way more efficient in developing e-Government capacities.

67. E-Government, in the sense of a virtualised state, is a complex assembly of legal, organizational, and technical measures. In the following text, we focus namely to basic initiatives in public information systems, core public sector data, identification and document delivery. Detailed explanation of online public services is provided in Part II of this monograph. Other elements of the Czech e-Government such as cybersecurity, electronic documents, etc. are discussed in specifically dedicated parts of this monograph.

§2. Public Information Systems

68. General rules regarding the development and deployment of public information systems are laid down in Public Information Systems Act No. 365/2000 Sb. The Act has undergone more than 30 revisions since it was adopted in 2000 and its technical quality is still far from perfect, including the clarity of definitions. The scope of application of the Act includes information systems in Czech public administration that are defined in Article 2(b) as (informal translation by DeepL): 'a functional unit or part thereof providing purposeful and systematic information activities for the purposes of public administration or the performance of other functions of the state or other public corporations. Each public administration information system includes data that are organised in such a way as to enable their processing and access, operational data, as well as technical and software means or other tools enabling the performance of information activities.' The Act covers also municipal and regional information systems but excluded from its scope are information systems of public institutions in security, defence, law enforcement, intelligence and financial regulation (CNB and fraud detection unit of the Ministry of Finance).[32]

69. The Act provides for administrative procedures of governmental approval for the development of public information systems as well as for their technical accreditation and other procedures that are mostly supervised by the Ministry of Interior. It also lays down basic rules for the operation of Czech POINTs, i.e., the central contact points of public administration.[33] These contact points offer a variety of administrative services including:

(1) Abstracts from public registries (e.g., criminal registry, drivers offence registry, land registry, trade registry etc.).

---

32. The list of exclusions is provided in s. 1 of the Act No. 365/2000 Sb.
33. *See* s. 8a of the Act No. 365/2000 Sb.

(2) Abstracts from and amendments to basic registries (*see* below).
(3) Filings to some administrative procedures.
(4) Administration of data mailboxes (*see* below).
(5) Conversion of documents (digital to paper or paper to digital).
(6) Identity verification.

70. The Czech POINTs are primarily physical places (offices) that are run by local and state authorities, embassies and even by some private entities such as notaries or banks. The information system of Czech POINTs is also used remotely by other entities that are entitled to conduct all or some of the above services either for their internal use (such as public universities) or for third persons (such as attorneys).

71. Another information system that is legislated in the Act No. 365/2000 Sb. is the Portal of Public Administration. The Portal and especially its part named Citizen's Portal was envisaged as the central place through which citizens could remotely access various e-Government services and applications run by various public offices and regional or municipal administrations. Besides electronic filing, the portal allows for automation of simple administrative tasks including the issue of personal documents (ID, driving licence etc.), tax filings etc.

72. It would be technically and legally possible to amend the portal with more complex administrative applications including those enabling for complete online handling of standard non-trivial administrative procedures (minor offences, building permits etc.). That, unfortunately, has not happened yet. In that sense, there were voiced great expectations with the introduction of the Act No. 5/2020 on the right for digital services that should have brought firm duties to the state administration regarding compulsory online proceedings. However, the Act only provides for mandatory digital communication (digital filing and serving of documents), but not for any mandatory portal-based complex digital handling of procedures.

73. The newest addition to specifically legislated public information systems are public cloud services. These were legally established by section 6i and following of the Act No. 365/2000 Sb. that provides for a mechanism of an inclusion of cloud services into the public cloud catalogue[34] and lays down a new category of state cloud that is provided by a public entity which in practice will mostly probably be one or more state companies. The Act also provides for general requirements that cloud services must meet in order to be eligible for public bodies.[35]

§3. Core Public Sector Data

74. The above architecture of public information systems is closely related to the concept of 'reference data' that serve as officially validated core data of the state

34. *See* s. 6k of the Act No. 365/2000 Sb.
35. *See* ss 6m and 6n of the Act No. 365/2000 Sb.

administration about persons and rights. Reference data are legislated as a special administrative category[36] and enjoy an official presumption of validity[37] which means that any activity, public or private, that relies on the content of these data is protected by law and deemed being in good faith. Reference data relate to natural persons (people), legal entities (corporate units), places (addresses, real estate), competences of public authorities and some administrative decisions (those that affect the reference data) and are organized into the following 'base registries'[38]:

- Registry of inhabitants.
- Registry of persons (legal entities, sole traders, public bodies).
- Registry of places.
- Registry of rights and duties.

75. Base registries are commonly administered by the Base Registry Administration that was established as relatively independent agency of the Ministry of Interior. The Base Registry Administration does not have general access to the content of the base registries, but it provides for technical functioning of the registries, their systemic relations and, most importantly, for the administration of access to the registries.

76. In general, public bodies have access to registries that they use while performing their tasks in public administration. The main purpose of granting access to public registries for various public bodies is to provide them with recent and accurate information and minimize the need for parties to administrative and other public proceedings to repeatedly submit or file such information for these proceedings. Consequently, the main benefit of the introduction of Base Registries from the viewpoint of parties of administrative or other proceedings is that when a form must be filled, relevant data either come pre-filled or the form is even not needed at all. Beneficial, yet still very limited, is also the use of access to the Base Registries by some public portal services that allow for fulfilling simple administrative tasks like filings for some personal documents (personal IDs or driving licenses), taxes, local duties (parking permits, fees for garbage disposal or dogs etc.)

77. Another benefit of the introduction of Base Registries is that people (or data subjects) have better control over the processing of their personal data by public authorities. That is because every access to Base Registries containing personal data of respective person is recorded and reports containing these records are sent to that person once in a year.

78. Besides obvious benefits for public authorities that arise from permanent availability of updated and verified data, Base Registries also helped to reduce transactional costs associated with document delivery (*see* below). However, as noted above, still only very few state or local authorities benefit from the availability of

36. *See* s. 2/b of the Act No. 111/2009 Sb.
37. *See* s. 4/4 of the Act No. 111/2009 Sb.
38. *See* s. 3 of the Act No. 111/2009 Sb.

Base Registries by incorporating their data into complex functional solutions to an extent that would correspond to their true potential.

§4. Identification

79. Trustworthy identification and authentication are necessary for the development and deployment of any public information system that includes an interaction with parties. So far, electronic identification was quite neglected by Czech public authorities, because advanced electronic signatures were considered sufficient to authenticate standard official communications. That corresponds to the traditional understanding of virtualization of public procedures in the Czech Republic as simple replacement of papers and post by electronic communications. Consequently, the task of developing efficient e-Government and e-Justice was so far mostly limited in the Czech Republic to enabling delivery and processing of electronic documents.

80. Only relatively recently, Czech public bodies realised that functioning electronic identification and authentication can provide for way more than just authorizing and serving of documents. In any case, going in the direction of complex procedural portals rather than corresponding and exchanging documents does not represent any overly progressive approach. It was always more efficient if parties had negotiated their cases with magistrates or other officials in person rather than exchanging letters. Correspondence, as a way of communicating with public authorities, developed only throughout modern ages mostly due to the multitude of administrative tasks and hardship in devoting proper administrative capacity to deal with every party of every administrative or court procedure in real time. In that sense, virtualised procedures allowing authenticated parties to interactively deal with respective authorities practically mean using modern technologies for overcoming the above capacity problem of public administration and providing, yet again, for computer-aided real-time interaction between a public authority and the parties.

81. Electronic means of identification and authentication that are accepted across the Czech public sector are at first those identification means that are accredited and notified under the eIDAS that currently (as of 2022) and include the Czech national ID cards and two private eIDs – the Starcos[39] and the MojeID.[40] In addition, there is NIA ID[41] and e-Government mobile key[42] which are relatively simple IDs provided by the state mostly for accessing e-government services.

39. *See* icaidentita.cz (in Czech). This eID is provided by a private company I.CA.
40. *See* mojeid.cz/en/. This eID is provided by CZ.NIC which is a private-law association of Information Society Service Providers (ISP) that also acts as the national domain name registry for .CZ ccTLD.
41. *See* info.identitaobcana.cz/ups/ (in Czech).
42. *See* info.identitaobcana.cz/mep/ (inc Czech).

82. Relatively recently, there was also introduced a bankID that primarily aims at enabling the use of officially accepted eID in public and private applications by existing clients of electronic banking. The advantage of bankID is that it was relatively seamlessly introduced by major Czech banks as a primary identification tool for electronic banking and so it is being used, unlike other eIDs, by quite remarkable percentage of the Czech population.[43] Downsides of bankID include the lack of eIDAS accreditation (which makes the Czech bankID officially accepted only in the Czech Republic), still very limited use other than for authenticating transactions in electronic banking and also some privacy concerns.[44]

83. EU eID was implemented Besides the EU eID, there are recognized also other identification and authentication means that developed for various causes over the time. Most important is the NIA ID.

§5. Document Delivery

84. We noted above that the Czech public administration still tends to consider digitization as simply replacing paper with electronic documents. Instead of developing swift interactive solutions for various administrative and other processes, major initiatives in e-government mostly focused on enabling parties only to electronically correspond (or exchange documents) with public sector bodies. It is then no surprise that officially recognized delivery of electronic documents represents a major issue.

85. Another reason for document delivery being quintessentially important agenda for the Czech e-Government is what literature describes as a 'delivery fetish' in the Czech public administration and judiciary. Official delivery formalities have grown so badly and became a matter of such unreasonable attention, misuse or even abuse that they became a matter of extended case law of all top Czech courts and are being analysed and discussed in thick law books.[45]

86. Reasons for the Czech legal practice and even academia being obsessed by document delivery are hard to find. Besides the still-present tradition of Communist legal culture of replacing content of rights by formalities, a relevant reason may be in actual functioning of the Czech legal counselling. While it is common in other jurisdictions for an attorney to be directly responsible for the client knowing about all relevant procedural information and documents (i.e., attorney being actively assisting official authorities in delivering and explaining relevant documents to the client), it is rather common for Czech attorneys to advice clients how to avoid document delivery in order to jeopardize respective procedures.

---

43. A report by the Ministry of Interior suggests the bankID being used by a majority of economically active Czech Population – *see* Klára Dlubalova, *Bankovní identitu má skoro polovina Čechů. Roste i zájem o datové schránky*, mvcr.cz.

44. *See* Pavel Loutocký & František Kasl, *Potenciál a úskalí identifikačních služeb bankovní identity*, Právník, vol. 160(12), p. 1038 (2021).

45. Mates.

87. Electronic document delivery started to develop in the Czech law in the form of mandatory introduction of 'electronic filing offices' to all public authorities. The 'filing office' meant in practice only a contact point, mostly an e-mail address, that acted as a mailbox for official correspondence. Public authorities had to make information about its 'electronic filing office' publicly available and had to provide for the 'filing office' being able to process electronic submissions and confirm their delivery by a reply signed by an authorized clerk.

88. The aforementioned strategic approach to the development of e-Government in the Czech Republic can be seen not primarily on the, rather obvious, introduction of mandatory e-mail addresses for official correspondence but on the process that follows a delivery of an electronic submission to a public authority. Considerable number of public authorities and all courts in most of proceedings still, after electronically confirming the delivery of respective submission to the sender, print it and file it into a paper file.

89. The biggest downside of e-mail delivery of official documents is that strict rules regarding procedural effects of delivery apply only in case when a document is delivered to a public authority. If a public authority tries to deliver a document to a party by e-mail, it is always required for a delivery to be legally relevant that the recipient confirms the delivery by a reply signed by a qualified electronic signature or by an advanced electronic signature based on a qualified certificate. Besides qualified electronic signing still not being overly popular in the Czech Republic, the biggest problem of this kind of delivery is that not all parties in all administrative and court proceedings are cooperative enough to actively confirm a reception of administrative or court documents.

90. Since 2008, the above problem was mitigated by the introduction of 'data mailboxes' ['*datové schránky*'] that act as officially recognized means of delivery of electronic documents. A document is legally considered delivered upon the recipient simply opening her mailbox. For many types of official documents, there also alternatively applies the legal fiction of delivery upon a document landing in a mailbox and its recipient not accessing her mailbox within ten days (similarly to some postal deliveries).

91. The pool of subjects, public and private, that have active data mailboxes steadily grows and the government gradually adds new types of subjects for whom data mailboxes are mandatory. That, together with allowing data mailboxes to be used also for provable delivering private documents, makes data mailboxes one of most successful Czech e-Government projects up to date.

92. Besides the above e-mail deliveries and data mailboxes, particular electronic documents can be also, based on specific legislation, legally delivered by other means. One of still very few examples are universities that are allowed to officially deliver some documents through their information systems. This type of delivery of electronic documents, i.e., through a filing system that also processes these documents, allows for submissions, assists parties with procedural actions, etc., is probably closest to proper understanding of virtualised procedure as indicated above. Documents are here not sent or received, but they are filed in a system to which all parties have permanent online access – and such a system may only notify parties by any convenient means including an sms, instant messaging service, etc., that there is something in their procedure that requires their attention.

Part I. Digital Market Regulation

Chapter 1. Legal Status of Standards and Technical Specifications

93. Highly specialized industries, such as IT, often cannot do without some form of regulation of what is the generally accepted minimum standard within the sector. That being said, legal norms as such, by their very nature, cannot regulate a perfectly concrete specification of procedures or parameters that are considered desirable by the legislator. Therefore, in many provisions, the law will refer to technical standards.

94. In business terms, technical standards facilitate the production and exchange of goods, create trust between producers and consumers, and help reduce production costs and remove market barriers. In many cases, technical standards are considered a decisive prerequisite for market acceptance.

95. This chapter deals with the nature and significance of technical standards, their types and alternatives, and introduces the purpose and role of technical standards (or their alternatives) in the legal system of the Czech Republic and in an international context.

96. The legal system of the Czech Republic recognizes several types of legislation with different legal force. At the apex are the Constitution and other constitutional laws, which have the highest legal force and can only be amended by constitutional law. Below them stands the general law. One further level below, implementing regulations are issued – decrees and regulations that are considered to be subordinate legislation and therefore, the principle of '*secundum et intra legem*' (i.e., according to the law and in accordance with it) must be observed.

97. The Czech Republic is also bound by international treaties. Under certain circumstances defined in the Constitution (Article 10a), those have a special status and in the case of dispute enjoy priority over domestic law, including even the constitutional law of the Czech Republic. EU regulations are directly applicable as well. Other requirements listed in EU law (Directives, Recommendations, Opinions) are binding in the Czech Republic only after their incorporation into national legislation.

98. The formal features of a legal norm include its statutory half-formation.[46] According to legal theory, the material features of a legal norm include, *inter alia*, its generality. That being said, legal norms as such, by their very nature, cannot regulate a perfectly concrete specification of procedures or parameters that are considered desirable by the lawmaker. Therefore, in many provisions, the legislation refers to technical standards – usually the Czech Technical Standards (ČSN). Reference to these documents is implemented in the legal regulation by means of the phrase 'standard value' or similar wording.

99. Czech technical standards are a special kind of written rules covering various areas of human activity. They contain a technical description of the parameters of products, constructions, materials and more complex units made from these constituent parts. They also contain information on generally accepted technical solutions, and basic legal requirements for structural, material, fire, hygiene, health and environmental safety. Technical requirements for products or services often result from international agreements by which the Czech Republic is bound – since the accession to the EU, these will most often be Directives as an instrument for harmonization of Member States' regulations.

100. Within Czech standardization, one can encounter three basic types of technical standard documents. These are the ČSN, ČSN EN, and ČSN EN International Organization for Standardization (ISO) standards, respectively. All of them are always accompanied by a numerical designation that identifies the document quite unambiguously. National legislation can only refer to national standards. On the other hand, standards issued in the EU as EN (European Norm) by a designated organization (ETSI, CE CENELEC, ISO) must be co-opted into Czech national standards.

101. Historically, ČSN standards used to be binding. Act No. 35/1957 Sb. on Technical Standardization stipulated that technical standards are valid for everyone to whom they apply and if a technical standard is not marked as recommended, it is binding. Later, Act No 142/1991 Sb. also imposed on legal and natural persons authorized to carry out business activities the obligation to comply in their activities with the provisions of Czechoslovak standards which were designated as binding in the Bulletin.

102. At present, ČSN are regulated by two acts: Act No. 20/1993 Sb. on ensuring the exercise of state administration in the field of technical standardization, and Act No. 22/1997 Sb. on technical requirements for products. Czech technical standards are now defined in a way that corresponds to the definitions used by international and regional standardization bodies, thus enabling them to have the same function as national standards of market economy countries and to be fully eligible, in particular, for the adoption of European standards. However, they are no longer legally binding unless they are referred to by law or subordinate legislation (decrees).

---

46. *See* the Judgment of the Constitutional Court of 13 Aug. 1997, Case No. IV.ÚS 1 67/97.

103. The Act on Technical Requirements for Products explicitly states that Czech technical standards are not generally binding. This was confirmed by the Constitutional Court of the Czech Republic in one of its decisions. According to the court, technical standards are considered qualified recommendations (as opposed to orders) and their use is strictly voluntary. However, the Constitutional Court also added that there are many cases in which compliance with the requirements of specific technical standards is required by law or decree. The obligation to comply with technical standards in certain activities may arise primarily on the basis of a legal regulation according to which Czech technical standards must be observed in the relations regulated by that regulation. In such cases, it is possible to speak of a certain binding character of the relevant standards.

104. The manner and form of such reference are regulated in the Government's legislative rules, specifically in the provision of Article 45a of the Government's legislative rules, which provides for indicative references (that are always given preference over exclusive references). Sponsored access is then provided not by the Czech Agency for Standardization, but by the competent Czech Ministry or other central administrative authority under whose jurisdiction the special legal regulation falls,[47] i.e., the special legal regulation that makes an indicative or exclusive reference to the technical standard.

105. A single authority has been entrusted with the responsibility of centrally ensuring their creation and supervision. However, the Office used its statutory authority[48] and established the Czech Agency for Standardization as a state-funded organization. Currently, it is the Agency that ensures the creation, publication and distribution of Czech technical standards and maintains a database of Czech technical standards and other technical documents.[49] The Agency is, *inter alia*, entitled to collect remuneration for the professional activities it performs and is also the administrator of the fee for the provision of Czech technical standards and other technical documents, the fee for access to the database and the fee for sponsored access to Czech technical standards and other technical documents.[50]

106. The Constitutional Court has expressed its view on compliance with technical standards through their purpose as follows: the purpose of compliance with detailed legal requirements is primarily the quality of products, protection of health and life of people, safety at work and technical equipment, fire protection, creation and protection of the environment, protection of property and other interests.[51] Compliance with technical standards is in many cases a decisive condition for market acceptance. The question of why standards are used, even if they are not legally binding, could therefore be answered by saying that their use is advantageous because they facilitate the production and exchange of goods and communication

47. *See* s. 6c/2 of the Technical Requirements Act.
48. *See* s. 5/2 of the Technical Requirements Act.
49. *See* s. 5/2 in fine of the Act on Technical Requirements.
50. *See* s. 5/3 of the Technical Requirements Act.
51. *See*, e.g., the Ruling of the plenary session of the Constitutional Court of 26 May 2009, No. Pl. ÚS 40/08.

between producers and purchasers. Technical standards also create trust between producers and consumers, help reduce production costs, remove market barriers, etc.

107. The Constitutional Court further added that references to a technical standard in legislation may, in terms of their strength, take the form of an exclusive (mandatory) or indicative reference. An exclusive reference establishes compliance with the technical standard referred to as *the* only way of complying with the relevant provision of the legislation in question. In the case of an indicative reference, compliance with the standard is *one* of the possible ways of meeting the requirements of the legislation. However, the general requirement of the legislation may be met in other ways.

108. When imposing a fine for non-compliance with an obligation arising from a ČSN, it is not sufficient for the administrative authority to merely state that a particular ČSN has been violated. The circumstances of the infringement must be examined in the proceedings as a question of fact. It is necessary to prove whether the ČSN applies to the particular case and whether the provision of the ČSN allegedly infringed is actually binding. As we have seen earlier above, the ČSN also contain provisions of a recommendatory nature and these are not mandatory. The same procedure must be followed in court proceedings.

109. On the basis of the decision-making practice of the Supreme Administrative Court[52] as well as EU case law,[53] Act No. 526/2020 Sb., amending Act No. 22/1997 Sb. on Technical Requirements for Products and on Amendments and Additions to Certain Acts and Act No. 90/2016 Sb. on the Assessment of Conformity of Specified Products When Placing Them on the Market, as amended, enacted free public access to technical standards.

110. Thus, the legal concept of sponsored access to Czech technical standards and other technical documents was introduced into domestic law with effect from 1 January 2021. The definition of sponsored access can be found in section 6c/1 of the Technical Requirements Act. It follows from the wording of this provision that sponsored access 'means the provision, for end users, of free access to a Czech technical standard or other technical document which is binding for the purposes specified in a special legal regulation, on the basis of registration in a manner allowing remote access'. In other words, not all technical standards or other technical documents are made available through sponsored access, but only those that are binding for the purposes specified in the specific regulation. In practical terms, therefore, anyone can access selected technical standards through sponsored access, subject to prior registration.

---

52. *See,* e.g., the Judgment of the Supreme Administrative Court of 28 May 2015, No. 1 As 162/2014 – 63.
53. *See,* e.g., Court of Justice of the European Union (CJEU): Case C-613/14, *James Elliott Construction Limited v. Irish Asphalt Limited* [2016] ECLI:EU:C:2016:821.

111. In terms of Article 297(1)(a) of the EC Treaty, interpreted in accordance with the principle of legal certainty, the Court of Justice of the European Communities (CJEU) ruled in C-160/20 Stichting Rookpreventie Jeugd and Others, published by the CJEU on 22 February 2022, that in the light of the wide discretion conferred upon the EU legislature in exercising its powers, where its action involves choices of a political, economic and social nature and where it has to carry out a comprehensive assessment and evaluation, the EU legislature may refer, in the acts which it adopts, to technical standards drawn up by a standardization body such as the ISO.

112. However, the Court stated that the principle of legal certainty requires that the reference to such rules be clear, precise and with foreseeable effects, so that the persons concerned can orient themselves in the legal situations and relationships covered by the jurisdiction of the EU.

113. In practice, therefore, as far as the applicability of ISO standards to enterprises is concerned, to the extent that those enterprises have access to the official and authentic version of the ISO standards through national standardization bodies, those standards can be applied to them. However, as regards the applicability of ISO standards to individuals, on the basis of the principle of legal certainty, those standards, which have become binding through a Union legislative act, can generally be applied to individuals only if they have themselves been published in the Official Journal.

114. Often, however, the requirements of ISO standards are incorporated into national legislation. For example, the Czech Cybersecurity Decree[54] is based on the ISO/IEC 27k series of standards. However, unlike the Decree, the standards are not directly binding on regulated entities and compliance with them (or possible certification) does not exempt regulated entities from complying with all requirements of the law and the Decree.

115. In business, in addition to references to ČSN or ISO, various clauses and certification are commonly used to briefly express the terms of the relationship and mutual rights and obligations, including technical specifications and the agreed standard, especially in sales contracts (e.g., on the dispatch of goods and the method of transport, on the payment of freight charges, on the obligation to insure the goods and to pay the relevant costs). The exact interpretation of frequently used clauses is being harmonized internationally.

116. In the IT sector, similar references are also increasingly included in employment contracts. International Data Company (IDC's) new white paper 'The Business Value of Red Hat Certification' highlights the importance of people skills for successful digital transformation. One of the key findings of the IDC study is the cost-benefit analysis of the study participants. The IDC return-on-investment

54. *See* Decree No. 82/2018 Sb., on Security Measures, Cybersecurity Incidents, Reactive Measures, Cybersecurity Reporting Requirements, and Data Disposal (the Cybersecurity Decree).

(ROI)) analysis shows a 365% appreciation over three years, with discounted IT infrastructure cost savings averaging at USD 2.95 million per organization over three years.[55]

117. The result of hiring certified staff, according to the study, is the ability to deploy new IT resources 23%–51% faster, with the kind of agility that forms the cornerstone of successful IT operations and digital transformation, as reported by the organizations surveyed.

118. The hiring of certified staff finds its positive reflection in public tenders for IT supplies and services, where there are often requirements for technical certifications through which the customer seeks to eliminate companies without the necessary know-how from the contracts.

119. In addition to the above-mentioned standards and certificates, clauses are also widely used in contracts for the supply of (in particular) IT services.

120. The possibility of applying rules of interpretation is enshrined in the provisions of section 1754 of the Civil Code, but it also follows from the principle of contractual freedom. Where parties incorporate clauses in their contract that are recognized by the rules of interpretation in use, it is presumed that the parties intended such clause to have the effect set out in the rules of interpretation. However, direct contractual provisions shall prevail over the interpretative rules.

121. Clauses are of particular importance in international trade but are also used in domestic trade. Among the most important are undoubtedly the Incoterms, which have become an established practice since 1936. The International Chamber of Commerce issues publications with up-to-date standards. The full text of the current Incoterms is also published for users by the Czech Chamber of Commerce. The most commonly used clauses today are Incoterms 2000, 2010 and 2020. If it is not specified which version is used, the latest version shall always be used.

122. In addition to the Incoterms, the new Intraterms (International Trade Terms), which build on the Incoterms, are beginning to be applied on an increasing scale.[56]

123. Apart from the above, various recommendations issued mostly by international organizations are an interesting example of industry regulation. Among the best known of these are the request for comments (RFCs) or best current practice (BCPs), issued by the Internet Engineering Task Force (IRTF). While they are 'just' recommendations, they are also the de facto standard due to their widespread use.

---

55. *See* The Business Value of Red Hat Training – An IDC Business Value White Paper, sponsored by Red Hat. *ROI Summary*, p. 17. (2020), https://www.redhat.com/rhdc/managed-files/tr-idc-business-value-training-analyst-material-f26718-202101-en.pdf.
56. *See* Adolf Hermann, *International Trade Terms*, p. 164 (RADIX Prague 1997).

124. Open Worldwide Application Security Project (OWASP) is an example of a set of recommendations so well written that even the official authorities recognize them. Another recommendation is issued by Senior Officials Group Information Systems Security (SOGIS), the advisory institute for information security managers, or ENISA (the EU Information Technology Security Agency). This organization seeks to provide advice within the EU on how to ensure that appropriate security rules have been put in place. In the context of cryptography rules, activities have been handed over to the European Network of Excellence in Cryptology (ECRYPT). This is due to the need for extensive expertise.

125. For the sake of completeness, one may also consider that technical standards and specifications, as well as various recommendations, will be reflected in the commercial practices or established practices of the parties.

126. In B2B relationships, a term admitting of different interpretations shall be given the meaning which it regularly has in such dealings. If, however, the other party is not a businessperson, then the party invoking a certain meaning must demonstrate that the other party had to be aware of such meaning.

127. Customary commercial usage, whether generally or in a given industry, shall be taken into account unless specifically ruled out in contract or in law. In the absence of any other agreement, the custom of the trade shall prevail over a provision of law which has no coercive effect, otherwise the entrepreneur may invoke the custom if they can prove that the other party must have known and understood the custom.

128. Trade practices are not legal norms, as they exercise no regulatory power on their own but only on the basis of the relevant statutory provision[57] or contractual agreement. In summary, commercial practices contain rules of conduct, compliance with which has legal consequences, but the implementation of the rules and the consequences do not arise from the practices themselves but from their connection to the text of the law or the contractual arrangement.

129. Somewhat different from business practices, but relevant to the field of IT, are so-called established best practices. Best practice is a general term for a formalized set of best practices in a particular field and industry, which are created on the basis of well-functioning feedback from the customer to the system integrator and IT system supplier. They basically reflect the experience with business process management, which is then reflected in the innovation of implementation methodologies, in the innovation of products themselves or their individual modules with modern management methods, or in the development of special tools. Best practice is a general term for a formalized set of best practices in a particular field and industry.

---

57. *See* Arts 9(2) and 558(2) CC.

130. Best practices set by defining authorities and large IT corporations complement the order set by states, which are unable to quickly and efficiently respond to constant industry changes with functioning regulation and rarely have the technical competence to ensure their implementation, even if they managed to create them in time. Said industry authorities are thus creating a source of law (of sorts), called *lex informaticae*.[58]

131. This creates hybrid governance structures between the public and private sectors, where public law sets minimum general standards and provides enforcement powers, while private para-legal regimes can provide detailed rules, first-level dispute resolution and enforcement mechanisms. An example is the Appropriate Children Age Code effective in the United Kingdom (UK) from 2 September 2020. The defining authorities were required to implement it by 2 September 2021, and smaller entities have been following suit, implementing the rules contained in that Code across the industry and turning them into best practice even before they are made mandatory. The Code sets a total of 15 standards for default design settings according to the age and level of risk of harm to the child. The aim is to compel companies active in online services (regularly used by children) to consider the best interests of children when processing their personal data.

58. *See* Van Boom et al., *Electronic Highways: On the Road to Liability, in Emerging Electronic Highways: New Challenges for Politics and Law. The Hague*, p. 153 (Victor Bekkers ed., Kluwer Law International, 1996).

Chapter 2. Legal Status of Standard Terms and Conditions

§1. Introduction

132. Vendors or service providers across all sectors, who often enter into the same type of contract repeatedly with a large number of different parties, make extensive use of what is called 'general terms and conditions' (GTCs) to bring simplicity, speed and flexibility to the contracting process.

133. In practice, GTCs are essentially generally formulated contractual templates that supplement the contract and the parties must abide by them – provided, however, that these terms are properly attached to the offer or are demonstrably known to the parties and subject to the proviso that the contract itself takes precedence over the terms and conditions. GTCs mainly deal with non-essential rights and obligations of the parties to the contractual relationship. In the case of the IT sector, GTCs will typically cover the permitted use of the technology, agreed tests, event-of-default procedures, details and limits of liability for defects, force majeure events, etc.

134. This chapter deals with the nature and significance of GTCs, and their purpose and role within the legal system of the Czech Republic. In addition to the legal regulation of this issue, the text specifically discusses the limits of the content of GTCs, their form, their position in relation to individual contracts, and the criteria for future amendments. In addition, a few words will be said on the specifics of GTCs in relation to the consumer, their role in the event of litigation, and the possibility of future use in the field of smart contracts.

§2. Defining GTCs

135. Section 1751 of the Civil Code provides that part of the content of the contract can be determined by reference to the GTCs which the offering party attaches to the offer or which are known to the parties. The deviating provisions in the contract take precedence over the wording of the GTCs.

136. According to Article 2.1.19: Principles of International Commercial Contracts – UNIDROIT, GTC are 'provisions which are prepared in advance for general and repeated use by one party and which are actually used without negotiation with the other party.'[59] Czech legislation, like the Vienna Convention, does not contain an explicit definition of GTCs, although the Civil Code often uses the term.

137. In practice, GTCs, or standard terms, are part of the contract and the parties must abide by them, provided, however, that these standard terms are properly

59. *See UNIDROIT Principles on International Commercial Contracts,* International Institute for the Unification of Private Law (UNIDROIT), s. 66. (2016), https://www.unidroit.org/wp-content/uploads/2021/06/Unidroit-Principles-2016-English-bl.pdf.

attached to the offer or are demonstrably known to the parties and subject to the proviso that the contract itself takes precedence over the terms and conditions. 'Standard terms known to the parties' are very often understood to include those issued by professional interest organizations.

138. GTCs can be characterized as indirect or ancillary contractual arrangements with a degree of abstractness from the contract itself. They are essentially generally formulated contractual templates that supplement the contract and rationalize and typify, in particular, repeated transactions. Standard terms and conditions are not contained in the text of the contract itself, but usually form a separate document.

139. Standard terms mainly deal with non-essential rights and obligations of the parties to the contractual relationship, e.g., agreed tests, details of liability for defects, force majeure events, billing procedures, acceptance procedures, etc., whereas the essential elements of the contract, without the negotiation of which the contract will not validly arise, are generally contained in the direct contractual arrangement, whether it be a written contract or e-mail communication between the parties that leads to the creation of the obligation. In theory, it is conceivable that the terms and conditions are negotiated orally, but the potential problems associated with proving their content make oral negotiation impractical.

§3. General Terms and Conditions in the Contracting Process

140. The terms and conditions should be worded intelligibly to ensure their shared understanding. In the event of a dispute, according to the established case law of the Czech courts and section 557 of the Civil Code, any ambiguous wording in the terms and conditions should be interpreted to the disadvantage of the party who used it first (i.e., usually, the author of the GTCs). It may be problematic if contractual partners undertake to trade according to the buyer's terms of purchase and at the same time according to the seller's terms of sale even though they are incompatible in certain points. In such a case, the contract is deemed concluded only to the extent that the terms of sale do not conflict.

141. The existence of GTCs should be explicitly brought to the attention of the business partner, who should be given the opportunity to read them, print them out and further dispose of them as they see fit. The terms and conditions, to the extent that their content is in accordance with applicable law, public order and good morals, become part of the contract when the parties agree to them. This consent does not always have to be in writing, in the form of a reference to the text of the terms and conditions in the contract itself. If, in principle, it is possible to conclude a contract orally or factually, reference to the other content of the contract contained in the terms and conditions may also be made in this fashion. However, the consent must be explicit. If the agreement of the parties to apply the terms and conditions is to be undisputed and demonstrable, it is of course appropriate and advisable to declare this in writing. In the event of a dispute, if one of the parties invokes provisions of the terms and conditions which it has submitted as documentary evidence, it must prove their authenticity, and in particular must show that these terms and conditions were applicable and in force and being referred to by the contract at the time. Therefore, in order to ensure that the entrepreneur is able to bear the burden of proof in similar cases, they should ideally attach the current version of the standard terms to the contract or the e-mail communication leading up to it.

142. A businessperson using GTCs in relation to a consumer should be even more vigilant, as there are stricter rules for consumer protection in this area. For example, in the context of consumer contracts, a clause establishing a contractual penalty or other similarly disadvantageous provision principally cannot be a part of the GTCs, but only of the consumer contract itself (i.e., the document to which the consumer affixes his signature).[60]

§4. Flexibility of General Terms and Conditions

143. Section 1752 of the Civil Code allows for the unilateral change of the terms and conditions on the assumption that a future change of the terms and conditions is possible, as foreseen by the main contract and therefore agreed by both parties. The change in the terms and conditions must then be notified to the other party in the manner agreed in the contract and the other party must be allowed to terminate the contract with sufficient notice to secure a new supplier. In effect, the contracting party is choosing between accepting the change or terminating the contract early.

144. According to settled case law,[61] it is not possible to insist that the contract be renewed whenever there is a change in the terms and conditions even if they only contain data and information immaterial to the contractual relationship, but it is possible to require that the wording of the relevant article of the contract will not prejudice a client who cannot react in time to changes in the terms and conditions, for example by terminating the contract before they are affected by changes that are disadvantageous to them.

145. Section 1753 of the Civil Code further provides that provisions in the terms and conditions which the other party could not have reasonably foreseen are null and void and produce no legal consequences. In practice, this will be the case in particular for provisions that go against the purpose of the contract or the obvious intentions of the parties. If the terms and conditions contain such provisions, they are disregarded by law. This rule applies not only to clauses whose own contents are unexpected, but also to clauses which are expressed in terms that are unclear to the other party or are set in small, hard-to-read print, if they modify or supplement the content of the main contract in a way that the other party could not reasonably have expected.

60. *See* Judgment of the Constitutional Court of 11 Nov. 2013, Case No. I. ÚS 3512/11.
61. *See* Judgment of the High Court in Olomouc of 11 Sep. 1997, Case Nos 2 A 5/97 et seq.

§5. SMART CONTRACTS AND GTCS

146. A specific situation will arise with the rapidly widening practice of smart contracts, based on blockchain technology, which promises to increase the efficiency of the contractual agenda, especially that of a routine and repetitive nature, leading to faster implementation of the law. Such a contract is concluded automatically by a computer program, based on an order that is triggered when predefined conditions are met.

147. A blockchain is a shared data structure that allows transparent and secure online storage and immediate transfer of information between users (the links of the blockchain). To secure data, the blockchain uses an algorithm to encode data into an immutable hash value. These values are stored as part of the contracting process, which increases the credibility of such a process, but also makes it inflexible in relation to future changes to the contractual terms.

148. Despite the rapid development in recent years, the use of smart contracts is thus limited for now to certain situations, typically following a previously reached contractual consensus, which are designed to ensure the agreed method of performance. In addition to exchanging data similar to a traditional contract, they can be used to register original works of artists, send and receive data, including data representing virtual property, to issue data representing rights (e.g., coupons, vouchers and other documents entitling to vote or to access certain functions) or to issue data representing assets.

§6. THE FUTURE OF SMART GTCS

149. If the smart contract is a 'continuation' of a traditional contract, or if GTCs are implemented, the parties will face difficulties in transferring legal clauses (some of which are vague and require interpretation) into computer code. Blockchain contracts should therefore not contain 'subjective clauses' – that is, terms whose meaning is subject to interpretation. This effectively restricts the applicability of blockchain technology to mass consumer or distributor contracts in particular, with clearly defined and quantified obligations without discretion.

150. If the orders in the blockchain are derived from the GTCs, the problem of terms that are subject to complex or subjective interpretation can be partially solved by defining the qualitative characteristics of the subject matter of the contract by reference to technical standards (*see* the introductory chapter). However, the issue of continuous changes in these technical standards, as well as legislative or economic factors, will remain problematic. In some cases, the solution is to introduce an additional order into the blockchain, linked to the condition that a change will occur (e.g., with respect to the purchase price, where the amount *x* may be released based on the code already written; if, for example, the condition of an inflation increase of n% is met, an additional amount *y* will be released). However, in the case of a change in the technical standards used, the condition would have to be much more complex to reflect the factual differences of the new document or specification compared to the original.

151. The field of smart contracts is relatively new and many of its pitfalls have not yet been satisfactorily addressed. For example, by allowing smart contract technologies to pseudonymize legal relationships, illicit financial transactions become possible, and so do covert unlawful activities that are difficult to detect from the outside – often due to the fact that, as mentioned above, the immutability of blockchain makes it impossible to respond flexibly to changes in legislation. Because of this, some voices within the professional community have cautioned that blockchain technology will require qualitatively new technical and legal regulatory interventions, even foreseeing the emergence of a new *lex numerica* or *lex cryptographica*.[62]

62. *See* Vincent Mignon, *Blockchains: Perspectives and Challenges, in Blockchains, Smart Contracts, Decentralized Autonomous Organizations and the Law*, 8–17 (Kraus D. et al., 2019).

Chapter 3. International Private Law Applied to the Online Environment

§1. Introduction

152. Czech private international law is regulated by Act No. 91/2012 Sb., Private International Law Act (hereinafter referred to as Czech PILA).[63] The Czech PILA entered into force on 1 January 2014 as part of the recodification of the Czech private law, with the Civil Code[64] and the Business Corporation Act.[65]

153. Procedural issues are further governed by the subsidiary applicable Civil Procedural Code,[66] the Enforcement Procedural Code[67] or the Special Judicial Proceeding Act.[68] Some procedural aspects of international commercial arbitration, such as rules of procedure or the relationship between arbitration courts (arbitrators) and civil courts, are governed by the Czech Arbitration Act (*see* further).[69]

154. The Czech Constitution[70] and the Charter of Fundamental Rights and Freedoms[71] contain fundamental principles of Czech law, such as equality of gender, race, religion, or political beliefs. These principles are applicable in the context of public policy reservation.[72]

155. The Czech PILA applies within the limits of certain promulgated international conventions and treaties binding on the Czech Republic[73] and of any directly applicable provisions of EU law.[74] The Czech Republic is a contracting party to international conventions aimed at the unification of private law[75] as well as international procedural law[76] and international commercial arbitration.[77] Apart from multilateral conventions, the Czech Republic is bound by several bilateral treaties concerning, *inter alia*, judicial assistance and cooperation in civil and commercial

63. The Czech PILA replaced the previous Act No. 97/1963 Sb., on Private International Law and the Rules of Procedure.
64. *See* Act No. 89/2012 Sb., Civil Code.
65. *See* Act No. 90/2012 Sb., Business Corporation Act.
66. *See* Act No. 99/1963 Sb., Civil Procedural Code.
67. *See* Act No. 120/2001 Sb., Enforcement Procedural Code.
68. *See* Act No. 209/2013 Sb., Special Judicial Proceedings Act.
69. *See* Act No. 216/1994 Sb., Arbitration Act.
70. *See* Act No. 1/1993 Sb., Czech Constitution.
71. *See* Act No. 2/1993 Sb., Charter of Fundamental Rights and Freedoms.
72. *See* s. 4 of the Czech PILA.
73. The preferential application of international conventions and treaties is expressly provided for in Art. 10 of the Czech Constitution.
74. *See* s. 2 of the Czech PILA.
75. United Nations Convention on Contracts for the International Sale of Goods (Vienna, 1980); Convention on the Contract for the International Carriage of Goods by Road (CMR, Geneva 1956); Convention concerning International Carriage by Rail (COTIF).
76. E.g., Convention of 30 Jun. 2005 on Choice of Court Agreements (2005, The Hague).
77. E.g., Convention on the Recognition and Enforcement of Foreign Arbitral Awards (1958, New York).

matters.[78] Therefore, the Czech PILA applies to issues falling outside the scope of the international conventions and EU regulations; its scope and applicability are consequently relatively limited.

156. The Czech PILA reflects the latest trends in European Private International Law.[79] It contains not only choice of law rules but also provisions on international jurisdiction and rules for recognition and enforcement of foreign judgments in a separate private law statute.

157. The Czech PILA is divided into nine Chapters encompassing 125 Sections. Chapters 1, 2 and 3[80] contain provisions regarding the general part of private international law and international procedural law, such as international mandatory rules, public policy reservation,[81] evasion of law,[82] general rules on international jurisdiction,[83] recognition and enforcement of foreign judgments,[84] classification[85] or determination and application of foreign law.[86] Chapter 4[87] is the most extensive; it regulates rules on jurisdiction, choice of law rules and recognition and enforcement of foreign judgments concerning individual types of legal relationships, such as legal capacity, legal actions, representation, statutes of limitation, family law, registered partnerships and similar relationships, rights in rem, succession, intellectual property rights, securities, investment tools and other documents and obligations (both contractual and non-contractual). Chapter 5 deals with judicial cooperation and assistance,[88] whereas Chapter 6 contains provisions for insolvency and bankruptcy proceeding.[89] Chapter 7 regulates international commercial arbitration, recognition, and enforcement of foreign arbitral awards.[90] Chapters 8 and 9 provide for transitional and final provisions.[91]

§2. Courts and Case Law

158. Private law disputes containing international (cross-border) element are not adjudicated by any specialized types of courts. Civil courts may decide cases with

78. Full list of international conventions and treaties is available on the website of the Ministry of Foreign Affairs of the Czech Republic (2.7.2022), https://www.mzv.cz/jnp/cz/zahranicni_vztahy/mezinarodni_smlouvy/index.html.
79. *See* Monika Pauknerová, *'Czech Republic' Encyclopaedia of Private InternationalLaw,* p. 2011 (Edward Elgar Publishing, 2017).
80. *See* ss 1 to 28 of the Czech PILA.
81. *See* ss 3 and 4 of the Czech PILA.
82. *See* s. 5 of the Czech PILA.
83. *See* ss 6 to 14 of the Czech PILA.
84. *See* ss 14 to 19 of the Czech PILA.
85. *See* s. 20 of the Czech PILA.
86. *See* s. 23 of the Czech PILA.
87. *See* ss 29 to 101 of the Czech PILA.
88. *See* ss 102 to 110 of the Czech PILA.
89. *See* ss 111 to 116 of the Czech PILA.
90. *See* ss 117 to 122 of the Czech PILA.
91. *See* ss 123 to 125 of the Czech PILA.

an international element, public notaries (e.g., successions) or registration offices (e.g.. births or marriages).

159. The Czech legal system is part of the continental legal system. As such, Czech law does not consider case law as a source of Czech law. However, the case law of the Supreme Court of the Czech Republic and the Constitutional Court of the Czech Republic regarding private international law has been widely respected in Czech law. The case law mainly contains the interpretation of fundamental principles and doctrinal issues of the Czech private international law, such as the existence of an international element in private law dispute,[92] the content and scope of the public policy reservation,[93] reciprocity[94] or determination and application of foreign law.[95]

160. Unfortunately, there is no relevant case law concerning the interpretation or application of the Czech PILA or of Czech private international law in the online context. This situation is due to the relative novelty of the Czech recodified legislation. Another reason is the preferential application of the EU law. Most case law deals with the autonomous interpretation of the EU regulations, especially Regulations Brussels I,[96] Brussels Ibis[97] or Brussels IIbis,[98] and related procedural provisions in the Czech Civil Procedural Code.[99]

161. In the context of online private international law, the Czech courts dealt mainly with the interpretation of Article 5(3) of the Brussels I Regulation (resp. Article 7(2) Brussels Ibis Regulation) in a dispute concerning unlawful administration of personal data on a website,[100] recognition and enforcement of a judgment rendered by a U.S. court in proceedings concerning infringement of personality

92. *See* the Judgment of the Supreme Court of 30 May 2017, Case No. 23 Cdo 5790/2016.
93. *See* the Judgment of the Constitutional Court of 29 Jun. 2017, Case No. I. ÚS 3226/16, and the Judgment of the Supreme Court of 18 Jul. 2016, Case No. 28 Ncu 187/2015-6.
94. *See* the Judgment of the Supreme Court of 5 Apr. 2017, Case No. 30 Cdo 4883/2016.
95. *See* the Judgment of the Constitutional Court of 2 Apr. 2012, Case No. Pl. ÚS 2/11, Judgment of the Supreme Court of 26 Sep. 2007, Case No. 25 Cdo 1143/2006, Judgment of the Supreme Court of 26 Jun. 2012, Case No. 33 Cdo 3117/2010 and 33 Cdo 3529/2010, Judgment of the Supreme Court of 31 Mar. 2016, Case No. 29 Cdo 1115/2014.
96. *See* Council Regulation (EC) 44/2001 of 22 Dec. 2000 on jurisdiction and the recognition and enforcement of judgments in civil and commercial matters.
97. *See* Regulation (EU) 1215/2012 of the European Parliament and of the Council of 12 Dec. 2012 on jurisdiction and the recognition and enforcement of judgments in civil and commercial matters.
98. *See* Council Regulation (EC) 2201/2003 of 27 Nov. 2003 concerning jurisdiction and the recognition and enforcement of judgments in matrimonial matters and the matters of parental responsibility, repealing Regulation (EC) No 1347/2000.
99. For a comprehensive database containing Czech legislation and case law in private international law please *see* InterLex – Decision Support and Training on Internet-related Private International Law, Find Law Module (2 Jul. 2022) https://interlex-portal.eu/en/index.html.
100. *See* Judgment of the Supreme Court of 7 Feb. 2017, Case No. 30 Nd 8/2017.

rights and defamation via a website[101] or an issue of jurisdiction and law applicable for a consumer contract concluded online.[102]

162. A similar respected position as case law holds doctrinal writings by private international law scholars, usually referred to in the cited case law.[103]

§3. General Private International Law

163. Previously, several provisions belonging to the general part of private international law, such as qualification, application of foreign law, incidental questions, or overriding mandatory rules, were dealt with only in the scholarly writings on the doctrine of private international law and corresponding case law.[104] With the recodification of Czech private international law, the first three chapters of the Czech PILA contain provisions on general issues of private international law. These chapters are further subdivided into general provisions, general provisions of international procedural law and general provisions of private international law.

164. These theoretical and doctrinal issues have their significance in the relationship between new technologies and law, particularly for the qualification (classification) of the factual background, interpretation of legal sources, application of foreign law based on conflict of law rules and the possibility of avoiding the application of foreign law because of the protection of public interests (public policy reservation or overriding mandatory provisions).

165. The Czech PILA contains an express provision on qualification (characterization). As a general rule, a legal assessment of a particular factual situation to find the applicable conflict of law rule is usually carried out according to Czech law (*lex fori* qualification).[105] Similarly, connecting factor contained in the respective conflict of law rule shall be assessed under Czech Law.[106] If legal provisions from more than one legal order are to be applied to a particular situation, the legal assessment of such provision may also include the consideration of the functions these provisions have within the framework of their legal system (functional qualification).[107]

---

101. *See* the Judgment of the Supreme Court of 22 Aug. 2014, Case No. 30 Cdo 3157/2013.
102. *See* the Judgment of the Regional Court in České Budějovice of 6 Feb. 2009, Case No. 5 Co 2864/2008.
103. *See* Zdeněk Kučera, *Mezinárodní právo soukromé*, 8. vyd (Doplněk 2012); Monika Pauknerová, *Evropské mezinárodní právo soukromé*, 2. vyd. (C.H.Beck 2013); Naděžda Rozehnalová, *Instituty českého mezinárodního práva soukromého* (Wolters Kluwer 2017); Naděžda Rozehnalová, Jiří Valdhans, Klára Drličková, Tereza Kyselovská, *Úvod do mezinárodního práva soukromého* (Wolters Kluwer 2017). The Czech PILA is based on a 'professorial draft' prepared by Professor-Emeritus Zdeněk Kučera, *see* above. In Monika Pauknerová, *'Czech Republic' Encyclopaedia of Private InternationalLaw* (Edward Elgar Publishing, 2017) p. 2010.
104. The 1963 PILA Act contained express provisions regarding only *renvoi* (s. 35) and public policy reservation (s. 36).
105. *See* s. 20/1 of the Czech PILA.
106. *See* s. 20/4 of the Czech PILA.
107. *See* s. 20/2 of the Czech PILA.

If the applicable law has been determined for the main situation (relation), the assessment of a particular situation (relation) or question connected to the main relation is usually also undertaken under that law (*lex causae* qualification).[108]

166. Czech private international law is based on the principle that conflict of law rules are binding for judges. If a conflict of law rule determines a foreign law as applicable law, a Czech judge is obliged to apply the foreign law.[109] The rules for determining and applying foreign law are provided in section 23 of the Czech PILA. Unless other provisions in the Czech PILA stipulate otherwise, the foreign law shall be applied ex officio the same way it is applied in the territory to which it applies. The relevant provisions of the foreign law shall be applied regardless of their systematic classification or public law nature, provided they are not contrary to the overriding mandatory provisions of the Czech law.[110]

167. Furthermore, the content of the foreign law which is to be applied under the provisions of Czech PILA shall be determined ex officio. The court shall apply foreign law as a law, not as a statement of facts under the principle of *iura novit curia.*[111] The court or public authority deciding upon matters covered by the Czech PILA shall undertake all necessary measures for such determination;[112] they may request the parties' cooperation or obtain the opinion of a qualified expert on foreign law.[113] The court or public authority may also request an opinion on foreign law from the Czech Ministry of Justice.[114] Czech law applies if the foreign law is not determined within a reasonable time or if such determination is impossible.[115]

168. Once a foreign law is determined according to the conflict of law rules, it shall be applied according to the above-mentioned rules. However, the Czech PILA provides rules for exception situations when the application of foreign law may be declined. In entirely exceptional cases, it shall be possible to decline the application of the law that should be applied under the provisions of the Czech PILA if it is inappropriate and contrary to a reasonable and fair settlement and expectations of the parties, and after due and reasonable consideration of all the circumstances of

108. *See* s. 20/3 of the Czech PILA.
109. *See* Rozehnalová Naděžda, Jiří Valdhans, Klára Drličková, Tereza Kyselovská, *Úvod do mezinárodního práva soukromého*, p. 85 (Wolters Kluwer 2017).
110. *See* s. 23/1 of the Czech PILA.
111. Czech courts are not obliged to know the content of any foreign law but they must find out its content. Petr Bříza, Zuzan Fišerová, *§ 23. Zákon o mezinárodním právu soukromém. Komentář*, 144.151 (C.H. Beck, 2014). Judgment of the Constitutional Court of 2 Apr. 2012, Case No. Pl. ÚS 2/11; Judgment of the Supreme Court of 26 Jun. 2012, Case No. 33 Cdo 3117/2010; Judgment of the Supreme Court of 26 Jun. 2012, Case No. 33 Cdo 3529/2010.
112. *See* s. 23/2 of the Czech PILA.
113. *See* the Judgment of the Constitutional Court of 2 Apr. 2012, Case No. Pl. ÚS 2/11; Judgment of the Supreme Court of 26 Sep. 2007, Case No. 25 Cdo 1143/2006; Judgment of the Supreme Court of 31 Mar. 2016, Case No. 29 Cdo 1115/2014.
114. *See* s. 23/3 of the Czech PILA.
115. *See* s. 23/5 of the Czech PILA.

the matter. Under such circumstances and provided that the rights of the third parties remain unaffected, a legal order is applied that is more favourable to such settlement.[116] In addition, if it is impossible to determine the law applicable under other provisions of the Czech PILA, the most closely connected law shall be applied unless the parties have chosen or have otherwise identified the application of a specific law.[117]

169. The Czech PILA also contains provisions on public policy reservation based on the same principles as in EU regulations and international conventions. The Czech PILA regulates *lex fori* overriding mandatory rules[118] and foreign overriding mandatory rules.[119]

§4. Jurisdiction

170. Czech courts have jurisdiction in proceedings when the Czech procedural provisions (mainly Czech Civil Procedural Code) stipulate a local jurisdiction[120] of a court in the territory of the Czech Republic unless any provision of the Czech PILA or any other relevant legislation provides otherwise.[121] Jurisdiction of the Czech Courts does not apply to persons, international organizations or institutions having immunity under public international law, international conventions, or Czech law.[122]

171. With the accession of the Czech Republic to the EU on 1 May 2005, the European (EU) private international law has become dominant in many fields, such as international civil procedure or conflict of law rules for contractual and non-contractual obligations. In many private law disputes, jurisdiction is generally determined according to EU regulations, particularly the Brussels Ibis Regulation, Brussels IIbis Regulation, Maintenance Regulation,[123] Insolvency Regulation[124] or Succession Regulation.[125] In some disputes, international jurisdiction may be ascertained under the Lugano Convention 2007,[126] bilateral treaties on judicial cooperation in civil matters or other specialized conventions, such as CMR Convention.

---

116. *See* s. 24/1 of the Czech PILA.
117. *See* s. 24/2 of the Czech PILA.
118. *See* s. 3 of the Czech PILA.
119. *See* s. 25 of the Czech PILA.
120. Local jurisdiction of Czech courts is governed by ss 84 to 89 of the Czech Civil Procedural Code.
121. *See* s. 6/1 of the Czech PILA.
122. *See* s. 7 of the Czech PILA.
123. *See* Council Regulation (EC) 4/2009 of 18 Dec. 2008 on the jurisdiction, applicable law, recognition and enforcement of decisions and cooperation in matters relating to maintenance obligations.
124. *See* Regulation (EU) 2015/848 of the European Parliament and of the Council of 20 May 2015 on insolvency proceedings.
125. *See* Regulation (EU) 650/2012 of the European Parliament and of the Council of 4 Jul. 2012 on the jurisdiction, applicable law, recognition and enforcement of decisions and acceptance and enforcement of authentic instruments in matters of succession and on the creation of a European Certificate of Succession.
126. Convention on jurisdiction and the recognition and enforcement of judgments in civil and commercial matters.

172. The Czech PILA is therefore applicable only to matters failing from the scope of the instruments mentioned above.[127]

§5. Law Applicable

173. In the area of conflict of law rules, the Czech PILA applies to issues falling outside the scope of legislation of EU regulations and international conventions unless these sources of law expressly allow the application of provisions contained in the Czech PILA.

174. Conflict of law rules to determine the law applicable in civil and commercial matters with international element can be found in Rome I Regulation,[128] Rome II Regulation,[129] Maintenance Regulation, Succession Regulation or in international conventions such as the Hague Convention on the Law Applicable to Traffic Accidents.[130] The Czech PILA applies to, *inter alia*, the personal status of corporations, intellectual property rights (as rights with *erga omnes* effects), unilateral legal acts and defamation and infringements of personality rights.

175. In the area of the law applicable to legal entities (corporations), the Czech PILA follows the incorporation principle. The legal personality and capacity of a legal entity (corporation) shall be governed by the law of the State under which it was incorporated (*lex loci incorporationis).* The applicable law shall also govern its trading name, internal relations, the relations between such an entity and its partners or members, their mutual relations and responsibility, a person responsible for acting on behalf of such entity, and it's winding up.[131]

176. The Czech PILA follows the generally acknowledged principle of territoriality contained in relevant intellectual property conventions and EU regulations for intellectual property rights. Intellectual property rights, as such are governed by the law of the State, which recognizes these rights and protects them (*lex loci protectionis*). Choice of law is not permitted. The *lex loci protectionis* is closely connected to the principle of territoriality and the notion that *'in the area of intellectual property rights, due to their absolute nature and erga omnes effects, conflict of law issues do not arise'*.[132] The law applicable, determined according to this provision,

127. For instance, Czech courts have exclusive jurisdiction to decide upon rights in the immovable property located in the territory of the Czech Republic (s. 68 of the Czech PILA).
128. *See* Regulation (EC) 593/2008 of the European Parliament and of the Council of 17 Jun. 2008 on the law applicable to contractual obligations (Rome I).
129. *See* Regulation (EC) 864/2007 of the European Parliament and of the Council of 11 Jul. 2007 on the law applicable to non-contractual obligations (Rome II).
130. Convention of 4 May 1971 on the Law Applicable to Traffic Accidents (Hague).
131. *See* s. 30/1 of the Czech PILA.
132. *See* Zdeněk Kučera et al., *Mezinárodní právo soukromé*, 8th ed., p. 272 (Aleš Čeněk – Doplněk, 2015).

governs issues of the creation of the right (e.g., conditions for granting the right), its content (rights and obligations associated with it), and the possibility to dispose of or transfer this right.

177. Law applicable to contracts related to intellectual property rights (typically international licence contracts) is determined according to the Rome I Regulation. Law applicable to infringements of intellectual property rights (typically online infringements of copyright or registered trademarks) is determined under the Rome II Regulation.[133]

178. Legal relations established by unilateral legal actions are governed by the law of the State in which the entity which has undertaken the unilateral legal act had its habitual residence or registered seat at the time of the legal action unless the entity has chosen another law.[134]

179. The Czech PILA has a vital role in certain non-contractual obligations. The Rome II Regulation expressly excludes from its scope non-contractual obligations arising out of violations of privacy and rights relating to personality, including defamation.[135] The Czech PILA contains conflict of law rules for this type of non-contractual relationship in section 101. This provision applies to the right to appearance and privacy, mental and physical integrity, honour, dignity, manifestations of a personal nature, and the private law aspects of personal data protection (e.g., the right for compensation for damage caused by unauthorized processing of personal data).[136]

180. This provision combines objective conflict of law criteria with the possibility of choice of law for the injured party. Unless otherwise chosen by the injured party, non-contractual obligations arising from violations of privacy and rights relating to personality, including defamation, shall be governed by the law of the State in which the violation occurred *(lex loci delicti commissi).* In the case of verbal defamation (slander), it will be the law of the State where the defaming information was said. In the case of defamation published in printed media (libel), it will be the law of the State where the perpetrator has their habitual residence or seat or the law of the State where copies of the media in question were circulated. Similarly, in the case of defamation via radio or TV broadcasting or online on the Internet, it shall be the law of the State of the operator, not, for example, the law of the State from

133. For detailed analysis of conflict of law rules for intellectual property rights, *see* Tereza Kyselovská, Pavel Koukal, *Mezinárodní právo soukromé a právo duševního vlastnictví – kolizní otázky,* p. 388 (Masarykova univerzita, 2019).
134. *See* s. 90 of the Czech PILA.
135. *See* Art. 1(2)(g) of the Rome II Regulation.
136. *See* Petr Bříza, *Komentář k § 101, in Zákon o mezinárodním právu soukromém. Komentář,* p. 573 (Petr Bříza et al., C.H.Beck, 2014). *Also see* ss. 81 et seq. of the Civil Code.

where the signal is broadcast or further disseminated, where the law of the State where the radio or TV broadcast was watched from[137] or where the information was accessible online.

181. The Czech PILA contains a limited choice of law rule in favour of the injured person. The choice of law could be made regarding the presumed outcome of the dispute, i.e., the presumed amount of damages. The injured party may choose the law of State in which (a) the injured party has their habitual residence or seat, (b) the infringer has their habitual residence or seat, or (c) where the result of the illegal conduct manifested itself, provided that the infringer could foresee such result.[138] The condition of foreseeability on the part of the infringer shall be examined objectively, i.e., with regards to the person of the infringer, their knowledge, experience, and consideration shall be given to all the circumstances of the case. If the infringer can prove that they could not foresee the consequences of their conduct in the State in question, it will not be possible to apply this provision.[139]

182. The choice of law can be made before or during proceedings. The latest moment up to which it is possible to make or change the choice during proceedings is regulated by the *lex fori* procedural rules.[140]

183. The scope of law applicable determined under this provision is broad; it applies to the prerequisites of a non-contractual obligation, delictual capacity, the basis and extent of liability, including the determination of persons who may be held liable for, the grounds for exemption from liability, any limitation of liability and any division of liability, he questions whether a right to claim damages or a remedy may be transferred, persons entitled to compensation for damage sustained personally, liability for the acts of another person, etc.[141]

§6. Recognition and Enforcement of Foreign Judgments

184. Recognition and enforcement of foreign judgments in the Czech Republic are primarily governed by EU regulations (Brussels Ibis Regulation, Brussels IIbis Regulation, Maintenance Regulation or Succession Regulation) and international conventions (Lugano Convention 2007 and bilateral treaties on judicial cooperation and assistance). The Czech PILA applies to foreign judgments falling outside the instruments mentioned above, mainly to judgments from Non-Member States of the EU or non-contractual States to bilateral international treaties.

137. *See* Jiří Valdhans, *Commentary on s. 101, in Zákon o mezinárodním právu soukromém* (Monika Pauknerová, Wolters Kluwer 2016).
138. *See* s. 101 of the Czech PILA.
139. *See* Jiří Valdhans, *Commentary on s. 101, in Zákon o mezinárodním právu soukromém* (Monika Pauknerová, Wolters Kluwer 2016).
140. *See* s. 95 of the Czech Civil Procedural Code.
141. Similarly to Art. 15 of the Rome II Regulation. Petr Bříza, *Komentář k § 101, in Zákon o mezinárodním právu soukromém. Komentář*, p. 575 (Petr Bříza et al., C.H. Beck, 2014).

185. The Czech PILA contains general provisions for recognition and enforcement of foreign judgments and special provisions for recognition and enforcement of certain foreign judgments. These provisions regulate the process of recognition, necessary documents, and grounds for refusal of recognition of a foreign judgment. The foreign judgments have legal effects in the Czech Republic, provided they have been final, have become legally effective and have been recognized by the Czech authorities.[142] Recognition of foreign judgments shall be refused on the grounds of not respecting the exclusive jurisdiction of Czech courts, on the grounds of *lis pendes, rei indicate*, breach of the procedural rights of the party against which the judgment is to be recognized, a manifest contradiction to the public policy or lack of reciprocity.[143]

§7. Arbitration

186. Rules on international commercial arbitration (such as arbitration agreement, the law applicable or recognition and enforcement of foreign arbitral awards) were previously enacted in the Arbitration Act. However, with the recodification of civil law, some of these rules were transferred into the Czech PILA.[144]

187. The Czech PILA expressly regulates issues such as determining the admissibility of an arbitration agreement in international commercial arbitration, the right of a foreigner to be designated as arbitrator in proceedings in the Czech Republic, and the determination of applicable law and recognition and enforcement of foreign arbitral awards. Arbitration proceedings are generally regulated by the Arbitration Act and procedural rules by arbitration courts.[145] The Czech Civil Procedural Code proportionally and adequately governs issues not expressly provided in these instruments.[146] Furthermore, the Czech Republic is contracting state to the New York Convention on Recognition and Enforcement of Foreign Judgments.

188. The admissibility of an arbitration agreement shall be governed by Czech law, i.e., the Arbitration Act. Other issues regarding an arbitration agreement shall be determined by the law of the State where an arbitral award is to be issued *(lex arbitri).*[147] The same applies to formal requirements for an arbitral award; nevertheless, it shall be sufficient if requirements of the law of the State where the intention of the parties were expresses were met.[148]

142. *See* s. 14 of the Czech PILA.
143. *See* s. 15 of the Czech PILA.
144. *See* Part 7, ss 117 to 122 of the Czech PILA.
145. In the Czech Republic are three permanent arbitration courts established by a special legislative act, Arbitration Court attached to the Economic Chamber of the Czech Republic and Agricultural Chamber of the Czech Republic, Prague Stock Exchange Arbitration Court, and International Arbitration Court of the Czech Commodity Exchange.
146. *See* s. 30 of the Arbitration Act.
147. *See* s. 117/1 of the Czech PILA.
148. *See* s. 117/2 of the Czech PILA.

189. Under the Czech Arbitration Act, the arbitration agreement shall be concluded in writing. Otherwise, it is invalid. However, the written form is fulfilled by electronic means that allow storage of their content and the identification of the contractual parties.[149] Therefore, it is possible to validly conclude an arbitration agreement using electronic communication means, such as e-mail; a qualified electronic or digital signature is not necessary.

190. A foreigner (a non-Czech citizen) may be designated as an arbitrator provided, they have full legal capacity under the law of the State of which they are a citizen *(lex patriae)*; it shall be, however, sufficient if the foreigner has full legal capacity under Czech law.[150]

191. The arbitration procedure is governed by the Czech Arbitration Act and the Czech Civil Procedural Code. The Czech Arbitration Act is relatively brief legislation and contains only basic rules determining the arbitral procedure, procedural rights and obligations of the parties and the arbitrators. The parties may agree on the procedure by which the arbitrators shall conduct the proceedings.[151] Parties may choose the place of arbitration,[152] how they will meet (in person or via videoconference), whether the proceeding will be based solely on written documents submitted by the parties (in written form or electronically), or whether the hearing will be necessary.

192. Procedural rules of arbitration courts regulate some aspects of arbitration proceedings. For example, the Arbitration Court attached to the Economic Chamber of the Czech Republic and the Agricultural Chamber of the Czech Republic offers online arbitration based on special procedural rules for online arbitration.[153] These online rules contain provisions on the place of rendering arbitral award (Prague), the format of submissions, case site where the dispute is conducted, method of communication between parties and arbitrators, examples of arbitration clauses, etc. This type of arbitration is conducted exclusively online using electronic communications.

193. Law applicable to the merits of the dispute shall be the law chosen by the parties; otherwise, it shall be determined under the Czech PILA (meaning under the EU regulations that are primarily applicable before the Czech PILA). *Renvoi* is permitted only if the parties have expressly agreed upon it. The Czech PILA also allows

149. *See* s. 3/1 of the Czech PILA.
150. *See* s. 118 of the Czech PILA. A foreigner may serve as an arbitrator in an international commercial arbitration under the Czech PILA Act. For domestic arbitration with no international element under the Czech Arbitration Act, only Czech citizens fulfilling conditions of s. 4 of the Czech Arbitration Act may be named as arbitrators.
151. *See* s. 19/1 of the Czech Arbitration Act.
152. *See* s. 17 of the Czech Arbitration Act.
153. *See* Additional procedures for online arbitration (online Rules), Arbitration Court attached to the Economic Chamber of the Czech Republic and Agricultural Chamber of the Czech Republic (3 Jul. 2022), https://en.soud.cz/rules/additional-procedures-for-on-line-arbitration-1st-june-2004.

arbitrators to decide the dispute based on the principles of justice, but they may do so only if expressly authorized by the parties.[154]

194. According to the Czech Arbitration Act, an arbitral award shall be passed by a majority of the arbitrators, made in writing and signed by at least a majority of the arbitrators.[155] An arbitral award may also be issued in electronic form. The Czech Arbitration Act does not specify which form of electronic signature must be used; an arbitral award shall be signed to enable unequivocal identification of the arbitrators who signed it.[156]

195. The Czech PILA contains special provisions for the recognition and enforcement of foreign arbitral awards.[157] The recognition shall be refused if no reciprocity is granted, the arbitral award Is not final or enforceable under the law of the State of its origin, was set aside in a State in which or under the law of which it was issued, is contrary to the Czech public policy or fulfils grounds for setting aside an arbitral award under section 31 of the Arbitration Act.[158] However, due to the existence of the more 'lenient' New York Convention, these provisions are not very often applied.

154. *See* s. 119 of the Czech PILA.
155. *See* s. 25/1 of the Czech Arbitration Act.
156. *See* Miloš Olík, *§ 25, in Zákon o rozhodčím řízení a o výkonu rozhodčích nálezů. Komentář* (Miloš Olík et al., Wolters Kluwer, 2019), available online at: www.noveaspi.cz.
157. *See* ss 120 to 122 of the Czech PILA.
158. *See* s. 121 of the Czech PILA.

Chapter 4. Competition Law Applied to the Digital Markets

§1. Introduction

196. In the Czech Republic, there is a set of rules on competition law in force since 1991. It is applicable to all branches of the economy, including the digital markets. The competition law deals with possible abuses of market power, both multilateral (anticompetitive agreements) and unilateral (abuse of dominant position), and with merger review. The Czech competition law is based on the EU one and the courts repeatedly held that it needs to be interpreted in line with EU law and jurisprudence. In addition to that, public authorities are prohibited from distorting competition by their activities. There is a specific governmental agency – the Office for the Protection of Competition [*Úřad pro ochranu hospodářské soutěže*] (UOHS) entrusted with the protection of competition and with enforcement of competition rules (hereinafter referred to as 'Czech Competition Authority' (CCA)).

197. Unlike in some other countries, there are no sector-specific competition rules concerning only digital markets (or any other specific sector), and the same general rules on competition thus apply throughout the economy.

198. At the same time, specific sectors are subject to a sector-specific regulation, aimed at promoting competition in areas where its intensity is not sufficient. Such a sector-specific regulation is in place also for the area of electronic communications, where, historically, the market used to be dominated by State monopolies and its development was not driven by market forces, but only by administrative directives. Specific regulation was, therefore, required in order to introduce competition into this market, in particular, to enable access of alternative operators. There is a specific governmental agency – the CTO [*Český telekomunikační úřad*] responsible for the enforcement of these rules.

199. The relationship between these two sets of rules and the two agencies enforcing them has not always been clear, as the same conduct of the same undertaking may be subjected to enforcement by both the agencies. As will be discussed in the Chapter below, the existence of sector-specific regulation does not prevent the CCA from exercising its powers.

200. In this Chapter, we will discuss general issues of Czech competition law, sector-specific regulation of electronic communications as far as it is concerned with promoting competition in digital markets and the relationship between these sets of rules. The enforcement of competition law will also be described. In addition to that, we will also outline the principal cases of enforcement of competition law in digital markets over the last ten years, i.e., in the period 2012–2021.

§2. Czech Competition Law and Its Enforcement

201. Czech competition law is contained in the Competition Act,[159] adopted in 2001, that covers both substantive provisions and procedural rules. It is based on the EU regulatory framework; the regulation of anticompetitive agreements corresponds in principle with Article 101 TFEU, abuse of dominant position with Article 102 TFEU and review of concentrations with the EU Merger Regulation.[160] All these provisions of the Competition Act, including the rules on procedure, have to be interpreted in line with EU competition law.[161] Conversely, the rule that public authorities may not distort competition does not have a direct mirror-image in the EU law.

202. As already mentioned above, the CCA is the only authority empowered to apply Czech competition law (*public enforcement*). In addition to that, it is also possible to raise competition-related claims before Czech civil courts (*private enforcement*), even though such cases of are still rare in practice. There are no specialized courts dedicated to private enforcement of competition law, general courts have jurisdiction in such cases. The enforcement of Czech competition law will be discussed in more detail below.

203. The Czech Competition Authority, in its current form, was created in 1996 by the Scope of Competence Act.[162] According to this Act, the main aim of the Competition Authority is to *support and protect the competition against its illegal restrictions.*[163] Additionally, apart from the enforcement of competition law, the CCA is also active in other areas broadly connected with undistorted competition. It is a central coordinating, advisory, consulting and monitoring authority in the area of State aid[164] and the supervisory authority for public procurement.[165] Since 2009, it has also been awarded a new competence concerning regulation of retail chains with significant market power.[166]

204. The Czech Competition Authority is both an investigative and adjudicative body. Its decisions are subject to full-jurisdictional review by administrative

159. *See* Act. No. 143/2001 Sb., on the Protection of Competition and on Amendment to Certain Acts (Act on the Protection of Competition), as amended ('Competition Act'), available in English at: http://www.uohs.cz/en/legislation.html.
160. *See* Council Regulation (EC) No. 139/2004 on the control of concentrations between undertakings (the EC Merger Regulation), OJ L 24, 20 Jan. 2004, 1.
161. *See* the Judgment of the Supreme Administrative Court of 25 Feb. 2009, Case No. 1 Afs 78/2008 (*Building Saving Banks*).
162. *See* Act No. 273/1996 Sb., on the Scope of Competence of the Office for the Protection of Competition, as amended ('Scope of Competence Act').
163. *Ibid.*, Art. 1(1).
164. *See* Act No. 215/2004 Sb., on Regulation of Relations in the Area of State Aid and on Amendment to the Act on the support of Research and Development, as amended.
165. *See* Act. No. 137/2006 Sb., on Public Contracts, as amended.
166. *See* Act No. 395/2009 Sb., on Significant Market Power in the Sale of Agricultural and Food Products and Abuse thereof.

courts,[167] specifically the Regional Court in Brno; legality of its judgments can then be scrutinized by the Supreme Administrative Court. All the decisions of the CCA are (in a non-confidential version) published on its website (in Czech only),[168] as are the court judgments reviewing them.[169]

205. As has already been observed, there are no sector-specific rules concerning the application of competition law in digital markets. Neither were we able to identify any specifics of competition policy in this area.

206. In the Annual Report for 2017, which mentioned as the likely focus for competition law agenda in 2018 also the competition law issues in the digital economy, the CCA stated that:

> The Office is going to concentrate on the enforcement of new phenomena in the field of competition law that follow from the developing digitalisation across all business sectors. Such digitalisation can be observed especially in the case of digital platforms, which disrupt and change the current thinking on the functioning of present economic relations. A big challenge in this regard will be the assessment of the functioning and behaviour of digital algorithms which have the ability of autonomous learning and which substitute human decision-making in some sectors. That will bring about a number of questions, for example, who would be liable for the potential infringement of competition law: the user of the algorithm or its designer; or how to assess a mutual agreement between two or more algorithms which would be contrary to competition law principles. The interest of the Office will also be focused on the issues of digital sales whether it be certain kind of production or services, or potentially on the Internet price comparison websites.[170]

207. Despite this proclamation, we have not been able to identify any significant shift in the CCA's policy. The CCA, however, repeated in its Annual Report for 2021 that it '*will closely monitor the activities in the area of digital markets and platforms*'.[171]

§3. Anti-competitive Agreements

208. The Competition Act stipulates in section 3/1 that all agreements between undertakings, decisions by associations of undertakings and concerted practices (hereinafter referred to as 'agreements') which have as their object or effect the distortion of competition shall be prohibited and void. Both horizontal (i.e., between

167. *See* Act No. 150/2002 Sb., Code of Administrative Justice, as amended.
168. Available at: https://www.uohs.cz/cs/hospodarska-soutez/sbirky-rozhodnuti.html.
169. Available at: https://www.uohs.cz/cs/hospodarska-soutez/soudni-prezkum-rozhodnuti.html.
170. *See* The CCA's Annual Report for 2017, p. 84 (own translation); available at: https://www.uohs.cz/cs/informacni-centrum/vyrocni-zpravy.html.
171. *See* The CCA's Annual Report for 2021, p. 57 (own translation); available at: https://www.uohs.cz/cs/informacni-centrum/vyrocni-zpravy.html.

competitors) and vertical (i.e., through the distribution chain) agreements are prohibited by this provision, regardless of their form. Agreements that have the distortion of competition as their object (e.g., price-fixing, market-sharing or bid rigging) are deemed to be illegal, without the necessity to prove their actual effect on competition.

209. Agreements with insignificant impact on competition, which do not have the distortion of competition as their object, are, however, not prohibited; the CCA has issued a notice clarifying when the impact is deemed to be insignificant, based on the market share of the undertakings concerned.[172] This exemption only covers the agreements that have the distortion of competition as their effect; conversely, by-object agreements are always prohibited, regardless of the market shares of the undertakings involved.

210. Even if agreements have as their object or effect the distortion of competition, they may still be exempted from the prohibition provided that they, at the same time:

(a) contribute to improving the production or distribution of goods or to promoting technical or economic progress while allowing consumers a fair share of the resulting benefit;
(b) do not impose on the undertakings restrictions which are not indispensable to the attainment of the objectives pursuant to letter (a) above;
(c) do not afford the undertakings the possibility of eliminating competition in respect to a substantial part of the market of goods, the supply or purchase which constitutes the objective of the agreement.[173]

211. While it is on the Competition Authority to prove that there is an agreement within the meaning of section 3/1 of the Competition Act, the undertakings concerned need to prove that the conditions for exemption according to section 3/4 of the Competition Act are fulfilled.[174] This is, however, only rarely the case in practice; as will be described below, the CCA was dealing only with by-object agreements over the last ten years, and it has never relied on this exemption with respect to them so far.

212. Certain categories of agreements may also be 'block-exempted'. In this case, it is not necessary to prove that all the conditions of Article 3(4) are fulfilled; it is sufficient only to show that the provisions of the agreement in question correspond with the requirements set by the block exemption. The CCA chose not to issue its own block exemptions; it instead declared that if an agreement fulfils the

172. Notice of the CCA on agreements of minor importance, which do not appreciably restrict competition (*de minimis*); available at: http://www.uohs.cz/en/legislation.html. The criterion is based on market share: horizontal agreements are not covered by the prohibition if the combined market share of their participants does not exceed 10 %, vertical ones, if the market share on any level of distribution does not exceed 15%.
173. Section 3/4 of the Competition Act.
174. *Ibid.*, s. 21d/1.

criteria set by the Commission (which is authorized to issue block exemptions from the EU law), and is, therefore, not prohibited by the EU competition law, it is also not prohibited by the Czech one.[175] The block exemptions cover both specific sectors of the economy (e.g., insurance) and specific types of commercial relationships (e.g., distribution agreements between producers and their distributors).[176]

213. Decisions on anticompetitive agreements constitute the vast majority of antitrust cases of the Competition Authority.[177] In the period 2012–2021, the Authority issued 74 such decisions, all of them by-object ones. The vast majority of agreements under investigation were horizontal ones (82%). The main focus of the authority is bid rigging, i.e., collusion in public procurement. As far as vertical agreements targeted by the CCA are concerned, most of them dealt with resale price maintenance, i.e., price-fixing by the supplier for the distributor.

214. Thus, even though several decisions of the authority address digital markets, both in bid rigging[178] or in online distribution,[179] the decisions' methodology generally followed the analysis employed in all other decisions on anticompetitive agreements and the fact that the conduct in question occurred in digital markets was from this perspective irrelevant.

215. The only significant 'digital' case was a decision against *Booking.com.*[180] The CCA investigated – as did many other EU competition authorities[181] – the parity clauses applied by Booking.com to the providers of accommodation. The CCA concluded that the wide parity clauses (which guaranteed that the offer the provider of accommodation made via Booking.com are at least as favourable as the most favourable offer made to anybody else) are anticompetitive vertical agreements that have the effect of restricting competition. By contrast, the narrow parity clauses (which enable the providers of accommodation to make a more favourable offer via other online platforms or via offline distribution channels) were found to be compliant with competition law. The CCA's findings were thus mostly in line with those

175. *Ibid.*, s. 4/1.
176. The EU block exemptions, as well as explanatory guidelines of the European Commission, are available at: https://ec.europa.eu/competition-policy/antitrust/legislation/block-exemption-regulations_en.
177. All the data for this Chapter are based on the statistics, contained in the CCA's annual reports, and on quantitative analysis of the decision making of the CCA, summarized in Michal Petr & Eva Zorková, *Kvantitativní analýza rozhodování soutěžního úřadu*, Antitrust, no. 3 (2018): 77; Michal Petr & Eva Zorková, *Rozšířená kvantitativní analýza rozhodování českého soutěžního úřadu*, Antitrust, no. 4 (2020): 88.
178. *See* in particular the decision of the CCA Ref. No. S257/2017/KD of 10 Feb. 2020 (*Data Transfers in Prerov*) and the decision of the Chairman of the CCA Ref. No. R221/2020/HS of 18 Aug. 2021 (*e-Government in Olomouc*).
179. *See,* e.g., decision of the Chairman of the CCA Ref. No. R84/2009/HS of 28 Jan. 2011 (*HUSKY*), concerning online sales of sport equipment.
180. *See* Decision of the Chairman of the CCA Ref. No. R219/2018/HS of 1 Nov. 2019 (*Booking.com*).
181. For details of this case on the EU level, *see,* e.g., *ECN Report on the Monitoring Exercise Carried out in the Online Hotel Booking Sector by EU Competition Authorities in 2016*, available at: https://ec.europa.eu/competition/ecn/hotel_monitoring_report_en.pdf.

of the French, Italian and Swedish competition authorities, which in parallel negotiated the commitments of Booking.com in 2015.

216. The Booking.com case was peculiar as far as commitments are concerned. The CCA opened the proceedings only after Booking.com committed itself to switch from wide parity clauses to narrow ones, which resulted in closure of the proceedings before French, Italian and Swedish competition authorities. As the commitments were EU-wide, it was generally believed that further investigation was not necessary, and indeed, other competition authorities in the EU brought their investigation to an end after the commitments were approved in France, Italy and Sweden. Conversely, the CCA was the only one to open formal investigation thereafter. As Booking.com had already modified its behaviour, no commitments were possible in the proceedings before the CCA. The CCA concluded that Booking.com's conduct before the commitments (i.e., wide parity clauses) was anticompetitive and imposed a fine; it also scrutinized its conduct after the commitments (i.e., narrow parity clauses) and concluded that the conduct was not anticompetitive.

217. The CCA's decision was recently endorsed by the Regional Court in Brno.[182]

§4. Abuse of Dominant Position

218. As far as unilateral conduct is concerned, the Competition Act prohibits abuse of dominant position of an undertaking. Such a position is defined as follows: *one or more undertakings jointly (joint dominance) shall be deemed to have a dominant position in the relevant market, if their market power enables them to behave independently to a significant extent of other undertakings or consumers.*[183] The Competition Act further stipulates that the Competition Authority *shall assess the market power on the basis of the amount of ascertained volume of sales or purchases in the relevant market for the goods in question (market share), achieved by the relevant undertaking or undertakings in joint dominant position during the period examined pursuant to this Act. Also on the basis of other indices, in particular the economic and financial power of the undertakings, legal or other obstacles for other undertakings to enter into the market, the level of vertical integration of undertakings, market structure and size of the market shares of their immediate competitors.*[184] It also postulates a safe harbour, according to which, unless proven otherwise, an undertaking or undertakings jointly shall be deemed not to be in a dominant position, if their share in the relevant market achieved during the examined period does not exceed 40%.[185] The CCA has not decided on a dominance below the 40% market share in the last ten years.

182. *See* Judgment of the Regional Court of 31 Jan. 2022, Case No. 30 Af 2/2020 (*Booking.com*).
183. *See* s. 10/1 of the Competition Act.
184. *Ibid.*, s. 10/2.
185. *Ibid.*, s. 10/3.

219. Not dominant position as such, but only its abuse is prohibited. The Competition Act does not define what is to be understood by abuse, it only states that *abuse of dominant position to the detriment of other undertakings or consumers shall be prohibited*, and includes a demonstrative list of practices deemed to be abusive.[186] Generally speaking, abusive would be such an exercise of market power that distorts competition and harms either other undertakings or consumers. It is possible to distinguish between exclusionary abusive strategies, whereby the dominant undertaking secures its position by forcing its competitors out of the market (or by prohibiting them from entering it), and exploitative ones, whereby the dominant takes advantage of its position in a way not perceivable on a functioning market, for example, by charging supra-competitive prices.

220. Compared to anticompetitive agreements, the enforcement activities of the Competition Authority in the area of abuse of dominance are very limited, with only 12 cases closed in the period 2012–2021. Out of these, only two may be considered to be connected with digital markets.

221. In 2018, a decision concerning refusal to allow access to data on public transportation timetables, deemed to constitute essential facility for services scheduling public transportation, was issued in the *CHAPS* case.[187] CHAPS is a private company, entrusted by the Czech Government to collect all the timetables of public personal transport by bus and rail; for those purposes, the transport operators are obliged to provide it with all the necessary data. CHAPS is thus the only company holding all the data on public transport in the Czech Republic. Thanks to that, it is able to provide services of finding the public transport connections.

222. The CCA decided that with respect to these data, CHAPS was a monopolist, and that it had abused its dominant position by refusing to provide access to it to other undertakings, in particular to Seznam.cz, the biggest Czech provider of online services, which led to a restriction of competition on the downstream services markets to the detriment of Seznam.cz and consumers. According to the CCA, Seznam.cz wanted to introduce potentially superior product to the existing search engine, which has been operated by CHAPS. However, by not allowing Seznam.cz to have access to the same data set that CHAPS had prevented Seznam.cz from doing so. This decision of the CCA was annulled by the Regional Court in Brno, but only on procedural grounds.[188] Materially the same decision is expected to be issued by the CCA in 2022.

223. The second case was concerned with a putative margin squeeze in broadband Internet access by *O2*. The CCA had been investigating this case for almost a decade, it nonetheless closed it in 2019, concluding that it had not accumulated enough information to prove that the dominant position was abused.[189] It is worth

186. *Ibid.*, s. 10/2.
187. *See* Decision of the Chairman of the CCA Ref. No. R 12/2006/HS of 16 Jan. 2018 (*CHAPS*).
188. *See* Judgment of the Regional Court of 25 Nov. 2020, Case No. 30 Afs 28/2018 (*CHAPS*).
189. *See* Decision of the CCA Ref. No. S109/2011/DP of 23 Jan. 2019 (*O2 margin squeeze*).

mentioning that a competitor to O2 on the retail level filed a private action for damages against O2, which was, however, dismissed by the courts of first and second instance; the case is still pending before the Supreme Court.

§5. Control of Concentrations

224. Merger control is based on the notification and *ex ante* clearance principle in the Czech Republic. If the annual turnover of the undertakings concerned exceed certain levels (*see* below), the concentration needs to be notified to the CCA and it cannot be implemented until the Competition Authority approves it.

225. What constitutes a concentration is defined in section 12 of the Competition Act; it includes mergers, acquisitions and other transactions whereby an undertaking acquires control over another one (or its part) on a lasting basis. Also, establishment of an undertaking jointly controlled by more undertakings that performs all functions of an autonomous economic entity is deemed to constitute a concentration; on the other hand, to the extent the establishment of a joint venture has as its object or effect coordination of competitive conduct of the undertakings controlling such a joint venture, such a coordination is assessed as an agreement according to section 3 of the Competition Act (*see* above). The CCA issued an explanatory notice clarifying which transactions under what conditions constitute a concentration.[190]

226. If a transaction constitutes a concentration and the annual turnovers of undertakings concerned exceed the thresholds specified in sections 13 and 14 of the Competition Act, it is subject to the approval of the CCA. A concentration shall thus be subject to the approval of the CCA if:

(1) the total net turnover of all undertakings concerned achieved in the last accounting period in the market of the Czech Republic exceeds CZK 1.5 billion [approximately EUR 60 million] and each of at least two of the undertakings concerned achieved in the market of the Czech Republic in the last accounting period a net turnover exceeding CZK 250 million [approximately EUR 10 million]; or
(2) the net turnover achieved in the last accounting period in the market of the Czech Republic:
  (a) in the case of a concentration pursuant to Article 12(1) at least by one of the parties to the merger;
  (b) in the case of a concentration pursuant to Article 12(2) by the acquired enterprise or a substantial part thereof;
  (c) in the case of a concentration pursuant to Article 12(3) by the undertaking, over whom the control is acquired; or

190. Notice of the CCA on the concept of concentration, available at: http://www.uohs.cz/cs/legislativa/hospodarska-soutez.html.

(d) in the case of a concentration pursuant to Article 12(5) by at least one of the undertakings establishing a joint venture.

(3) is higher than CZK 1.5 billion [approximately EUR 60 million] and at the same time the worldwide net turnover achieved in the last accounting period by another undertaking concerned exceeds CZK 1.5 billion [approximately EUR 60 million].

227. The CCA has issued two explanatory notices on the procedure of turnover calculation.[191]

228. If these notification thresholds are fulfilled, the concentration must be notified to the CCA; the notification takes place on a special form, issued as a decree by the Authority.[192] An administrative fee of CZK 100,000 [approximately EUR 4,000] has to be paid to the CCA.[193]

229. In the course of the proceedings, the CCA assesses whether the notified concentration may result in a substantial distortion of competition in the relevant market, particularly because it would result in creating a dominant undertaking or strengthening of its position. If the combined share of all undertakings concerned in the relevant market does not exceed 25%, it is presumed that their concentration does not result in a substantial distortion of competition.[194]

230. Usually, the notified concentration will be reviewed in thirty days (Phase I review); if the Competition Authority does not issue any decision within this deadline, the concentration is deemed to be approved.[195] If, however, the CCA finds that the concentration raises serious concerns as to a significant distortion of competition, it will inform the parties to the proceedings within the thirty-day deadline that it is continuing the proceedings;[196] the final decision is then to be reached within five months after the proceedings have been initiated (Phase II review).[197]

231. If the concentration raises serious concerns, the undertakings concerned may propose commitments in order to maintain effective competition in the relevant market; such commitments may be both behavioural (i.e., the undertakings commit themselves to behave in a specific way) and structural (i.e., the undertakings commit themselves to change their structure, for example, to divest a specific part of their commercial activities). The CCA would, in such a case, make its decision approving the concentration conditional on fulfilment of the commitments.[198]

191. Notice of the CCA on the notion of 'undertakings concerned' and on calculation of turnover, available at: http://www.uohs.cz/en/legislation.html.
192. *See* Decree of the Competition Authority No. 294/2016 Sb., stipulating details relating to the notification of a concentration of undertakings, as amended ('Decree on Concentrations').
193. *See* Act No. 634/2004 Sb., on Administrative Fees, as amended; Item 63 of an attachment thereof.
194. *See* s. 17/3 of the Competition Act.
195. *Ibid.*, s. 16/2.
196. *Ibid.*
197. *Ibid.*, s. 16/5.
198. *Ibid.*, s. 17/4.

232. If the distortion of competition is less likely, a simplified procedure may take place. According to section 16a/1 of the Competition Act, simplified notification of a concentration may be filed in case of a concentration when:

(a) none of the undertakings involved is operating in the same relevant market, or their combined share in such a market does not exceed 15%, and at the same time none of the undertakings concerned is operating in the market vertically connected to the relevant market in which another undertaking operates, or their share in every such market does not exceed 25%; or
(b) the undertaking acquires exclusive control over the joint venture in which it has participated in joint control so far.

233. The undertakings concerned then only need to submit a shortened version of the notification form;[199] the proceedings take up to twenty days.[200] The CCA has issued an explanatory note clarifying which concentrations can be assessed in such a simplified procedure and how it is to be conducted.[201]

234. In order to avoid any unnecessary problems during the course of the proceedings, where the time limits are rather tight, the undertakings may discuss their envisaged merger with the CCA even before the notification.[202]

235. Based on the Annual reports of the CCA,[203] there were 459 merger decisions issued in the period 2012–2021, i.e., less than fifty every year. The overwhelming majority of these (almost 70%) were approved in the simplified procedure, where the competition authority does not raise any competition concerns at all, the rest (26%) were approved in Phase I, where the analysis is very limited and no competition concerns are mentioned. Only twenty-one cases were adopted by a Phase II decision. In ten cases, the CCA adopted commitments of the merging parties. Even though several concentrations reviewed during this period of time concerned digital markets, it is not possible to discuss them in detail due to the limited analysis, included in the CCAs simplified-procedure or Phase-I decisions.

236. The only significant exception in this regard was the case *Rockaway Capital/Heureka Shopping*,[204] where a private equity company acquired control over a major Czech price comparison website (Heureka.cz) and other related online businesses, while the acquiror at that time controlled one of the major Czech online shopping malls (mall.cz). The CCA held that the market share of Heureka.cz on the

199. *See* Decree on Concentrations, Annex No. 2.
200. *See* s. 16a/3 of the Competition Act.
201. Notice of the CCA on the simplified procedure of merger assessment, available at: http://www.uohs.cz/cs/legislativa/hospodarska-soutez.html.
202. Notice of the Competition Authority on pre-notification contacts with merging parties, available at: http://www.uohs.cz/en/legislation.html.
203. Annual reports of the Competition Authority are available at: http://www.uohs.cz/en/information-centre/annual-reports.html.
204. *See* Decision of the CCA Ref. No. S13/2016/KS of 16 May 2016 (*Rockaway Capital/Heureka Shopping*).

market of price comparison websites in the Czech Republic was in the range of 45%–55%[205] and there was a concern that after the acquisition by Rockaway Capital, the said price comparison website would start preferring other online businesses controlled by Rockaway Capital, in particular the mall.cz. Furthermore, there was a concern that Heureka.cz would ask participating online shops to provide excessive data about their customers which might be used to favour Rockaway Capital businesses. In order to overcome those concerns, the acquirer proposed commitments which the CCA accepted and eventually approved the concentration. The commitments were meant to provide transparency (a clear link between Heureka.cz and other Rockaway Capital activities were to be published visibly on the website) and non-discrimination of independent sellers (especially prescribed number of positions of recommended shops and minimum number of search results) as well as to limit the possibility to gather excessive data. With regard to the gathering of data, Heureka.cz was not allowed to oblige sellers to provide other data than the underlying customers' e-mail addresses and nor was it allowed to provide benefits to those who provided more data or to disadvantage those who did not.

§6. Supervision over Public Authorities

237. On the basis of an amendment to the Competition Act in 2012, the CCA now makes sure that the competition is not distorted not only by activities of undertakings, but also of public authorities, exercising their public powers. Public authorities are defined very broadly and include: (i) state administration authorities in the exercise of state administration; (ii) local government authorities in the exercise of self-government and the transferred state administration; and (iii) self-governance authorities in the exercise of transferred state administration.[206]

238. Public authorities are prohibited from unjustifiably distorting competition, in particular by favouring a particular undertaking or group of undertakings, by excluding them from competition or by excluding competition in the market;[207] these terms are not further defined. Conversely, decision-making of public authorities and granting State aid is not covered by this provision.[208]

239. Should the CCA find that a public authority distorted the competition and that there was an infringement, it may impose a fine up to CZK 10 million [approximately EUR 400,000].[209] If the public authority in question is subordinated to another one (e.g., a governmental agency subordinated to a specific ministry), the CCA shall also inform such a superior authority.[210]

205. The precise figure of the market share is not available in the publicly accessible decision.
206. *See* s. 1/1/d of the Competition Act.
207. *Ibid.*, s. 19a/1.
208. *Ibid.*, s. 19a/2.
209. *Ibid.*, s. 22aa.
210. *Ibid.*, s. 19a/4.

240. Sector-specific regulators are not exempted from this regulation and the CCA may thus in principle exercise supervision over their activities.; for example, the Czech Competition Authority received several complaints against the Czech Telecommunications Authority concerning the auction for 5G frequencies, but no formal proceedings were opened. The CCA declared in its Annual Report for 2020 that it will concentrate of this topic,[211] it has, however, not taken any enforcement action yet.

241. The decisions issued by the CCA in this area have so far only concerned municipal decrees on location of slot-machines within their territories.[212] We will therefore not discuss this topic any further.

§7. FAILURE TO COMPLY WITH COMPETITION LAW

242. When an undertaking concludes an anticompetitive agreement or abuses its dominant position, the CCA will initiate proceedings, governed by the Competition Act and the Code of Administrative Procedure,[213] in conjunction with the Act on Administrative Offences.[214] A fine of up to 10% of the annual turnover may be imposed on an undertaking in breach of the law.[215] If, however, the undertaking in question confesses it breached the law, its fine shall be decreased by 20% (settlement).[216]

243. In case of secret horizontal cartels, the undertakings participating in them may avoid the fine if – broadly speaking – they provide the CCA with evidence previously unknown to it, which will enable it to prove the infringement.[217] The details of this *leniency programme* are set out in a notice of the CCA.[218]

244. In parallel with the fine, the CCA may impose remedial measures, the aim of which is to restore effective competition in the market;[219] such measures would be of a behavioural nature, for example, to change existing contracts in a certain way.

---

211. The CCA's Annual Report for 2020, p. 61; available at: https://www.uohs.cz/cs/informacni-centrum/vyrocni-zpravy.html.
212. *See, e.g.*, the decision of the Chairman of the CCA Ref. No. R7/2017/HS of 13 Nov. 2017 (*Bílina*).
213. *See* Act No. 500/2004 Sb., Code of Administrative Procedure, as amended.
214. *See* Act No. 250/2016 Sb., on Liability for Administrative Offences and on Proceedings Concerning Them, as amended.
215. *See* s. 22a of the Competition Act; in cases of decisions of associations of undertakings, the fine may go up to 10% of the annual turnover of their members.
216. *Ibid.*, s. 22ba/2. For further details, *see* the Competition Authority's notice on settlement procedure, available at: http://www.uohs.cz/cs/legislativa/hospodarska-soutez.html.
217. *See* s. 22ba of the Competition Act.
218. Leniency programme of the Competition Authority is available at: http://www.uohs.cz/en/competition/antitrust/new-leniency-programme.html.
219. *See* s. 20/4 of the Competition Act.

245. In case of *bid rigging*, a prohibition to participate in public tenders for up to three years may also be imposed in addition to the fine.[220] First, such a prohibition was imposed in 2021 in a case concerning bid rigging in the area of logistics.[221]

246. In case a merger was implemented without the approval decision of the CCA or not in accordance with it, the Competition Authority decides on measures indispensable to re-establish effective competition in the relevant market; in particular, it may impose on the undertakings concerned an obligation to sell stakes, to transfer an enterprise or a part thereof acquired on the basis of a concentration or to discharge the contract, on the basis of which the concentration was realized, or to implement other adequate measures necessary for re-establishing effective competition.[222] In this case, the remedial measures may, thus, be both behavioural and structural.

247. For the sake of completeness, it also ought to be mentioned that from a civil law point of view, legal acts contrary to the Competition Act, in particular contracts, are null and void.[223] In cases of disputes, it is on civil courts – not the Competition Authority – to decide on the validity of individual contracts or the particular provisions thereof. Those harmed by anticompetitive conduct may also seek damages.[224] A special act on damages,[225] implementing an EU directive,[226] was issued to facilitate their claims. Private enforcement of competition law is, however, still extremely rare in the Czech Republic.[227]

248. Finally, involvement in a horizontal cartel may also constitute a crime of natural persons;[228] an imprisonment of up to eight years may be imposed for such a crime.[229] The authors are aware of an ongoing criminal investigation concerning bid rigging in the ICT markets, connected with an above-mentioned CCA decision on bid rigging in case of e-government.

220. *Ibid.*, s. 22a/4.
221. Decision of the Chairman of the CCA Ref. No. R115/2021/HS of 29 Oct. 2021 (*Logistics*).
222. *See* s. 18/5 of the Competition Act.
223. *See* s. 580/1 of the Act. No. 89/2012 Sb., Civil Code, as amended.
224. *Ibid.*, s. 2990.
225. *See* Act No. 262/2017 Sb., on damages claims in case of competition law infringements.
226. *See* Directive (EU) 2014/104/EU of the European Parliament and of the Council of 26 Nov. 2014 on certain rules governing actions for damages under national law for infringements of the competition law provisions of the Member States and of the EU.
227. In detail, *see* Michal Petr & Eva Zorková, *Soukromé prosazování v České republice*, (Antitrust, no. 2 2016): I.
228. *See* s. 248/2 of the Act No. 40/2009 Sb., *Criminal Code*, as amended.
229. *Ibid.*, s. 248/4.

§8. Czech Competition Law and Sectoral Regulation

249. The Act on Electronic Communications[230] will be discussed in detail in a separate Chapter below. For the sake of completeness, it is, however, necessary to make a few comments from the perspective of competition law.

250. First of all, the Act on Electronic Communications regulates the conduct of enterprises with significant market power, which are defined in the same way as dominant undertakings according to competition law.[231] Second, the Czech Telecommunications Authority regularly conducts analyses of relevant markets, in order to ascertain whether the markets are effectively competitive;[232] again, the relevant markets are defined in the same way as in competition law.[233] Third, the Czech Telecommunications Authority is empowered to impose obligations on enterprises, including price regulation.[234] And finally, the Telecommunications Authority may impose specific behavioural obligations on enterprises with significant market power, that are in practice very similar with the prohibition to abuse dominant position, e.g., non-discrimination or obligation to enable access to specific pieces of infrastructure,[235] and in case these obligations are not heeded, impose sanctions.[236]

251. Thus, it cannot be excluded that the Competition Authority and the Telecommunications Authority would analyse the same markets in a different way, e.g., define different relevant markets, assess the market power of an individual undertaking in a different way (dominant/ non-dominant) or disagree on the level of competition in a specific market. To prevent this unwelcome outcome, the Act on Electronic Communications contains specific provisions on cooperation between these authorities.[237] Still, discrepancies may prevail.

252. First, it is possible that a conduct endorsed or even imposed by one of the Authorities would be found to be illegal according to the other. In an older case concerning interconnection agreements among cell-phone operators, an agreement endorsed by the Telecommunications Authority was found anticompetitive by the Competition Authority.[238]

253. And second, it is possible that both the Authorities would scrutinize the same conduct of the same undertaking, and both would find it illegal and impose a

230. *See* Act No. 127/2005 Sb., *on Electronic Communications*, as amended.
231. *Ibid.*, s. 53.
232. *Ibid.*, s. 51.
233. *Ibid.*, s. 52.
234. *Ibid.*, ss 54 et seq.
235. *Ibid.*, s. 51/6.
236. *Ibid.*, s. 118.
237. *Ibid.*, s. 111.
238. *See* Decision of the Chairman of the CCA ref. No. R406/2015/HS of 22 Dec. 2015 (*Internconnection Agreements*). This decision concerns an arrangement from 2002, the previous decisions of the CCA were annulled by courts. Even this judgment was recently annulled by the court, not on the merits but because the case was time-barred; *see* Regional Court's judgement Ref. No. 62 Af 23/2016 of 29 Apr. 2021 (*Internconnection Agreements V*).

fine; would that be in line with the *ne bis in idem* principle? The authors are not aware of any such a case in the area of electronic communications, similar case, however, happened in the energy sector, where the regulation is in principle the same; according to the Supreme Administrative Court, 'double' punishment for the same conduct by two competent Authorities is not in breach of that principle.[239]

254. During the last ten years, the authors have not noticed any significant disagreement between the Competition Authority and the Telecommunications Authority, or the imposition of sanctions for the same conduct by both of them; it thus seems that the above-mentioned rules on coordination between them are sufficient.

239. *See* the Judgment of the Supreme Administrative Court of 18 Dec. 2007, Case No. Komp. 3/2006 (*Competences of the Czech Energy Authority*).

Chapter 5. Regulation of the Electronic Communications Market

§1. Legal Framework of Electronic Communications

255. The basic legal regulation of electronic communications in the legal system of the Czech Republic consist currently in the Act No. 127/2005 Sb. on electronic communications and on amendments to Certain Related Acts (AEC). One of the main reasons for the adoption of the AEC was the need to implement the EU regulatory framework for electronic communications consisting of the Framework Directive and related special directives.[240]

256. Effective 1 May 2005, the AEC replaced the previous Telecommunications Act[241] adopted in 2000, the most visible change being the replacement of the term 'telecommunications' with 'electronic communications'. The change reflected technological developments, in particular the convergence that had occurred between telecommunications, media and information technologies in the interim, with all electronic communications services and networks, i.e., fixed and wireless networks, including cable television and satellite networks as well as optical networks enabling signal transmission, being included in the common definition.

257. As a result of these technological changes, it was necessary to unify the regulation of all transmission networks and at the same time to separate transmission regulation from content regulation. This is why the AEC also states explicitly that it '*does not apply to the content of services provided over electronic communications networks, such as the content of radio and television broadcasting, financial services and certain information society services*',[242] subject to the exceptions expressly provided for in the AEC.

258. Since its adoption in 2005, AEC has been the subject of a total of 52 amendments. The most recent major amendment was the transposition of Directive (EU) 2018/1972 of the European Parliament and of the Council of 11 December 2018 establishing the European Electronic Communications Code, implemented by

240. The regulatory framework for electronic communications consisted of: Directive 2002/21/EC on a common regulatory framework for electronic communications networks and services (Framework Directive), Directive 2002/20/EC on the authorization of electronic communications networks and services (Authorization Directive), Directive 2002/19/EC on access to, and interconnection of, electronic communications networks and associated facilities (Access Directive), Directive 2002/22/EC on universal service and users' rights relating to electronic communications networks and services (Universal Service Directive), Directive 2002/58/EC concerning the processing of personal data and the protection of privacy in the electronic communications sector (Directive on privacy and electronic communications). The regulatory framework was followed by Commission Directive 2002/77/EC on competition in the markets for electronic communications networks and services.
241. *See* Act No. 151/2000 Sb. on Telecommunications and on Amendments to Other Acts.
242. *See* s. 1/2 AEC Subject of activity.

Act No 374/2021 Sb.[243] In addition to this transposition, the amendment also introduced two unrelated but very important changes, namely in the area of telemarketing and the regulation of the use of cookies. In the area of telemarketing, the amendment significantly tightened the possibilities of telemarketing contacting of natural and legal persons by replacing the existing opt-out principle (under which it was possible to contact by telephone for marketing purposes anyone who did not indicate in a phone directory that they did not wish to be contacted) with the opt-in principle with effect from 1 January 2022, with a transitional period until 30 June 2022. The regulation of cookies has removed the previous inaccurate transposition of Directive 2002/58/EC on privacy and electronic communications[244] with effect from 1 January 2022, so now the opt-in principle also applies to most cookies and the data controller is obliged to obtain consent of the data subject for the processing of personal data in the form of cookies.

259. The AEC is followed by a number of implementing regulations, the most important of which are regulations setting the amount and method of calculating fees for the use of radio frequencies[245] and regulating the frequency band allocation plan[246] (the national frequency table).

§2. Czech Telecommunications Office

260. The AEC established the CTO as the central administrative authority for the performance of state administration in matters provided for by this act, including market regulation and setting conditions for business in the field of electronic communications and postal services. The CTO has a separate chapter in the state budget of the Czech Republic. The Office thus established became the legal successor of the former CTO established by the previous Telecommunications Act;[247] the Office retained its original name after the AEC came into force, although the AEC otherwise generally introduced the new term 'electronic communications' instead of the former term 'telecommunications'. As stated in the explanatory memorandum to the government's draft AEC, '*For practical reasons, the regulatory authority is being established under the name of the Czech Telecommunications Office (already the*

243. *See* Act No. 374/2021 Sb., amending Act No. 127/2005 Sb., on electronic communications and amending certain related acts (Electronic Communications Act), as amended, and certain other acts.

244. *See* Directive 2002/58/EC, as amended by Directive 2009/136/EC, required in the Art. 5(3) Member States to ensure that '*the use of electronic communications networks to store information or to gain access to information stored in the terminal equipment of a subscriber or user is only allowed on condition that the subscriber or user concerned is provided with clear and comprehensive information in accordance with Directive 95/46/EC, inter alia about the purposes of the processing, and is offered the right to refuse such processing by the data controller*', within the transposition deadline of 25 May 2011. The Czech Republic did not fully implement this requirement until the recent amendment to the AEC.

245. *See* Government Regulation No. 154/2005 Sb. on the determination of the amount and method of calculation of fees for the use of radio frequencies and numbers.

246. *See* Decree No. 105/2010 Sb., on the frequency band allocation plan (national frequency table).

247. *See* Act No. 151/2000 Sb., on Telecommunications and on Amendments to Other Acts.

established name).' However, some experts had a different view on the matter and pointed out that '*This law establishes a new regulatory authority. It is not, as would be logically correct given the subject matter of the law, the "Office for Electronic Communications", but again the Czech Telecommunications. A new institution with an old and factually inaccurate name, but with a completely new mission...*'[248]

261. By establishing the CTO as a separate administrative authority, the AEC fulfilled the requirements for the independence of the CTO that resulted from Directive 2002/21/EC on a common regulatory framework for electronic communications networks and services (Framework Directive), now replaced by Directive (EU) 2018/1972 of the European Parliament and of the Council of 11 December 2018 establishing the European Electronic Communications Code. Of course, Directive 2018/1972 also contains a requirement for regulatory independence, *see* Article 6, according to which '*Member States shall guarantee the independence of national regulatory authorities and of other competent authorities by ensuring that they are legally distinct from and functionally independent of, any natural or legal person providing electronic communications networks, equipment or services*'. This independence is also respected by Act No 2/1969 Sb. on the establishment of ministries and other central government bodies of the Czech Republic, which lists the CTO among the central government bodies.[249]

262. The AEC also contributes to ensuring the independence of the CTO by clearly defining the CTO's relations with the Ministry of Industry and Trade of the Czech Republic and other authorities and by regulating the competence of the ministry as an administrative authority in the field of electronic communications. As follows from the Act on the Establishment of Ministries and Other Central Bodies of State Administration of the Czech Republic, the Ministry of Industry and Trade is the central body of state administration for, *inter alia*, '*electronic communications and postal services, with the exception of matters entrusted to the competence of the Czech Telecommunications Office*'. According to the AEC, the ministry submits to the government proposals for fundamental documents relating to electronic communications, such as the draft state policy on electronic communications or proposals for the main principles of state policy in electronic communications and ensures international relations in the field of electronic communications, including representation of the Czech Republic in the bodies of the EU.

I. CTO Council, Organization of the Office

263. The CTO is headed by the Council of the Office. This collective body was first introduced by the AEC as 'a five-member Council of the Office, with one of its

248. *See* Zdeněk Vaníček et al., *Zákon o elektronických komunikacích Komentář*, p. 77 (Linde Praha a.s. 2014).
249. *See* s. 2/11 of Act No. 2/1969 Sb. on the Establishment of Ministries and Other Central Bodies of State Administration of the Czech Republic, as amended, which includes the CTO among 'other central bodies of state administration', in addition to 'central bodies of state administration headed by a member of the government', as these are defined in s. 1 of the aforementioned Act.

members as the Chairman of the Council, the AEC also established a mechanism for the gradual replacement of the members of the Council, whereby the members are appointed and dismissed by the Government on the proposal of the Minister of Industry and Trade for a five-year term of office, so that one of the members is appointed each year',[250] with the Chairman being appointed for a maximum period of three years. However, the gradual rotation of Council members as envisaged by the AEC, i.e., the appointment of one member every year, is not always observed in practice.

264. In order to ensure the independence of the CTO, the AEC allows for the removal of a Council member by the Government only in specified cases. These include gross or repeated minor breaches of duty, illness permanently preventing the member from performing his/her duties, or cases where the member has not performed his/her duties for more than six months or no longer meets the conditions for appointment to the Council in force at the time of his/her appointment.

265. The AEC reserved to the CTO Council 'the approval of statutory documents and the adoption of fundamental decisions (on measures of a general nature, on price, on the designation of a universal service provider, on the designation of an undertaking with significant market power and on the imposition of obligations on that undertaking, as well as on appeals against decisions issued in the first instance by the Chairman of the Council)'.[251] According to the AEC, the Council of the Office also approves specified documents such as the Statute of the CTO, the CTO's plan of activities, the draft budget or draft implementing legislation.

266. Within the internal structure of the CTO, 'The organisational structure of the Office comprises three sections – the Internal Affairs Administration Section, the Regulatory Section and the Consumer Protection and Control Section. These sections are further subdivided into departments, divisions and separate units. The Consumer Protection and Control Section includes regional departments (regional detached offices of the Office) – the department for the Prague region, the department for the South Bohemia region, the department for the North Bohemia region, the department for the West Bohemia region, the department for the North Moravia region, the department for the South Moravia region and the department for the East Bohemia region.'[252]

250. *See* Miroslav Uřičař, *Administration and regulation of electronic communications, in Encyklopedie českých právních dějin. Volume XV.* p. 11 (Karel Schelle, Jaromír Tauchen eds., Vydavatelství a nakladatelství Aleš Čeněk, s.r.o. in co-edition with KEY Publishing s.r.o. 2019).

251. *See* Miroslav Uřičař, *Administration and regulation of electronic communications, in Encyklopedie českých právních dějin. Volume XV.* p. 11 (Karel Schelle, Jaromír Tauchen eds., Vydavatelství a nakladatelství Aleš Čeněk, s.r.o. in co-edition with KEY Publishing s.r.o. 2019).

252. *See* Zuzana Chudomelová et. al., *Zákon o elektronických komunikacích. Komentář*, p. 18 (Wolters Kluwer ČR 2016).

II. Relationship of the CTO to Other Authorities

267. The AEC explicitly regulates cooperation of the CTO with other authorities at national and international level. Domestically, the CTO cooperates with the UOHS, the Radio and Television Broadcasting Council (RRTV), the Office for the Protection of Personal Data (UOOU) and the National Office for Cyber and Information Security (NCISA); the CTO and these authorities provide each other with proposals, information and other forms of cooperation necessary for the performance of their tasks.

268. Given the extensive tasks of the CTO in the area of electronic communications market regulation, cooperation between the CTO and the UOHS is particularly important. The CTO, as the sector regulator, carries out *ex ante* regulation of pre-defined markets, including regular reviews of these markets. Therefore, in the framework of cooperation between the CTO and the UOHS, the AEC explicitly provides for cooperation in the definition of relevant markets and in the conduct of analyses of relevant markets; in certain other matters affecting the protection of competition, the CTO is obliged to consult the UOHS. In particular, the AEC requires the CTO to allow the UOHS to take a position before the CTO issues a decision in analyses of relevant markets and before imposing a sanction for a breach of such a decision, as well as in the conduct of analyses of relevant markets. Similarly, the CTO is obliged to consult with the RRTV on draft measures concerning radio or television broadcasting and certain other measures in this area, and with the UOOU on measures concerning the protection of personal data.

269. At the international level, the CTO cooperates with the European Commission, the national regulatory authorities of the EU Member States, the European Network and Information Security Agency (ENISA), the Body of European Regulators for Electronic Communications (BEREC) and the North Atlantic Treaty Organization (NATO). The CTO's cooperation with the European Commission, BEREC and the national regulatory authorities in the form of consultations and comments on defined measures plays an especially important role in the regulation of electronic communications.

§3. Regulation of Electronic Communications

270. Regulation of electronic communications is sector-specific regulation based on the assumption that there is not full competition in the electronic communications sector. AEC therefore explicitly assumes that sectoral regulation is temporary. Therefore, the main purpose of regulation is defined by AEC as replacing the missing effects of competition, creating conditions for the proper functioning of competition and for the protection of users and other market participants until a fully competitive environment is achieved.

271. The importance of regulation in the electronic communications sector is emphasized in the AEC by the fact that the AEC lists regulation as part of the exercise of state administration in the electronic communications sector, alongside the conditions of doing business and the conditions of performing communication activities in this area. Also, in the definition of the term 'regulation', AEC emphasizes the achievement of a competitive environment as the main objective, defining regulation as '*the direction of communication activities and relations in order to achieve and maintain a competitive environment, to protect the electronic communications market, including the protection of users of electronic communications services*';[253] AEC envisages that regulation will be implemented by issuing decisions, measures of general nature and opinions.

272. To meet the main objectives of electronic communications regulation, the Ministry of Industry and Trade and the CTO promote competition in the provision of electronic communications networks and services and associated facilities. According to the AEC, the Ministry and the CTO are to achieve this in particular by ensuring, in their decision-making, that users obtain maximum benefits in terms of service choice, price and quality, and that competition in the electronic communications sector, including content transmission services, is not distorted or restricted, and by ensuring the efficient management and effective use of radio frequencies and numbers. In order to ensure the management and efficient use of radio frequencies, the CTO manages the radio spectrum in accordance with the harmonization objectives of the EU and in accordance with the obligations arising from international treaties or from the Czech Republic's membership in international organizations.

273. In defining the competence of the CTO, the AEC 'does not distinguish between strictly regulatory activities and other activities within the scope of the state administration in the field of electronic communications. However, the activities that are typically regulatory include, in particular, conducting analyzes of relevant markets, identifying undertakings with significant market power and imposing obligations on these undertakings, issuing decisions on prices and exercising price control, or deciding on imposing an obligation to amend a contract for a publicly available electronic communications service or for providing a connection to a public communications network'.[254] 'nerozlišuje mezi striktně regulačními činnostmi a mezi ostatními činnostmi v rámci výkonu státní správy v oblasti elektronických komunikací. Mezi činnosti typicky regulační však patří zejména provádění analýz relevantních trhů, určování podniků s významnou tržní silou a ukládání povinností těmto podnikům, vydávání rozhodnutí o ceně a vykonávání kontroly cen, či rozhodování o uložení povinnosti změnit smlouvu pro veřejně dostupnou službu elektronických komunikací nebo pro zajištění připojení k veřejné komunikační síti'.

274. One of the main activities in the field of electronic communications regulation is the regular analysis of relevant markets. In general, in electronic communications markets '*competition law, including appropriate remedies, is to be applied*

253. *See* s. 2/4/d of the AEC.
254. *See* Radim Polčák et al., *Právo informačních technologií*, p. 515 (Wolters Kluwer ČR 2018).

primarily. Only if these remedies are insufficient to address the problem and there is no effective competition in a particular market with one or more undertakings with significant market power, regulators are entitled to impose ex ante obligations. The imposition of remedies should therefore be preceded by an analysis of effective competition, including an assessment of the prospects for the permanence of any identified deficiencies.'[255] *'má být uplatňováno primárně právo hospodářské soutěže, včetně příslušných nápravných opatření. Teprve pokud tato nápravná opatření k řešení daného problému nepostačují a na určitém trhu s jedním, či více podniky s významnou tržní silou neexistuje účinná hospodářská soutěž, mohou regulační orgány ukládat povinnosti ex ante. Ukládání nápravných opatření by tak měla předcházet analýza účinné hospodářské soutěže, včetně vyhodnocení perspektivy trvalosti případných zjištěných nedostatků'.*

275. Prior to the analysis itself, the CTO shall define, by means of a measure of a general nature, the relevant product or service markets whose characteristics may justify the imposition of regulatory obligations. In doing so, the CTO shall take into account decisions, recommendations and guidelines of the European Commission. This is followed by an analysis of the relevant markets, the results of which the CTO consults, *inter alia*, with the UOHS, whose opinion is then published. If the relevant market is not effectively competitive, the CTO shall identify the undertaking with significant market power on the basis of the analysis and impose obligations on it to remedy the situation. The AEC *'lists the measures that the CTO may impose in this way – these include transparency obligations (disclosure of information, in particular on network access or interconnection), non-discrimination obligations (equivalent conditions in the provision of access or interconnection), obligations related to price regulation and others. As a last resort, where the CTO concludes that the "standard" obligations imposed have not led to effective competition, the CTO may impose an extraordinary measure – a functional separation obligation – on an undertaking with significant market power. This consists in separating or transferring the activities related to the wholesale provision of access services to a separate, independently operated economic unit. A higher form of separation, structural separation, i.e. separation not only to a separate economic unit but directly to another legal entity with a different ownership structure, is envisaged by the Electronic Communications Act as a voluntary decision. In practice, such a structural separation took place in the case of O2 Czech Republic a.s. by a decision of its general meeting in 2015, by which the company was split up in the form of a spin-off with the creation of one new company, Česká telekomunikační infrastruktura a.s.'.*[256] *'vyjmenovává opatření, která ČTÚ takto může uložit – patří mezi ně povinnost průhlednosti (uveřejňování informací zejména o přístupu k síti nebo propojení sítí), povinnost nediskriminace (rovnocenné podmínky při poskytování přístupu nebo propojení), povinnosti související s regulací cen a další. V krajním případě, kdy dle závěru ČTÚ uložené "standardní" povinnosti nevedly k dosažení účinné hospodářské soutěže, může ČTÚ uložit podniku s významnou tržní silou mimořádné opatření – povinnost funkční separace. Ta spočívá v oddělení, či*

255. *Ibid.*, p. 508.
256. *Ibid.*, p. 509.

převedení činnosti spojené s velkoobchodním poskytováním služeb přístupu na oddělenou, nezávisle provozovanou hospodářskou jednotku. S vyšší formou separace, strukturální separací, tedy s oddělením nejen na oddělenou hospodářskou jednotku, ale přímo na jinou právnickou osobu s odlišnou vlastnickou strukturou, počítá zákon o elektronických komunikacích jako s dobrovolným rozhodnutím. V praxi takováto strukturální separace proběhla u společnosti O2 Czech Republic a. s. rozhodnutím její valné hromady v roce 2015, kterým došlo k rozdělení společnosti formou odštěpení se vznikem jedné nové společnosti Česká telekomunikační infrastruktura a. s.'

§4. Rights and Obligations of Operators Subscribers and Users, Consumer Protection

276. In this chapter, the authors deal with selected rights and obligations of entrepreneurs, subscribers and users in the field of electronic communications, including obligations and corresponding rights under consumer protection. Among the most important obligations imposed in the AEC on undertakings in the operation of electronic communications networks and the provision of electronic communications services are those related to the interconnection of electronic communications networks and access to these networks. According to the authors' assessment, the obligations imposed on undertakings to ensure consumer protection and the rights of consumers and other persons corresponding to these obligations, whose protection the lawmaker has in some cases equated with consumer protection, are equally important both in terms of scope and impact on the services provided. In connection with the two areas mentioned above, it is also necessary to mention the specific regulation of dispute resolution contained in the AEC; many of the disputes resolved by the CTO concern precisely these areas, i.e., in the case of disputes between undertakings, there are often disputes concerning interconnection or access to the network, and in the case of disputes between an undertaking and a subscriber, disputes concerning consumer protection or, more broadly, the protection of subscribers' rights.

§5. Interconnection and Access to Electronic Communications Networks

277. Access to networks, facilities and services, including network interconnection, is one of the important elements ensuring the promotion of competition in the electronic communications sector, according to the AEC. Access to an electronic communications network is defined by the AEC as the making available of resources or services to another undertaking for the purpose of providing electronic communications services. Access may also be used to transmit information society services or content transmission services. Access to an electronic communications network includes, in particular, access to network elements and associated resources, access to physical infrastructure or software systems, access to networks for roaming purposes and other situations defined in the AEC.[257] One of the forms of access to a network is also interconnection according to the AEC– the interconnection point between these networks is then the access point; however, in most cases the AEC uses the terms 'access to an electronic communications network' and 'network interconnection' in parallel, side by side.

278. The interconnection between two electronic communications networks is based on a written contract, with the aim of enabling communication between users of both networks or enabling access to services provided on one of the networks; in practice, the interconnection may be direct or indirect (via another network). The legal regulation of interconnection and access to networks in the AEC is characterised by a high degree of regulatory intervention, including, among other things, the obligation to negotiate an interconnection, the obligation to submit the concluded contract to the CTO, the regulation of the price for access or interconnection, the determination of the formalities of the contract by an implementing regulation[258] and, last but not least, the possibility of the CTO's interference in the negotiations on the conclusion of the contract. '*The CTO enters into negotiations on its own initiative or at the initiative of one of the parties. The CTO shall communicate to the parties its opinion on the disputed parts of the draft contract or on the refusal by the undertaking providing the publicly available electronic communications service. If the access or interconnection contract is nevertheless not concluded, either party may request the Authority to adjudicate their dispute.*'[259]

§6. Consumer Protection

279. The AEC includes consumer protection among the basic objectives of regulation when it sets obligation of the CTO to promote the interests of end users, in particular by ensuring a high level of consumer protection in its activities.[260] It reflects the fact that '*the performance of communication activities falls largely within the sphere of public law, which corresponds to the relatively strong interference of legal regulation in the contractual freedom of the parties*', the reasons for such interference '*can be seen in the need to protect the consumer, but also in the need to ensure the technical functioning of services and the protection of limited resources*'.[261]

280. The ACK regulates broadly the rights of consumers in connection with the conclusion of contracts for the provision of publicly available electronic communications services, including extensive information obligations towards the consumer prior to the conclusion of the contract, limitations on the duration of contracts, the

---

257. *See* s. 78 of the AEC.
258. The mandatory elements of the draft contract are regulated by Decree No. 158/2005 Sb., which establishes the minimum elements of a draft contract for access to or interconnection of public communications networks.
259. *See* Barbora Vlachová, *Zákon o elektronických komunikacích. Komentář*, p. 260 (C.H.Beck, 2016).
260. *See* s. 5/3/b of the AEC.
261. *See* Jiří Vaníček, *Zákon o elektronických komunikacích. Komentář*, p. 296 (Linde Praha a.s. 2014).

possibility of their termination by the consumer, obligations in connection with the offer of packages of services and others. A number of these rights explicitly apply not only to consumers but more broadly to subscribers of electronic communications services under the AEC. A significant number of amendments to the AEC in recent years have also further extended consumer rights. Also, as of the date of completion of this text, the most recent major amendment to the AEC, adopted in 2021,[262] has largely focused on further enhancing consumer protection, the primary purpose of which was to transpose the European Electronic Communications Code into Czech law.[263]

§7. Dispute Resolution

281. The specific dispute resolution provisions contained in the AEC relate to the areas of consumer protection and interconnection and network access discussed above. This regulation covers the dispute resolution of (1) subscriber disputes and (2) disputes between persons carrying out communication activities (many of which in practice relate to interconnection or access to networks). Subscriber disputes are disputes between a person carrying out a communication activity and a subscriber or user, as the case may be, on the basis of a claim by either party to the dispute, provided that the dispute relates to obligations imposed by or under the AEC.[264] For both types of disputes, the AEC provides for a time limit of four months for the issuance of a decision, six months in particularly complex cases, and only ninety days for the issuance of a decision in a dispute initiated at the request of a consumer (the time limit may be extended in particularly complex disputes).

282. Disputes between persons carrying out communication activities shall be decided by the Chairman of the Council if the dispute concerns obligations imposed by or pursuant to the AEC. The lawmaker has decided to assign this agenda directly to the Chairman of the Council, as '*it is a relatively substantial agenda with a potential impact on the entire electronic communications sector, and therefore its management and decision-making should be subordinated to this seriousness.*'[265] If the CTO concludes, following an oral hearing involving all parties to the dispute, that other means of resolution would better contribute to the timely resolution of the dispute, the CTO is entitled to refuse to adjudicate the dispute. Where such disputes involve the performance of a monetary obligation, an arbitration agreement for their resolution may also be concluded.

262. *See* Act No. 374/2021 Sb., amending Act No. 127/2005 Sb., on electronic communications and amending certain related acts (Electronic Communications Act), as amended, and certain other acts.
263. The obligation of EU Member States to implement the European Electronic Communications Code into the national law is derived from the Directive (EU) 2018/1972 of the European Parliament and of the Council of 11 Dec. 2018 establishing the European Electronic Communications Code.
264. *See* s. 129 of the AEC.
265. *See* Zuzana Chudomelová et al., *Zákon o elektronických komunikacích. Komentář*, p. 424 (Wolters Kluwer ČR 2016).

283. In practice, this includes disputes initiated by service providers seeking payment for services provided, as well as disputes in cases where the service provider has not satisfied the complaint and the subscriber or user has filed an application with the CTO to initiate proceedings to object to the handling of the complaint. End subscribers or users are entitled to file such an application with the CTO within one month of the date of receipt of the complaint or the expiry of the time limit for its settlement; this is a time limit for expiry and the right to file an application ceases to exist in case of a futile expiry of the time limit. In addition to the above-described dispute resolution, the Czech legal system also provides for an out-of-court mechanism for the settlement of consumer disputes; the CTO is the subject of such disputes.

284. In the case of subscriber disputes, the CTO decides only such disputes between a person carrying out a communication activity and a subscriber or user that relate to obligations imposed by or on the basis of the AEC. '*Providers of electronic communications services provide a number of services that are not electronic communications services and thus do not fulfil this feature (in practice, these are logos, ringtones,* etc.*), so the CTO does not adjudicate disputes over their payment. A similar problem applies to disputes over the payment of the price of goods sold by providers of electronic communications services to subscribers (typically mobile phone or other communications equipment), the payment of contractual fines or other related payments, and also disputes over the payment of the price of third-party services offered and billed to the subscriber by the provider of electronic communications services. The delimitation of the boundary between disputes which the CTO is entitled to decide and disputes which the general courts are competent to decide has been the subject of many court decisions. The matter has also been decided on several occasions by a special panel established pursuant to Act No 131/2002 Sb., on the adjudication of certain competence disputes, whose decisions are now applied in practice to determine this boundary.*'[266] '*Poskytovatelé služeb elektronických komunikací poskytují řadu služeb, které nejsou službami elektronických komunikací, a tento znak tak nenaplňují (v praxi jde o loga, vyzváněcí melodie a další), spory o jejich úhradu tedy ČTÚ nerozhoduje. Obdobný problém se týká sporů o úhradu ceny zboží prodávaného poskytovateli služeb elektronických komunikací účastníkům (typicky telefonní přístroje, či jiná komunikační zařízení), o úhradu smluvních pokut, či jiných souvisejících plateb a také sporů o úhradu ceny služeb třetích stran, které jsou nabízeny a také vyúčtovávány účastníkovi poskytovatelem služeb elektronických komunikací. Vymezení hranice mezi spory, které je oprávněn rozhodovat ČTÚ, a spory, k jejichž rozhodování jsou příslušné obecné soudy, bylo mnohokrát předmětem soudního rozhodování. Ve věci několikrát rozhodoval také zvláštní senát zřízený podle zákona č. 131/2002 Sb., o rozhodování některých kompetenčních sporů, jehož rozhodnutí jsou dnes v praxi aplikována na určení této hranice.*'

---

266. *See* Radim Polčák et al., *Právo informačních technologií*, p. 533 (Wolters Kluwer ČR 2018).

§8. Security of Networks and Services, Protection of Personal Data

285. The security of electronic communications networks and services, including ensuring the confidentiality of communications and also including the protection of personal data, plays an important role in the legal regulation of electronic communications contained in the AEC, and its importance in practice continues to grow with regard to the development of electronic communications services and the related technical possibilities that electronic communications networks and services provide in practice. AEC regulates this area comprehensively, replacing the previous partial regulation of the protection of telecommunications secrecy and the protection of personal and intermediary data.

286. In view of the importance of this area, the lawmaker has primarily imposed certain obligations on the CTO as a regulatory authority in the AEC. Among the basic objectives of the regulation is the obligation of the CTO to promote '*the interests of end users, in particular by ... promoting the preservation of the integrity and security of public communications networks*' and '*contributing to ensuring a high level of protection of personal data and privacy*'.[267] In addition to the general obligation of persons providing public communications networks or a publicly available electronic communications services to ensure the security and integrity of their network and the security of the services they provide, the AEC also imposes on such persons the obligation to adopt technical and organizational rules ensuring '*a level of security appropriate to the level of risk present, in order to prevent or minimise the impact of security incidents on users and on networks and services*'.[268] In addition, in the event of a serious breach of network and service security and loss of network integrity, such persons are obliged to '*inform the CTO, the entities operating the emergency communication centres and users in an appropriate manner and without delay*';[269] in such cases, the CTO may inform the public in an appropriate manner or impose a disclosure obligation directly on the person concerned. In appropriate cases, the CTO is entitled to inform the competent authorities in other EU Member States as well as the ENISA.

287. Among the specific measures provided for in the AEC with the aim of ensuring the security and integrity of networks, the CTO is also authorized to impose on persons operating a public communications network or providing publicly available electronic communications services the obligation to carry out a security audit by a qualified independent entity. In the event of a significant threat to the security and integrity of a public communications network or an electronic communications service, the CTO is authorized to impose an obligation on such persons to take specific measures. According to the AEC, requirements for network security are also to be included in contractual relations between providers of electronic communications services and subscribers, where the AEC stipulates, as part of the information provided prior to the conclusion of the contract, the obligation of

267. *See* s. 5/3/c and f of the AEC.
268. *See* s. 98/1 of the AEC.
269. *See* s. 98/4 of the AEC.

providers to inform the consumer, *inter alia*, about the type of measures that the provider may take in response to security incidents or when a threat or vulnerability is detected.[270]

288. Also in the area of personal data protection, the AEC sets out some specific obligations for undertakings providing publicly available electronic communications services. In this case, AEC juxtaposes personal data and traffic and location data. With regard to the definition of these categories of data, it is clear that in practice, traffic data will in many cases constitute one of the categories of personal data, but not always, especially since traffic data also concern subscribers who are legal persons; location data will always be personal data at the same time.[271] In addition to data protection, the AEC also defines obligations aimed at ensuring the confidentiality of communications; this concept (of confidentiality of communication) replaced the former protection of telecommunications secrecy long established in previous legislation. The protection of the confidentiality of communications is also ensured in the Czech legal system in the area of criminal law, specifically by the provision of Article 182 of the Criminal Code,[272] which regulates the criminal offence of Breach of the secrecy of transmitted messages. The liability of service providers for the content of information transmitted or stored by them is defined in the Act No. 480/2004 Sb.

289. In order to ensure the protection of personal, traffic and location data and the confidentiality of communications, providers of publicly available electronic communications services are primarily obliged to '*ensure technically and organisationally the security of the service provided with regard to the protection of personal data of natural persons in accordance with a special legal regulation, the protection of traffic and location data and the confidentiality of communications of natural and legal persons in the provision of this service.*'[273] Further specific obligations for providers include the obligation to draw up internal technical and organizational rules to ensure data protection and confidentiality of communications, the obligation to inform affected subscribers of the specific risk of a breach of network security in relation to data protection and the obligation to establish internal procedures for dealing with requests for access to users' personal data.

290. The protection of confidentiality of communications in the AEC is broadly defined and includes the conditions for the protection of traffic and location data, the conditions for interception and recording of messages, the definition of the Data Retention obligation, i.e., the obligation to retain traffic and location data for a

270. *See* point A e) Annex 1 to the AEC.

271. Pursuant to s. 90 of the AEC, traffic data means '*any data processed for the purpose of transmission of a message over the electronic communications network or for its billin*', while location data is defined in s. 91 of the AEC as '*any data processed on an electronic communications network or by an electronic communications service that determines the geographic location of a telecommunications terminal equipment of a user of a publicly available electronic communications service*'.

272. *See* Act No. 40/2009 Sb., Criminal Code, as amended.

273. *See* s. 88/1 of the AEC.

period of six months for the purpose of their possible request by authorized authorities, and others. The procedural conditions for interception and recording of messages (resp. the conditions for 'interception and recording of telecommunications traffic') and the conditions for discovery of the stored traffic and location data by law enforcement authorities are laid down in the Criminal Procedure Code.[274] The Code of Criminal Procedure also contains a subsequent information obligation, according to which the person concerned must be informed of the order for interception or the discovery of traffic and location data after the final conclusion of the case. On the basis of the information provided in this way, the person concerned is entitled to initiate a judicial review of the lawfulness of the order for interception and recording of telecommunications traffic or the order for discovery of traffic and location data.

§9. Construction of Electronic Communications Networks

291. The lawmaker recognizes the importance of the construction of electronic communications networks, the building of their elements and the establishment and operation of communication lines in the AEC, therefore the introductory provisions of the AEC explicitly provide that '*the provision of a public communications network, the provision of a publicly available electronic communications service, the deployment of high-speed electronic communications networks pursuant to the Act on Measures to Reduce the Costs of Building High-Speed Electronic Communications Networks and the provision of electronic communications networks for state security purposes are carried out in the public interest.*'[275] Furthermore, the AEC also instructs the Ministry of Industry and Trade and the CTO to promote '*efficient investment in the upgrade of existing infrastructure or the construction of new infrastructure, including very high capacity networks*' as part of the objectives and guiding principles of regulation.[276]

292. The above-mentioned principle, according to which the provision of a public communications network is carried out in the public interest, is manifested by the authorization of the operator of a public communications network to establish and operate elements of this network (overhead or underground lines, support points, antenna masts, etc.) on the land or building of others, subject to the fulfilment of specified conditions. In order to ensure the exercise of these rights, the network operator is obliged to conclude an agreement on the establishment of an easement or another type of agreement, usually a lease agreement.

293. Among the specific measures to protect electronic communications networks contained in AEC is the obligation of operators of machines, devices and equipment to prevent interference to electronic communications networks and services by radio frequency energy, including interference caused by electromagnetic

274. *See* Act No. 141/1961 Sb., on Criminal Procedure (Criminal Procedure Code), as amended.
275. *See* s. 7/2 of the AEC.
276. *See* s. 5/4/c of the AEC.

shielding or reflections of electromagnetic waves by buildings. For a similar purpose, the AEC establishes protection zones for underground and overhead communication lines and protection zones for radio equipment and radio directional links and prohibits certain activities in these protection zones.

§10. Other Legislation in the Sector of Electronic Communications

294. The AEC regulates the area of electronic communications almost comprehensively, so apart from the AEC, there are only some specific legal regulations in the Czech legal system regulating partial areas of electronic communications or areas related to electronic communications. These include, in particular, the Act on Certain Information Society Services (ACISS) and the Act on Measures to Reduce the Costs of Deploying High-Speed Electronic Communications Networks, which are briefly mentioned below, and also the Act on the Operation of Radio and Television Broadcasting and on Amendments to Other Acts[277] and Act on on-demand audiovisual media services,[278] which are both discussed separately in Chapter 6.

I. Act on Certain Information Society Services

295. A regulation closely related to AEC is the Act No. 480/2004 Sb., on Certain Information Society Services[279] ('Act No. 480/2004 Sb.'). In addition to the AEC, this act is also very closely linked to the Act on the Protection of Personal Data, where it regulates, in particular, obligations in the dissemination of commercial communications. The Act No. 480/2004 Sb. transposed the Directive on Electronic Commerce[280] into the Czech legal System, in the field of electronic communications it regulates mainly the liability and the rights and obligations of persons providing information society services.

296. As for the term 'information society service' itself, the Act No. 480/2004 Sb. defines it to mean 'any service provided by electronic means at the individual request of a user made by electronic means, usually for a fee; a service is provided by electronic means if it is sent via an electronic communications network and retrieved by the user from an electronic data storage device. In view of the priority

277. *See* Act No. 231/2001 Sb. on the Operation of Radio and Television Broadcasting and on Amendments to Other Acts, as amended.
278. *See* Act No. 132/2010 Sb. on on-demand audiovisual media services and on amendments to certain acts (Act on on-demand audiovisual media services), as amended.
279. *See* Act No. 480/2004 Sb. on Certain Information Society Services and on Amendments to Certain Acts (Act on Certain Information Society Services), as amended.
280. *See* Directive 2000/31/EC of the European Parliament and of the Council of 8 Jun. 2000 on certain legal aspects of information society services, in particular electronic commerce, in the internal market (Directive on electronic commerce).

of European law and the need for a euroconform interpretation, no differences will have to be sought between the definition under the eCommerce Directive and the Czech law'.[281]

297. The Act No. 480/2004 Sb. significantly limits the liability of intermediary service providers for the content of information transmitted, for the content of information automatically temporarily intermediated and for the storage of the content of information provided by the user, service providers are not obliged under this Act to supervise the content of information transmitted or stored by them or to actively search for facts and circumstances indicating illegal content of information.[282] In this context, it is necessary to mention the tendencies of recent years to impose the obligation of special supervision both in legislative proposals and in the judicial sphere, but so far, from the point of view of the Czech legal system, these are only tendencies.[283]

II. Act on Measures to Reduce the Costs of Deploying High-Speed Electronic Communications Networks

298. Another legal norm, which also does not fall exclusively within the electronic communications laws, but in this case also within the field of construction laws, is the Act on measures to reduce the costs of deployment of high-speed electronic communications networks and on amendments to certain related acts;[284] this is also a transposition of EU law.[285] With this law, the CTO '*has acquired a new competence: thanks to the adoption of the Act on Measures to Reduce the Costs of Deploying High-Speed Electronic Communications Networks, it has become a single point of information for providing information on existing passive infrastructure, and at the same time it has the power to resolve disputes arising under this Act*'.[286] Within the framework of the rules for the deployment of high-speed electronic communications networks, i.e., electronic communications networks enabling the provision of connection services with a speed of at least 30 Mbps, particularly relevant obligations in this Act include the obligation to provide data on the physical infrastructure to authorized persons and the obligation of access to this infrastructure by authorized persons. Physical infrastructure includes pipes, masts, cable ducts, collectors, as well as buildings, antenna carriers, towers and supporting structures, etc.; the authorized persons are the operators of the public communications network and the obliged authorities.

---

281. *See* Miroslav Uřičař, Vladan Rámiš et al., *Obecné nařízení o ochraně osobních údajů. Komentář*, p. 269 (C. H. Beck 2021).
282. *See* s. 6 of the Act on Certain Information Society Services.
283. For more details, *see* Martin Maisner, *Zákon o některých službách informační společnosti. Komentář*, pp. 99 ff (C.H.Beck 2016).
284. *See* Act No. 194/2017 Sb. on measures to reduce the costs of the deployment of high-speed electronic communications networks and on amending certain related acts, as amended.
285. This Act transposed into Czech law the Directive 2014/61/EU of the European Parliament and of the Council of 15 May 2014 on measures to reduce the costs of building high-speed electronic communications networks.
286. *See* Czech Telecommunications Office, Annual Report 2017.

Chapter 6. Regulation of Broadcasting Activities (Audiovisual Services)

§1. LEGAL FRAMEWORK

299. The basic legal regulation governing the conditions of radio and television broadcasting in the Czech legal system is Act No. 231/2001 Sb. on the operation of radio and television broadcasting and on amendments to other acts, as amended ('Broadcasting Act'). This Act '*regulates the exercise of state administration in the field of radio and television broadcasting*', i.e., it primarily establishes the Council for Radio and Television Broadcasting (RRTV), regulates the granting of licences to operate radio and television broadcasting, the registration of retransmissions and certain other areas. The RRTV is the regulatory authority in the field of broadcasting and in the field of on-demand audiovisual media services – the Broadcasting Act established the RRTV as the central administrative authority exercising state administration in the field of radio and television broadcasting and retransmission and, following amendments to the Broadcasting Act, also in the field of on-demand audiovisual media services, the conditions of which are not regulated by the Broadcasting Act but by a separate regulation.

300. It is already clear from this definition of the RRTV that Broadcasting Act is very closely related and followed by the other key regulation in this area – the Act on on-demand audiovisual media services[287] ('Act No. 132/2010 Sb.'). This Act regulates the conditions for the provision of on-demand audiovisual media services, i.e., those services which are information society services,[288] for which '*the provider of the on-demand audiovisual media service has editorial responsibility*' and whose main objective is '*the provision of programmes to the public for the purpose of information, entertainment or education*' and which allow '*viewing programmes at a time chosen by the user and at his individual request on the basis of a catalogue of programmes drawn up by the provider of the on-demand audiovisual media service*'.

§2. ACT ON THE OPERATION OF RADIO AND TELEVISION BROADCASTING

301. According to the reasoning of the draft Broadcasting Act, the main reason for the adoption of Broadcasting Act as 'a new legal regulation of the operation of radio and television broadcasting ... was the compatibility of the Czech legal regulation in this area with the secondary law of the European Community in the field of television broadcasting, namely Council Directive No 552 of 3 October 1989 on the coordination of certain provisions of the laws and administrative regulations of

287. *See* Act No. 132/2010 Sb. on on-demand audiovisual media services and on amendments to other acts (Act on on-demand audiovisual media services), as amended.
288. According to s. 2/a of the Act No. 480/2004 Sb., an information society service is '*a service provided by electronic means at the individual request of a user made by electronic means, generally provided for a fee; a service is provided by electronic means if it is sent via an electronic communications network and retrieved by the user from an electronic data storage device*'.

the Member States relating to the operation of television broadcasting "television without frontiers", as amended by Amendment No 36 of 30 June 1997'.[289] With effect from 4 July 2001, Broadcasting Act replaced the previous Act on the operation of radio and television broadcasting[290] adopted in 1991. This previous law on radio and television broadcasting had already made it possible in the Czech Republic to 'create a dual broadcasting system – i.e., the coexistence of the public and private sectors',[291] and this system is still in operation under the subsequent legislation – Broadcasting Act. In fact, this act 'essentially follows the division between public and private broadcasters, but the dividing criterion between these entities is based on the type of authorisation under which they are entitled to broadcast. The law therefore distinguishes between broadcasters who operate these broadcasts on the basis of special legislation'[292] – these are Czech Television and Czech Radio.

302. The Broadcasting Act applies to statutory broadcasters, licensed broadcasters and broadcasters of retransmission. The RRTV grants a licence for the operation of radio and television broadcasting distributed by transmitters, satellites, cable systems and special transmission systems for a fixed period of time – a maximum of eight years for radio broadcasting and a maximum of twelve years for television broadcasting. A licence may be granted only upon application, subject to the conditions laid down by law, and generally there is no legal entitlement to a licence.[293] The distribution of retransmitted radio and television broadcasts via an electronic communications network is subject to registration of the operator of such broadcasts, which, according to the Broadcasting Act, must be a '*simultaneous, complete and unchanged distribution to the public*' of such broadcasts of '*original radio and television programmes or substantial parts thereof*', via electronic communications networks.[294] The essence of retransmission is that '*an operator takes over a programme (or a substantial part thereof), including related services, from another, primary licensed operator and then distributes that programme simultaneously, that is*

289. For details, *see* the Reasoning of the Parliamentary Proposal for the Issuance of the Act on the Operation of Radio and Television Broadcasting, Parliamentary Document No. 717/0, sent to MPs on 19 Sep. 2000. Available from www.psp.cz.
290. Act No. 468/1991 Sb., on the operation of radio and television broadcasting.
291. Ministry of Culture of the Czech Republic. *Rozhlasové a televizní vysílání v ČR*. Available from https://www.mkcr.cz/rozhlasove-a-televizni-vysilani-v-cr-484.html.
292. *See* Aleš Rozehnal, *Mediální zákony Komentář* (Wolters Kluwer ČR, a.s., 2007).
293. For more details, *see* Helena Chaloupková, Petr Holý & Jiří Urbánek, *Mediální právo. Komentář*, p. 555 (C. H. Beck 1st ed. 2019): Broadcasting Act '*distinguishes between a licensing procedure announced by the Council, in which several applicants may submit an application for a licence (which was particularly relevant in view of the former limited capacity of technical means in analogue broadcasting), and a procedure initiated at the initiative of the applicant for a licence (Sec. 25), where only one applicant is a party to the procedure and where the question of ensuring and specifying the technical aspects of broadcasting (including, for example, the radio frequency usage diagram for terrestrial digital broadcasting programmes transmitted via transmitters) is up to the applicant. If the licensing procedure is initiated by the applicant for a licence, then, provided that the applicant complies with the statutory conditions and requirements (Sec. 25/3) and that the applicant has not had its licence revoked or registration cancelled in the previous five years for breach of the Act (Sec. 17/3), it is legally entitled to the licence*'.
294. *See* ss 2/1/b and 26 et seq. of the Broadcasting Act.

at the same time as the licensed entity, in its entirety and without change, to the public. The Czech version of a foreign language broadcast is also considered to be an unchanged takeover broadcast, which is particularly important in terms of the takeover of foreign programmes'.[295]

303. In order to ensure plurality of information in broadcasting, Broadcasting Act restricts the possibility of holding more than one licence for analogue nationwide television broadcasting and, similarly, more than one licence for analogue nationwide radio broadcasting. For the same reason, Broadcasting Act prohibits a nationwide analogue radio broadcaster from participating in or merging with the business of another operator. Similarly, these restrictions and prohibitions apply to nationwide digital television broadcasting and digital radio broadcasting, where the maximum number of licences held by one natural or legal person is limited to two. Further restrictions are also imposed by the Broadcasting Act on local and regional broadcasting and on the establishment of programme networks.

§3. Rights and Obligations of Radio and Television Broadcasters and Retransmission Operators

304. The main elements of the definition of a broadcaster under the Broadcasting Act include setting up the programme, determining the organization of the broadcasting and editorial responsibility for the broadcasts and the initial dissemination of the programme and related services; in the case of a retransmission operator, this includes deciding on the composition of the programmes of the broadcaster and their dissemination in their complete and unaltered form. The rights of both the broadcaster and the retransmission operator include, in particular, the right to broadcast programmes freely and independently, the broadcaster shall provide objective and balanced information and separate opinion or evaluative commentary from information of a news nature.

305. In general, the operator is responsible for the content of the broadcast and is obliged to observe the legal restrictions – according to Broadcasting Act, the programmes must not promote war or incite hatred, they must not contain subliminal messages, the operator is obliged not to include programmes that may seriously impair the physical, mental or moral development of children and minors, and to observe certain other obligations in relation to the programme composition. In addition, the broadcaster has a legal obligation under Broadcasting Act to provide a balanced offer for all citizens, including members of minorities. As A. Rozehnal points out, some of the obligations of a broadcaster do not apply to a retransmitted broadcaster, since the latter does not set up the programme and also certain other elements of the definition of a broadcaster do not apply to it. Moreover, '*the retransmitted broadcaster has no possibility to influence the original broadcast, it*

295. *See* Helena Chaloupková, Petr Holý & Jiří Urbánek, *Mediální právo. Komentář*, p. 555 (C. H. Beck 1st ed. 2019).

only has the possibility to stop broadcasting in order to prevent a breach of this obligation'. However, in view of the absolute nature of its responsibility for the content of the broadcast, the retransmitted broadcaster '*cannot claim that it was unaware of the content of the retransmitted broadcast*'.[296]

306. In relation to events of significant social importance,[297] the Broadcasting Act imposes certain special obligations on broadcasters, in particular it prohibits them from using exclusive rights to the detriment of a substantial part of the public in the Czech Republic, which would be '*deprived of the possibility of watching the event live or recorded in a nationwide television broadcast in unencrypted form and without a special fee*'.[298] A broadcaster that has obtained exclusive rights to broadcast an event of increased public interest also has obligations under the Broadcasting Act towards other broadcasters established in EU Member States.

307. Operators are obliged to keep recordings of all programmes, including other parts of the broadcast, in broadcast for at least thirty days and to make them available to RRTV upon written request. Certain other obligations of broadcasters in relation to the promotion of European production, as well as obligations in the field of commercial communications, advertising, sponsorship and product placement under the Broadcasting Act, are discussed below together with similar obligations of providers of on-demand audiovisual media services under the Act No. 132/2010 Sb.

§4. Broadcast Content

308. As stated above, the broadcaster and the retransmitted broadcaster have the right to broadcast programmes freely and independently. Within this framework, according to Broadcasting Act, the content of programmes can only be interfered with on the basis of and within the limits of the law. Such cases include the protection of persons affected by the content of the broadcast; this provision was inserted in Broadcasting Act to transpose the Television Without Frontiers Directive.[299] In order to ensure the protection of persons affected by the content of radio

296. *See* Aleš Rozehnal, *Zákon o provozování rozhlasového a televizního vysílání Komentář*, p. 656 (Wolters Kluwer ČR, 2008).

297. According to the Broadcasting Act, such an event is '*an event listed in the List of Events of Major Social Importance, which is established by the Ministry by decree after consultation with the Council* (RRTV)', as well as an event declared by a Member State of the European Communities and announced in the Official Journal of the European Communities and an event declared by a Member State of the Council of Europe and published in accordance with an international treaty. The decree in question is Decree No 233/2001 Sb. of the Ministry of Culture issuing the List of Events of Major Social Importance; these events are currently the Olympic Games, the World and European Football Championships and the Ice Hockey and Athletics World Championships, within the defined scope.

298. *See* s. 33 of the Broadcasting Act.

299. *See* Council Directive 89/552/EEC of 3 Oct. 1989 on the coordination of certain provisions laid down by Law, Regulation or Administrative Action in Member States concerning the pursuit of television broadcasting activities.

or television broadcasts, the Broadcasting Act contains institutes similar to the Press Law,[300] i.e., the right of reply and the right of additional communication. '*The right of reply and the right to publish an additional communication are common in European media law and apply in our legal system to both print and electronic media. These institutes are enshrined in both the Press Law and the Law on the Operation of Radio and Television Broadcasting.*'[301] The right of reply may be invoked against a communication published in a radio or television broadcast if the communication contains a factual allegation which affects, in the case of a natural person, his or her honour, dignity or privacy and, in the case of a legal person, its name or reputation. At the request of the person concerned, the broadcaster shall publish the reply. The additional communication shall apply in the case of a communication about criminal or misdemeanour proceedings which has been published in the broadcast. The natural or legal person against whom the proceedings have been brought may, after the final conclusion of the proceedings, request the publication of information on the outcome of the proceedings. The broadcaster shall also be obliged to comply with the request in this case, otherwise the person concerned shall be entitled to claim the right to have the reply or additional communication published before a court.

309. Broadcasting Act regulates the protection of the source and content of information in radio and television broadcasting and guarantees a natural or legal person who '*has participated in the acquisition or processing of information for publication or published*' in a broadcast the right '*to refuse to provide a court, other state authority or public administration body with information on the origin or content of such information*', as well as the right '*to refuse to produce or release items from which the origin or content of such information could be ascertained*'.[302]

§5. Act on On-Demand Audiovisual Media Services

310. The Act No. 132/2010 Sb. was adopted only after relatively long time following the legislation on television and radio broadcasting, as a response to technological developments that brought services unforeseen by the existing legislation. According to the Ministry of Culture of the Czech Republic, on-demand audiovisual media services are a newly regulated segment of services '*similar to television broadcasting, but differing in their characteristics in that the user chooses what to watch and when to watch it from the offer presented*'. These services are similar to television broadcasting, but '*are provided to the user at a time of his or her choice – on-demand audiovisual media services. The subject matter of these services is the*

300. *See* Act No. 46/2000 Sb. on Rights and Obligations in the Publication of Periodicals and on Amendments to Certain Other Acts (Press Act), as amended.
301. *See* Aleš Rozehnal, *Zákon o provozování rozhlasového a televizního vysílání Komentář*, p. 656 (Wolters Kluwer ČR, 2008).
302. *See* s. 41 of the Broadcasting Act.

provision of programmes such as movies, recordings of sporting events, sitcoms, documentaries, children's programmes or original television plays'.[303]

311. The Act No. 132/2010 Sb. was adopted as a new piece of legislation, so it does not contain the 'classic' repeal provisions, whereby a legislation repeals the previous legislation it replaces; there was no prior legislation in this area. As further stated by the Ministry of Culture of the Czech Republic, '*The Act implements the European Directive on audiovisual media services (2007/65/EC), which responded to the imbalance in audiovisual market regulation. As on-demand services were not qualified as television broadcasting, even though they offered the same or similar content, the regulatory framework in force until then was modified. The difference between the two services lies in the way the service is provided. When the user decides on the viewing time, choosing the programme from a catalogue drawn up by the service provider, it is an on-demand audiovisual media service. By contrast, television broadcasting means that the broadcaster provides the same programme to everyone at the same time.*'[304]

312. In view of the fact that the provision of on-demand audiovisual media services is not subject to a licence, the lawmaker has defined in the Act No. 132/2010 Sb. the obliged persons to whom the law applies. These are providers of on-demand audiovisual media services who are considered to be established in the Czech Republic or who, although they are not considered to be established here or in another EU Member State, use for the provision of these services equipment for the transmission of a signal to a satellite located in the Czech Republic or the capacity of a satellite belonging to the Czech Republic, subject to other conditions.[305] The RRTV keeps a register of providers of on-demand audiovisual media services; providers are obliged to notify the RRTV of the facts specified by law.

§6. Obligations of Providers of On-Demand Audiovisual Media Services

313. Providers of on-demand audiovisual media services have certain obligations under the Act No. 132/2010 Sb. similar to the obligations of radio and television broadcasters under the Broadcasting Act. In particular, the Act No. 132/2010 Sb. imposes an obligation on providers of on-demand audiovisual media services to ensure that the service does not contain messages that deliberately influence the subconscious or incite hatred. In the case of a service whose content may seriously impair the physical, mental or moral development of children and adolescents, the

303. *See* Ministry of Culture of the Czech Republic. *Audiovizuální mediální služby na vyžádání.* Available from https://www.mkcr.cz/audiovizualni-medialni-sluzby-na-vyzadani-485.html.
304. *See* Ministry of Culture of the Czech Republic. *Audiovizuální mediální služby na vyžádání.* Available from https://www.mkcr.cz/audiovizualni-medialni-sluzby-na-vyzadani-485.html.
305. *See* s. 3 of the Act No. 132/2010 Sb.

provider is obliged to ensure that it is not normally accessible to children and adolescents. Providers are also obliged to keep recordings of all programmes and audiovisual commercial communications for at least thirty days and to make them available to RRTV on written request. The Act No. 132/2010 Sb., like the Broadcasting Act, imposes certain additional obligations on providers of on-demand audiovisual media services to promote European production, as well as obligations in the areas of commercial communications, programme sponsorship and product placement; for ease of comparison, we list these obligations under both laws together later in this chapter.

§7. Council for Radio and Television Broadcasting

314. As mentioned in the introduction to this chapter, the Broadcasting Act established the Broadcasting Council as the regulatory authority in the field of broadcasting with effect from 4 July 2001, and subsequently, under the Act No. 132/2010 Sb., the RRTV also became the regulatory authority in the field of on-demand audiovisual media services. RRTV was established under the Broadcasting Act by transformation from the previous Council of the Czech Republic for Radio and Television Broadcasting.[306]

315. RRTV is a central administrative authority based in Prague, the Act on the Establishment of Ministries and Other Central Bodies of State Administration of the Czech Republic lists the RRTV among the central bodies of state administration.[307] According to Broadcasting Act, the RRTV primarily supervises '*the preservation and development of the plurality of programme offerings and information in the field of radio and television broadcasting and retransmission*'[308] and ensures the content independence of broadcasting and performs other tasks stipulated by law.

I. Composition and Organization of the RRTV

316. The RRTV has a total of thirteen members appointed and dismissed by the Prime Minister on the proposal of the Chamber of Deputies for a term of office of six years. The RRTV elects and dismisses a chairman and three vice-chairmen from among its members; the chairman manages the activities of the RRTV and acts on its behalf. According to the Broadcasting Act, the Council Office is a body of the

306. The Council of the Czech Republic for Radio and Television Broadcasting was established by Act No. 103/1992 Sb. on the Council of the Czech Republic for Radio and Television Broadcasting, this Council operated in cooperation with the Federal Council for Radio and Television Broadcasting.
307. Act No. 2/1969 Sb. on the Establishment of Ministries and Other Central Bodies of State Administration of the Czech Republic, as amended, lists RRTV in s. 2/13 among 'other central bodies of state administration', in addition to the 'central bodies of state administration headed by a member of the Government' defined in s. 1 of this Act.
308. *See* s. 4/2 of the Broadcasting Act.

RRTV, which provides professional, organizational and technical support for the activities of the RRTV; the head of the Council Office is appointed and dismissed by the RRTV.

II. Competence of RRTV

317. The RRTV's competence is primarily to supervise compliance with legal regulations in the field of radio and television broadcasting, in the field of on-demand audiovisual media services and compliance with the conditions contained in decisions on granting licences or in decisions on registration, and to decide on licences to operate radio and television broadcasting – i.e., to grant, amend and withdraw licences and to decide on registrations to operate retransmission – to issue, amend and revoke registration decisions. The RRTV also monitors the content of radio and television broadcasting as well as the content of on-demand audiovisual media services and exercises other competences according to Broadcasting Act, Act No. 132/2010 Sb. and other laws. According to the Act on Advertising Regulation,[309] the RRTV is also the competent authority to supervise compliance with this act for advertising disseminated in radio and television broadcasting and in on-demand audiovisual media services and for sponsorship in radio and television broadcasting and in on-demand audiovisual media services. As stated by A. Rozehnal in his commentary on Broadcasting Act, '*Certain obligations of advertisers are laid down both in this act and in the Act on Advertising Regulation. However, this does not mean that two administrative penalties can be imposed on a broadcaster for the same breach of obligations by two different supervisory authorities. Indeed, the Council for Radio and Television Broadcasting is the body with exclusive competence to supervise broadcasters' obligations regarding advertising.*'[310]

III. Relationships of the RRTV to Other Bodies

318. The Broadcasting Act expressly regulates the cooperation between the RRTV and the CTO, which is very close with regard to the competence of both authorities and includes mutual provision of opinions, consents and other forms of cooperation envisaged by law. The cooperation concerns mainly the licensing procedure, in which RRTV requires the opinions of the CTO as well as the use of frequencies for analogue radio and television broadcasting and certain other issues. According to the Electronic Communications Act, the RRTV and the CTO also '*shall provide each other with suggestions, information and other forms of cooperation necessary for the performance of the tasks assigned to them by the legislation*'.[311]

---

309. *See* Act No. 40/1995 Sb., on the regulation of advertising and on amending and supplementing Act No. 468/1991 Sb., on the operation of radio and television broadcasting, as amended, as amended.
310. *See* Aleš Rozehnal, *Zákon o provozování rozhlasového a televizního vysílání Komentář*, p. 656 (Wolters Kluwer ČR, 2008).
311. *See* s. 112/1 of the Electronic Communications Act.

319. The Broadcasting Act and similarly also the Act No. 132/2010 Sb. stipulate the obligation of the RRTV to provide the Ministry of Culture of the Czech Republic with data necessary for the purposes of fulfilling the obligations arising for the Czech Republic from international treaties and from membership in international organizations, if the Ministry requests such data. According to the Broadcasting Act, the Government of the Czech Republic and state administration bodies shall cooperate with the RRTV in broadcasting matters, the Broadcasting Act obliges these bodies to always request the opinion of the RRTV in broadcasting matters and to provide the RRTV with the necessary cooperation within the limits of their competence. At the national level, the RRTV also cooperates with legal entities exercising self-regulation in one of the RRTV's fields of competence.

320. At the international level, the RRTV cooperates with the EU authorities and with the regulatory authorities of EU Member States, with which it exchanges information and performs other tasks resulting from the Czech Republic's membership in the EU. According to the Broadcasting Act, in the field of regulation of television broadcasting and in the field of regulation of on-demand audiovisual media services, the RRTV also cooperates with the competent authorities of countries that are not Member States of the EU or parties to the European Convention on Transfrontier Television. Finally, RRTV also participates in the activities of international organizations – the European Platform of Regulatory Authorities (EPRA), the European Regulators Group for Audiovisual Media Services (ERGA),[312] the Central European Regulatory Forum (CERF)[313] and the Contact Committee of the Audiovisual Media Services Directive.

§8. SUPPORT OF THE EUROPEAN WORKS

321. Both Broadcasting Act and Act No. 132/2010 Sb. impose obligations on broadcasters and on-demand audiovisual media service providers respectively to promote European works. As A. Rozehnal comments, '*The primary objective of the extension of the range of regulated entities is to maintain a fair competitive environment for broadcasters and for providers of new on-demand audiovisual media services, which have generally been less regulated to date. In the absence of regulation of the new players, broadcasters could find themselves at an economic disadvantage because they would have to comply with relatively strict rules that would not apply to their newer competitors.*'[314] Broadcasting Act defines a European work as a work originating in an EU Member State and, subject to other conditions, also a work originating in a State party to the European Convention on Transfrontier

312. ERGA was established by European Commission Decision C(2014) 462 of 3 Feb. 2014 (currently under Art. 30b of the revised Audiovisual Media Services Directive) as a High Level Group with an advisory voice, issuing opinions at the request of the Commission.
313. Established by the Cooperation Agreement of 10 Dec. 2009, it currently includes the regulatory authorities of the Czech Republic, Hungary, Poland, Romania, Serbia, Slovakia and Slovenia.
314. *See* Aleš Rozehnal, *Zákon o provozování rozhlasového a televizního vysílání Komentář*, p. 350 (Wolters Kluwer ČR, 2008).

Television[315] or a work co-produced under an audiovisual contract concluded between the European Communities (EC) and a third State.[316] This definition contained in Broadcasting Act is also referred to in Act No. 132/2010 Sb.

322. In order to promote 'European works and European independent and contemporary works', broadcasters are obliged to reserve for European works more than half of the total broadcasting time of each of their programmes (excluding the time allocated for news programmes, sport events, competitions, teletext, advertising and teleshopping). This obligation is also fulfilled by spending at least 10% of the broadcaster's programming budget on the production or purchase of European works produced by independent producers. Broadcasting Act further develops this obligation by setting mandatory shares for new European works.

323. The provider of an on-demand audiovisual media service is obliged to reserve at least 10% of the total number of programmes on offer, with the exception of news, competition and sports programmes, in a calendar year for European works, subject to feasibility. It may also fulfil this obligation by spending at least 1% of the total revenue from the service in a calendar year on '*the creation of European works or the acquisition for consideration of rights to use European works by means of an on-demand audiovisual media service*'.[317]

§9. Marketing and Advertising Obligations

324. The Broadcasting Act sets out certain restrictions on commercial communications for broadcasters. These are defined by the Broadcasting Act as advertising, teleshopping and sponsorship and, in the case of television broadcasting, product placement or other display meeting the definition criteria set by the Broadcasting Act. Broadcasters are thus prohibited from including certain types of commercial communications in their broadcasts, in particular those that are not easily recognizable, those that promote behaviour that endangers health or safety or behaviour that is grossly prejudicial to the protection of the environment, hidden commercial communications, religious and atheistic commercial communications, commercial communications containing subliminal messages and certain others, including an explicit prohibition on commercial communications relating to cigarettes, other tobacco products, electronic cigarettes or their refills. According to the Broadcasting Act, the truthfulness of the information contained in commercial communications is the responsibility of their sponsor and, if this cannot be determined, of the broadcaster.

---

315. European Convention on Transfrontier Television, as amended by the Protocol amending the European Convention on Transfrontier Television, promulgated under No. 57/2004 Sb. of International Treaties.
316. *See* s. 46 of the Broadcasting Act.
317. *See* s. 7 of the Act No. 132/2010 Sb.

325. When including advertisements, teleshopping and sponsor designations in the broadcast, the broadcaster is obliged to ensure, in particular, that advertisements and teleshopping are easily recognizable and that their inclusion does not undermine the integrity of the programme or the rights of rightsholders. The Broadcasting Act also lays down details concerning the volume level of the broadcast of advertising, teleshopping and sponsor identification, the frequency of interruptions of certain programmes by advertising or teleshopping spots, it also defines the time span of advertising and teleshopping in television and radio broadcasts, including special arrangements applicable to broadcasters by law, and lays down certain other obligations.

326. In addition to these general conditions, the Broadcasting Act contains specific regulation of two types of commercial communications, namely commercial communications concerning erotic services, erotic products and human medicines or food supplements to promote sexual performance, for which the Broadcasting Act defines the details of their timing in broadcasting, and commercial communications concerning alcoholic beverages – here the Broadcasting Act establishes certain content restrictions on these commercial communications, in particular the prohibition of their targeting specifically children and minors, the depiction of children and minors consuming alcoholic beverages, etc.

327. In the case of sponsorship of programmes and product placement,[318] Broadcasting Act also applies certain other rules, such as the prohibition of influencing the content and chronological order of programmes, in order to preserve the editorial responsibility and independence of the broadcaster, the prohibition of sponsorship of news and political-publicity programmes or the prohibition of placement of products from two categories – cigarettes, other tobacco products, electronic cigarettes, etc. and medicinal products or medical procedures available in the Czech Republic only on prescription.

328. Similarly, the Act No. 132/2010 Sb. also imposes certain obligations on service providers in relation to audiovisual commercial communications, sponsorship and product placement. However, it states that '*The rules are more relaxed in this case than for television broadcasting. Stricter rules governing audiovisual commercial communications do not seem justified in the case of on-demand audiovisual media services.*'[319] Audiovisual commercial communications[320] must be easily recognizable, must not violate human dignity, contain or promote discrimination, or

318. Product placement is defined by the Broadcasting Act in s. 2/2/b as any form of '*inclusion of a product, service, trademark relating to a product or service or mention of a product or service in a programme for remuneration or similar consideration*'.

319. *See* Aleš Rozehnal, *Zákon o provozování rozhlasového a televizního vysílání Komentář*, p. 350 (Wolters Kluwer ČR, 2008).

320. According to s. 2/1/e of the Act No. 132/2010 Sb., an audiovisual commercial communication means '*a visual sequence with or without sound which is intended to promote, directly or indirectly, the goods or services of a person carrying out an economic activity, or his image to the public, and which accompanies a programme or is included in a programme for remuneration or*

encourage behaviour that endangers health, safety or the environment. Certain commercial communications are expressly prohibited by the Act No. 132/2010 Sb. – the prohibition applies to covert audiovisual commercial communications and to communications relating to certain specific products, including cigarettes, other tobacco products, electronic cigarettes, etc., medicinal products or medical procedures available in the Czech Republic only on prescription, and commercial communications indicating that the country of origin of the food is the Czech Republic, unless the requirements under a specific law are met. Special restrictions on audiovisual commercial communications apply in order to protect children and minors.

329. The Act No. 132/2010 Sb. provides for restrictions on the sponsorship of on-demand audiovisual media services and programmes similar to those applicable in this area under the Broadcasting Act. The content of on-demand audiovisual media services and programmes must not be influenced by their sponsorship in such a way as to affect the editorial responsibility and independence of the provider, there is a prohibition on sponsoring news and political-publicity programmes and certain other restrictions. The Act No. 132/2010 Sb. also sets out conditions and restrictions on the product placement in programmes, and explicitly prohibits certain forms thereof.

§10. Act on the Czech Television and Act on the Czech Radio

330. By its nature, the legislation governing public Broadcasting is related to the regulation of radio and television Broadcasting; in the Czech Republic this is the Act on the Czech Television[321] and the Act on the Czech Radio.[322] As stated by the Ministry of Culture of the Czech Republic, '*The Czech Television and the Czech Radio are broadcasters by law with specific public service tasks. Both operators are independent of the State, do not receive any State subsidies and their activities are financed by income from radio and television licence fees and income from their own business activities (in particular the sale of advertising time, but also income from copyright, rental of equipment* etc.*). The Czech Television and the Czech Radio provide a service to the public by producing and distributing television and radio programmes, respectively, as well as other multimedia content and additional services.*'[323]

331. The Czech Television Act established the Czech Television as a legal entity with its own property, which provides a service to the public by '*producing and distributing television programmes, or other multimedia content and additional services throughout the territory of the Czech Republic in order to meet the democratic,*

similar consideration or for the purpose of self-promotion; an audiovisual commercial communication may take the form, in particular, of advertising, sponsorship or product placement'.

321. *See* Act No. 483/1991 Sb., on the Czech Television, as amended.

322. *See* Act No. 484/1991 Sb., on the Czech Radio, as amended.

323. *See* Ministry of Culture of the Czech Republic. Public broadcasting in the Czech Republic. Available from https://www.mkcr.cz/rozhlasove-a-televizni-vysilani-v-cr-484.html.

social and cultural needs of society and the need to preserve media plurality';[324] the Act set out specific tasks for the Czech Television within this 'public service in the field of television broadcasting'. The Act on the Czech Television established the Council of the Czech Television as the body '*through which the public's right to control the activities of the Czech Television is exercised*'. The Council has fifteen members, elected and recalled by the Chamber of Deputies of the Parliament of the Czech Republic, so that '*important regional, political, social and cultural currents of opinion*' are represented on the Council.[325] The law defines the financial sources of the Czech Television as mainly television fees and income from its own business activities.

332. Similarly to the case of the Czech Television, the Act on Czech Radio established the Czech Radio as a legal entity managing its own assets. According to the Act, the Czech Radio also provides a service to the public by '*producing and disseminating radio programmes and, where appropriate, other multimedia content and additional services throughout the territory of the Czech Republic*'[326] and, unlike the Czech Television, also abroad. Similarly to the Council of the Czech Television, under the Act on the Czech Radio, the Council of the Czech Radio is the body '*through which the public's right to control the activities of the Czech Radio is exercised*'. The Council has nine members, elected and dismissed by the Chamber of Deputies of the Parliament of the Czech Republic, with the same objectives as in the case of the Council of the Czech Television. The financial resources of the Czech Radio are also defined by law in a similar way to those of the Czech Television, i.e., mainly in terms of radio fees and income from its own business activities; in the case of the Czech Radio, moreover, the costs associated with radio broadcasts abroad are covered by the Czech Republic from the state budget.

§11. ADVERTISING REGULATION ACT

333. Another legal norm related to the regulation of radio and television broadcasting is the Advertising Regulation Act. As can be seen from the text earlier in this chapter, the Broadcasting Act as well as the Act No. 132/2010 Sb. impose a number of obligations on broadcasters and on-demand audiovisual media service providers respectively in the area of advertising, including teleshopping, sponsorship and product placement. The Advertising Regulation Act provides for the regulation of advertising of certain products such as tobacco products, human medicines, alcoholic beverages and others, as well as the regulation of unfair commercial practices and comparative advertising. The communication media through which advertising is disseminated are defined in the Act as the means by which advertising is transmitted – these include, in addition to periodicals, computer networks, audiovisual media, posters, leaflets and others, also radio and television broadcasting and

324. *See* s. 2 of the Act on the Czech Television.
325. *See* s. 4 of the Act on the Czech Television.
326. *See* s. 2 of the Act on the Czech Radio.

on-demand audiovisual media services. As already mentioned above in the definition of the competence of the RRTV, the RRTV supervises compliance with the Advertising Regulation Act in the defined areas.

§12. Act on Electronic Communications

334. As already mentioned in the chapter *Regulation of the electronic communications market*, in response to the technological developments of the previous years and in particular the convergent tendencies between the fields of telecommunications, media and information technology, the legal system of the Czech Republic has unified the regulation of all transmission networks, newly referred to as 'electronic communications', instead of the previous term 'telecommunications' with a narrower meaning, with the adoption of the Electronic Communications Act with effect from 1 May 2005. At the same time, this legislation clearly separated the regulation of transmission contained in Electronic Communications Act from the regulation of content primarily regulated in Broadcasting Act.[327]

335. Electronic Communications Act defines the electronic communications network as transmission systems that enable the transmission of signals, including, but not limited to, radio and television broadcasting networks and cable television networks, regardless of the type of information transmitted,[328] and other provisions contained in Electronic Communications Act similarly explicitly contemplate radio and television broadcasting. In the context of the adjustment of frequency plans, the Electronic Communications Act provides the CTO with the possibility to limit the principle of technological neutrality in cases necessary, *inter alia*, for '*the pursuit of public interest objectives such as the protection of life and health, the promotion of social, regional or territorial cohesion or the promotion of cultural and linguistic diversity and media pluralism, such as the provision of broadcasting services*'.[329] The Electronic Communications Act also regulates fees for the use of radio frequencies, including for frequency bands used for the dissemination and transmission of radio and television broadcasting. The regulation of transmission contained in the Electronic Communications Act also covers other areas relating to broadcasting, including the power of the CTO to impose obligations for the dissemination of designated radio and television programmes and services in the public interest, including the establishment of conditions for access to digital television and radio broadcasting services in the framework of the regulation of interconnection and access to electronic communications networks and associated facilities, or including the power of the CTO to impose obligations for the immediate elimination of interference to the reception of radio or television broadcasts.

---

327. As stated in the explanatory memorandum to s. 1 of the Government's draft Act on Electronic Communications (Parliamentary Document No. 768/0, later adopted as Act No. 127/2005 Sb.), '*In accordance with EC law, the content of services provided in the form of, for example, text, image, sound or video, i.e. in particular radio and television broadcasting, the provision of content on the Internet, etc., is generally excluded from the scope of the Act.*'.
328. *See* s. 2/2/b of the Electronic Communications Act.
329. *See* s. 16a/2/f of the Electronic Communications Act.

336. We have already mentioned the cooperation between the CTO and the RRTV above. Beyond that we can also mention, for example, the CTO's obligation to inform the RRTV without delay even in cases where it grants only a short-term authorization for a broadcasting service or in the case of granting or extending an authorization for experimental purposes in a frequency band reserved exclusively for a radio service.

Chapter 7. Regulation of Online Interactive Services

§1. Introduction

337. Online interactive services are an important part of the Czech Republic's economy, which is illustrated by the data of the Czech Statistical Office for 2021. 79% of Czech homes own a personal computer or a tablet and 83% of homes have access to the Internet. Ninety percent of Czech Internet users connect to the internet daily.

338. Social media have an established position in the Czech population considering they are used by 56% of individuals older than 16 years. The online environment also presents a widely utilized space for looking for information about goods and services; 89% of Czech Internet users use it for these purposes.

339. Regarding entertainment, most people read news on news servers – 76% of the Czech population, or 92% of Internet users. 58% of the Czech population use the Internet for watching videos on services such as YouTube, 49% for listening to music.

340. Purchasing over the Internet experienced significant growth between 2020 and 2021 due to the COVID-19 pandemic. In the three months preceding the survey, 57.5% of the Czech population made a purchase on the Internet, 37% of which made six or more purchases. A third of people who bought goods or services online in 2021 ordered them through foreign e-shops.

§2. Regulation Overview

341. The regulation of online interactive services in the Czech Republic can be divided into three categories: (i) regulation affecting legal persons and/or businesses in general, (ii) specific Czech regulation of online interactive services (usually issued on the basis of and with little to no differences from EU regulations), and (iii) EU regulation of online interactive services not specific to the Czech Republic.

342. General conditions for carrying on a trade in the Czech Republic are laid down in Act No. 455/1991 Sb., on licensed trade (the Trade Licensing Act), as amended. Foreign persons, i.e., those with their residence or registered seat outside of the Czech Republic, may usually carry on trade under the same conditions and to the same extent as a Czech person. Trades are divided into two categories: notifiable trades, which may be carried on once they have been notified, and permitted trades, requiring a concession. Some trades, e.g., the provision of travel agency services or brokerage activities in the energy sector (as of 1 July 2022), have additional requirements covered by special acts. In some cases, professional or other competence is required by law.

343. Considering that information society services providers (ISSPs) enter into legal relations with their customers, general contractual law set out by Act No. 89/2012 Sb., Civil Code, as amended ('Civil Code'), applies as well. This needs to be considered, *inter alia*, in the service's terms and conditions, and relates mostly to consumer protection (*see* Part III, Chapter 6). Naturally, competition law applies as well (*see* Part I, Chapter 4).

344. Regarding online interactive services, the core of their specific regulation is covered by Act No. 480/2004 Sb., on certain information society services and on amendments to some acts ACISS, as amended . The ACISS is the Czech transposition of Directive 2000/31/EC of the European Parliament and of the Council of 8 June 2000 on certain legal aspects of information society services, in particular electronic commerce, in the Internal Market (Directive on electronic commerce) ('E-commerce Directive'). The ACISS mostly covers the responsibilities and rights and obligations of ISSPs and the dissemination of commercial communications.

345. A notable portion of Information Society Services Providers (ISSP) regulation in the Czech Republic, however, originates directly from EU regulations. Regulation (EU) 2016/679 of the European Parliament and of the Council of 27 April 2016 on the protection of natural persons with regard to the processing of personal data and on the free movement of such data, and repealing Directive 95/46/EC General Data Protection Regulation (GDPR) will usually apply. In P2B (platform-to-business) scenarios, ISSPs must be compliant with Regulation (EU) 2019/1150 of the European Parliament and of the Council of 20 June 2019 on promoting fairness and transparency for business users of online intermediation services ('P2B Regulation'). This will affect, again, the service's terms and conditions. Other regulations may apply in specific fields, e.g., Council Regulation (EC) No 428/2009 of 5 May 2009 setting up a Community regime for the control of exports, transfer, brokering and transit of dual-use items.

346. In terms of EU legislation, there are several new regulations in various stages of the legislative process which are relevant to ISSPs. These are in particular, (i) Regulation of the European Parliament and of the Council on a single market for digital services (Digital Services Act) and amending Directive 2000/31/EC, (ii) Regulation of the European Parliament and of the Council on contestable and fair markets in the digital sector (Digital Markets Act), (iii) Regulation of the European Parliament and of the Council on European data governance (Data Governance Act), or (iv) Regulation of the European Parliament and of the Council on harmonized rules on fair access to and use of data (Data Act).

§3. Notable Transpositions and Adaptations of EU Legislation

I. E-commerce Directive Transposition (ACISS)

347. The E-commerce Directive is transposed into several different acts within Czech legislation. Section 1 (Establishment and information requirements) and section 3 (Contracts concluded by electronic means) of the directive are transposed into the Civil Code and relate to consumer protection (*see* Part III, Chapter 6). Section 4 (Liability of intermediary service providers) is transposed into the ACISS and is covered in Part III, Chapter 7.

348. Section 2 of the directive covers the dissemination of commercial communications and regulated professions and is partially transposed also in the ACISS. The baseline is an opt-in regime, i.e., the user's information may be used for the dissemination of commercial communication by electronic means only in the case of users who previously consented to this. An exception in the form of an opt-out regime applies where the ISSPs obtain the user's information in connection with the sale of a product or service in accordance with GDPR.

349. Regarding commercial communications related to ISSPs, the transposition in the ACISS essentially copies the E-commerce Directive. That is without prejudice to the general conditions for such, i.e., compliance with the professional rules applies in addition to the relevant regime (opt-in/opt-out) and other conditions.

II. Cookies

350. Information is key in various endeavours and online services are no different. For ISSPs, a lot of important user information is acquired via cookies. Their usage is regulated by Directive 2002/58/EC of the European Parliament and of the Council of 12 July 2002 concerning the processing of personal data and the protection of privacy in the electronic communications sector (Directive on privacy and electronic communications), which has been transposed into Act No. 127/2005 Sb., on electronic communications and amendments to some acts (Electronic Communications Act), as amended.

351. There used to be an opt-out regime for cookies, but as of 1 January 2022, the Electronic Communications Act has been amended to change the regime into opt-in, in accordance with the change in the Directive on privacy and electronic communications.

352. In the first half of 2022, the Czech Office for personal data protection started to monitor compliance in cookies usage by websites operators. The office has identified a number of shortcomings that ultimately violate data protection. In the first half of the year, the office gave operators time to adapt to the new legislation but in the future, the office will approach operators who are in breach of the legislation to take remedial action. If such is not done, the office will utilize sanctions, primarily of a financial nature.

353. The main deficiencies identified by the inspections of the office are, *inter alia*, use of non-technical cookies without consent, disproportionately long validity of cookies in relation to their purpose, the absence of an option to opt-out of the use of non-technical cookies in the first layer of the cookie bar, poor categorization of cookies, absence of information on the specific cookies used, difference in the visibility of the buttons for agreeing and disagreeing to the use of non-technical cookies, incorrect classification of cookies, information about cookies in a foreign language, or cookie bars which make it difficult or impossible to read the website.

III. Platform-to-Business

354. The specifics of intermediation services are regulated by the directly applicable P2B Regulation. The Czech adaptation has not been finalized, yet – an amendment of the ACISS is currently in the legislative process. The amendment mainly defines particular infringements and associated sanctions, as well as designating the authority responsible for supervising compliance with the P2B Regulation (the Czech Telecommunication Office).

Chapter 8. Regulation of Cryptography and Dual-Use Goods

355. The Czech Republic has no domestic laws and regulations applicable to cryptography. As a result, no mandated insecurity or any key escrow mechanism is in effect. Furthermore, no proposals in this area are being prepared or seriously considered.

356. However, some cryptography technology falls within the scope of the existing legal framework of dual-use goods. As a result, conditions restrict its free trade (export, import).

357. The legal framework of dual-use goods is highly harmonized at the EU level. Therefore, the Czech legal framework is, to a large extent (scope, use of EU authorization mechanisms etc.), formed by the Regulation (EU) 2021/821 of the European Parliament and of the Council of 20 May 2021 setting up a Union regime for the control of exports, brokering, technical assistance, transit and transfer of dual-use items ('Regulation 2021/821'). The national legislation, specifically Act No. 594/2004 Sb., implementing the ECregime for the control of exports, transfer, brokering, and transit of dual-use items ('Act No. 594/2004 Sb.') covers the control mechanisms, activity of brokers and provision of brokering services, transit of dual-use goods, rights and obligations on the export of dual-use goods from the territory of the Czech Republic, and rights and obligations of persons importing the dual-use goods into the territory of the Czech Republic.[330]

358. Act No. 594/2004 Sb. is periodically amended to reflect the development of EU legislation. However, the current version of the Act still contains references to the Council Regulation (EC) No. 428/2009 of 5 May 2009 setting up a Community regime for the control of exports, transfer, brokering and transit of dual-use items, although this regulation was already repelled by the Regulation 2021/821.[331] This was to be solved by a technical amendment to the Act No. 594/2004 Sb. However, the amendment was not yet passed.

359. The scope of the legal regime of dual-use goods *vis-á-vis* cryptography is governed solely by Regulation 2021/821. As a result, cryptography falls into dual-use goods Category 5 Part 2 (Information Security).[332]

360. Concerning scope, it is essential to note that the Czech Ministry of Trade and Industry [*Ministerstvo průmyslu a obchodu*], as the responsible body, can impose restrictions on trade on goods that are not specified as dual-use goods in Regulation 2021/821. This mechanism, the 'catch-all principle,'[333] is a part of the

330. *See* ss 1/1 and 1/2 of Act No. 594/2004 Sb.
331. *See* Art. 31 of Regulation 2021/821.
332. *See* Annex I of Regulation 2021/821.
333. *See* Art. 4 of Regulation 2021/821.

EU legal regime, taking into account embargoes and special measures aimed at specific countries. A list of special measures mirrors the imposed EU measures.[334] However, some of the measures from before the Czech EU membership are still in effect. An example of such a measure is Act No. 99/2000 Sb., on the prohibition of supplies to the Bushehr nuclear power plant, which prohibits the trade of any services, documentation or information directly or indirectly supplying the Bushehr nuclear power plant in Iran.[335] Summary information about these special measures is made available on the website of the Ministry of Industry and Trade, specifically its Licencing Office [*Licenční správa*] ('Ministry').[336]

361. Act No. 594/2004 Sb. recognizes four types of authorizations for export of dual-use goods:

(1) Union general export authorization.[337]
(2) National general export authorization.[338]
(3) Individual export authorization.[339] and
(4) Global export authorization.[340]

362. General export authorizations (both Union and national) are the primary means for exporting dual-use goods. If no general export authorization is available, exporters can apply for individual or global export authorization. These authorizations are obtained through the procedure governed by Czech national law.[341] If there is a general export authorization available, exporters must register for its use through the procedure governed by Czech national law.[342] Additionally, brokers are required to apply for permission to provide brokering services.[343] Related definitions (exporter and export, broker and brokering services) are not provided by Czech law but follow the existing EU framework.[344]

363. Union general export authorization is an export authorization allowing export to specific countries, which is available to all the exporters who respect conditions and requirements listed in Regulation 2021/821.[345] There are eight Union general export authorizations available (designated as EU001 to EU008). Three (EU001, EU007 and EU008) will be covered in more detail since they are relevant to the export of cryptography.

---

334. E.g., measures against Russia following the Council Regulation No. 833/2014 or Iran following the Council Regulation No. 267/2012.
335. *See* s. 1 of Act No. 99/2000 Sb., on the prohibition of supplies to the Bushehr nuclear power plant.
336. *See* https://www.mpo.cz/dokument40596.html.
337. *See* Art. 12(1)(d) of Regulation 821/2021 and s. 4/a of Act No. 594/2004 Sb.
338. *See* Art. 12(1)(c) of Regulation 821/2021 and s. 4/b of Act No. 594/2004 Sb.
339. *See* Art. 12(1)(a) of Regulation 821/2021 and s. 7/2 of Act No. 594/2004 Sb.
340. *See* Art. 12(1)(b) of Regulation 821/2021 and s. 7/3 of Act No. 594/2004 Sb.
341. *See* s. 8 of Act No. 594/2004 Sb.
342. *See* s. 6 of Act No. 594/2004 Sb.
343. *See* s. 7 of Act No. 594/2004 Sb.
344. *See* Arts 2(2), 2(3), 2(7), 2(8) of Regulation 821/2021.
345. *See* Annex 2 of Regulation 821/2021.

364. EU001 covers the export of all dual-use goods to Australia, Canada, Iceland, Japan, New Zealand, Norway, Switzerland, Liechtenstein, the United Kingdom and the United States. As a result, this Union general export authorization also includes cryptography export to listed states. EU007 covers intra-group export of software and technology (hence it includes cryptography) to Argentina, Brazil, Chile, India, Indonesia, Israel, Jordan, Malaysia, Mexico, Morocco, Philippines, Singapore, South Africa, South Korea, Thailand and Tunisia. This authorization allows the export of software and technology to a company wholly owned and controlled by the exporter (subsidiary) or to a company directly and wholly owned and controlled by the same parent company as the exporter (sister company).

365. EU008 is Union global export authorization entirely focused on cryptography. First, it permits the export of cryptography items using published or commercial cryptographic standards that have been approved or adopted by internationally recognized standard bodies. Second, it permits the export of cryptography items not employing cryptographic standards designed for government use (e.g., TETRA, TETRAPOL, P25). Third, it permits the export of cryptography items where the user cannot easily change the used cryptographic functionality. All three criteria have to be fulfilled cumulatively. Furthermore, EU008 cannot be used to export goods to Afghanistan, Armenia, Azerbaijan, Belarus, Cambodia, Central African Republic, China (including Hong Kong and Macao), Congo, Democratic Republic of the Congo, Egypt, Eritrea, Georgia, Iran, Iraq, Israel, Kazakhstan, Kyrgyzstan, Lebanon, Libya, Malaysia, Mali, Mauritius, Mongolia, Myanmar/Burma, North Korea, Oman, Pakistan, Qatar, Russia, Saudi Arabia, Somalia, South Sudan, Sudan, Syria, Tajikistan, Turkmenistan, United Arab Emirates, Uzbekistan, Venezuela, Yemen, Zimbabwe. Additionally, EU008 is unavailable for export to states subjected to arms embargoes or restrictive measures of the EU applying dual-use goods.

366. The Czech Republic issued no national general export authorization.

367. Any exporter desiring to rely on the Union general export authorization or national general export authorization (should it be issued in the future) must register with the Ministry. Registration has to contain a designation of the general export authorization to be used by an exporter.[346] The registration procedure requires submission of the original or an officially certified copy of an extract from the Commercial Register not older than ninety days, and the original or an officially certified copy of the document proving the authorization to engage in business activity related to the export of dual-use goods (if it was issued).[347] The Ministry is required to confirm the registration within ten days.[348]

368. Successful registration carries with it obligations. First, every exporter is required to notify the Ministry of any changes in the information submitted upon

346. *See* s. 6/2 of Act No. 594/2004 Sb.
347. *See* s. 6/3 of Act No. 594/2004 Sb.
348. *See* s. 6/4 of Act No. 594/2004 Sb.

registration within fifteen days.[349] Second, the exporter is to apply for termination of registration if it has not exported dual-use items for one year.[350] Additionally, the exporter is to submit, at any time on request from the Ministry, the complete data on exports made under the general export authorization.[351]

369. In case of export of dual-use goods for which neither the Union general export authorization nor the national general export authorization is available, the Ministry can, upon request, issue an individual export authorization or a global export authorization.[352]

370. The individual export authorization allows the export of dual-use goods specified in the authorization to one country either in one shipment or in partial shipments based on the contractual agreement between the exporter and its foreign partner.[353] By its nature, the individual export authorization covers one contract for which it is granted. On the other hand, global export authorization allows a continuous export of dual-use goods of the same nature into one or multiple countries for which it is granted.[354]

371. Exporter is required to submit an application for individual export authorization or global export authorization to the Ministry.[355] The application needs to be accompanied by an original or an officially certified copy of an extract from the Commercial Register not older than ninety days, and the original or an officially certified copy of the document proving the authorization to engage in business activities related to the export of dual-use goods (if it was issued).[356] Furthermore, an import certificate from the competent authority of the importing state or a declaration by the foreign end-user with information on the specific purpose of the use of dual-use goods must be attached, as well as a declaration that the dual-use goods will not be subsequently exported without the consent of the Czech Republic (as the exporting country).[357] Further information may be required by the Ministry for the purpose of adequately understanding and overseeing the specific transaction.[358] Finally, the application must contain either a proposal or a contract between the exporter and its foreign partner. This document has to contain an exact specification

349. *See* s. 6/5 of Act No. 594/2004 Sb.
350. *See* s. 6/6 of Act No. 594/2004 Sb.
351. *See* s. 6/7 of Act No. 594/2004 Sb.
352. *See* s. 7/1 of Act No. 594/2004 Sb.
353. *See* s. 7/2 of Act No. 594/2004 Sb.
354. *See* s. 7/3 of Act No. 594/2004 Sb.
355. *See* s. 8/1 of Act No. 594/2004 Sb.
356. *See* s. 8/2/a of Act No. 594/2004 Sb.
357. *See* s. 8/2/b of Act No. 594/2004 Sb.
358. *See* s. 8/2/c of Act No. 594/2004 Sb.

of the dual-use goods to be exported, including their quantity.[359] Application forms are published in bylaws.[360]

372. Exporter applying for global export authorization must prove that it can validate the end-use of individual shipments exported under the requested global export authorization.[361] If the application is rejected because the applicant could not fulfil this condition and sufficiently prove its ability to monitor individual shipments, the exporter is entitled to apply for individual export authorization.[362] This requirement primarily distinguishes between single and continuous exports, as the continuous export places more emphasis on exporter's experience and internal controlling mechanisms.

373. There are multiple grounds for the rejection of the application. Submitting an incomplete application (e.g., not accompanied by one of the mandatory attachments) will result in the rejection of the application by the Ministry.[363] The application is also to be rejected if the applicant engaged in unauthorized export or other administrative offences related to the trade of dual-use goods in the past.[364] Furthermore, the Ministry is to reject the application whenever the rejection is in line with the foreign policy and security interests of the Czech Republic.[365] Finally, the Ministry will reject the application if the end-user (or the end-use) specified in the application did not provide sufficient guarantees that the dual-use goods will not be used in connection with weapons of mass destruction, missile systems capable of delivering such weapons or for military purposes.[366]

374. The Ministry can also revoke once granted authorization on several grounds. Mainly if the authorization was granted based on false or incomplete information or if conditions upon which the authorization was granted were not fulfilled.[367] In case of a change of circumstances under which the authorization was granted, the Ministry can either revoke or amend existing authorization.[368] The

359. *See* s. 8/3 of Act No. 594/2004 Sb.
360. *See* s. 7/4 of Act No. 594/2004 Sb. and Annex 1 of the Government Decree No. 344/2010 Sb., laying down the form to applications or individual and global export authorizations, applications for authorization of brokering services and applications for international import certificates for dual-use goods and technology.
361. *See* s. 8/4 of Act 594/2004 Sb.
362. *See* s. 8/5 of Act 594/2004 Sb.
363. *See* ss 9/2/a, and 9/3/a of Act No. 594/2004 Sb.
364. *See* ss 9/2/b, 9/2/c, 9/3/b and 9/3/c of Act No. 594/2004 Sb.
365. The Ministry must receive such information from the relevant state authorities, e.g., the Ministry of Defence, the Ministry of Foreign Affairs or intelligence agencies. *See* s. 9/2/d and s. 9/3/d of Act No. 594/2004 Sb.
See also Recital 16 of Regulation 2021/821.
366. *See* ss 9/2/e and 9/3/e of Act No. 594/2004 Sb.
367. *See* s. 10/1 of Act No. 594/2004 Sb.
368. *See* s. 10/3 of Act No. 594/2004 Sb.

Ministry can also temporarily suspend granted authorization for a period necessary to investigate further whether a ground for revocation or amendment of the authorization exists.[369]

375. Generally speaking, it is possible to review the decisions of administrative bodies. A decision can be subjected to administrative review (e.g., through appeal) and subsequently to judicial review (action against the decision of an administrative body). However, the law excludes explicitly Ministry's decision to grant, reject, suspend, amend or revoke an authorization from these review procedures.[370]

376. The individual and the global export authorization are issued in two copies. One copy is, for customs purposes, accompanied by the depreciation certificate.[371] Anyone granted the authorization must to return the copy with the depreciation certificate to the Ministry no later than fifteen days after the authorization expiry or the shipment delivery. Any exceptions from this rule are individual and are part of the specific authorization granted by the Ministry. If the authorization is not used for the intended purpose, the exporter must return both copies of authorization to the Ministry with an explanation of why the authorization was not used.[372]

377. The law requires authorized subjects (exporters, brokers) to archive any records and commercial documents for at least five years starting from the 31st December of the year the service was provided.[373] Furthermore, the authorized subject is obliged to secure a declaration of the end-use of dual-use goods if required and present (upon Ministry's request) a delivery verification document issued by the competent authority of the country of import.[374] The verification document confirms the reception of the dual-use goods in the authorized country of destination. It provides the Ministry with information about the use of any given authorization.

378. Besides the export authorizations, special rules exist for:

(a) Technical assistance.
(b) Intra-Union transfer of dual-use goods.
(c) Transit.

379. Technical assistance is defined in Czech law[375] in the same manner as in Regulation 2021/821.[376] Providing technical assistance requires individual export authorization granted by the Ministry[377] if the technical assistance: (1) is provided

369. *See* s. 10/2 of Act No. 594/2004 Sb.
370. *See* s. 10/5 of Act No. 594/2004 Sb.
371. *See* s. 7/1 of Act No. 594/2004 Sb.
372. *See* s. 11/2 of Act No. 594/2004 Sb.
373. *See* s. 11/4 of Act No. 594/2004 Sb.
374. *See* s. 11/5 of Act No. 594/2004 Sb.
375. *See* s. 12/2 of Act No. 594/2004 Sb.
376. *See* Art. 2(9) of Regulation 2021/2021.
377. *See* s. 12/1 of Act No. 594/2004 Sb.

outside of the territory of the EU; (2) requires cross-border movement of persons; and (3) relates to chemical, biological and nuclear weapons or missile systems capable of delivering such weapons, or countries subjected to weapons embargo.[378] Furthermore, individual export authorization is not required if the technical assistance is provided in the form of publicly available information or as part of the fundamental (non-applied) scientific research.[379]

380. Regulation 2021/821 requires authorization for the intra-Union transfer of dual-use goods for transfers of specific items in Category 5 Part 2 (Information security) used in the cryptanalysis.[380] Furthermore, the Czech Republic can issue bylaws requiring authorization for the intra-Union transfer of other dual-use goods, unspecified by Regulation 2021/821.[381] Authorization for intra-Union transfers follows requirements for individual or global export authorizations.

381. Transit is the transport of non-Union dual-use goods through the customs territory of the Union with the destination outside the customs territory of the Union.[382] Under Czech law, transit can be prohibited,[383] and the dual-use goods in transit can be seized.[384] The Ministry can prohibit the transit upon reasonable suspicion[385] that the goods are to be used or could be used in connection with chemical, biological or nuclear weapons or missile systems capable of delivering such weapons or for military end-use in a country subjected to an arms embargo.[386] Such a prohibition is excluded from the administrative and judicial review.[387] Furthermore, the customs authority can seize the dual-use goods upon reasonable suspicion[388] that the goods are to be used or could be used in connection with chemical, biological or nuclear weapons or missile systems capable of delivering such weapons or for military end-use in a country subjected to an arms embargo.[389]

382. While most of the legal framework of trade of dual-use goods is concerned with export, the Ministry also issues international import certificates. The certificate grants an additional layer of control in the international trade of dual-use goods and is issued upon application submitted by the importer.[390] The process is similar to the application for individual and global export authorization.[391]

378. *See* s. 12/4 of Act No. 594/2004 Sb.
379. *See* s. 12/6 of Act No. 594/2004 Sb.
380. *See* Art. 11 and Annex IV of Regulation 2021/821.
381. *See* s. 13/1 of Act No. 594/2004 Sb.
382. *See* Art. 2(11) of Regulation 2021/821.
383. *See* s. 13b of Act No. 594/2004 Sb.
384. *See* s. 13a of Act No. 594/2004 Sb.
385. *See* recital 16 of Regulation 821/2021.
386. *See* s. 13b/1 of Act No. 594/2004 Sb. Further, *see* Art. 4(1) and Art. 4(2) of the Regulation 821/2021.
387. *See* s. 13b/2 of Act No. 594/2004 Sb.
388. *See* recital 16 of Regulation 2001/821.
389. *See* s. 13b/1 of Act No. 594/2004 Sb. Further, *see* Art. 4(1) and Art. 4(2) of the Regulation 2021/821.
390. *See* ss 14/1, 14/2 and 14/4 of Act No. 594/2004 Sb.
391. *See* ss 14/5 and 14/6 of Act No. 594/2004 Sb.

383. Overall, the oversight over the dual-use goods regime is granted to the customs authority, which is the Customs Administration of the Czech Republic [*Celní správa České republiky*]. The Ministry can also require customs authority to conduct preliminary verification of information provided in the application for individual export authorization, global export authorization, individual export authorization for technical assistance, intra-Union transfer or international import certificate.[392] Furthermore, custom authority is expressly granted powers to enter business premises and inspect business files.[393] It is also authorized to control the transfer of dual-use software and technology by electronic means, fax or telephone to a destination outside of the EU.[394]

384. There are three groups of administrative sanctions related to the trade of dual-use goods. The first group is concerned with proper record keeping (under Regulation 2021/821 and Act No. 594/2004 Sb.) and designation of dual-use goods upon transport.[395] The second group focuses mainly on engagement in unauthorized activities (export, brokering services, technical assistance, violation of the decision prohibiting transit).[396] Finally, the third group focuses on less severe violations, such as exporting dual-use goods under the Union global export authorization without the required registration.[397] Sanctions for offences from the first and the third group can be up to CZK 5,000,000 (approx. EUR 200,000) and for offences from the second group up to 20,000,000 (approx. EUR 800,000).

385. Additionally to administrative offences, the trade of dual-use goods has a criminal liability dimension. Exporting dual-use goods without proper authorization is punishable by three to eight years in prison.[398] Furthermore, obtaining export authorization based on false or incomplete information is punishable by up to two years in prison.[399] Finally, violating the integrity of records or documents necessary for authorizing the export of dual-use goods is also punishable by up to two years in prison.[400] It is important to note that criminal liability for these crimes is not excluded under Act No. 418/2011 Sb., on Criminal liability of legal persons and proceedings against them.[401] As a result, companies can be criminally liable similarly to natural persons.

---

392. *See* s. 16/2 of Act No. 594/2004 Sb.
393. *See* s. 16/3 of Act No. 594/2004 Sb.
394. *See* s. 16/4 of Act No. 594/2004 Sb.
395. *See* s. 17/1 of Act No. 594/2004 Sb.
396. *See* s. 18/1/a, 18/1/b, 18/1/c, 18/1/d, 18/1/e, 18/1/f of Act 594/2004 Sb.
397. *See* s. 18/1/g, 18/1/, 18/1/i of Act No. 594/2004 Sb.
398. *See* s. 262 of the Criminal Code.
399. *See* s. 264/1 of the Criminal Code.
400. *See* s. 264/2 of the Criminal Code.
401. *See* s. 7 of Act No. 418/2011 Sb., on Criminal liability of legal persons and proceedings against them.

Part II. Online Public Services

Chapter 1. E-government Legal Framework

§1. Introduction

386. The Czech e-Government infrastructure has been developing gradually. Unfortunately, it suffers from many issues, including a lack of strategic foresight and expertise, corruption and vendor lock-in issues. The framework consists of multiple legal acts providing a basic structure to carry out the e-Government services. Additionally, it consists of decrees and guidelines implementing the basic structure into the day-to-day activity of public administration bodies. The most important legislation, which is going to be covered in this chapter, contains these acts:

(1) Act No. 365/2000 Sb., on information systems of public administration.
(2) Act No. 499/2004 Sb., on archiving and filing services.
(3) Act No. 300/2008 Sb., on electronic acts and authorized document conversion.
(4) Act No. 111/2009 Sb., on Basic Registers (BRs).
(5) Act No. 222/2016 Sb., on the Collection of Laws and International Treaties (CLA) and the preparation of legislation published in the collection of laws and international treaties.
(6) Act No. 12/2020 Sb., on the right to digital services.
(7) Act No. 35/2021 Sb., on the collection of legal regulations of self-government units and certain administrative bodies.

387. These acts were amended on many different occasions. The e-Government landscape was often not developed with clear foresight and logical planning. Additionally, in some areas, more modern legal instruments have already superseded the first generation of legislation. As a result, this chapter will be organized with broader e-Government aspects and concepts in mind. As such, the gradual development will be less apparent, but the state of e-Government in the Czech Republic will be more readily available.

§2. Rights to Digital Services

388. Act No. 12/2020 Sb., on the right to digital services (ARDS) is a recent addition to the Czech e-Government legal framework. Additionally, it is quite controversial and, in some opinions, redundant. While it was presented to the public as a significant step developing the e-Government infrastructure, some argue that most of the rights granted by ARDS were already present in law but not diligently applied.[402]

389. For example, ARDS grants natural and artificial persons the right to act digitally toward public bodies. In return, it creates an obligation for public bodies to accept digital submissions and to provide digital services.[403] Strictly speaking, the right to act digitally existed in the Czech Republic even before ARDS, mainly through the data mailbox infrastructure (Act No. 300/2008., on electronic acts and authorized document conversion). However, ARDS has, at least on paper, the potential for far-reaching consequences on the development of the Czech e-Government infrastructure. While it codifies specific rights concerning electronic communication and e-Government services, it also provides an obligation to digitize all the government services that can be meaningfully digitized. Additionally, it provides a specific time frame to achieve the desired state.

390. ARDS required the government to establish the Catalogue of Services as a part of the Register of Rights and Obligations by 1st February 2021. Subsequently, government services listed within the Catalogue that can be meaningfully digitized have to be provided digitally by 1st February 2025. Given the development and deployment of e-Government infrastructure, this is a highly ambitious time frame carrying specific issues. As of now, the Catalogue of Services is not yet finished. Unfortunately, some administrative bodies did not understand the reason for its inception and did not commit to the idea of fast and systematic digitization of their various agendas.[404]

391. Additionally, ARDS granted specific rights. The right to use digital services and the corresponding obligation of public administration bodies to provide digital services[405] was already mentioned. It also established the right to act via data mailboxes, sending electronic documents signed by digital signatures, or Information Systems of Public Administration (ISA) enabling authentication by electronic means.[406] Furthermore, ARDS granted the right to receive confirmation of the digital act from the public administration body,[407] the right to replace the non-digital officially certified signature by digital means,[408] or the right to use electronic identification and authentication[409] when dealing with the authorities. It also established an obligation for public administrative bodies not to require the data it already has

402. *See* Pavel Mates, *Právo na digitální služby*, Revue pro právo a technologie, vol. 11, no. 21, p. 74 (2020).
403. *See* s. 1 of ARDS.
404. *See* Zdeněk Zajíček, František Korbel, Dalibor Kovář et al., *Zákon o právu na digitální služby. Komentář,* p. 4 (C. H. Beck 2021).
405. *See* s. 3 of ARDS.
406. *See* s. 4 of ARDS.
407. *See* s. 5 of ARDS.
408. *See* s. 6 of ARDS.
409. *See* s. 12 of ARDS.

access to,[410] which is still widespread practice by some authorities. Mates claims most of these rights existed even before ARDS, and the issue was not their non-existence but mainly their non-enforcement.[411]

392. ARDS also contains the right to technological neutrality, which is an obligation of public authorities to make any service or data available for use regardless of specific platform or technology. Understandably, this right is not unlimited. Technological neutrality has to be observed where it is not economically unviable or when barred by the security issues preventing the neutrality.[412] In a way, this is an interesting right, as it is closely related to ARDS prohibiting forcing natural persons to use digital services.[413] This is a manifestation of a dilemma faced by many countries worldwide. The effort to develop their e-Government infrastructure must ensure that the part of the population with a lower level of digital literacy is not excluded by such development from accessing government services.[414] In a way, ARDS requires the government to adjust to the needs of modern society but protects natural persons from being forced to use digital means of communication. However, in this area, ARDS only *expressis verbis* states what is already implicitly contained in anti-discriminatory[415] or EU law.[416]

393. While the impact of ARDS is now limited, the 1 February 2025 might have a paradigm-altering impact on the landscape of e-Government. After that date, natural and artificial persons can enforce the rights granted by ARDS. Eventually, they might sue for compensation for any harm they may suffer due to the government's failure to provide digital services.[417] Unfortunately, delays, lack of understanding and commitment tied to other issues, such as lack of funding, can lead to last-minute digitization efforts, which can have serious negative consequences. Understandably, the public is split about the potential of ARDS. The act brought forth many enthusiasts and many sceptics. One of the main points of criticism emphasizes the act to be vague, declaratory and significantly lacking in effective enforcement mechanisms.[418]

---

410. *See* s. 7 of ARDS.
411. *See* Pavel Mates, *Právo na digitální služby*, Revue pro právo a technologie, vol. 11, no. 21, p. 74 (2020).
412. *See* s. 13 of ARDS.
413. *See* s. 14/1 of ARDS.
414. *See* Zdeněk Zajíček, František Korbel, Dalibor Kovář et al., *Zákon o právu na digitální služby. Komentář*, p. 4 (C. H. Beck 2021).
415. *See* Act No. 198/2009 Sb., on equal treatment and on the legal means of protection against discrimination.
416. *See* Art. 107 of the Treaty on the Functioning of the EU.
417. *See* Zdeněk Zajíček, František Korbel, Dalibor Kovář et al., *Zákon o právu na digitální služby. Komentář*, p. 5 (C. H. Beck 2021).
418. *See* Pavel Mates, *Právo na digitální služby*, Revue pro právo a technologie, vol. 11, no. 21, p. 87 (2020).

§3. PUBLIC INFORMATION SYSTEMS

394. Act No. 365/2000 Sb., on ISA is one of the focal pieces of e-Government legislation. ISA provides the framework guiding the development of ISA (such as Information System of Basic Registers (ISBR) or the ORG Converter), as well as for their technical accreditation and other procedures that the Ministry of Interior mostly supervises. Additionally, ISA established the Portal of public administration [*Portál veřejné správy*],[419] network of points of public administration (Czech POINT, *Český Podací Ověřovací Informační Národní Terminál*),[420] and the cloud computing catalogue.[421]

395. The Portal of public administration ('Portal') is an information system of public administration providing access to the information published by public bodies and a platform for communication with public bodies. Its administrator is the Ministry of Interior.[422] The Portal serves these purposes mainly in social security, health services, public finances, subsidies, public procurement procedures, state statistical services, evidence and identification of persons, and creation and publication of legal acts.[423] Communication with public bodies is available via data mailboxes, authorized access to information systems of public administration, or applications administered by public bodies.[424] Additionally, the Portal allows natural persons to file information about their official documents, such as ID card or driver's licence. It then notifies the person about the upcoming expiration of such a document.[425] Furthermore, one of its services allows applying for a new driver's licence in case of its expiration. However, this is an example of highly selective service provided through the Portal, as only some governmental agendas or services are digitized to an extent allowing the use of Portal.

396. One of the significant benefits of the Portal is the evidence of life scenarios [*Životní události*] and the list of public administration services [*Služby veřejné správy*]. The former provides individuals with guidance regarding particular life situations, such as sickness, death of a relative, loss of a job and others. These scenarios make navigating related legal provisions and governmental services easier. The latter provides an overview of governmental services in different areas (e.g., taxes, digital citizenship, or culture and media). This overview serves as a database allowing disambiguation of different concepts in law, concerned authorities, and their powers and responsibilities.

397. The network of contact points of public administration, Czech POINT, provides a range of services to both natural and artificial persons. The whole infrastructure aims to establish a dense-enough network for communication with the

419. *See* s. 8a of ISA.
420. *See* s. 6g of ISA.
421. *See* s. 6k of ISA.
422. *See* s. 6g/1 of ISA.
423. *See* s. 6g/2 of ISA.
424. *See* s. 6g/3 of ISA.
425. *See* s. 6g/5 of ISA.

state, where data can be obtained and verified, documents can be officially certified and paper documents can be converted into electronic form and vice versa. The pilot stage of the Czech POINT network started in 2007. Since its official start in 2008, the network has gradually developed in the number of access points and the scope of provided services. The network contains 7,344 physical places (offices) both in the Czech Republic and abroad. These places include mainly municipalities but also offices of regional governments, notaries, embassies, or post offices.[426]

398. The Czech POINT network allows:

- to obtain authorized excerpts from databases such as Land Register, Commercial Register, Trade Register, Criminal Register, Driver's Record Card, List of Qualified Suppliers, Insolvency Register, ePrescription;
- to submit documents required for registration under the Trade Act and to the Car Wreckage module of the Waste Management Information System;
- to obtain excerpts from basic registers and to amend data in these registers;
- to administer data mailboxes;
- authorized conversion of documents from paper to electronic form and from electronic to paper form; and
- to verify identity.

399. The seemingly random pattern of provided services (especially concerning the submission of documents required for registration) points out the gradual and haphazard nature of the development of e-Government infrastructure in the Czech Republic.

400. Additionally, the Czech POINT network provides remote access to other entities (Czech POINT@office), such as public bodies, universities or attorneys, which require some of the services either for their internal use or are legally allowed or mandated to provide these services to the public.

401. Since 2021, the newest addition to the framework is the information system of cloud computing[427] administered by the Ministry of Interior[428] and the related cloud computing catalogue.[429] ISA now provides conditions that public authorities must fulfil to run their cloud-based information system. Authorities may only use cloud computing services that are either provided:

- by a state cloud computing provider or by a cloud computing provider listed in the cloud computing catalogue; or
- within the framework of vertical or horizontal cooperation under the public procurement legislation; or

426. *See* s. 8a/2 of ISA.
427. *See* s. 6j/1 of ISA.
428. *See* s. 6j/2 of ISA.
429. *See* s. 6j/1 of ISA. This provision was in ISA since 2020 but was significantly amended in 2021.

– within the framework of a general exemption from the obligation to award a public contract in a tender.[430]

402. The cloud computing catalogue contains notices about cloud computing demands of public administration bodies, publishes cloud computing offers, and lists cloud computing providers and cloud computing services used by public administration bodies.[431]

403. As these provisions were recently either newly added or substantively amended, we are currently within the interim period. Such a period allows the use of cloud computing services based on existing contracts without the need to fulfil the new requirements. However, the interim period is going to conclude in 2023. Therefore, since 1 January 2024, all cloud computing services must be acquired and operated in compliance with ISA. Overall, this legislation provides a centralized procurement procedure. Additionally, mandating the use of cloud computing services only from the catalogue makes it easier for individual public bodies to develop further services and be more aware of their security properties.[432]

§4. Basic Registers

404. Basic registers (BRs) established by Act No. 111/2009 Sb., on basic registers (BRA) are one of the cornerstones of the e-Government in the Czech Republic. BRs were to become piloted starting 1 July 2010 and planned to become operational starting 1 July 2011. However, due to various issues typical for Czech e-Government efforts, the deployment was delayed, and BRs became operational only on 1 July 2012. Their *raison d'être* was streamlining the ineffective and inefficient practice of government bodies relying on their own (often paper-based) registers by providing centralized (available to all administrative bodies), interconnected and paperless architecture containing basic data.

405. Additionally, before the introduction of BRs, paper-based registers were often not legally binding, and citizens were repeatedly required to fill in their data and confirm their correctness with a signature. BRA also fixed this issue by establishing the term 'reference data'. Reference data are legally presumed to be correct until proven incorrect or a reasonable doubt arises regarding their correctness.[433] The reference data editor (employee of public authority) is responsible for ensuring the data entered in BRs are identical to the data contained in official (e.g., birth certificate, ID card).[434] Additionally, the editor is required to enter the reference data in

430. *See* s. 6l/1 of ISA.
431. *See* s. 6k of ISA. *See also* Decree No. 433/2020 Sb. and Decree No. 316/2021 Sb.
432. *See* Decree No. 315/2021 Sb.
433. *See* s. 4/4 of BRA.
434. *See* s. 4/2 of BRA.

the BR or to update the reference data based on newly presented documents without delay (or within three working days).[435] In case of doubts, the reference data editor can mark it as 'incorrect'. For the duration of the mark, such data shall be deemed only informative.[436]

406. BRA established four following registers:

- Basic Register of Inhabitants ('Register of Inhabitants', often abbreviated ROB in Czech).
- Basic Register of Artificial Persons, Sole Traders, and Public Authorities ('Register of persons'. ROS).
- Basic Register of Territorial Identification, Addresses and Real Estate Property ('Register of Territorial Identification', RUIAN).
- Basic Register of Agendas, Public Authorities, Private Users of Data and Certain Rights and Obligations ('Register of Rights and Obligations', RPP).

407. The Register of Inhabitants contains reference data on natural persons who are: citizens of the Czech Republic, foreigners residing in the Czech Republic (based on permanent residence or long-term visas), citizens of EU countries and members of their families (based on permanent residence or who were issued the confirmation of temporary residence for longer than three months), foreigners who were granted international protection (asylum or temporary protection), or other categories of persons when the law requires.[437] These data include name, gender, addresses for delivery of official documents, date and place of birth, date and place of death, citizenship information, ID card information (including expiration dates), marital status, data mailbox number and others. Additionally, the Register of Inhabitants contains other (non-reference) data[438] allowing more accessible communication with an individual, such as mobile phone numbers, data necessary for electronic identification and authentication, or serial numbers of electronic signature certificates. Data are deleted after fifty years from the death of the individual.[439] The Ministry of Interior administers the Register of Inhabitants.[440]

408. The Register of Persons contains reference data on artificial persons, organizational units of artificial persons, organizational units of the state, sole traders, foreign persons (meaning foreign artificial persons or sole traders with residence outside of the Czech Republic) or trusts. These data include corporate name or designation of similar purpose, identification of the statutory body, designation of natural persons authorized to act in their stead, legal form, identification number, address and others. Given the variety of types of persons listed in the Register of Persons, the list of reference data is extensive and diverse. The variety is reflected in the assignment of many different bodies as editors responsible for different reference

435. *See* s. 4/3 of BRA.
436. *See* s. 4/4 and 4/5 of BRA.
437. *See* s. 17 of BRA.
438. *See* s. 18/2 of BRA.
439. *See* s. 22/1 of BRA.
440. *See* s. 20/1 of BRA.

data.[441] The reference data also reflect various life cycle stages and include data about, e.g., insolvency, sequestration or liquidation. The Czech Statistical Office administers the Register of Persons.[442]

409. The Register of Territorial Identification contains reference data on state and its regions, territorial elements, territorial units of registration, buildings (including, e.g., number of apartments in the building, whether the building is connected to gas services or whether it is serviced by an elevator), unique addresses and others. Given the wide variety of reference data in this register, BRA provides detailed rules about the types of reference data available on different entities.[443] All the data within the Register of Territorial Identification are marked on the state maps or on the digital maps of public administration, consisting of the cadastral map, orthophoto map, and technical map of settlement (where available).[444] This register is administered by the State Administration of Land Surveying and Cadastre.[445] Unlike other basic registers, the Register of Territorial Identification is remotely available to the public.[446]

410. Finally, the Register of Rights and Obligations has a specific position and fulfils a specific role. This register contains data about access rights and authorization of individual entities to display or edit the data in the three other registers. Specific agendas and related administrative powers must be registered with the Ministry of Interior for administrative bodies to be granted access to reference data.[447] More importantly, the Register of Rights and Obligations maintains logs containing who, when, and for what purpose displayed or edited the reference data within the Register of Inhabitants, Register of Persons or Register of Territorial Identification.[448] As a result, the Register of Rights and Obligations serves, in a way, as the data source for the ISBR. ISBR maintains the integrity of the data contained in all the basic registers and ensures the communication infrastructure necessary to access these data.[449] Access rights and authorizations are managed based on the reference data contained in the Register of Rights and Obligations. The Ministry of Interior administers the Register of Rights and Obligations.[450] ISBR is administered by the Administration of Basic Registers, a single-purpose administrative body established by BRA and subordinate to the Ministry of Interior.[451] It is worth noting that the

441. *See* ss 24/a and 24/b of BRA.
442. *See* s. 28/1 of BRA.
443. *See*, e.g., ss 33, 34 and 35 of BRA.
444. *See* s. 36 of BRA.
445. *See* s. 30/2 of BRA.
446. *See* s. 30/1 of BRA.
447. *See,* e.g., ss 53, 54, 55, 56 and 57 of BRA.
448. *See* s. 7/4 of BRA.
449. *See* s. 7/2 of BRA.
450. *See* s. 49/1 of BRA.
451. *See* ss 6/1 and 7/1 of BRA.

Administration of Basic Registers does not have access to the reference (and non-reference) data within basic registers – or more precisely, the Register of Rights and Obligations does not list it as an entity with access to data – as its role is to provide technical support and maintenance.

411. Personal data protection was one of the significant issues related to introducing BRs into the e-Government landscape. BRs contain a significant amount of personal data. Therefore, the architecture formed by BRA granted a significant role to the Office for Personal Data Protection. One of the starting points of BRs was to shift away from using birth certification numbers to identify citizens. Birth certification numbers unravel certain information about an individual (date of birth, gender). BRs use semantics-free identifiers. However, semantics-free identifies are different between individual agendas or groups of agendas. Therefore, an individual is identified by different semantics-free identifiers within different agendas or information systems. The Office for Personal Data Protection was tasked with creating an information system to convert different identifiers to ensure interoperability of the whole infrastructure. This information system, the ORG Converter, serves as an interface allowing the conversion of semantics-free identifiers between different agendas. However, the ORG Converter contains no reference (or non-reference) data. Overall, this element of the e-Government infrastructure mitigates the risk of identity theft.

§5. Delivery

412. Delivery of electronic documents is a quintessential concern of the Czech e-Government. There are three different methods available, each with its specifics: e-mail, data mailboxes and transaction portals.[452]

413. The delivery via e-mail started to develop in Czech law with the mandatory introduction of 'electronic filing offices' by the (now defunct) Decree No. 496/2004 Sb., on electronic filing offices. The electronic filing office served as a contact point – mainly just a dedicated e-mail address – for official correspondence from the public to the administrative body. Information about the electronic filing office was mandatorily published on the official webpage. As a result, administrative bodies had to be able to process electronic submissions and confirm their delivery. Understandably, the whole procedure was cumbersome and technologically unsophisticated. However, for some administrative bodies, it served as a first incentive to engage in electronic communication with the public. Nowadays, some administrative bodies accompany the announcement of the e-mail address for official

452. This distinction was introduced by Lechner. *See* Tomáš Lechner, *Elektronické dokumenty, in Právo informačních technologií* 252–253 (Radim Polčák et al., Wolters Kluwer ČR 2018).

communication, warning that e-mail communication is globally considered non-guaranteed. Therefore, the e-mail might not be delivered to the public body and, as a result, might not have the intended legal consequences.[453]

414. Additionally, Lechner states explicitly that this delivery method is problematic due to uncertainty about the content of the message that is to be delivered. The text intended to cause legal consequences can be included in the body of the e-mail or its attachment.[454] According to Lechner, the question of e-mail delivery is: what is signed and what is delivered (hence should be signed). It is possible to sign the e-mail as a whole. However, the format (EML) is not included in the eIDAS Regulation. As such, it cannot be signed by a legally recognised qualified or advanced electronic signature based on a qualified certificate.[455]

415. The Czech Constitutional Court ruled on the issue of the delivery of signed e-mails together with unsigned attachments. The court emphasized that e-mail is a unified container for delivery.[456] It stated that while it is preferable to sign both the e-mail and the attachment, delivering an unsigned attachment should not be considered a ground for refusal of the submission.[457] Another uncertainty related to delivery via e-mail is establishing the delivery time. Rules are specified, for example, in Decree No. 259/2012 Sb., on details of filing service, which requires the administrative body to confirm the reception of an e-mail while specifying the exact time of reception.[458]

416. Individual acts contain specific rules for the delivery of documents to parties via e-mail. For example, Act No. 500/2004 Sb., on administrative procedure, specifies that it is possible to deliver the document via e-mail if it can speed up the proceedings.[459] The document is delivered only if the recipient confirms the reception by replying and signing the reply. Subsequently, the time of the reply is the time of the delivery of the document.[460] If reception of the document is not confirmed by the next working day, the administrative body moves on to deliver through other means.[461] Act No. 99/1963 Sb., on civil procedure, provides similar rules but grants three days for confirmation.[462]

---

453. *See*, for example, information of the District Court in Ústí nad Orlicí at https://www.justice.cz/web/okresni-soud-v-usti-nad-orlici/-/elektronicka-podatelna.
454. *See* Tomáš Lechner, *Elektronické dokumenty, in Právo informačních technologií*, p. 253 (Radim Polčák et al., Wolters Kluwer ČR 2018).
455. *Ibid.*
456. *Ibid. See also* the Judgment of the Constitutional Court of 13 May 013, Case No. IV. ÚS 4787/12.
457. *See* paragraph 19 of the Judgment of the Constitutional Court of 13 May 2013, Case No. IV. ÚS 4787/12.
458. *See* s. 4/5 of Decree No. 259/2012 Sb.
459. *See* s. 19/4 of Act No. 500/2004 Sb.
460. *See* s. 19/9 of Act No. 500/2004 Sb.
461. *Ibid.*
462. *See* s. 47/3 of Act No. 99/1963 Sb.

417. While this delivery method is legally possible, it is not overly popular for delivering to public bodies and is not flexible enough for delivering to other subjects (e.g., natural persons, artificial persons).

418. By Act No. 300/2008 Sb., on electronic acts and authorized document conversion (EAA), the delivery via data mailboxes is provided as a unique national solution. It was designed to deliver documents from public bodies and to them.[463] There are four types of data mailboxes prescribed by law: data mailbox of a natural person,[464] data mailbox of sole traders,[465] data mailbox of an artificial person,[466] and data mailbox of a public body.[467]

419. Data mailboxes can be established upon request – this is the case of natural persons, artificial persons not listed in the Public Register or most sole traders. Furthermore, data mailboxes are established automatically, e.g., for artificial persons listed in the Public Register, public bodies, sole traders in specific businesses, such as attorneys-at-law or insolvency administrators. However, the rules for automated mailbox assignment will change significantly after 1 January 2023. The scope of subjects with automatically created mailboxes will also include natural persons. If, at any point after 1 January 2023, a natural person uses an electronic identity (bank ID, electronic ID) when communicating with a public body, a data mailbox will be automatically created.[468] It stems from the assumption that if a natural person can communicate using an electronic identity, he or she can use the data mailbox. Data mailboxes are intended as a primary mean of communication with public bodies, and non-digital communication is a relic that will be removed with the growing level of digital skills and awareness.

420. It needs to be emphasized that having a data mailbox implies using it. Subjects which have been automatically created a data mailbox are required, e.g., to submit the tax declaration via the data mailbox. Similarly, public bodies must deliver official documents to these subjects primarily via the data mailbox and not through standard post services to their physical address.[469] In 2011, this rule was contested at the Constitutional Court. The obligation to communicate via data mailboxes was claimed to be unconstitutional due to imposing additional costs on companies, such as the cost of Internet connectivity. Constitutional Court rejected this argumentation, stating that there is no objective impossibility to obtain Internet access. Additionally, the court stated that the mere necessity to pay for Internet access could not make the data mailboxes unconstitutional.[470]

---

463. *See* s. 2 of EAA.
464. *See* s. 3 of EAA.
465. *See* s. 4 of EAA.
466. *See* s. 5 of EAA.
467. *See* s. 6 of EAA.
468. *See* Act No. 261/2021 Sb., which amended s. 3 of Act No. 300/2008 Sb.
469. *See* s. 17 of EAA.
470. *See* the Judgment of the Constitutional Court of 21 Jul. 2011, Case No. III. ÚS 1513/11.

421. Data mailboxes have been operational since 1 July 2009 as part of the Information system of data mailboxes, administered by the Ministry of Interior[471] and operated by the Czech Post (state-owned provider of post services). A unique and identified person (natural, artificial) operates every data mailbox.[472] Therefore, any action via the data mailbox is legally presumed to be signed,[473] even when no electronic signature is used.

422. Furthermore, EAA laid down rules to establish the time of delivery. The moment the message is sent is the date (and time) of technically sending the message, and the moment the message is made available to the recipient is the date (and time) of reception.[474] However, this does not mean the message is legally delivered and can cause legal consequences. EAA states that the message is delivered when the authorized user logs into the data mailbox.[475] If there is no log-in within ten days since the message's technical delivery (reception) into the respective data mailbox, the message is legally delivered by the tenth day since its reception.[476] However, this applies only when the message is delivered to natural or artificial persons, not public bodies.

423. Concerning the moment the message is delivered to the public body, EAA remains silent. This shortcoming was addressed relatively shortly after the deployment of data mailboxes. In 2008, the Supreme Administrative Court ruled that the moment of delivery to the public body is identical to the time of technical reception of the message.[477]

424. One issue with data mailboxes was the legal consequences of multiple individuals accessing the same unique data mailbox. Besides persons for whom was the data mailbox created (authorized person),[478] persons whom the authorized person authorized can use the data mailbox (person with credentials).[479] The Supreme Court ruled that any action via the data mailbox is signed by the authorized person, regardless of the person with credentials undertaking the action. This rule applies even if the person with credentials was not authorized, per internal guidelines or instructions of an artificial person, to represent the authorized person and act in its stead.[480]

---

471. *See* s. 14/2 of EAA.
472. *See* s. 8 of EAA. *See also* Tomáš Lechner, *Elektronické dokumenty, in Právo informačních technologií,* p. 256 (Radim Polčák et al., Wolters Kluwer ČR 2018).
473. *See* s. 18/2 of EAA.
474. *See* Tomáš Lechner, *Elektronické dokumenty, in Právo informačních technologií,* p. 256 (Radim Polčák et al., Wolters Kluwer ČR 2018).
475. *See* s. 17/3 of EAA.
476. *See* s. 17/4 of EAA.
477. *See* the Judgment of the Supreme Administrative Court of 15 Jul. 2010, Case No. 9 Afs 28/2010.
478. *See* ss 8/1 to 8/5 of EAA.
479. *See* s. 8/6 of EAA.
480. *See* the Judgment of the Supreme Court of 5 Jan. 2017, case No. Plsn 1/2015.

425. Finally, the third method of delivery, via transaction portals, stems from the inability (or unwillingness) of the Czech law to distinguish between electronic identification (as an authentication mechanism) and electronic signature (as a method to express the will). The distinction is the main starting point of the eIDAS Regulation, but it seems to be lost on some of the e-Government services provided in the Czech Republic.[481] This is evident mainly in taxation. For example, Act No. 280/2009 Sb., on tax procedure, allows documents to be delivered based only on identification and does not require the expression of will through the electronic signature.[482] From this, Lechner concludes that the Czech administration bodies consider identification (authentication) of users sufficient to deem the document legally delivered.[483]

§6. Conversion

426. A mechanism for authorized conversion was established and is provided within the Czech POINT network to allow the existence of documents independently of their form.[484] The authorized conversion of documents was introduced by EAA[485] and has been available since 1st July 2009. According to EAA, the authorized conversion means both (a) the conversion of documents in paper to a document contained in a data message, conformity verification of the content of those documents, and the attachment of authentication clause; and the (b) conversion of the document contained in the data message into a document in paper form, conformity verification of those documents, and attachment of the authentication clause.[486] On occasion, the definition is criticised for being old-fashioned and (understandably, given the time frame) not in line with eIDAS Regulation or even with the more recent case law of the Supreme Court.[487]

427. The authorized conversion consists of three steps: conversion of the form, verification of conformity between the two forms (which is a subjective assessment)[488], and attachment of an authorization clause certifying the conformity. Additionally, every authorization is recorded by the Ministry of Interior as part of the information system connecting the Czech POINT network[489] and by the converting

481. *See* Tomáš Lechner, *Elektronické dokumenty, in Právo informačních technologií*, p. 256 (Radim Polčák et al., Wolters Kluwer ČR 2018).
482. *See* s. 71/1/b of Act No. 280/2009 Sb.
483. *See* Tomáš Lechner, *Elektronické dokumenty, in Právo informačních technologií*, p. 256 (Radim Polčák et al., Wolters Kluwer ČR 2018).
484. Additionally, authorized conversion is provided by attorneys according to s. 25c of Act No. 85/1996 Sb.
485. *See* s. 22 of EAA.
486. *See* s. 22/b of EAA.
487. *See* Tomáš Lechner, *Elektronické dokumenty, in Právo informačních technologií*, p. 261 (Radim Polčák et al., Wolters Kluwer ČR 2018).
488. *Ibid.*
489. *Ibid.*, pp. 261–262.

authority in the book of authorized conversions.[490] Information allowing the identification (and verification) of the individual conversion in these records is also part of the authentication clause.

428. Authorized conversions are provided either upon request[491] or ex officio.[492] It is worth noting that there is a difference between the conversion process upon request and ex officio. EAA states that converting an electronic document not signed by the recognised electronic signature or seal upon request is impossible. On the other hand, ex officio conversion of such documents is possible. However, this has to be explicitly stated within the authentication clause.[493]

429. Act No. 499/2004 Sb., on archiving and filing services, provides a conversion mechanism alternative to that introduced by EAA.[494] However, this mechanism is only available for the internal needs of the public administration body. This conversion is conducted in the information system of the filing services, which ensures the authenticity of the document's origin, its integrity, legibility of the document, and the security of the process of conversion or change of data format.[495] Furthermore, every conversion must be recorded within a transaction protocol that allows searching and selecting individual records. This requires some formal authentication record, similar to the book of authorized conversions, to exist.[496]

§7. Promulgation

430. One of the less remarkable stories of the development of e-Government in the Czech Republic is an effort to establish electronic publication of laws. Act No. 222/2016 Sb., on the CLA and the preparation of legislation published in the CLA, introduced a new method of publishing laws. CLA places the Electronic Collection of Laws ('eCollection') on par with the traditional publishing method (paper-based Collection of Laws). Before CLA, the Collection of Laws was the only legally binding source of legislation. Database ran by the Ministry of Interior, which published laws online, was considered only informative and not legally binding. CLA grants the eCollection legal consequences,[497] which aims to increase accessibility and comprehensibility of the applicable law.

431. However, the eCollection is still not available. CLA was published in July 2016 and was initially scheduled to become effective on 1 January 2020. By that

490. *Ibid.*, p. 262.
491. *See* s. 23/1 of EAA.
492. *See* s. 23/2 of EAA.
493. *See* Tomáš Lechner, *Elektronické dokumenty, in Právo informačních technologií*, p. 262 (Radim Polčák et al., Wolters Kluwer ČR 2018).
494. *See* s. 69a of Act No. 499/2004 Sb.
495. *See* s. 69a/1 of Act No. 499/2004 Sb.
496. *See* Tomáš Lechner, *Elektronické dokumenty, in Právo informačních technologií*, p. 263 (Radim Polčák et al., Wolters Kluwer ČR 2018).
497. *See* s. 1/2 of CLA.

date, the Ministry of Interior should have made the related infrastructure operational. However, the date of effect of CLA was pushed forward multiple times. Act No. 277/2019 Sb. amended CLA and put the date of effect to 1 January 2022. Subsequently, Act No. 261/2021 Sb. pushed the date to 1 January 2023. Finally, Act No. 177/2022 Sb., set the date to 1 January 2024. Significant landmarks in the development and procurement of the related infrastructure are expected to be met by the end of 2022, but there is still a significant amount of scepticism and uncertainty surrounding this effort. The eCollection is administered by the Ministry of Interior.[498] Based on CLA, the eCollection has to be remotely accessible to the public,[499] and also published as open data.[500] To prevent the digital divide barring people without e.g., access to the Internet or digital skills from acquainting themselves with the applicable law, municipalities will, during office hours, provide free access to the eCollection.[501]

432. The eCollection is divided into two parts: (1) the portal containing binding electronic versions of legal acts and (2) the database of legal acts. While the former is to be filled gradually with newly issued legal acts, the latter is to be filled with legal acts published in the Collection of Laws prior to CLA's effectiveness.[502] Unfortunately, this establishes a two-tier platform, as the database of legal acts published prior to CLA's effectiveness is not going to be legally binding, but only informative. As a result, eCollection is going to be a reliable (and legally binding) source only for legal acts published after CLA's effectiveness, which is significantly diminishing the overall value of eCollection.

433. Additionally, the database of legal acts has to contain ineffective legislation published after 1945.[503] The system is to be linked with EU sources, such as EUR-Lex or N-Lex, which is going to further increase its value by aggregating links to other related legislation, even if it is not coming from national lawmakers.

434. Another e-Government effort within CLA is eLegislation. The system should provide modern tools for law-making. For example, it should allow the preparation of amendments to existing legislation by typing the changes through the interface directly into existing laws.[504] Amendments in the form required for Parliament's approval are to be generated automatically based on the typed changes. Additionally, published amendments are to be accompanied by legally binding summary texts. This is a considerable development compared to the previous practice, where summary texts are publicly unavailable, and in the rare instance of their availability, they are not legally binding.

498. *See* s. 6/1 of CLA.
499. *See* s. 6/2 of CLA.
500. *See* s. 6/3 of CLA.
501. *See* s. 27 of CLA.
502. *See* s. 6/4 of CLA.
503. *Ibid.*
504. *See* s. 17 of CLA.

435. Regional legislation pursued a similar aim of achieving a modern way of publishing legal acts. Surprisingly enough, this remained (and remains) mostly unnoticed. Act No. 35/2021 Sb., on collection of legal regulations of self-government units and certain administrative bodies, became effective on 1 January 2022. It established a new Collection of Legal Regulations of Self-government Units and Certain Administrative Bodies ('Collection of Legal Regulations'). The Collection of Legal Regulations contains decrees and regulations issued by regional self-governments, as well as legislation issued by administrative bodies.[505] It is mandatory to use the collection to publish laws[506] and to accompany these documents with metadata.[507] The collection is administered by the Ministry of Interior,[508] and is freely and remotely accessible.[509] Aims of its introduction are similar to the eCollection: to strengthen legal certainty, to ensure actual (and not only presumed) awareness of the local legislation, and to ensure accessibility of the legislation. Despite all the differences between the Collection of Legal Regulations and the eCollection, the swift implementation of the Act No. 35/2021 Sb., and the perceived smoothness of establishing the related infrastructure were surprising.

505. *See* s. 1/1 of Act No. 35/2021 Sb.
506. *See* s. 2/1 of Act No. 35/2021 Sb.
507. *See* s. 2/3 of Act No. 35/2021 Sb.
508. *See* s. 1/2 of Act No. 35/2021 Sb.
509. *See* s. 1/3 of Act No. 35/2021 Sb.

Chapter 2. Legal Framework for eHealth

436. The effort to develop eHealth applications in the Czech Republic to modernize the Czech healthcare system spans over two decades. The effort is marked by ambitious state-wide projects but achieved only limited regional successes. One of the most ambitious and controversial state-wide projects was [Internetová Zdravotní Knížka Pacienta *(IZIP)*] intended to allow sharing of health records over the Internet between healthcare providers and patients, and between healthcare providers themselves. The project was piloted in 2002. However, it was cancelled by the Ministry of Health ('Ministry') in 2012 because of its claimed uselessness and dysfunctionality. To this day, IZIP is widely understood as a benchmark for the complicated development of eHealth services in the Czech Republic. However, there are successes – albeit, as mentioned, mainly confined to regions. These include, e.g.:

(1) eMeDocs *(exchange Medical Documents System)*, which allows sharing of health records between healthcare providers in the Highland region [*Kraj Vysočina*];
(2) emergency Card, which allows sharing of health data between hospitals and medical emergency service providers in the Pilsen region [*Plzeňský kraj*];
(3) meDiMed (*Metropolitan Digital Imaging System in Medicine*) for sharing information and images from diagnostic devices between health service providers.

437. Additionally, there is also a development in state-wide projects focusing on particular issues, such as:

- ePrescription [*eRecept*], which allows health service providers to issue prescriptions and patients to collect their medication;[510]
- shared medication list [*Sdílený lékový záznam*] storing information about ePrescriptions issued and vaccinations administered to patients, and allowing sharing of these data between health service providers;[511]
- system for electronic evidence of temporary incapacity to work [*eNeschopenka*], which allows issuing of confirmation of temporary incapacity to work and sharing of data between individuals, employers, Czech Social Security Administration [*Česká správa sociálního zabezpečení*], and general practitioners.[512]

438. However, until 2021, no unified eHealth legal framework or related central eHealth infrastructure was available. The absence of a comprehensive legal framework was often criticized as the main reason for the ineffective development of eHealth in the Czech Republic, with the lack of central infrastructure, legal

510. *See* ss 81 and 81a of Act No. 378/2007 Sb., on pharmaceuticals.
511. *See* s. 81d of Act No. 378/2007 Sb., on pharmaceuticals.
512. *See* ss 56 and 57 of Act No. 187/2006 Sb., on sickness insurance.

definitions of roles and assignment of responsibilities, standards of communication or rules governing the transfer of health records being the starkest examples.[513]

439. The effort leading up to the development of the eHealth legal framework started in 2016 with the publication of the National eHealth Strategy of the Czech Republic 2016–2020.[514] Subsequently, it culminated in August 2021 when Act No. 325/2021 Sb., on eHealth ('eHealth Act' or 'Act') was finally published. The first part of eHealth became effective on 1 January 2022, with its further provisions to become effective on 1 January 2023, 1 July 2023, 1 January 2024 and 1 January 2026. To reflect this gradual enrolment of the eHealth Act, we describe the legal framework as consisting of three distinct phases.

440. In the first phase, mainly the definitions related to the architecture of the eHealth infrastructure and provisions regarding the cooperation between the emerging eHealth infrastructure and the existing eGovernment databases come into effect. This phase includes all the provisions of the eHealth Act, which came into effect on 1 January 2022.[515] The second phase contains provisions becoming effective on 1 January 2023 and 1 July 2023. These include mainly the functioning of the eHealth infrastructure, as on 1 January 2023, the whole infrastructure will become operational.[516] Additionally, since 1 July 2023, data in databases included in the eHealth infrastructure are presumed correct[517] by health service providers, who will also be obligated to designate staff with access to the eHealth infrastructure.[518] Finally, the third phase includes provisions coming into effect on 1 January 2024 and 1 January 2026. Starting 1 January 2024, health service providers must use the eHealth infrastructure when providing health services.[519] Additionally, health service providers will be required to monitor access to the eHealth infrastructure from their information systems and, since 1 January 2026, follow the standards issued by the Ministry under the eHealth Act.[520]

441. The eHealth Act follows the following five principles, which help us to frame the role it is to play in the Czech healthcare system:[521]

- Priority of decentralised solutions: The eHealth Act does not establish any central repositories of health records and minimalizes centralization of data about

513. *See Explanatory Memorandum of eHealth Act, general part*, Ch. 1 (p. 30), available at https://www.psp.cz/sqw/text/tiskt.sqw?O=8&CT=1163.
514. *See The National eHealth Strategy of the Czech Republic*, 2016–2020, available at https://www.dataplan.info/img_upload/7bdb1584e3b8a53d337518d988763f8d/national_ehealth_strategy__v0.2_en.pdf.
515. *See* ss 1 to 3, 6, 7/1, 7/2, 9, 19/1, 19/2, 21/1, 23/1, 25, 28, 38, 39, 40, 42 to 45 of eHealth Act.
516. *See* ss 5, 7/3, 8, 10 to 15, 16/1, 16/2, 16/3, 18, 19/3, 20, 21/2, 22, 23/2, 24, 26, 27, 29 to 37 of eHealth Act.
517. *See* ss 16/4 and 17 of eHealth Act.
518. *See* s. 5 of eHealth Act.
519. *See* ss 4/b, 4/c, 4/d of eHealth Act.
520. *See* s. 4/a of eHealth Act.
521. *See Explanatory Memorandum of Act eHealth Act, general part*, Ch. 2 (p. 31), available at https://www.psp.cz/sqw/text/tiskt.sqw?O=8&CT=1163.

health professionals.[522] Centralization is to be done only at the level of basic eHealth infrastructure, which is the Integrated data interface [Integrované Datové Rozhraní (IDI)] .
- Emphasis on voluntary implementation: the development and deployment of eHealth infrastructure in the Czech Republic must respect the right to privacy, and any data centralization is to be done only following explicit authorization by law. Additionally, the implementation of eHealth is to be, to a maximum degree, voluntary. It is to be done primarily through non-mandatory and gradual implementation of eHealth tools by health service providers to reflect their readiness level.
- Respect for existing processes: the eHealth Act does not aim to restructure the processes and practices in the Czech healthcare system, both in providing health services and reporting these services to health insurance providers. The explanatory memorandum explicitly states: *'[the eHealth Act] is "only" about digitisation, and not the creation of a new "parallel" healthcare system.'*[523]
- Respect towards existing institutional roles: the eHealth Act does not alter the existing modes of interaction between agents and institutions (health service providers, health professionals, patients, Ministry, and health insurance providers).
- Personal data protection: the eHealth Act is, understandably, concerned with the processing of personal data, particularly special category data. As such, it declared its adherence to the existing legal obligations in personal data protection.

442. In terms of scope, the eHealth Act regulates eHealth services provided by telecommunication and information technology and stipulates conditions for the safe sharing of data[524] (including, but not limited to, health records). Furthermore, the eHealth Act regulates the rights and obligations of patients, healthcare providers, healthcare workers, health insurance and other persons, and the jurisdiction of the Ministry.[525] Additionally, the Act contains the legal definition of eHealth, which is both providing and using:

- services and information systems of the IDI;
- services connected to the IDI; and
- information systems of health service providers serving to record and transfer electronic health records; including
- information systems allowing remote access to patients.[526]

443. The definition's scope already hints at the extent of eHealth services to be deployed in the Czech Republic in the near future.

---

522. The extent of personal data about healthcare professionals processed in registers was already subject to review by the Constitutional Court. *See* the Judgment of the Constitutional Court of 10 Nov. 2020, Case No. Pl. ÚS 33/16.
523. *See Explanatory Memorandum of Act eHealth Act, general part*, Ch. 2 (p. 31), available at https://www.psp.cz/sqw/text/tiskt.sqw?O=8&CT=1163.
524. *See* s. 1/1 of eHealth Act.
525. *See* s. 1/2 of eHealth Act.
526. *See* s. 2/1 of eHealth Act.

444. The eHealth Act comes into effect in three distinct phases. The first phase of deployment of the eHealth framework is mainly concerned with definitions and authorization, allowing collaboration with other e-Government services. The eHealth Act establishes the patient identifier[527] and the health professional identifier[528] as unique identifiers serving to identify both the patient and the health professional when providing or being provided with health services or in the health records. These identifiers are meaningless (semantics-free), which follows the previous decision of the Czech government to gradually shift away from using birth identification numbers to identify citizens in e-Government databases.[529] Other key terms of the eHealth framework include:

- master data: data contained in the master health registers;[530]
- eHealth standards: standards for maintaining and transmitting electronic health records as well as their security;[531]
- recording entity: any person which is allowed to insert data in master health registers;[532]
- authorized person: any person which is allowed to use the services of the IDI through its information system;[533]
- designated staff: a natural person employed or is in a similar relationship to the authorized person and who has been granted access rights to the authorized person's information system using the IDI.[534]

445. According to the eHealth Act, the IDI (Integrated Data Interface) consists of the master health registers,[535] trust services,[536] central eHealth services,[537] and the Activity Log.[538] However, except for the master health registers, the first phase does not go simply beyond mentioning that these components are to exist. Further specifications and related obligations are part of the subsequent phases. The Act designates the Ministry as the administrator of the IDI. The Institute of Health Information and Statistics of the Czech Republic (IHIS) is its operator. Finally, the Act also declares the IHIS as a processor of eHealth data under the GDPR.[539]

446. Within the first phase, the Act also established the three master health registers, specifically the Master Register of Health Service Providers,[540] the Master

527. *See* s. 2/2 of eHealth Act.
528. *See* s. 2/3 of eHealth Act.
529. *See* Vladimíra Těšitelová et al., *Elektronizace zdravotnictví řečí paragrafů*, p. 52 (Ústav zdravotnických informací a statistiky ČR 2021).
530. *See* s. 2/4 of eHealth Act.
531. *See* s. 2/6 of eHealth Act.
532. *See* s. 3/a of eHealth Act.
533. *See* s. 3/b of eHealth Act.
534. *See* s. 3/c of eHealth Act.
535. *See* s. 7/1/a of eHealth Act.
536. *See* s. 7/1/b of eHealth Act.
537. *See* s. 7/1/c of eHealth Act.
538. *See* s. 7/1/d of eHealth Act.
539. *See* s. 7/2 of eHealth Act.
540. *See* ss 19/1 and 19/2 of eHealth Act.

Register of Health Professionals,[541] and the Master Register of Patients.[542] These registers contain the data necessary for identifying of every patient and health professional. Besides identifiers, which the Ministry will administer during the second phase,[543] master health registers will be partially filled by cooperation between the Ministry and the Ministry of Interior and the Police of the Czech Republic. The Ministry of Interior and the Police of the Czech Republic are to provide the data from other e-Government databases.[544] The rest of the data for the initial feed (or synchronization) of the master health registers are to be obtained from the existing databases maintained by the IHIS, namely the National Register of Health Service Providers[545,546] and the National Register of Health Professionals.[547]

447. Finally, the first phase also contains provisions delineating the obligations of the Ministry regarding the development of the eHealth infrastructure. Besides traditional assignments, such as that of conceptual and strategic management of eHealth,[548] the Ministry is called to manage the standardization of eHealth processes,[549] as well as to prepare and issue eHealth standards that health service providers will be required to comply with in the third phase of the eHealth Act's deployment.[550] Additionally, the Ministry is to issue certificates for advanced electronic signatures, sectoral system certificates for access to the IDI, and sectoral personal certificates authenticating health professionals when accessing the eHealth services.[551]

448. The second phase requires Ministry to make the IDI and its components operational and available[552] starting 1 January 2023. A substantial batch of provisions concerned with the practical functioning and access to master health registers,[553] trust services,[554] central eHealth services[555] and the Activity Log,[556] comes into effect on said date.

449. The Ministry starts to process the data of health service providers, health professionals and patients to the extent specified in relevant provisions and for a limited period. In the case of the Master Register of Health Service Providers, the data are processed for ten years after the expiration of authorization to provide

541. *See* s. 21/1 of eHealth Act.
542. *See* s. 23/1 of eHealth Act.
543. *See* s. 13/1 of eHealth Act.
544. *See* s. 6/1 of eHealth Act.
545. Some IHIS documents use the term 'National Register of Healthcare Providers'.
546. *See* ss 72/1/c, 74 and 75 of Act 372/2011 Sb., on health services and conditions of their provision.
547. *See* ss 72/1/d, 76 and 77 of Act 372/2011 Sb., on health services and conditions of their provision.
548. *See* s. 38/2/a of eHealth Act.
549. *See* s. 38/2/b of eHealth Act.
550. *See* s. 38/2/c of eHealth Act.
551. *See* s. 38/2/d of eHealth Act.
552. Note s. 9 of eHealth Act states that the IDI is not publicly available unless stated otherwise.
553. *See* ss 7/3, 8, 10 to 15, 16/1, 18, 19/3, 19/4. 20, 21/2, 21/3, 21/4, 22, 23/2, 24 of eHealth Act.
554. *See* ss 7/3 and 26 of eHealth Act.
555. *See* ss 27 to 36 of eHealth Act.
556. *See* s. 37 of eHealth Act.

health services.[557] In the Master Register of Health Professionals, data are stored and processed for ten years after the death of the respective professional.[558] The Master Register of Patients contains personal data for fifty years since the patient's death.[559]

450. Apart from master health registers, the IDI contains trust services, central eHealth services and an Activity Log. All of these will be made operational during the second phase as well.

451. Trust services included in the eHealth Act consist of the following:[560]

- the system providing sectoral electronic time stamps;
- the system providing remote use of sectoral advanced electronic time stamps;
- service for issuing sectoral certificates for an advanced electronic signature;
- service for issuing sectoral system certificates for access to the IDI; and
- services for issuing sectoral personal certificates for access to the IDI.

452. Similarly, central eHealth services specified in the eHealth Act will include the following:[561]

- services allowing viewing of master data in the master health registers;
- services allowing entry of data into the master health registers;
- exchange network services: the service will allow a secure transfer of electronic health records through the securely encrypted communication channel.[562] This service is to be accessed by health service providers and health insurance providers to fulfil their legal obligations;[563]
- consent management system: the service will contain a track record of consent given by a patient to third persons or consents that were later revoked;[564]
- the eHealth Portal: the web portal through which the Ministry will manage access of recording entities and authorized persons to the IDI, offer eHealth services and provide information about the services provided, as well as publish web and mobile phone applications;[565] and

557. *See* s. 8/3/a of eHealth Act.
558. *See* s. 8/3/b of eHealth Act.
559. *See* s. 8/3/c of eHealth Act.
560. *See* s. 26/1 of eHealth Act.
561. *See* s. 27/1 of eHealth Act.
562. *See* s. 30 of eHealth Act.
563. For obligations, *see*, e.g., Act No. 372/2011 Sb., on health services and conditions of their provision, or Act No. 48/1997 Sb., on public health insurance. These exchange mechanisms already exist, but the eHealth act is to establish a new secure communication channel guaranteed by the state.
564. *See* s. 32/1 of eHealth Act.
565. *See* s. 35/1 of eHealth Act.

- catalogue of eHealth services: this catalogue will contain an overview of central eHealth services, a list of web and mobile phone applications published at the eHealth Portal and a list of eHealth services provided by health service providers.[566]

453. Finally, the Activity Log will provide internal operational and security services by recording, storing, and transmitting information about activities performed via the IDI by recording entities, authorized persons, and designated staff.[567] Activity Log will contain data for two years since the data creation.[568]

454. Starting the second phase, the IHIS will be legally obligated to develop the IDI Operations Documentation.[569] This documentation will serve as a basic standard ensuring the interoperability of the information systems which the recording entities and authorized persons will deploy and use to access the IDI. The eHealth Act will require the documentation to contain:

- the description of the interface and requirements for communication of recording entities and authorized persons with the IDI;
- the form of healthcare professional's and patient's identifier in which it is provided to authorized persons;
- the process of issuing sectoral certificates for advanced electronic signatures and system/personal certificates for accessing the IDI for health service providers;
- the description of the service providing sectoral electronic time stamps and remote sealing services;
- the process, method, structure and format for entering personal and other data into master health registers; and
- the characteristics of the identity management system for the designated staff, including rules for assignment, change and termination of credentials.

455. Recording entities and authorized persons will access the IDI through their information systems – either developed in-house or, more likely, purchased. One of their obligations will be to ensure these information systems are fully compatible with the IDI and fully compliant with the published IDI Operations Documentation.[570] The mode of access of such an information system to the IDI depends on the legal nature of the recording entity or authorized person. A legal person or sole trader will access the IDI through its information system equipped with a sectoral system certificate. The access will be automated or conducted manually by the designated staff.[571] Natural persons will access the IDI through means of electronic identification by using the eHealth Portal.[572] Health professionals are going to

566. *See* s. 36 of eHealth Act.
567. *See* s. 37/1 of eHealth Act.
568. *See* s. 8/3/d of eHealth Act.
569. *See* s. 10 of eHealth Act.
570. *See* s. 5/b of eHealth Act.
571. *See* s. 11/1/a of eHealth Act.
572. *See* s. 11/1/b of eHealth Act.

access the IDI by using personal certificates.[573] Recording entities and authorized persons will be obligated to appoint a designated staff and validate their identity before allowing them to access the IDI.[574]

456. The third phase consists of health service providers being obligated to use the eHealth infrastructure when providing health services. Starting 1 January 2024, health service providers must use the master data in master health registers.[575] Additionally, they will be required to record identifiers of health professionals employed (or in a similar relationship) by the provider,[576] identifiers of patients who are provided with health services by the provider,[577] and activities of all the designated staff logged in the information system using the IDI.[578]

457. As part of the third phase, the final piece of the eHealth Act will come into effect on 1 January 2026 and will require health service providers to comply with the eHealth standards issued by the Ministry. It is worth noting that the original draft of the eHealth Act required this obligation to become effective only on 1 January 2032. This unusually long *vacatio legis* was reasoned due to a lack of preparedness on the side of general practitioners, partially due to their age structure.[579] However, this was changed within the legislative process. The first argument was the critical nature of the deployment of eHealth services to maintain the level of healthcare available in the Czech Republic. The second argument was the requirement to strengthen the resilience toward cyberattacks against the eHealth infrastructure.[580] Health service providers serve in this instance as end-users of the eHealth infrastructure. Therefore, such a delayed onset of obligations to comply with (security) standards developed by the Ministry would have negatively affected the secure deployment and functioning of the eHealth services in the Czech Republic.

458. The eHealth Act as a framework deploying eHealth infrastructure is a long-desired piece of legislation. The Working Group for the eHealth Act was established in 2017 after many aspirations and failures. Finally, in 2020 a consensus was reached regarding the implementation of the 'elementary phase of eHealth' in the legislation. The development was, undoubtedly, sped up by COVID-19. However, it was also allowed by scaling back on the scope of eHealth deployment in this initial phase.[581] As a result, further development in eHealth is expected over the next several years as further consensus is reached. In part, the development will take shape in bylaws and standards based on the eHealth Act. The eHealth Act is an

573. *See* s. 11/1/c of eHealth Act.
574. *See* s. 5/a/1 of eHealth Act.
575. *See* s. 4/b of eHealth Act.
576. *See* s. 4/c/1 of eHealth Act.
577. *See* s. 4/c/2 of eHealth Act.
578. *See* s. 4/d of eHealth Act.
579. *See* Vladimíra Těšitelová et al., *Elektronizace zdravotnictví řečí paragrafů*, p. 256 (Ústav zdravotnických informací a statistiky ČR 2021).
580. *See Amendment to the government bill on eHealth*, proposed by Petr Třešňák and Olga Richterová, available at https://www.psp.cz/sqw/text/orig2.sqw?idd=191762&pdf=1.
581. *See* Vladimíra Těšitelová et al., *Elektronizace zdravotnictví řečí paragrafů*, p. 258 (Ústav zdravotnických informací a statistiky ČR 2021).

extraordinary piece of legislation – perhaps not in its scope, extent and novelty, but because it presents a solid first step in developing eHealth in the Czech Republic.

Chapter 3. Online Voting

459. In the Czech Republic, online voting was seriously discussed. However, this possibility to cast a ballot was never implemented. This chapter will describe the effort aiming to introduce online voting, which took place between 2008 and 2014.

460. In April 2008, the director of the Czech Statistical Office [CSU and the Minister of the Interior signed the Memorandum of Understanding on Cooperation in the Design, Development, Testing, and Implementation of the Electronic Election System ('Memorandum').[582] The Memorandum established a common ground for two bodies mainly involved in managing the elections in the Czech Republic. The Ministry of Interior is the central state administration body in elections. Regarding this role, its main task is to prepare electoral legislation and coordinate elections.[583] On the other hand, CSU is an electoral body responsible for developing binding guidelines for determining and processing election results and procuring software for processing and publishing the results of elections.[584] By signing the Memorandum, both bodies agreed to submit complex material stemming from the pilot project and proposals for necessary legislative changes to the Government and the Parliament by the end of 2009.

461. In terms of content, the memorandum was hardly ground-breaking. Online voting would allow them to cast their votes from within their homes or public places with Internet access. It was not intended to replace the classic ballot but to exist in parallel. The pilot was to be conducted outside of elections as a proof-of-concept system aiding in developing documentation and subsequent drafting of legal requirements.

462. The development of online voting following the Memorandum was unusually opaque, with only limited information available to the public. However, in October 2012, the Government acknowledged the document *Information on Electronic Voting*[585] ('Information') prepared by the Ministry of Interior. The Information shed some light on what happened in online voting between 2009 and 2012.

463. Pursuing the Memorandum, the CSU and the Ministry of Interior established a project team consisting of voting, IT, and security experts. The team supposedly prepared a document titled *Substantive Concept of Electronic Voting*

582. *See Memorandum of Understanding on Cooperation in the Design, Development of a Solution, Testing, and Implementation of the Electronic Election System* of 7 Apr. 2008, available at https://www.czso.cz/documents/10180/23201319/memorandum_mv_csu.pdf/1b7a1452-2319-45c8-ab1e-48cbed3372e1?version=1.0.

583. *See* s. 12/1/l of Act No. 2/1969 Sb., on Ministries and other Central State Administration Bodies of the Czech Socialist Republic.

584. *See* s. 4/1/p of Act No. 89/1995 Sb., on State Statistical service.

585. *See Information on Electronic Voting* of 20 Jul. 2012, file No. 164/12, available at https://www.mvcr.cz/volby/soubor/priloha-1-informace-o-elektronickem-zpusobu-hlasovani.aspx.

('Concept'), which concluded the first phase of developing online voting mechanisms. The following second phase consisted of developing technical infrastructure, and the final third phase focused on developing the legislation.[586] The Information is publicly available as a result of the second phase. On the other hand, the Concept (the main result of the first phase) is not publicly available.

464. The Information contained a schedule for deploying online voting in the Czech Republic. The pilot was planned for 2015, with the first use of online voting planned for 2016 in Senate elections in two districts.[587]

465. The Government acknowledged the existence of the Information.[588] However, the Information was explicitly requested by the Government[589] and was not prepared only to be acknowledged. The Information also called for a decision of whether to pursue one of the three possibilities. The Government was to decide whether:

- not to pursue the online voting further and not to organize a pilot in 2015;
- to organize a pilot in 2015 and assign the task of organizing the pilot to the ministry of Interior;
- not to pursue online voting further but to develop voting infrastructure to allow for future deployment of online voting. However, the Government did not approach the issue as its priority. As a result, no decision was made on further action.

466. In a way, this lukewarm sentiment was surprising. The Government only acknowledging the Information had previously prioritised online voting in its Coalition Agreement.[590] The Coalition Agreement has set forth the goal to *'start the preparation of an online voting project so that it can be piloted in 2012 and fully implemented starting the elections to the Chamber of Deputies of the Parliament in 2014.'*[591] The schedule within the Information was already delayed compared to the Coalition Agreement timeline. However, this did not encourage the Government to take a more active stance.

467. The Information outlined fundamental principles of the intended online voting mechanism. The online voting was to:

586. *See Information on Electronic Voting*, p. 3.
587. Out of the total 81 districts for Senate elections, online voting was to be piloted in District No. 34 (Liberec) and District No. 61 (Olomouc).
See Information on Electronic Voting, pp. 26–27.
588. *See* Results of the Government meeting of 17 Oct. 2012, available at https://www.vlada.cz/cz/media-centrum/tiskove-zpravy/vysledky-jednani-vlady--17--rijna-2012--99851/.
589. *See* Resolution of the Government of the Czech Republic from 14 Mar. 2012, No. 151, available at https://apps.odok.cz/attachment/-/down/KORN97AU7TXU.
590. *See Coalition Agreement* of 12 Jul. 2010, available at https://www.vlada.cz/assets/media-centrum/dulezite-dokumenty/koalicni_smlouva_ods_top09_vv.pdf.
591. *See Coalition Agreement*, p. 22. Translated by J.H.

- be an alternative to traditional voting;
- be in the form of remote online voting;
- be implemented as voting over the Internet;
- allow voters to vote multiple times, only counting the last ballot cast, to prevent family voting;
- ensure secrecy of the ballot and prevent the possibility of casting two votes;
- ensure that no third person and no election body can find out how the voter voted;
- ensure that the vote cannot be altered undetected;
- allow a high level of security for the identification and authentication of the voter;
- allow determining whether all valid votes have been counted correctly;
- share information about how the system works publicly.[592]

468. Ballots in online voting were to be cast through the Information System of Data Mailboxes. A single-purpose data mailbox, Election Data Mailbox, would have been established and assigned to individual voters to ensure ballot secrecy.[593] However, the effort to implement online voting did not continue after the change of Government in 2014.

469. Some lawmakers occasionally mention the idea of online voting. However, the idea seems not to be taken seriously anymore. In 2019, the Draft Law on Election Administration was proposed,[594] expressly containing the phrase *'the electronic voting is not expected'* in its explanatory memorandum.[595] While the proposal was not enacted, it was re-introduced by the next Government in 2022.[596] Its explanatory memorandum contains the exact phrase which might be perceived as symptomatic of the state of online voting in the Czech Republic.

470. In 2020 and 2021, elections were affected by COVID-19. The possibility of casting a ballot in a drive-in was introduced to allow participation of voters in quarantine resulting from COVID-19 infection.[597] In a way, this can dilute the highly conservative approach toward the election in the Czech Republic. Regardless, online voting is most probably very far off.

592. *See Information on Electronic Voting*, pp. 10–11.
593. *Ibid.*, pp. 16–17.
594. *See* Draft Law on Election Administration (2019), available at https://apps.odok.cz/veklep-detail?pid=KORNBH2MHKS9.
595. *See Explanatory Memorandum of Draft Law on Election Administration*, p. 68 (2019). Translated by J.H.
596. *See* Draft Law on Election Administration (2022), available at https://apps.odok.cz/veklep-detail?pid=ALBSCERHSHDS.
597. *See* ss. 8 ff. of Act No. 350/2020 Sb., on special voting methods in the 2020 regional and Senate elections. *See* ss. 8 ff. of Act No. 296/2021 Sb., on special voting methods in the Chamber of Deputies of the Parliament of the Czech Republic in 2021.

Chapter 4. Other E-government Services

471. One of the fastest developing areas of e-Government is regional self-government. However (and surprisingly), it is at the same time an area where the legislation shows significant weaknesses concerning future development.

472. The two largest cities in the Czech Republic, Prague (also a capital) and Brno offer the widest variety of services through their platforms.

473. Portal of Citizen of Prague [*Portál Pražana*][598] allows logging in through electronic or banking identity or data mailbox. It is mainly concerned with self-government issues and allows to pay waste management and dog ownership fees, submit various forms, book an appointment with an official or manage parking permits. The Portal is still undergoing further development, with various other services under construction, such as a specific module for business owners, rental of municipal flats or self-government subsidies.

474. BrnoiD[599] provides similar services upon registration. For example, it allows citizens to pay a waste management fee, manage their parking permits, or renew a cemetery lease contract with the city cemetery. Additionally, it allows the management of long-term public transportation tickets (because the city of Brno owns the public transportation company) or accounts in the city library [Knihovna Jiřího Mahena].

475. Regional self-government services are gaining traction and are being developed in other cities and villages. However, the development is always tied to the available funding and services reaching a critical mass of users to provide a benefit. As a result, major cities have a better starting position.

476. However, the existing legislation shows major weaknesses and may eventually limit self-governments' efforts to develop their e-Government platforms and services further. For example, for the electronic form provided by self-government to access the data from basic registers, the self-government authority must request the Ministry of Interior to register the relevant digital service in the Catalogue of Services (as part of the Register of Rights and Obligations). However, the Ministry will register the authority (and service provided by it) only if a specific legal provision requests such activity. Such a limit presents a significant issue since most of the digital services provided by self-governments are provided not because the law mandates it but because it is citizen-friendly and reasonable.[600]

598. *See* https://www.portalprazana.cz/.
599. *See* https://www.brnoid.cz/.
600. Similarly Zdeněk Zajíček, František Korbel, Dalibor Kovář et al. Zákon o právu na digitální služby. Komentář, p. 3 (C. H. Beck 2021).

Part III. Online Transactions

Chapter 1. Electronic Contracting

477. Electronic contracting, as such, is not specifically regulated in Czech legislation. Therefore, it is necessary to proceed primarily from the general legislation on concluding contracts (with partial specifics within the electronic environment), which is regulated by Act No. 89/2012 Sb., the Civil Code, as amended ('Civil Code'), and then apply the given conclusions to situations where contracting occurs in the electronic environment.

478. Primarily, it is necessary to proceed from the fact that section 559 of the Civil Code provides for the formlessness of legal act: 'everyone has the right to choose any form for a legal act unless they are restricted in their choice of form by agreement or law'. However, unless the manifestation of intent is captured more permanently (quite typically when the contract is made orally), the testimonial value of the legal obligation may diminish over time.

479. Due to the aforementioned time degradation, there is often a requirement for a prescribed form of conclusion of the contractual obligation itself between the parties – the requirement of a written form. This is typically required in the case of disposal of immovable property,[601] in order to establish a certain level of protection for one of the parties (typically in the context of consumer protection),[602] in the case of selected types of representation, acts related to the activities of legal persons,[603] etc.[604]

480. The written form is generally preserved if it is possible to (1) capture the content of the legal act (it is a written text/the writing) and (2) this legal act was signed by the one who acted.[605]

481. The writing (document), as a text container, informs about a given legal act and is able to resist the loss of informational value and thus carry, to some extent,

601. *See* s. 560 of the Civil Code.
602. *See* ss 1810 of the Civil Code et seq.
603. For example, s. 123/2 of the Civil Code or s. 6 of Act No. 90/2012 Sb., on Business Corporations, as amended.
604. Specific examples are given here rather indicatively, as the legislation always explicitly mentions and further elaborates on this requirement in the specific case.
605. *See* s. 561/1 of the Civil Code.

reliable information about what has been agreed. As Polčák points out, 'writing is not even a manifestation of the will but only its external phenomenal form. Thus, if the will is expressed in writing, this means that its expression takes the form of a text, i.e., words captured by using writing.'[606] Such a condition is undoubtedly fulfilled also in the case of the use of electronic communication tools (e.g., using e-mail or in the form contracting or 'click' method of concluding contracts), especially in the context of the provision in section 562/1 of the Civil Code: 'the written form is preserved even in the case of a legal act performed by electronic or other technical means enabling the content of the act to be captured ...'. It is thus the capture of the content that is essential, which is undoubtedly made possible by electronic means (the electronic form of a legal act is thus a subset of the written act). It will then be a question of the specific situations in which it will be assessed whether the content has been sufficiently captured.[607] In this context, then, the provisions that discuss the status and reliability of private and public instruments are indicative. In the case of a private instrument, it is emphasized that 'the onus is on anyone who relies on a private instrument to prove its authenticity and accuracy'.[608] In contrast, in the case of a public instrument, it is emphasized that 'where a fact is confirmed in a public instrument, this constitutes, with respect to any person, a full proof that the instrument originates from the body or person that established it, a full proof of the time of drafting the instrument, as well as of a fact which the originator of the public instrument confirmed as having occurred or having been performed in his presence until the contrary is proved.'[609] The above-mentioned is further supported by the fact that both the document (information carrier in any form),[610] the writing (capturing the text)[611] and the instrument as defined in the Civil Code by their nature and by the legal regulation do not contradict the fact that they cannot exist in electronic form. However, in the case of the concept of an instrument, this is not as clearly derived from section 3026/1 of the Civil Code: 'unless excluded by the nature of the document, the provisions of this Act on instruments also apply by analogy to other documents irrespective of their form'.

482. The signature is the second prerequisite for fulfilling the written form of the legal act. 'The signature should, in particular, fulfil the function of identifying the person who has performed the legal act ...'.[612] According to section 561/1 of the

606. *See* Radim Polčák, *Elektronické právní jednání – změny, problémy a nové možnosti v zákoně č. 89/2012 Sb,* Bulletin advokacie, n. 10, p. 36 (2013).
607. Korbel and Melzer add that the written form is equivalent to the electronic form and the limitation will be mainly in the technical possibilities of recording on paper. František Korbel & Filip Melzer, *Písemnost, elektronický a biometrický podpis v elektronickém právním jednání*, Bulletin advokacie, n. 12, p. 31 (2014).
608. *See* s. 565 of the Civil Code.
609. *See* s. 568/1 of the Civil Code.
610. A document is defined in Czech law as 'any written, visual, audio or other recorded information, whether in analogue or digital form, which has been created by the originator or has been delivered to the originator'. s. 2/e of Act No. 499/2004 Sb., on Archives and Records Management and on Amendments to Certain Acts, as amended.
611. As stated above.
612. *See* Petr Lavický et al., *Občanský zákoník I. Obecná část. (§ 1-654). Komentář,* p. 2021 (C. H. Beck 2014).

Civil Code, a different legal regulation determines how a document may be electronically signed in the case of a legal act performed by electronic means. This 'other' legislation is represented by the eIDAS Regulation.[613] This will be discussed in more detail in the next chapter. However, in the present context, it should be noted that an electronic signature is defined under Article 3(10) of the eIDAS Regulation as 'data in electronic form which is attached to or logically associated with other data in electronic form and which is used by the signatory to sign'. However, a possible lower level of assurance in the authentication and identification of a person signing with a 'simple' electronic signature (compared to, for example, the level of assurance offered by the qualified electronic signature) does not imply the impossibility of using such a signature and fulfilling the legal requirements.

483. This has also been gradually confirmed by Czech case law. The Supreme Court of the Czech Republic has stated in the past that the form method of concluding a contract does not meet the requirement of written form because it was not accompanied by an advanced (*sic!*) electronic signature.[614] However, the courts have departed from this view. They have gradually confirmed, for example, that both a unique password or ID tied exclusively to one person[615] and a simple signature in an e-mail will satisfy the statutory requirements for a written form.[616] Nevertheless, court decisions where it is mentioned without further consideration, that an e-mail cannot satisfy the written form requirement because it has not been electronically signed continue to appear. However, the context of the particular decision showed that the court did not understand the broad definition of a 'simple' electronic signature and, in fact, considered only higher levels (advanced etc.) to be recognized as electronic signature.[617]

484. In the Czech environment, moreover (and especially recently), the opinion that it is not necessary to electronically sign the document (i.e., the signature of such document is not required) to fulfil the requirement of the written form is increasingly emerging. This is based on the wording of section 562/1 of the Civil Code, where, in addition to the above-discussed requirement to capture the content of the legal act, it is explicitly stated that the written form is furthermore preserved in the case of 'designation of the person acting.' Thus, it will be sufficient if the requirement to designate the person acting is fulfilled[618] by whatever means – for example, using an agreed e-mail address.

---

613. *See* Regulation (EU) No. 910/2014 of the European Parliament and of the Council of 23 Jul. 2014 on electronic identification and trust services for electronic transactions in the internal market and repealing Directive 1999/93/EC, OJ L 257, 28.8.2014.
614. *See* the Judgment of the Supreme Court of 30 Oct. 2009, Case No. 33 Cdo 3210/2007.
615. *See* the Judgment of the Regional Court in České Budějovice of 27 Mar. 2015, Case No. 24 Co 696/2015.
616. *See* the Judgment of the Supreme Court of 16 May 2019, Case No. 23 Cdo 3439/2018.
617. *See* the Judgment of the Supreme Court of 22 May 2019, Case No. 26 Cdo 1230/2019.
618. *See* Adam Jareš, *(Ne)podepisování elektronického právního jednání*, Soukromé právo, n. 5, pp. 20 et seq. (2019).

485. Therefore, based on the above stated, when concluding a contract using electronic means, the written form will be observed after the two conditions mentioned above (the writing and the signature) have been fulfilled. In connection with the above, we state that compliance with the written form occurs much more frequently than the parties may presume. 'Thus, whereas in offline shopping we generally conclude purchase contracts by implication, in a similar e-shop contract there is usually a mutual expression of intent to conclude a purchase contract in writing …'.[619]

486. With regard to the form of the legal act itself, we would like to point out that, unless the form is prescribed directly by law, section 564 of the Civil Code provides that when the parties agree on a particular form of the act by contract, the content of the act may be changed in another form (if it is not against the law), unless this is excluded by mutual agreement of the parties. However, if the parties have not determined the form of the legal act, the form of the original obligation must be respected.[620]

487. The specific terms and conditions applicable to electronic contracting are typically associated with a situation where one of the parties is in a weaker position – typically a consumer.[621] The legal regulation of consumer protection related to the conclusion of consumer contracts is regulated by sections 1810 et seq. of the Civil Code,[622] and the basic premise is that an arrangement that deviates from the law in terms of consumer protection is disregarded.[623] Furthermore, the consumer must be adequately informed and educated; thereby, their protection should be increased by the extensive information obligation imposed on businesses at the pre-contractual stage.[624] Furthermore, the general rules specify prohibited and unreasonable terms[625] or regulate the right of withdrawal.[626]

488. The legislation also concerns distance contracting and, specifically, the conclusion of consumer contracts in electronic form. The purpose of this regulation[627] is, in particular, to compensate for the fact that the consumer does not have the opportunity to physically see the goods. It should be noted that the legislation on distance contracting also applies, for example, to contracting by telephone.

---

619. *See* Radim Polčák, *Elektronické právní jednání – změny, problémy a nové možnosti v zákoně č. 89/2012 Sb*, Bulletin advokacie, n. 10, p. 37 (2013).
620. *See* the Judgment of the Supreme Court of 10 Feb. 2015, Case No. 32 Cdo 451/2013.
621. The term 'consumer' is defined by s. 419 of the Civil Code.
622. This issue draws heavily e.g., from Directive on certain aspects of the sale of consumer goods and associated guarantees (1999/44/EC), OJ L 171, 7.7.1999, Directive 2011/83/EU of the European Parliament and of the Council of 25 Oct. 2011 on consumer rights, OJ L 304, 22.11.2011.
623. *See* s. 1812/2 of the Civil Code.
624. *See* ss 1811, 1820, 1826 and others of the Civil Code.
625. *See* ss 1813 et seq. of the Civil Code.
626. *See* s. 1818 of the Civil Code.
627. *See* s. 1820 of the Civil Code.

489. Only the specific regulation of electronic contracting[628] reflects online contracting. This regulation reflects, in particular, the need to provide information on the technical processing of the contract, on its storage, or any codes of conduct to which the entrepreneur may be bound. The consumer should also be informed of the various technical steps leading to the conclusion of the contract, as well as how to pay for the order. In general, distance contracting is also covered by the possibility of withdrawing from the contract without giving a reason within fourteen days of receiving the order, free of charge, provided that the value of the goods or services has not been reduced by the consumer.[629]

490. Moreover, in connection with the above stated, the Directive on the digital content and digital services[630] and the Directive on certain aspects of contracts for the sale of goods[631] were to be implemented in the Czech law.[632] However, at the moment, the amendment is still in the legislative process. These directives should be implemented, in particular in sections 2389a–2389s of the Civil Code, and should define the requirements related to the distribution of digital content or regulate differently the possibility of withdrawal from a contract concluded at a distance (and by explicitly mentioning that the provisions in question also apply to services, not only to goods).[633]

491. The use and specific nature of smart contracts bring specific challenges within Czech law. First of all, its technological aspect must be perceived, where it is a software solution, the use of which may (or may not) lead to the effective conclusion of a contract. This is mainly caused due to the use of blockchain technology, which is based on a chain of transaction records that are technologically (cryptographically) interconnected.[634] The problems related to the Czech (but potentially also any other) legal regulation are primarily those that the requirements related to the legal regulation of contracting (as discussed above) may not be complied with. One of the distinctive features present in the context of entering into a smart contract (typically by sending tokens) is the implicit acceptance of the smart contract offer. Not only does this fail to satisfy one of the requirements for a written form by Czech law, as the contract is not signed, but also, in the smart contract environment, it is typically difficult to actually identify a specific party (so there is a

628. *See* ss 1826 et seq. of the Civil Code.

629. *See* s. 1829 of the Civil Code.

630. *See* Directive (EU) 2019/770 of the European Parliament and of the Council of 20 May 2019 on certain aspects concerning contracts for the supply of digital content and digital services, OJ L 136, 22.5.2019.

631. *See* Directive (EU) 2019/771 of the European Parliament and of the Council of 20 May 2019 on certain aspects concerning contracts for the sale of goods, amending Regulation (EU) 2017/2394 and Directive 2009/22/EC, and repealing Directive 1999/44/EC, OJ L 136, 22.5.2019.

632. The directives should have been transposed into Czech law by 1 Jan. 2022, but this did not happen.

633. *See* the current status here: *Parliamentary print 994, Amendment to the Civil Code – EU*, Parliament of the Czech Republic, Chamber of Deputies (21 Apr. 2022), https://www.psp.cz/sqw/historie.sqw?o=8&t=994.

634. *See* more on the definition here: Nick Szabo, *Smart Contracts: Building Blocks for Digital Markets* (21 Apr. 2022), https://www.fon.hum.uva.nl/rob/Courses/InformationInSpeech/CDROM/Literature/LOTwinterschool2006/szabo.best.vwh.net/smart_contracts_2.html.

missing link also in connection with designating the person as mentioned above), due to the fact that there is no immediate linking of an address to a specific person; concluding the contract can thus be described as rather pseudonymized, as the specific negotiation can be at least partially linked through the associated metadata. The Czech law does not explicitly respond to these facts.

Chapter 2. Electronic Signatures

492. The electronic signature as a tool, the requirements imposed on it and the related legislation are not only essential for electronic contracting, as mentioned above, but also closely related to dealing with electronic documents in general, their authenticity and the provision of an adequate tool for the needs of electronic legal acting. Its essential feature is to enable (with a certain degree of reliability) the determination or identification of the signatory, the creation of a signature as an expression of the will of the person acting and also the related liability regime of the signatory.[635]

493. Historically, the legal regulation concerning electronic signatures in the Czech Republic was contained in the Act No. 227/2000 Sb., on Electronic Signature and on Amendments to Certain Other Acts ('the Act on Electronic Signature'), which was created in parallel with the European Directive on Electronic Signatures.[636] However, the Czech law already corresponded to the European regulation at that time[637] and, in addition, regulated several other trust services, which were, e.g., electronic marks (*sic!*) and electronic time stamps, which were regulated at the European level only much later by the eIDAS Regulation.

494. Currently, the issue of electronic signatures is regulated by the eIDAS Regulation, which is supplemented at the national level by Act No. 297/2016 Sb., the Act on Trust Services for Electronic Transactions, as amended ('the Act on Trust Services').[638]

495. According to the eIDAS Regulation, electronic signatures can be de jure divided into three categories according to the level of trust; a fourth category is specifically introduced in Czech legislation: 'simple' electronic signature; advanced electronic signature;[639] qualified electronic signature; recognized electronic signature (Czech specificity).

§1. 'Simple' Electronic Signature

496. 'Simple' electronic signature is defined by the eIDAS Regulation in Article 3(10) as 'data in electronic form which is attached to or logically associated with

635. These characteristics are then specifically reflected in the legal regulation of the advanced electronic signature, which will be described later.
636. *See* Directive 1999/93/EC of the European Parliament and of the Council of 13 Dec. 1999 on a Community framework for electronic signatures, OJ L 13, 19.1.2000.
637. The Czech Republic joined the EU on 1 May 2004.
638. eIDAS Regulation is also supplemented by the Act No. 250/2017 Sb. Electronic Identification Act, as amended, however, this act is not that relevant further for this text.
639. The Czech version of the eIDAS Regulation uses a rather confusing translation for this type of signature, which, when translated back into English, has the following meaning: 'guaranteed electronic signature'.

other data in electronic form and which is used by the signatory to sign'[640] as indicated above. It is clear from this broad definition that such an electronic signature does not necessarily (and usually will not) reliably prove the identity of the signatory (and it is also not the legal condition). However, in conjunction with metadata such as records of communications within the information system and other data, it can and often does provide sufficient evidence of the signatory's intent.[641] It is important to emphasize that this type of signature is characteristic only for electronic legal acting, as de facto there is no analogy for it in the 'paper' form (here we are talking about the handwritten signature, which in the electronic environment is considered to be represented by qualified electronic signature)[642,643]

497. Specific examples of such electronic signatures include scanned signatures embedded in an electronic document, signing the text within an e-mail message, using an online e-commerce platform to purchase goods online, or using dynamic biometric signatures. All these signatures fulfil the above definition in the eIDAS Regulation, but it is clear that the level of trustworthiness of such signatures is on a different level. Thus, it will always depend on the specific assessment of the situation and the evaluation of the circumstances and the associated data/metadata that can prove with a certain degree of confidence (usually quite low) who is the person acting. In this context, however, it is important to note that no electronic signature (even a 'simple' one) 'shall not be denied legal effect and admissibility as evidence in legal proceedings solely on the grounds that it is in an electronic form or that it does not meet the requirements for qualified electronic signatures.'[644]

§2. Advanced Electronic Signature

498. Advanced electronic signature under Article 26 of the eIDAS Regulation must satisfy the following: '(a) it is uniquely linked to the signatory; (b) it is capable of identifying the signatory; (c) it is created using electronic signature creation data that the signatory can, with a high level of confidence, use under his sole control; and (d) it is linked to the data signed therewith in such a way that any subsequent change in the data is detectable':

(a) The condition of a unique link with the signatory is aimed at the fact that the advanced electronic signature can be linked to a specific person, and therefore, it is possible (but not necessary) to identify the person. The uniqueness means

640. Interestingly, the definition of this type of signature in the aforementioned Directive 1999/93/EC emphasizes that the data was intended to be used for 'authentication', now it is the data that the signatory uses to sign. It is thus an extension of the applicability of the regulation with the intention of performing some legally significant act, rather than focusing on the authentication of that acting.
641. This is also confirmed by the s. 7 of the Act on Trust Services.
642. *See* Art. 25(2) of the eIDAS Regulation.
643. *See* Peter Lechner, *Elektronické dokumenty, in Právo informačních technologií*, p. 233 (Radim Polčák et al., Wolters Kluwer 2018).
644. *See* Art. 44(1) of the eIDAS Regulation.

that the person cannot deny that the signature (or certificate) belongs to them and is aimed at their identification. This requirement is logically closely related to point (c) since such a signature must then be under the person's exclusive control. The requirement of a unique link to the signatory is also reflected in the fact that the advanced electronic signature should be inseparable from the document being signed and must be attached by means which ensure that it cannot be separated (e.g., a 'simple' signature in an e-mail will not satisfy this requirement) or altered (*see* point (d)).

(b) The condition on enabling identification of the signatory means that the identification itself need not lead to a unique (unquestionable) identification, but a person being uniquely distinguishable from others in a given context. Furthermore, it should be stressed that the wording refers to the possibility of identification, not to the necessity of identification (here, the eIDAS Regulation leaves room for specific needs when setting up the functionality of an advanced electronic signature). The requirements for the electronic signature set out in points (a) and (b) fulfil the need to ensure that the electronic signature is linked to the person who created it (the signatory) and that the recipient of the document to which the electronic signature is attached can identify the person who issued the document. However, an advanced electronic signature (due to the lower standards imposed on its creation) cannot be perceived as a handwritten signature per se (this requirement is fulfilled by a qualified electronic signature under Article 25(2) of the eIDAS Regulation). This does not exclude the possibility of introducing specifically different national legislation (this has not been done in the Czech Republic so far).

(c) The condition of exclusive control of the data by means of which the signature was created aims mainly to the fact that the creation and use of data are always fully dependent on the signatory and on the data to which they attach it. An electronic signature must not be created automatically without the direct expression of the free will of the signatory to create such a signature. Exclusive control of an electronic signature means choosing an approach that ensures the identification of the signatory to which only the signatory has access. Such access is then typically secured technically using asymmetric cryptography.

(d) The requirement of detecting a subsequent change to the data states that the advanced electronic signature is attached to the data signed by this signature in such a way that any subsequent change to the data can be detected. This means that the signature is linked to the data (which is important, *inter alia*, for condition ad (a)) in such a way that any change is detectable (and again, quite typically, as mentioned above, on the basis of asymmetric cryptography due to the properties resulting from the use of this technology). However, the eIDAS Regulation does not mention a specific tool or technology but only sets out a requirement to ensure immutability (or a requirement to detect change) due to the need to maintain a technology-neutral approach within the legislation.

499. The Czech legislation does not specify other requirements for an advanced electronic signature. It, however, introduces a specific national instrument – a recognized electronic signature, which will be discussed below. Particular examples include various commercial certificates and, where appropriate, the service provided under the Czech bank identity (BankID SIGN).[645]

§3. Qualified Electronic Signature

500. A qualified electronic signature is 'an advanced electronic signature that is created by a qualified electronic signature creation device, and which is based on a qualified certificate for electronic signatures'[646] and it is a signature with the highest level of trustworthiness and the possibility of identification of a given person. The qualified creation device itself is intended to ensure a high level of data confidentiality and also the fact that the data associated with the electronic signature cannot leave the creation device[647]– a hardware solution in the form of a token, card or hardware chip is a very typical solution (but there are also various server-based software solutions as well).[648] It is clear from the definition itself that, in very simplified terms, this is a higher level of advanced electronic signature, but one that is stored on a qualified medium and based on the qualified requirements of a single pan-European certification scheme, given that only this level of signature is recognized by all Member States without further means.[649] The eIDAS Regulation lays down specific requirements for the issuance and use of qualified electronic signatures. These include, in particular, requirements for qualified certificates for electronic signatures,[650] requirements for qualified creation devices for creating electronic signatures[651] and requirements for the qualified trust service provider itself.[652] There are currently three qualified trust service providers that can issue qualified certificates for electronic signatures in the Czech Republic, which are available to the general public: První certifikační autorita, a. s., Česká pošta, s. p. and eIdentity a. s.[653]

---

645. To *see* more for example here: Pavel Loutocký & František Kasl, *Potenciál a úskalí identifikačních služeb bankovní identity*, Právník, vol. 160, n. 12, p. 1045 et seq. (2021).
646. *See* Art. 3(12) of the eIDAS Regulation.
647. A qualified creation device is defined in Art. 3(23) of the eIDAS Regulation in conjunction with Annex II and further specified by implementing acts and technical standards. These are in particular Commission Implementing Decision (EU) 2016/650 of 25 Apr. 2016 laying down standards for the security assessment of qualified signature and seal creation devices pursuant to Arts 30(3) and 39(2) of Regulation (EU) No. 910/2014 of the European Parliament and of the Council on electronic identification and trust services for electronic transactions in the internal market.
648. The list of issued qualified creation devices for creating electronic signatures in the Czech Republic is available on the website of the Ministry of the Interior here: *List of issued qualified means for creating electronic signatures in the Czech Republic*, Ministry of Interior of the Czech Republic (22 Apr. 2022), https://www.mvcr.cz/clanek/seznam-vydavanych-kvalifikovanych-prostredku-pro-vytvareni-elektronickych-podpisu-v-ceske-republice.aspx.
649. *See* Art. 25(3) of the eIDAS Regulation.
650. *See* Annex I of the eIDAS Regulation.
651. *See* Annex II of the eIDAS Regulation.
652. *See* Arts 20 et seq. of the eIDAS Regulation. These requirements are the same for all Member States.
653. A list of qualified trust service providers and of qualified trust services is available here: *List of qualified trust service providers and qualified trust services provided*, Ministry of Interior of the

501. According to the specifics of section 5 of the Act on Trust Services, the Czech legal regulation states that only qualified electronic signatures can be used when signing an electronic document that is legally acted upon by the state, a self-governing territorial unit or legal entities established by the state or by law.[654]

§4. 'Recognised' Electronic Signature

502. 'Recognised' electronic signature is a Czech specificity introduced by the Act on Trust Services. It should be noted that this term was also used under the old, no longer effective legislation; historically, it was de facto the electronic signature that we now associate with a qualified electronic signature. The current legislation has thus introduced some opacity into the issue and problems understanding which electronic signatures are there. Section 6/2 of the Act on Trust Services states that 'a recognised electronic signature means an advanced electronic signature based on a qualified certificate for electronic signature or a qualified electronic signature.' Thus, an advanced electronic signature based on a qualified certificate,[655] as opposed to a qualified electronic signature, does not have to be stored on a qualified medium/creation device (discussed above). An advanced electronic signature based on a qualified certificate thus loses its level of trustworthiness,[656] and, in addition, this type of signature will not be recognised by any other Member State as it does not reach the level of a qualified electronic signature. This signature is then only usable by a private entity when dealing with a public entity (as mentioned above, public entities can only electronically sign using a qualified electronic signature).

503. The question, which has been addressed by the Czech courts,[657] has been whether some form of electronic signature is able to meet the legal requirement of

---

Czech Republic (22 Apr. 2022), https://www.mvcr.cz/clanek/seznam-kvalifikovanych-poskytovatelu-sluzeb-vytvarejicich-duveru-a-poskytovanych-kvalifikovanych-sluzeb-vytvarejicich-duveru.aspx.

654. These are the public signatories.

655. This type of signature is partly assumed for national use according to Art. 27 of the eIDAS Regulation and was created as a kind of compromise for the use of this type of signature when dealing with public authorities. The same applies to electronic seals under Art. 37 of the eIDAS Regulation. *See* more: Alessio Zaccaria, Martin Schmidt-Kessel, Reiner Schulze & Alberto M Gambino. *EU eIDAS regulation: Regulation (EU) 910/2014 on electronic identification and trust services for electronic transactions in the internal market : article-by-article commentary*, p. 232 (C. H. Beck 2020).

656. In general, it is thus necessary to take into account different levels of evidential reliability for all the discussed levels of electronic signatures. The Municipal Court in Prague commented on this in its judgment as follows: 'The Czech court identifies a signatory with an electronic signature with a significant level of trust only when using a qualified, advanced and recognised signature, which are regulated in the eIDAS Regulation and in the national legislation. While the court is obliged to accept all other electronic signatures as evidence, without further allegations and evidence, it cannot be considered that these other electronic signatures are the signature of the person (allegedly) acting.' Judgement of the Municipal Court in Prague of 8 Jul. 2020, Case No. 18 Co 187/2020.

657. *See* the Judgment of the Supreme Administrative Court of 30 Jul. 2019, Case No. KSPH 64 INS 26339/2015, 29 NSR 133/2017-B-36.

official signature verification.[658] Qualified or recognised electronic signatures have not been able to meet this requirement per se under Czech law until recently; it had to be explicitly stated that, for example, in the case of electronic submissions, it is possible for official signature verification to be replaced by a recognised electronic signature. As of 1 June 2022, under section 6 of Act No. 12/2020 Sb., on the Right to Digital Services and Amendments to Certain Acts, it is newly regulated that in such a case, where a legal regulation provides for the requirement of official signature verification, 'it shall be deemed to have been fulfilled by the use of a recognised electronic signature if it can be verified, using data from the basic population register … or the public administration portal, that the qualified certificate for electronic signature, on the basis of which the signatory has created a recognised electronic signature on the document, belongs to the signatory.' Thus, it will no longer be necessary to rely on special legislation, but this requirement will generally be fulfilled using a recognised electronic signature (i.e., as defined above, using an advanced electronic signature based on a qualified certificate for electronic signature or a qualified electronic signature).

658. It is a specific institute that increases the certainty of the signatory's identification in 'paper' form; it is used, for example, when registering or changing data in public registers.

Chapter 3. Trust Services

504. According to Article 3(16) of the eIDAS Regulation (which is directly applicable in all EU Member States), electronic services are generally provided for a fee and consisting of: '(a) the creation, verification, and validation of electronic signatures, electronic seals or electronic time stamps, electronic registered delivery services and certificates related to those services, or (b) the creation, verification and validation of certificates for website authentication; or (c) the preservation of electronic signatures, seals or certificates related to those services.'[659]

505. It should be noted that a revision of the eIDAS Regulation is currently under preparation,[660] which proposes to extend trust services to include electronic attestation of attributes, the electronic archiving of electronic documents and the recording of electronic data into an electronic ledger.[661]

506. In the case of these trust services, the eIDAS Regulation emphasizes in general terms that they must not be deprived of their evidentiary effects on the sole ground that they are electronic.[662]

507. Among the trust services, this chapter will focus on services related to the use of electronic seals, electronic time stamps, electronic registered delivery services and a related Czech specificity – data boxes; we will also discuss website authentication services.[663]

§1. Electronic Seal

508. The electronic seal is another electronic trust service following the electronic signature. The eIDAS Regulation introduces (similarly to the electronic signature) three levels of trust for electronic seals, while the Czech legislation

659. An overview of all qualified providers in each Member State is available here: *EU Trust Services Dashboard, Trusted List Browser*, European Commission (12 May 2022), https://esignature.ec.europa.eu/efda/tl-browser/#/screen/home.
660. Proposal for a Regulation of the European Parliament and of the Council amending Regulation (EU) No 910/2014 as regards establishing a framework for a European Digital Identity, 2021/0136(COD), 3.6.2021 ('the Proposal on Amending eIDAS Regulation').
661. *See* draft revised Art. 3(16) of the Proposal on Amending eIDAS Regulation. However, due to the ongoing legislative process, we will not elaborate further on these newly regulated services as proposed.
662. Specifically, Art. 25(1) of the eIDAS Regulation applies to electronic signatures, Art. 35(1) of the eIDAS Regulation applies to electronic seals, Art. 41(1) of the eIDAS Regulation applies to electronic time stamps and Art. 46 of the eIDAS Regulation applies to the handling of electronic documents in general.
663. Issues related to the regulation of the electronic signature have been discussed separately in the previous chapter. Archiving, which is only reflected in the revision of the eIDAS Regulation, will be specifically addressed in the Czech legal environment in Chapter 5: Law of evidence in the digital environment, as well as the authorized conversion of documents.

specifically introduces a fourth. These are: (a) 'Simple' electronic seal; (b) Advanced electronic seal;[664] (c) Qualified electronic seal; (d) Recognised electronic seal (Czech specificity).

(a) 'Simple' electronic seal is defined under Article 3(25) of the eIDAS Regulation as 'data in electronic form, which is attached to or logically associated with other data in the electronic form to ensure the latter's origin and integrity'. In contrast to the definition of an electronic signature, a seal thus guarantees the origin and integrity of the data to which it is linked – this instrument does not demonstrate the expression of the will of a specific person and is typically created as part of an automated process. Czech legislation used a similar instrument before the introduction of the eIDAS Regulation – it was the 'electronic mark'. It was similar in concept to the electronic seal, but unlike it, it could be used by both a natural person and a legal person.[665]

(b) Advanced electronic seal, like an advanced electronic signature, must meet more stringent requirements. An advanced electronic seal shall be uniquely associated with the creator of a seal; allow the identification of the creator of a seal (but not of the natural person who used this instrument); be created using electronic seal creation data that can be used by the creator of a seal with a high level of confidence to create an electronic seal under their control, and be attached to the data to which it relates in such a way that any subsequent change to the data can be detected.[666] The creator of a seal is then defined as 'a legal person who creates an electronic seal',[667] so that the seal cannot be used, for example, by a self-employed natural person. All the requirements for an advanced electronic seal, except the third requirement (creation of the seal using data that the legal person can use with a high level of confidence to create the seal), are similar to the requirements for an advanced electronic signature, leading to the use of similar technologies for signing and sealing. The wording of the third condition then shows that it is a different type of security. In the case of an advanced electronic signature, it is that each creation of a signature is an independent expression of the will of the signatory, and therefore each specific use of data to create a signature (signing) is under the control of the signatory. 'With an advanced electronic seal, security is at the level of the creation process. The creator of a seal is not expected to authorise each individual creation

664. The Czech version of the eIDAS Regulation also uses a rather confusing translation (similar to electronic signature) for this type of seal, which, when translated back into English, has the following meaning: 'guaranteed electronic seal'.

665. An electronic mark has generally been defined under s. 2/c of the Act on Electronic Signature as 'data in electronic form that are attached to or logically associated with a data message and that meet the following requirements: 1. they are uniquely associated with the designating person and enable their identification by means of a qualified system certificate, 2. have been created and attached to the data message by means of electronic tagging tools which the tagging person can maintain under his exclusive control, 3. are attached to the data message to which they relate in such a way that any subsequent modification of the data can be detected.' Thus, according to that definition, the instrument was more akin to a guaranteed electronic seal in its nature.

666. *See* Art. 36 of the eIDAS Regulation.

667. *See* Art. 3(24) of the eIDAS Regulation.

of an electronic seal, as this typically occurs through an automated process, which must therefore be secured at the process level.'[668]

(c) Qualified electronic seal represents (like a qualified electronic signature) the highest level of the instrument and is subject to 'the presumption of integrity of the data and of the correctness of the origin of that data to which the qualified electronic seal is linked'.[669] It is then defined, similarly to an electronic signature, as an advanced electronic seal that is created by a qualified electronic seal creation device and is based on a qualified certificate.[670] However, its purpose is to confirm the integrity of the sealed document and its origin, not the will of the (legal) person. Examples of the use of this seal in the Czech Republic include, for example, the confirmation of receipt of a document within an electronic filing service, its use in authorized document conversion or the sealing of outputs from a public administration information system.[671]

(d) Recognised electronic seal is as a Czech specificity defined (again, similarly to recognised electronic signature) as 'an advanced electronic seal based on a qualified certificate for an electronic seal or a qualified electronic seal.'[672] This type of electronic seal poses similar conceptual problems as already mentioned in the case of a recognised electronic signature. Also, a recognised electronic seal (based on a qualified certificate) does not have to be stored on a qualified medium as compared to a qualified electronic seal. Thus, similar to a recognised electronic signature, an advanced electronic seal based on a qualified certificate has a reduced level of trust and will not be recognized by any other Member State. Recognised electronic seals can then only be used by a private entity when dealing with a public entity.[673]

§2. Electronic Time Stamp

509. An electronic time stamp, as an additional trust service instrument, generally demonstrates that the electronic document to which the stamp was attached existed at a given point in time. Other tools – a signature or a seal – are not capable of reliably proving this fact. However, an electronic time stamp can be linked to an electronic signature or seal to provide a comprehensive tool where the stamp is capable of proving the existence of a signature or seal in addition to the point in time. The electronic time stamp was also introduced in the Czech legislation by the Act on Electronic Signature. However, it explicitly mentioned only qualified time stamps.[674] According to the current legislation in the eIDAS Regulation, two levels

668. *See* Peter Lechner, *Elektronické dokumenty, in Právo informačních technologií*, p. 238 (Radim Polčák et al., Wolters Kluwer 2018).
669. *See* Art. 35(2) of the eIDAS Regulation.
670. *See* Art. 3(27) of the eIDAS Regulation.
671. *See* more: *Methodological Guideline on Electronic Signatures and Seals for Public Originators*, Ministry of Interior of the Czech Republic (13 May 2022), https://www.mvcr.cz/soubor/metodicky-material-k-problematice-peceteni-zsvd.aspx. pp. 13 et seq.
672. *See* s. 9/2 the Act on Trust Services.
673. *See* s. 9/1 the Act on Trust Services.
674. *See* the definition in s. 2/r of the Act on Electronic Signatures.

are introduced for the time stamp – electronic time stamp (simple) and qualified electronic time stamp. An electronic time stamp is defined as 'data in electronic form which binds other data in the electronic form to a particular time establishing evidence that the latter data existed at that time.'[675]

510. Qualified electronic time stamp in accordance with Article 42 of the eIDAS Regulation shall (a) associate the date and time with the data in such a way as to reasonably prevent the possibility of undetectable alteration of the data; (b) be based on an accurate time source; and (c) be signed using an advanced electronic signature, sealed using the advanced electronic seal of a qualified trust service provider or by another equivalent method:

(a) In relation to the first requirement, a qualified electronic time stamp, therefore, provides reliable evidence that, in the event of a change of data within a document, this can be detected. This is similarly provided for in the case of a qualified electronic signature or seal – but in more detail and less volatile for these instruments.
(b) The requirement to establish a qualified electronic time stamp on an accurate time source (which is associated with coordinated world time) then ensures a reliable indication of the time represented by the time stamp; these requirements must then be ensured by the trust service provider based on technological procedures.
(c) The last requirement related to the signing of the time stamp with an advanced electronic signature or sealing with an advanced electronic seal may be somewhat problematic. Indeed, in practice, 'it is not conceivable to create qualified electronic time stamps that would be associated with their signing, where the interaction of a specific natural person expressing their will in this way is required.'[676] Thus, most often, an advanced electronic seal will be used to seal time stamps (and not the entire document).[677]

§3. Electronic Registered Delivery Service

511. Electronic registered delivery service as another trust service is defined under Article 3(36) of the eIDAS Regulation as 'a service that makes it possible to transmit data between third parties by electronic means and provides evidence relating to the handling of the transmitted data, including proof of sending and receiving the data, and that protects transmitted data against the risk of loss, theft, damage or any unauthorised alterations'. At this general level, it is conceivable that not only within the Czech Republic, various delivery systems capable of generating reliable logs and records of the various activities that take place in the handling of electronic documents will meet the requirements. In the Czech Republic, the general

675. *See* Art. 3(33) of the eIDAS Regulation.
676. *See* Peter Lechner, *Elektronické dokumenty, in Právo informačních technologií*, p. 240 (Radim Polčák et al., Wolters Kluwer 2018).
677. *Ibid.*

features of this service are fulfilled, among others, by the system of data boxes, which are specific and used only within the Czech Republic and will be discussed further below. Data received and sent under these services must not be denied legal effect and must not be rejected as evidence simply because they are in electronic form.[678]

512. Article 44 of the eIDAS Regulation establishes a qualified level for electronic registered delivery services. In addition to the above stated, it must be provided by a qualified service provider; it must enable the sender and the recipient to be identified with a high degree of reliability; the sending itself is secured by means of an advanced electronic signature so that changes to the data can be detected (if they occur, both the sender and the recipient must be notified); the time of sending is then stamped by a qualified electronic time stamp, etc. Due to the specific approach in the Czech Republic, this type of qualified service is not provided and mentioned data boxes are not falling within such a system.[679,680] However, in the other Member States, these services are available, namely in Belgium, Italy, Germany, Spain, France, the Netherlands, Poland and Slovenia.[681] 'Member States should remain free to define other types of trust services in addition to those making part of the closed list of trust services provided for in this Regulation, for the purpose of recognition at a national level as qualified trust services.'[682] This possibility has been used, among others, by the data box system in the Czech Republic.

§4. Data Box

513. Data boxes are, as already indicated above, a specific service for trusted delivery – but not a qualified (*sic!*) one. It is a purely Czech instrument that was primarily introduced to make communication with public authorities more efficient. However, it also enables communication between private entities.[683] The legal regulation of this issue is contained in Act No. 300/2008 Sb., on Electronic Acts and Authorised Conversion of Documents, as amended ('the Act on Electronic Legal Acts').[684] In addition to public administration bodies, the data box is also established free of charge for legal entities, natural persons and self-employed persons.

678. *See* Art. 43(1) of the eIDAS Regulation.

679. This is also indirectly confirmed by the list of qualified trust service providers available for the Czech Republic here: *EU Trust Services Dashboard, Trusted List Czech Republic*, European Commission (13 May 2022), https://esignature.ec.europa.eu/efda/tl-browser/#/screen/tl/CZ.

680. *See also* commentary at: Josef Donát, Martin Maisner, Robert Piffl, *Nařízení eIDAS: Komentář*, 163–164 (C.H. Beck 2017).

681. A list of all available providers of qualified electronic registered delivery services in each Member State is available after filtering here: *EU Trust Services Dashboard, Trusted List Browser*, European Commission (13 May 2022), https://esignature.ec.europa.eu/efda/tl-browser/#/screen/search/type/1.

682. Alessio Zaccaria, Martin Schmidt-Kessel, Reiner Schulze & Alberto M Gambino, *EU eIDAS regulation: Regulation (EU) 910/2014 on electronic identification and trust services for electronic transactions in the internal market: article-by-article commentary*, p. 329 (Beck 2020).

683. *See* s. 2/1 of the Act on Electronic Legal Acts.

684. Data boxes have been in operation since 1 Jun. 2009 and are operated by the Česká Pošta, s.p.

Public authorities, legal persons, but also some other entities[685] are always obliged to use it (once they are entered into the relevant register), and they must primarily use it for all communications where one of the entities is a public authority. For natural persons and self-employed persons, it is now established only at their request. From 1 January 2023, however, a data box will be automatically established for a self-employed person after they have been entered into the relevant register, and for a natural person when they 'use for the first time a means of electronic identification issued under a qualified electronic identification system'.[686]

514. A data box is therefore established for a pre-determined entity, through which it performs actions that are unambiguously linked to the natural person who performed them. Moreover, the fiction of signature is explicitly established, i.e., an act performed through a specific natural person (whether acting on behalf of a legal person or as a natural person) is to be regarded as an 'act in writing and signed.'[687] Thus, the person concerned does not need to possess a qualified certificate for signing.[688] In addition, in order to streamline communication in public administration, all public authorities are obliged to deliver primarily to the data boxes of the addressees.[689] This means that if a given entity has a data box, it must be primarily delivered to that data box; such delivery 'shall have the same legal effect as personal delivery to the hands'.[690,691]

515. Delivery within data boxes is specifically regulated in relation to the moment of delivery to the addressee's data box. The moment of delivery is defined as the moment when the data message is available in the addressee's data box (in the case of a public administration body)[692] or the moment when the addressee logs into the data box (in the case of any entity other than a public administration

685. These include attorneys, statutory auditors, tax advisors, insolvency practitioners, expert witnesses, court interpreters and court translators pursuant to s. 4(3) of the Act on Electronic Acts.
686. *See* amended s. 3 and 4 pursuant to Act No. 261/2021 Sb., Amending Certain Acts in Connection With Further Computerization of Procedures of Public Administration Bodies.
687. Section 18/2 of the Act on Electronic Legal Acts.
688. This was also confirmed, for example, by the Judgment of the Constitutional Court of 19 Jan. 2016, Case No. II. ÚS 3042/14. The Judgment of the Constitutional Court of 12 Feb. 2014, Case No. IV. ÚS 1829/13, or the Judgment of the Constitutional Court of 7 Mar. 2016, Case No. II. ÚS 289/15, confirmed that it is not necessary to sign even an attachment sent from a data box by a given person (on the contrary, if the person for whom the data box was established sends a data message on behalf of someone else, it must already be electronically signed). These conclusions were also summarized by the Judgment of the Supreme Court of 5 Jan. 2017, Case No. Plsn 1/2015.
689. *See* s. 17/1 of the Act on Electronic Legal Acts.
690. *See* s. 17/6 of the Act on Electronic Legal Acts.
691. In this context, it should also be noted that Czech judiciary practice has often been criticised for excessive formalism in its approach to the issue of data boxes (and in general regarding the area of electronic documents). In one particular case, the Supreme Court of the Czech Republic ruled that it was in order for a natural person to act as an executive for a housing association through a data box that had been set up for him as a natural person, since the housing association itself did not have a data box. Nevertheless, the data box set up for the natural person sufficiently identified that person and he could act for the housing association through the data box set up for that natural person. The Judgment of the Supreme Court of 27 Oct. 2020, Case No. 27 Cdo 143/2020.
692. *See,* e.g., the Judgment of the Supreme Court of 5 Jan. 2017, Case No. Plsn 1/2015.

body).[693] 'Every login to the data box by an authorised person is fully recorded, which is another important attribute of the overall credibility of this instrument.'[694] If a natural person, a self-employed person or a legal entity does not log into the data box 'within 10 days from the date on which the document was delivered to the data box, the document shall be deemed to have been delivered on the last day of this period'[695] (thus, the fiction of delivery occurs, which, however, can be claimed ineffective in cases provided for by law). However, this fiction does not arise if the public administration authority fails to deliver the document to the data box, even though it has been set up (e.g., instead of delivering to the data box, it chooses to deliver via a postal service provider). If, however, the entity in question logs into the data box after the period within which the fiction of delivery should normally occur, then delivery is effective at that moment. The case law has also dealt with delivery to an inappropriate data box, as a person may have multiple data boxes (e.g., both as a natural person and as a lawyer). Even in the case of delivery to an inappropriate data box (i.e., delivery to a different data box than the one to which it should be delivered in connection with the role or status of the person concerned), there is no fiction of delivery occurring and it is delivered only at the moment of logging into the data box.[696] In addition, the data box may then be accessed by a person authorized to do so (to the extent specified by the person for whom the data box was set up) in addition to the person for whom it was set up.[697] This authorization is established by the person for whom the data box has been set up by designating it after logging in as part of the settings in the data box system (no further specific authorization is required). The Supreme Court then stated that a procedural act made by means of a data box by an authorized person 'has the same effect as a procedural act made in writing and signed by the person for whom the data box was set up.'[698]

516. In conclusion, it should be stressed that data boxes not only guarantee and prove delivery in a trustworthy manner, they also provide information on the time of sending and receipt,[699] and also fully ensure the preservation of the secrecy of letters.

§5. Website Authentication Services

517. As the last of the trust-building tools, we describe website authentication services. These should provide a means by which 'a visitor to a website can be

693. *See* s. 17/3 of the Act on Electronic Legal Acts.
694. *See* Peter Lechner, *Elektronické dokumenty, in Právo informačních technologií*, p. 258 (Radim Polčák et al., Wolters Kluwer 2018).
695. *See* s. 18a/3 of the Act on Electronic Legal Acts.
696. *See* the Judgment of the Supreme Administrative Court of 15 Jul. 2010, Case No. 7 Asf 46/2010-51, or more on that in the Judgment of the Supreme Court of 5 Jan. 2017, Case No. Plsn 1/2015.
697. *See* s. 8/6 of the Act on Electronic Legal Acts.
698. *See* the Judgment of the Supreme Court of 5 Jan. 2017, Case No. Plsn 1/2015.
699. For more on the specific information recorded within the data box system, *see* s. 14 of the Act on Electronic Legal Acts.

assured that there is a genuine and legitimate entity standing behind the website.'[700] Thus, using an issued certificate authenticates the website and links it to the individual or entity to which the certificate is issued.[701] In the context of qualified services, the certificate must be issued by a qualified provider and meet specific requirements, such as, in particular, an indication of the security of the website and the link to the person to whom the certificate was issued (including authentication), information about the organization and certification authority that issued the certificate, the name of the certified domain or the validity period of the certificate.[702] However, the specific use of qualified certificates for websites under the eIDAS Regulation is rather difficult to ascertain. The list of specific providers is quite numerous; however, according to the information we obtained from some providers of these services in the Czech Republic, this qualified instrument is not much used. This is probably due to the fact that the use of this tool does not bring many advantages compared to other traditionally established tools (often provided by the bodies outside the EU),[703] the process of issuing qualified certificates is procedurally more complex, and it is a voluntary tool.

700. *See* Recital 67 of the eIDAS Regulation.
701. *See* the definition under Art. 3(38) of the eIDAS Regulation.
702. *See* Annex IV of the eIDAS Regulation for details.
703. *See*, for example, information provided by ENISA in the past: *Qualified Website Authentication Certificates,* The European Union Agency for Cybersecurity Commission, pp. 33–34 (13 May 2022), https://www.enisa.europa.eu/publications/qualified-website-authentication-certificates.

Chapter 4. Online Financial Services

§1. Introduction

518. Czechs have always been relatively positive about and open to innovation, including financial innovations introduced by so-called FinTech companies.[704]

519. One example to demonstrate Czechs' inclination towards new technologies could be payment services, especially retail payments. Based on published statistical data, in 2020 already, more than half (54%) of retail transactions were cashless, with a presumed further decrease in cash payments in 2021 (also due to the coronavirus pandemic). Furthermore, contactless payments have always been prevalent in the Czech Republic, and 2021 was no different. According to information published by Mastercard, in 2021, approximately (i) 98% of payment cards distributed in the Czech Republic allowed contactless payments, and (ii) 96% of retail payments were contactless (initiated either by card, smartphone, or wearables). This trend also affects the acquirers' side, as 93% of retailers already accept contactless payments. The coronavirus pandemic has also led to the increased usage of *'Buy Now, Pay Later'* payment solutions in e-commerce (in the Czech Republic offered e.g., by Twisto or Equa bank) or QR code payments in restaurants (Qerko).

520. Having said that, the Czech FinTech market is still relatively undeveloped and thus offers business opportunities. The most popular FinTech products in the Czech Republic include P2P lending, with several successful projects focused on P2P lending being founded in the country in recent years (e.g., Zonky), crowdfunding services (e.g., HitHit and Startovač), digital payment services (e.g., Spendee and Twisto), and investment services (e.g., Portu, Fondee or Bondster). Thus, below, we provide an overview of the essential areas of online financial services, and we also mention one of the obstacles that online financial services providers must tackle when developing their products – i.e., AML obligations.

§2. Regulation of Online Financial Services in the Czech Republic

521. In the Czech Republic, at the moment, apart from a few exceptions, there is no specific regulation that would apply to financial services only because they were provided online.

522. Therefore, online financial services providers must first and foremost follow the rules laid down by the relevant sectoral legislation – e.g.,: Act No. 21/1992 Sb., on Banks (Act on Banks); Act No. 370/2017 Sb., on Payment System; Act No.

704. The term FinTech, as we perceive it today, refers to a field situated at the intersection of finances and information and communication technologies. It can concern technical innovations applied to the classic model of financial institutions as well as entirely new instruments that disrupt the finance market and, with their flexibility, redraw the boundaries formerly strictly defined by traditional players on the market.

256/2004 Sb., on Capital Market Business; Act No. 240/2013 Sb., on Management Companies and Investment Funds; Act. No. 257/2016 Sb., on Consumer Credit; Act 277/2009 Sb., on Insurance; Act. No. 170/2018 Sb., on Distribution of Insurance and Reinsurance; etc. – as well as relevant EU legislation. Guidelines (and other soft law) issued by the relevant regulatory authorities such as the (CNB), the European Banking Authority, the European Securities and Markets Authority, and others play an important role also.

523. Apart from the above, financial services providers must also adhere to the rules laid down by the personal data protection regulations (especially GDPR), AML regulation (*see also* below), or for example, legislation in the area of consumer protection.

524. Given the diversity in business models and the related wide range of legal regulations that could apply in connection with the specific activities of various entities operating on the market for financial services, it would go beyond the scope of this publication to comment on each potential scenario. However, we provide below further information concerning payment services, crowdfunding, Distributed Ledger Technology (DLT), and cryptocurrency and loan services. At the end of this section, we also mention the approach of the CNB (Czech National Bank) to financial innovation.

I. Payment Services

525. Payment services make up probably the largest FinTech market segment in the Czech Republic, with e.g., a continuous increase in cashless (digital) payment solutions.[705]

526. In the Czech Republic, payment services are regulated by the Payment Services Act. However, many (in fact most of the) Czech regulatory requirements are based on EU law or are influenced by EU-wide developments, which allow foreign

705. Based on the data published by the CNB in accordance with EU Regulation 1409/2013, the following can be concluded for 2020: (i) The number of payment cards issued by banks only was almost 14 million (the population of the Czech Republic is less than 11 million), while on the other hand the number of ATMs remained the same/slightly decreased; (ii) An increase in the number of payment transactions can be witnessed, with approx. 911 million payment orders initiated through Internet banking (i.e., approx. 15 million more than in 2019) and 1,5 billion transactions initiated with payment cards (i.e., approx. 200 million more than in 2019). On the other hand, the number of cash withdrawals from ATMs decreased to approx. 140 million transactions (more than 30 million fewer transactions than in 2019); (iii) A similar trend can be seen regarding the amounts of payment transactions initiated. In 2020, credit transfers initiated through Internet banking amounted to approx. CZK 154 billion (i.e., approx. CZK 5 billion more than in 2019); however, there was a decrease in direct debits to approx. CZK 168 billion (i.e., approx. CZK 23 billion less than in 2019). As for payment card transactions, there was a significant increase to approx. CZK 926 billion (i.e., approx. CZK 120 billion more than in 2019).

countries to set up their businesses in the Czech Republic without the need for significant changes in their business models. This also applies in the case of online payment services.

527. As regards payment services, it should be pointed out that following the revised Payment Services Directive (PSD2), the Payment Services Act is one of the financial regulations that regulates certain financial services provided only via the Internet – i.e., so-called payment initiation services and account information services.[706]

528. The account information service allows clients, through the online platforms of 'third-party' apps, to access 'their' data about a payment account managed by another entity (e.g., data about the balance, saved templates, or transaction history), all for the more convenient and interactive handling of money. An implied possibility of the account information service is thus the aggregation of information from multiple accounts at multiple banks within one application and its monitoring, analysis, and processing into a format with added value for the user or for the accessing and assessment of such data by credit companies when assessing clients' creditworthiness (*see also* below).

529. The payment initiation service is primarily an alternative to online card payment, where banks undertake to proceed according to the client-payer's instructions, sent to such banks through an intermediary (payment initiation service provider). This intermediary is the application, which the client provided with information about their payment account and which communicates with the client's payment account through an Application Programming Interface (API).

530. An important obligation introduced by PSD2 was also strong customer authentication. The entity authorized to provide payment services (typically a bank, but also a different payment services provider) must, in certain situations, authenticate the user using two or more elements categorized as knowledge (something only the user knows), possession (something only the user possesses) and inherence (something the user is). However, the set of possible solutions is primarily limited by the condition of mutual independence of the elements used, where the breach of one does not compromise the reliability of the whole. This change has had a significant impact on e-commerce, especially, as e.g., authentication solutions based on credit card details and SMS OTPs (one-time-passwords) do not meet the requirements for strong customer authentication.[707]

---

706. Providers of these new services rely on their statutory right to require access (under specific conditions) to payment accounts held by banks or other account servicing payment service provider (ASPSP). If this access is not facilitated, ASPSP is in breach with its legal obligations for which it may be sanctioned – *see, e.g.*, CNB's decision of 17 Feb. 2022, Case No. 2022/17352/570.

707. The CNB has already sanctioned payment services providers for not complying with strong customer authentication obligations – *see, e.g.,* CNB's decision of 18 Feb. 2022, Case No. 2022/17682/570.

II. Crowdfunding

531. Crowdfunding represents an alternative form of financing for those who seek funds, as well as a form of investing, whereby multiple investors come together through an Internet platform to raise the target amount required for the realization of a specific project. The legal nature of the investment may vary, with investors most often providing debt financing (credit/loans) to those seeking funding, but they may also acquire a share in the company.

532. The popularity of crowdfunding in the Czech Republic has been rising steadily, although the supply can be viewed as limited compared to other EU Member States. The crowdfunding platforms active in the Czech Republic include, e.g., Hithit, Startovač, Fundlift, and Penězdroj, but also the slightly different business models of Zonky or Bondster.

533. As for regulation, at the moment, there is no specific Czech regulation applicable to crowdfunding platforms. However, this does not mean that no regulations apply.

534. Firstly, crowdfunding platform provider activities may fall within the scope of the Regulation (EU) 2020/1503 on European crowdfunding service providers for business (European Crowdfunding Service Provider Regulation – (ECSPR)). If so, the provider needs to obtain the relevant licence under the ECSPR. It should be noted that ECSPR is one of the regulations that target online financial services specifically since it applies exclusively to Internet-based crowdfunding platforms (*see* the definition of crowdfunding platform which pursuant to Article 2(1)(d) of the ECSPR '*means a publicly accessible internet-based information system operated or managed by a crowdfunding service provider*').

535. Also, please do note that although there may be no specific regulation applicable to crowdfunding platforms, providers that are not covered by the ECSPR, depending on their business model, may fall within the scope of other financial regulations, e.g., in the area of payment services (Act on Payment Services) or investment services (Act on Management Companies and Investment Funds).[708] Additionally, anti-money laundering and data protection regulations must be complied with.

708. Failure to appropriately assess legal aspects of the specific product/business model and subsequent failure to comply with the applicable legislation (esp. to acquire the necessary license) may give rise to liability for legal offence – *see,* e.g., CNB's decision of 27 Jan. 2022, Case No. 2022/10114/570.

III. DLT and Cryptocurrencies

536. At the moment, there is no specific regulation applicable to DLT-based or cryptocurrency-based products, nor is there (with one exception in the AML Act) any express mention of DLT or cryptocurrencies in Czech Republic law.[709]

537. This may also be the result of the CNB's approach *'do not protect, do no harm'*, adopted in 2017 already, which will probably not change until the newly proposed EU legislation targeting DLT and cryptocurrencies is passed.

538. Thus, for instance, for buying or selling exchange tokens (the term used by the CNB with respect to cryptocurrencies/virtual currencies) in one's own name for Czech crowns or other fiat currency, or for the execution of payments between buyers and sellers solely for the purpose of paying for the purchased exchange tokens, no specific licence is needed (and none can be given as the CNB does not recognize this as a regulated activity).

539. However, a licence is needed for trading in cryptocurrencies derivatives, managing the assets of investors invested in cryptocurrencies, and transferring funds in connection with the organization of trades with cryptocurrencies. Having said that, there is no special licence regarding cryptocurrencies: the entity that wants to perform regulated activities involving cryptocurrencies needs to obtain an appropriate license, e.g., for an investment company/fund under the Czech Act on Management Companies and Investment Funds (transposing both AIFMD and MiFID II in parts regarding investment firms) or for a payment services provider pursuant to ZPS.

540. Irrespective of the above-mentioned regulatory nature, an entity providing services related to cryptocurrencies (virtual assets) is an obliged entity pursuant to the Czech AML Act (*see also* below). Also, it is necessary, pursuant to Article 28(1) of the Trade Licensing Act, to obtain trade authorization for the *'Provision of services related to virtual assets.'*

IV. Loan Services

541. The shift to the online world has also affected the market for loan services. Not only that most Czech banks have already digitized their loan products and thus allowed their clientele to conclude the most common loan agreements entirely online (with certain exceptions such as mortgage loan agreements), but this has also allowed the creation of entirely digital FinTech companies with business models built around loan services.

709. On the other hand, already in several cases the Czech courts concluded that cryptocurrencies cannot be viewed as currencies, but they need to be legally qualified as intangible assets – at least for tax purposes, *see, e.g.,* Judgment of the Regional Court in Brno of 17 Feb. 2022, Case No. 30 Af 29/2020-48, or of 24 Mar. 2022, Case No. 30 Af 41/2020-49.

542. FinTechs usually provide clients an alternative to financing from traditional credit or financial institutions (in those cases where traditional credit or financial institutions are not interested in providing the required loan), but their business models are also different – e.g., some FinTechs allow third parties to invest in loans already provided by credit providers to businesses or consumers (e.g., Zonky and Bondster) or to invest in receivables of various natures (e.g., Roger), thus opening the factoring services sector to the general public.

543. Depending on the product/business model, different legislation may again apply. However, as with other financial services, there is no specific regulation that would apply only if the services were provided online.

544. Therefore, the general rules must be followed, which in the case of the Czech Republic means that the regulatory implications in the Czech Republic differ depending on whether the debtor is a consumer or not. B2B (or C2B) loans are not specifically regulated, on the other hand, B2C loans (consumer loans) fall within the scope of the Consumer Credit Act, which implements in Czech law the Consumer Credit Directive and the Directive On Credit Agreements for Consumers Relating to Residential Immovable Property.

545. One of the obligations imposed on credit providers by the Consumer Credit Act that should be mentioned is the obligation to assess the consumer's creditworthiness – i.e., its ability to repay the loan. Since the Consumer Credit Act does not specify how this obligation can or must be fulfilled, recently, credit providers have become more interested in the digitalization of this process. One of the methods now used includes using a payment account information service pursuant to PSD2 – i.e., the credit provider acquires a history of the consumer's payment transactions and assesses the consumer's creditworthiness/verifies the information provided by the consumer regarding its income and expenses.[710]

V. The Approach of the Czech Regulatory Authority

546. The CNB – as the regulatory authority primarily responsible for supervision over the market for financial services – has adopted a proactive approach as it is aware of the potential of innovation based on the application of digital technologies to streamline the functioning of all sectors of the financial market, enhance the provision of financial services and foster a stronger and more resilient real economy of the Czech Republic.

710. However, whether these new methods will become widely used in future will also depend on the relevant authorities' views on their sufficiency and/or appropriateness for assessment of consumer's creditworthiness – as for the current approach of CNB, *see, e.g.,* CNB's decision of 7 Jun. 2022, Case No. 2022/55689/570.

547. One of the steps taken by the CNB was thus to establish a new specialized communication channel targeted specifically at queries regarding financial innovation. The CNB calls this channel simply the 'FinTech contact point.'

548. Through the FinTech contact point, the CNB wants to promote the introduction of innovative technologies to the Czech financial market, it aims to facilitate more active communication between market players and the regulatory authority and allow them to resolve unclear regulatory issues more flexibly.

§3. AML Regulation

549. In addition to selected sectoral regulations, financial service providers are usually obliged to take into account also regulation in the area of combating money laundering and terrorist financing – in the Czech Republic contained in particular in Act No. 253/2008 Sb., on Selected Measures against the Legitimization of Proceeds of Crime and Financing of Terrorism (AML Act).

550. In general, the AML Act stipulates extensive obligations for the obliged entities, both in the area of client identification and verification when performing individual trades or transactions within a long-term business relationship (be it in terms of the method or scope of this identification and verification), and in the area of preventing suspicious trades by conducting risk assessments related to the services provided and drafting internal operation principles aimed at the effective management of the risk of legalization of proceeds from crime and financing of terrorism, or the subsequent reporting of suspicious trades and cooperation with the relevant authorities and entities.[711]

551. However, the most crucial obligation that financial service providers must fulfil is the obligation to identify their clients appropriately. Failure to comply with this obligation may result in a fine of up to 10% of net annual turnover.

552. The strict requirements set out in the AML Act in the area of client identification are often challenging to meet, especially in the case of digital financial services where all communication with the client is conducted online/remotely. Currently, the Czech AML Act effectively allows two ways of online/remote client AML identification.

553. The first option is to identify the client by electronic identification means pursuant to eIDAS with a high level of trustworthiness or by means of the so-called bank identity.

711. As recently confirmed by the Czech Supreme Court, AML Act's goal is to protect the soundness of the financial system as such and to promote its resilience against AML risks, not to protect individuals. Therefore, individuals cannot sue AML obliged persons for damages caused or not prevented due to their failure to comply with AML Act (e.g., to identify and prevent suspicious transaction) – *see* the Judgement of the Supreme Court of 17 May 2022, Case No. 25 Cdo 418/2022.

554. Bank identity is an electronic identification means pursuant to eIDAS with a substantial level of trustworthiness issued by a bank in compliance with specific conditions set out in Act No. 21/1992 Sb., on Banks. From the user's point of view, identification via bank identity works in the same way as the process of logging into Internet banking, which *inter alia* means that it is based on strong authentication according to PSD2. The advantage of this method of client AML identification is that it is a full substitute for *face-to-face* identification and is thus applicable to all types of clients and business relationships, regardless of the level of AML risk.

555. The second possible option and also one of the most frequently used methods of online AML identification in the Czech Republic is the so-called 'penny payment'. This method of AML identification is prevalent in the Czech Republic, as up until recently, it was de facto the only possible method of online AML identification. However, its attractiveness declined after the latest amendments to the AML Act, which further complicated the process of penny payment AML identification. Also, unlike e.g., bank identity, this method of AML identification is not allowed without further limitations – it may not be used in case of clients or transactions that pose an increased risk of abuse for the laundering of proceeds of crime or terrorist financing.

556. An obliged person wishing to AML identify its client through this method must ensure that the following requirements in particular are met: (i) the client must provide the obliged person with a copy of its identity card and of one other supporting identity document (e.g., a driving license); (ii) the contents of the contract concluded between the obliged person and the client must be in written form; (iii) the client must provide the obliged entity with credible evidence of the existence of a payment account held in its name with a credit institution or a foreign credit institution operating in the territory of a member state of the EU or a state forming part of the European Economic Area (EEA); (iv) the first payment executed in line with such contract concluded between the obliged person and the client must be made through the account referred to in point (iii); and (v) when making such payment, the client must add to it information about its purpose and also identify the obliged entity as well as itself (to the extent of name and surname) – e.g., *'opening a current account at Bank B, Jan Novák.'*

557. Other methods of online identification – e.g., video identification, identification using biometrics, etc., – are not prohibited by the AML Act but are only allowed to be used in case of clients and business relationships (transactions) that pose a low risk of abuse to launder the proceeds of crime or terrorist financing.

Chapter 5. Law of Evidence in the Digital Environment

§1. Electronic Evidence in Private Law

558. The Czech law generally does not contain special legal provisions about the requirements imposed on the taking of electronic evidence as opposed to evidence in other forms. However, this should not be considered problematic. In the context of the private law regulation of section 125 of Act No. 99/1963 Sb., Civil Procedure Act, as amended ('the Civil Procedure Act'), provides that 'all means by which the state of the case may be established, in particular the examination of witnesses, expert reports, reports and statements of authorities, natural or legal persons, notarial or executor's records and other documents, inspection and examination of the parties... may serve as evidence.' The level of evidentiary reliability of a particular piece of evidence is thus essential. It determines the admissibility and evidentiary power of the evidence based on the principle of the free evaluation of evidence.

559. In private law, the issue of evidence is generally contained in the context of the procedural rules under sections 120–136 of the Civil Procedure Act. Evidence in private law is governed at a general level by fundamental principles such as the impartiality of the court and the judges, the equality of the parties,[712] the presence of the public, and the economy of the entire procedure, or is bound by the principle of disposition and the principle of uniformity of proceedings (arbitral order).[713] However, these principles are not specific to evidence but permeate the entire civil procedure.

560. The specific principle to be considered in the given context (with emphasis on the issues of electronic evidence in private law) is the principle of adjudication, according to which, in the context of contentious proceedings (which permeate the civil process), the evidence provided by the parties is considered in particular.[714] The parties are thus primarily producing the evidence (on the basis of the dispositive principle); they are de facto forced to present the evidence in their own interest. Suppose the evidence is incomplete or must be regarded as insufficient. In that case, the court will draw the party's attention to it (which follows from the principle of the free evaluation of evidence).[715]

561. In our view, another fundamental principle in the presented context is the principle of the free evaluation of evidence, which is enshrined in particular in section 132 of the Civil Procedure Act: 'the court shall evaluate the evidence according to its discretion, each piece of evidence individually and all the evidence in its

712. The non-discrimination principle is then specifically stated in s. 133a of the Civil Procedure Act.
713. On these and other principles, *see* Radka Zahradníková, *Civilní Právo Procesní* pp. 55 et seq. (Vydavatelství a nakladatelství Aleš Čeněk 2018), or Alena Winterová et al., *Civilní právo procesní – Část první: Řízení nalézací* pp. 219 et seq. (Linde 2014).
714. Karel Svoboda, Petr Smolík, Jiří Levý & Jiří Doležílek et al., *Občanský soudní řád. Komentář* p. 611 (C. H. Beck 2021).
715. Section 132 of the Civil Procedure Act.

context; in doing so, it shall take carefully into account everything that has come to light during the proceedings, including what the parties have said.' It follows from the above that it is not stipulated what credibility, form, and evidentiary power each piece of evidence is to have; the evaluation and the evidentiary power of the evidence rest with the judge (who must explain from what evidence they are basing their evaluation). Evidence obtained in violation of legal procedures (e.g., where the consent of the person captured on the recording is absent) cannot be accepted.[716] 'If the court assesses that the evidence is admissible ..., it gives the individual piece of evidence its formal evidentiary power... For example, it assesses the credibility of witnesses or the authenticity of documents. Finally, it considers its substantive evidentiary power, i.e., its relevance to establishing the relevant facts.'[717]

562. The court must consider the evidence provided (in the context of the principle of the free evaluation of evidence), and must, where appropriate, give reasons why it was not produced (or was produced but not reflected in the decision). If the court fails to do so, it will be assessed as the omission of the evidence, which causes a defect in the evidence procedure leading to the violation of the right to a fair trial.[718] Omitted evidence can be divided into situations where: (i) the evidence was not produced but should have been produced;[719] (ii) the evidence was not produced but was required by law or the nature of the proceedings to be produced;[720] (iii) the evidence was produced but was not considered on the facts;[721] or (iv) the evidence was produced and considered but inappropriately or illogically.[722,723]

---

716. *See* more in the Judgement of the Supreme Court of 14 Aug. 2018, Case No. 21 Cdo 1267/2018.
717. *See* Karel Svoboda, Petr Smolík, Jiří Levý & Jiří Doležílek et al., *Občanský soudní řád. Komentář* p. 645 (C. H. Beck 2021).
718. *See* more in the ruling of the Constitutional Court of the Czech Republic: II. ÚS 182/02, 11 Nov. 2003.
719. In such cases, if the court did not produce the proposed evidence, the party to the proceedings 'ultimately did not have adequate evidentiary scope and opportunity to prove the factual allegations relevant to the causal link in the case at hand'. Thus, the problem may not be that the evidence is not produced, if it was evidence that is not relevant to the findings of fact. For more on this, *see*, for example, the Judgement of the Constitutional Court of 3 Sep. 2014, Case No. I. ÚS 4793/12.
720. In this case, the court has a duty to actively determine the facts due to the inquisitorial nature of the proceedings. This has been confirmed, *inter alia*, in the Judgement of the Supreme Court of 1 Oct. 2014, Case No. 8 Tdo 1189/2014, where the court stated that arbitrary evaluation of evidence without an acceptable rational logical basis and making factual findings that have no proper support in the evidence is inadmissible.
721. In this case, it is a situation 'where the evidence adduced in the proceedings has not been produced in the reasoning of the substantive decision, either negatively or positively, in establishing its factual basis, i.e. the court has not made it the subject of its deliberations and assessment, although it has been duly carried out'. For more on this, *see* the Judgement of the Constitutional Court of 23 Sep. 2005, Case No. III. ÚS 359/05.
722. This involves the implementation of an evidentiary procedure that has not been carefully and fully described, leading to unconvincing reasoning, illogical conclusions were drawn from the evidence due to questionable evaluation, or the evidence was produced in an illogical manner. For more information, *see* the ruling of the Constitutional Court of the Czech Republic: II. ÚS 226/06, 11 Mar. 2010.
723. In more detail, *see also* Radim Polčák et al. *Elektronické důkazy v trestním řízení* pp. 35 et seq. (Masarykova univerzita 2015).

563. The principle of free evaluation of evidence is followed by another principle under which the court decides based on the established facts and is bound by the parties' submissions.[724] This is not so much a historical application and division of substantive and formal truth principles but rather a requirement that the court should determine the factual (not, according to the former rules, 'real/true') state of affairs. The defects relating to questions of fact are, in turn, largely associated with the taking of evidence and have their basis in the defective application of procedural rules.[725]

564. As the last of the selected principles closely related to evidence, we consider as the vital the principle of the directness of evidence. According to section 122(1) of the Civil Procedure Act, this is the principle where the court comes out of the evidence that it has produced (the exception being the taking the evidence outside the hearing or making of the evidence through the requested court).[726] Thus, under this principle, evidence is in the vast majority of cases made by the court deciding the case at the hearing.

565. According to the aforementioned section 125 of the Civil Procedure Act, the specific means of evidence are then listed only demonstratively. The evaluation of specific evidence will be carried out according to the nature of this evidence (e.g., a recording from an electronic system in the form of an electronic document bearing one of the aforementioned trust services tools will be provided to the court as a document; a video recording will be presented by its reproduction, etc.).

566. The specific types of evidence are then, according to the Civil Procedure Act, indicatively divided into several categories: (a) witnesses;[727] (b) expert reports;[728] (c) documents[729] and (d) inspection.[730] Of course, the questioning of the parties themselves[731] is also relevant. Still, their subjective bias and, therefore, limited testimonial value in the litigation in question must be perceived:

(a) A witness may be a natural person who is not a party to the proceedings. A witness shall be obliged to appear and testify truthfully about the facts relevant to the court proceedings and not to conceal anything upon summons by the court. A witness may appear in court without a subpoena, affecting their credibility. 'They may refuse to testify only if it would cause danger of criminal prosecution to themselves or persons close to them...'.[732] The right to refuse to give testimony does not mean that the witness does not have to appear in court; it is

724. *See* s. 153/1 of the Civil Procedure Act.
725. *See* Karel Svoboda, Petr Smolík, Jiří Levý & Jiří Doležílek et al., *Občanský soudní řád. Komentář* p. 726 (C. H. Beck 2021).
726. *See* s. 122/2 of the Civil Procedure Act.
727. *See* s. 126 of the Civil Procedure Act.
728. *See* s. 127 and 127a of the Civil Procedure Act.
729. *See* s. 129 of the Civil Procedure Act.
730. *See* s. 130 of the Civil Procedure Act.
731. *See* s. 131 of the Civil Procedure Act.
732. *See* s. 126 of the Civil Procedure Act.

only at the trial itself that the court decides on the merits of the refusal to give testimony based on the reasons given by the witness. When a witness is summoned, the credibility is first examined. The witness testifies about the facts based on which the witness was brought before the court. Finally, they answer questions from the court, the parties or an expert (suggestive, capricious or unrelated questions to the subject matter of the proceedings cannot be admitted).

(b) An expert witness is appointed by the court when it is necessary to assess facts on which an expert report is required (i.e., it is not general knowledge or skills), and at the same time, the report of the public authority is not sufficient, (or there is doubt about this report).[733] An expert witness is usually appointed at the parties' request but may also be appointed by the court without a request. The conditions for the performance of expert activities are laid down in Act No. 254/2019 Sb. on Expert Witnesses, Expert Offices and Expert Institutes,[734] based on which a list of expert witnesses in individual fields is also maintained.[735] The expert report is usually drawn up in writing, however, the expert witness is usually questioned afterwards. In addition to the cover page and the terms of reference, the content of the expert report consists mainly of the preparation of the report itself, which includes a list of documents and source data, a description of the procedure and methodology for evaluating the subject matter under examination (e.g., forensic procedures assess the acquisition of specific electronic evidence) and the conclusions, evaluation and ideally a clear answer to the question under investigation. This is supplemented by an expert clause identifying the expert witness and their field of expertise. The expert report is recorded in the register of expert reports[736] (in electronic form, the expert report must be signed with a qualified electronic signature).[737] The court evaluates the expert report based on the principle of free evaluation of evidence, which does not mean that it should have *a priori* higher evidentiary power than other testimonial evidence.

567. Therefore, the court has a legal obligation to bring in an expert witness (expert body) whenever expertise and experience is needed to assess a certain fact.[738] Thus, the expert witness (if called) assesses expert questions of fact, while the court assesses primarily questions of law (which it cannot waive) or of a fact,

---

733. The expert report of the public authority is preferred for reasons of economy of proceedings.
734. According to this legislation, the expert witness must have clean criminal record, have adequate background (technical, instrumental, etc.) and, above all, be professionally qualified. This means that they have attained an appropriate university degree and at least five years of active experience or have obtained a professional certificate of competence. They then take an entrance examination in the relevant field and, if successful, are then entered on the list of experts after taking the oath.
735. The list is maintained by the Ministry of Justice of the Czech Republic and is available through this portal: *Znalci*, Justice.cz (1 Jun. 2022), https://znalci.justice.cz/.
736. 'The register of assessments is a public administration information system and is maintained in a manner allowing remote access.' s. 29/1 of Act No. 254/2019 Sb., on Expert Witnesses, Expert Offices and Expert Institutes.
737. In more detail, *see* Karel Svoboda, Petr Smolík, Jiří Levý & Jiří Doležílek et al., *Občanský soudní řád. Komentář* p. 635 (C. H. Beck 2021).
738. This follows, *inter alia*, from s. 127 of the Civil Procedure Act.

which do not require an expert report (for which the expert is called).[739] A situation may then arise in the proceedings where there are reasonable doubts as to the completeness of the expert's report or as to the correctness of the procedure and conclusion chosen by the expert witness. If these doubts are not removed by the hearing of the expert witness who prepared the report, and they continue to exist, the court may order a revised expert report (even on the basis of a party's demand) within the court's discretion and discretion to evaluate the evidence.[740,741]

568. In examining witnesses, expert witnesses, and the parties themselves, the court may carry out this act using video conferencing equipment (both at the party's request and the court).[742] The hearing takes place at any place (at another court where video conferencing equipment is available or at another place using a mobile solution) after notification of the place and time. The interviewee is then identified by the authorized judicial officer or another official, and the person in charge also checks the course of the entire interrogation, which is recorded:

(c) 'Evidence by a document shall be produced by the President of the Court Chamber reading it or a part of it at the hearing, or by communicating its contents, or, if sufficient, by providing it for inspection by the parties.'[743] It is then also relevant from an evidentiary perspective whether the document is seen as a private or public document, which was discussed in Chapter 1 (Electronic contracting). If the document is in electronic form, the above principle enshrined in Article 46 of the eIDAS Regulation must be taken into account: 'An electronic document shall not be denied legal effect and admissibility as evidence in legal proceedings solely because it is in electronic form.' In practice, however, it is unfortunately still the case that electronic documents are sometimes still converted into 'paper' forms for evidentiary purposes, but this can easily reduce their evidentiary reliability and eliminate other related information (metadata).
(d) In the case of the taking of evidence by inspection, the inspection of the object under examination may be considered at the court if it is possible to transport it there; if not, the assessment shall take place where the object is located. The object of inspection, in general, may be any tangible object, movable or immovable, animate or inanimate. The judge conducts the search in court directly with their senses (e.g., they assess the testimonial value of a video recording). This examination is recorded in a report, and a record may also be made of it. In the case of an on-site inspection, the judge or an authorized person, in the presence

739. The fact that it is necessary to separate the expert's assessment of factual conclusions from the court's assessment of legal conclusions is emphasized by the Judgement of the Supreme Court of 7 Jan. 2009, Case No. 28 Cdo 171/2008. This is then dealt with in the case of *lege artis* assessment, for example, in the Judgement of the Supreme Court of 26 Nov. 2016, 25 Cdo 4223/2009.
740. *See* s. 127a of the Civil Procedure Act.
741. *See* the Judgement of the Constitutional Court of 3 Jun. 2010, Case No. III. ÚS 1336/10. For more details on the issues of the review report, *see*, for example the Judgement of the Supreme Court of 12 Aug. 2014, Case No. 32 Cdo 1124/2014.
742. Such a procedure occurs in particular if such an action could be carried out only with difficulty or at an unreasonably high cost. s. 39 of the Civil Procedure Act.
743. *See* s. 129 of the Civil Procedure Act.

of persons present at the court hearing, also carries out an inspection with their senses (e.g., assessing the specifics of the equipment's connection to the system). Such an inspection may also be recorded, supposing the object is in possession of someone else (or has not been provided to the court, and it is clear that it is used as evidence). In that case, the court may then invite third parties to provide the object (or to be granted the possibility to access the property, etc.). If this obligation is not fulfilled, it may be enforced by means of orderly fines.

569. Typical electronic evidence in private law proceedings based on the above stated can be considered as, for example, electronic documents proving someone's will or decision, evidence of the content of websites,[744] lawfully acquired and used records of communication (e-mail, messenger, including the location of devices), records from other devices (recordings, video recordings, access records, device diagnostic data, stored data on device), but more generally also records and metadata located and generated within electronic systems.

570. Within private law, the Czech legal system has a rather unique legal regulation concerning electronic evidence of records located within reliable systems. It is contained in section 562/2 of the Civil Code, and it is provided that 'the records of data on juridical acts in the electronic system are presumed to be reliable if they are recorded systematically and sequentially, and if they are protected against alterations.' If a record has been made in the operation of an enterprise and the other party invokes it to his advantage, the record is presumed to be reliable. Thus, a rebuttable legal presumption is established (the law, therefore, allows for the possibility of proving the contrary) of the authenticity and accuracy of the recorded data if they are recorded by the relevant system systematically and sequentially and, furthermore, that they are protected against alterations. The burden of proving the unreliability of the records is, therefore, on the person who disputes the reliability of the data, provided that it is not disputed (or confirmed) that the system in question generally operates reliably.

571. In the case of the rebuttable legal presumption of systematic and sequential data recording, it means that the system does not record data randomly, illogically or chaotically, but that the data are recorded continuously and in such a way that they follow each other. In this case, the data will therefore be considered reliable.

572. In the case of a rebuttable legal presumption under which data are presumed to be protected against alteration, the standard to be achieved for this is not and cannot be specified. The minimum level of protection against changes is

744. With regard to the reliability of the evidence, the Supreme Administrative Court emphasized that when the content of a website is captured only in print (i.e., in the sense of a print screen), some graphic elements that may contain full text may be lost. There may also be a significant loss of evidentiary reliability; ideally, in order to preserve all relevant information, it is therefore necessary to consider the use of tools leading to the archiving of the website at a given moment in time. For more on this, *see* the Judgement of the Supreme Administrative Court of 28 Aug. 2016, Case No. 1 As 80/2016-30.

assumed to be a situation where the system is secured to such a level that it cannot be compromised by normal user intervention. That is to say, the user will not be able to interfere with the records of legal acting without the use of special hardware or software tools to potentially disrupt the standard functioning of the electronic system and break its protection.[745] 'It is therefore not the document itself, but the system by means of which we prove its authenticity or authenticity.'[746] This is provided, however, in the case that the system itself works correctly and reliably (which must be demonstrated in the event of a challenge).

§2. ARCHIVING

573. Archiving is an essential element of the handling of electronic documents. It is primarily regulated by Act No. 499/2004 Sb., on Archiving and Records Management and Amendments to Certain Acts, as amended ('the Act on Archiving'). It is undeniable that, in general, the testimonial value of a document may be lost over time. 'In the case of documents in digital form, preservation also means ensuring the authenticity of the origin of the documents, the integrity of their content and their legibility...'[747] Similarly to the case of documents in 'paper' form, the risks associated with the legibility of data formats over time,[748] the degradation of the physical medium[749] and, in particular, the risks related to the limitation of the validity of security features must be perceived in the case of electronic documents.

574. It is precisely in the case of risks related to the limitation of the validity of security features (their validity is limited to a specific time period) that their most significant pitfalls must be perceived because the legal regulation related to long-term archiving is currently not regulated by the eIDAS Regulation.[750,751] Within the framework of Czech legislation dealing with the issue of archiving, it is possible to choose several approaches. However, the most appropriate is applying different

745. *See* Petr Lavický et al. *Občanský zákoník I. Obecná část. (§ 1-654). Komentář* pp. 1803–1804 (C. H. Beck 2014).

746. *See* Radim Polčák, *Elektronické právní jednání – změny, problémy a nové možnosti v zákoně č. 89/2012 Sb*, Bulletin advokacie, n. 10 p. 39 (2013).

747. *See* s. 3/5 of the Act on Archiving.

748. Specific risks are obsolescence of formats or limitations in their handling in relation to their protection (which should be overcome by formats chosen as standard in the Open Data policy). For more detail on this, *see* Peter Lechner *Chapter 5: Elektronické dokumenty* in *Právo informačních technologií,* p. 264 (Radim Polčák et al, Wolters Kluwer 2018).

749. Within this risk, it is necessary to use data backup and reflect specific legal or procedural requirements.

750. Article 34(1) of the eIDAS Regulation provides the regulation for the preservation of qualified certificates by qualified service providers, but this is aimed at enabling the long-term verifiability of electronic security features with the knowledge that trustworthiness is reduced after the end of the validity of the certificate. However, this applies only to the security element itself and certainly not to the archiving of the electronic document as whole.

751. However, a revision is currently underway in the form of the Proposal on Amending eIDAS Regulation. The forthcoming proposal would, *inter alia*, introduce electronic archiving services and qualified electronic archiving services. *See* more in proposed Art. 3(47) and Art. 45g of the Proposal on Amending eIDAS Regulation.

solutions that synergistically combine technical and procedural measures.[752] The solution can be represented by these approaches: (a) re-stamping, the use of (b) transaction protocols or the (c) use of trusted repositories:

(a) Re-stamping is one of the essential technical solutions leading to the long-term archiving of electronic documents. This procedure is based on the principle that a newly qualified time stamp is attached to an electronic document stored in a digital archive before the expiry of the certificate on which the previous (qualified) time stamp is based. This results in the chaining of these instruments, where the last attached (valid) qualified time stamp proves the validity of the previous one(s).[753]
(b) The Act on Archiving, in relation to electronic filing systems,[754] mentions the maintenance of a transaction protocol as one of the functionalities of the filing service in section 70(2)(h). A transaction protocol is a record of data relating to the operations carried out within an electronic filing system by the entities using that system, or it records data generated by the electronic filing system itself.[755] The logging and other information thus make it possible to trace, check and retrospectively verify the operations and activities carried out by users of the electronic filing system. The details of the maintenance of the filing systems and the specific requirements involved are mentioned in the national standard.[756] 'To further enhance the credibility of the entire system, the transactional approach is supplemented by the important subsequent step of fixing the status of the transaction protocol in the form of digital documents...[757] Most often, storage is done once a day, always for the previous day.'[758] Such a document is further provided with an 'electronic signature or electronic seal followed by a qualified

752. *See* Peter Lechner *Chapter 5: Elektronické dokumenty* in *Právo informačních technologií*, p. 265 (Radim Polčák et al, Wolters Kluwer 2018).
753. The disadvantage of this technical solution is that it is not resistant to possible revocation of the certificate on which the electronic time stamp is based. Peter Lechner *Chapter 5: Elektronické dokumenty* in *Právo informačních technologií*, p. 266 (Radim Polčák et al, Wolters Kluwer 2018).
754. In this system, the file service is maintained by public organizations and entities, as well as by state-owned entities, with some differences (some entities may also maintain the file service partly in paper form). *See* ss 63 et seq. of the Act on Archiving. In addition, there is a new obligation to maintain a comprehensive electronic filing service, through an attested system, as of 31 Jan. 2023, pursuant to Act No. 261/2021 Sb., Amending Certain Acts in Connection with Further Computerization of Procedures of Public Authorities.
755. A specific overview of the recorded operations is available here: *Spisová služba v otázkách a odpovědích*, Národní archive (2 Jun. 2022), https://www.nacr.cz/verejnost/2-predarchivni-pece/verejnopravni-puvodci/spisova-sluzba-otazky-odpovedi.
756. *See Národní standard pro elektronické systémy spisové služby*, Ministerstvo vnitra České republiky (2 Jun. 2022), https://www.mvcr.cz/clanek/narodni-standard-pro-elektronicke-systemy-spisove-sluzby.aspx.
757. This is a .pdf or .xml format. *See* requirement 5.3.3 of the national standard for more details: *Národní standard pro elektronické systémy spisové služby*, Ministerstvo vnitra České republiky (2 Jun. 2022), https://www.mvcr.cz/clanek/narodni-standard-pro-elektronicke-systemy-spisove-sluzby.aspx, p. 40.
758. *See* Peter Lechner *Chapter 5: Elektronické dokumenty* in *Právo informačních technologií*, p. 267 (Radim Polčák et al, Woltes Kluwer 2018).

electronic time stamp',[759] according to clause 5.3.2 of the national standard. The trustworthiness of such a protocol is therefore determined by its regular automated generation[760] and the use of security features, and these documents are then again registered back within the system (thus chaining multiple archiving-related tools).

575. Archiving using transaction protocols also occurs partially in the case of the use of data boxes, but only if data messages are processed within electronic filing systems, while the Data Vault provided within the data box system can be used to archive other messages.[761] The presumption of integrity, which is applied to any public administration information system (one of which is the data box),[762] is then applied for the period before long-term storage use.[763]

(c) It is precisely the approach related to the presumed integrity of the system used in the context of trusted repositories. This is a system for storing data in such a way as to ensure its long-term trustworthiness and availability. This principle, which is based on a specific legal requirement, is used, for example, by the National Digital Archive, as part of the National Archive,[764] where it is stipulated that the digital archive for stored data 'shall ensure the preservation of the integrity of its content and its legibility'[765] or, in this case, by the aforementioned data repository system.

576. For the needs of proving, it is also possible to use private electronic archives that preserve selected websites at a specific time period and are thus able to prove their existence retrospectively even if the website is no longer available. Such archives vary in nature and are provided by different subjects – for example, by non-profit organizations,[766] or they are part of the state institutions.[767] Courts take into account the evidentiary nature of such archives specifically and consider and assess their reliability and evidentiary power.[768]

---

759. Interestingly, the national standard does not explicitly set a requirement for a qualified electronic signature or seal, but the context shows that these should also reach this level.
760. In particular, this is requirement 7.2.5 of the national standard. *Národní standard pro elektronické systémy spisové služby*, Ministerstvo vnitra České republiky (2 Jun. 2022), https://www.mvcr.cz/clanek/narodni-standard-pro-elektronicke-systemy-spisove-sluzby.aspx, p. 52.
761. *See Datový trezor*, Datové schránky (3 Jun. 2022), https://www.datoveschranky.info/aditivni-sluzby/datovy-trezor.
762. *See* s. 14/1 of the Act on Archiving.
763. Measures corresponding to the security requirements to ensure the confidentiality, integrity and availability of information processed in public administration information systems result primarily from s. 5a/2 and 5b/1 of Act No. 365/2000 Sb., on Public Administration Information Systems and on Amendments to Certain Other Acts, as amended.
764. *See* s. 15/3 of the Act on Archiving.
765. *See* s. 46/3/a of the Act on Archiving.
766. *See About the Internet Archive*, Internet Archive (2 Jun. 2022), https://archive.org/about/.
767. In the Czech Republic, this service is provided by the National Library of the Czech Republic. *Webarchiv preserves Czech web*, the National Library of the Czech Republic (2 Jun. 2022), https://www.webarchiv.cz/en/contact.
768. In one case, the Supreme Administrative Court used evidence provided by a website that was no longer available, but which was archived by the foreign Internet archive provider – archive.today

577. In connection with the archiving of electronic documents, the aforementioned provision of section 562/2 of the Civil Code can also be considered, but with the difference that it will always be necessary to take into account the fact that in case of need (challenge) it will have to be proven by the system operator that it is a reliable system (subsequently, based on a rebuttable presumption, it will be possible to consider the individual recorded data as reliable).

§3. Authorized Document Conversion

578. Within this chapter, we consider it essential to discuss above all previously mentioned also the authorized document conversion, which leads to preserving the integrity of the document and its reliability in the event of a change of its form (typically from paper to electronic or vice versa) and thus ensures mutual 'compatibility', data integrity and usability of these two forms.[769] For a reliable transition from one form to the other, the instrument of the authorized conversion of documents has been introduced in the Czech legislation, which is enshrined in sections 22 et seq. of the Act on Electronic Acts. It is thus defined that authorized conversion means 'the complete conversion of a document in documentary form into a document contained in a data message or data file[770] ... in a manner ensuring the conformity of the content of those documents and the attachment of a clause on the execution of the conversion ..., or the complete conversion of a document contained in a data message into a document in documentary form in a manner ensuring the conformity of the content of those documents and the attachment of a clause.'

579. Independent authorities carry out the conversion – these are public administration contact points[771] and attorneys[772] who certify that the output document corresponds in content to the input one. A record is then made of each authorized document conversion carried out to verify the conversion. The conversion itself is then carried out either at the request of the subject (thus provided as a service) or ex officio (i.e., in connection with the needs and activities of the public authority concerned).[773]

(the archive was located under an Icelandic domain at that time). In decided case, the Court used that archive to prove that a particular person had been listed as a contact person during relevant period of time, even though that person claimed otherwise, which was one of the key facts for the assessment of the case. For more on this, *see* in particular paragraph 47 of the Judgement of the Supreme Administrative Court of 4 Oct. 2017, Case No. 14 Kse 1/2017.

769. In the case of copying an electronic document, there is no point in talking about specific tools for preserving the originality of the original electronic document, since by definition the electronic document is copied identically. However, there may potentially be a need to convert the format of the electronic document to another, in which case it may be appropriate to use conversion.

770. It should be noted that the law is based on old terminology and it should be emphasized that the term data message or data file should ideally be replaced by the term electronic document.

771. It is an information system used by contact points not only for conversion but also for a wide range of other operations in connection with the performance of public administration. For more information *see Co je to Czech POINT?,* Ministerstvo vnitra České republiky (3 Jun. 2022), https://www.mvcr.cz/clanek/co-je-czech-point.aspx.

772. *See* s. 23/1 of the Act on Electronic Acts.

773. *See* s. 23/2 of the Act on Electronic Acts.

Chapter 6. Consumer Protection (Online Sales and Online Services)

§1. Sale of Goods Directive, Digital Content Directive and Their Transposition into the Czech Law

580. At the level of EU law, Directive 1999/44/EC of the European Parliament and of the Council of 25 May 1999 on certain aspects of the sale of consumer goods and associated guarantees (Consumer Sales and Guarantees Directive) had provided the basis for the online sale of goods and the provision of services online until the end of 2021. The directive primarily defined the contractual parties (consumer *v.* seller) and regulated terms such as consumer goods, producer, guarantee, and repair (remedy). The legal regulation of consumer protection safeguards and B-2-C obligations has not been transposed into a special legislation in the Czech law, but is contained in the Czech Civil Code, which has been in force since 1 January 2004.[774]

581. On 20 May 2019, the European Parliament and the Council of the EU adopted two directives on specific aspects of digital sales. These are Directive (EU) 2019/770 of the European Parliament and of the Council on certain aspects of contracts for the supply of digital content and services ('Digital Content Directive') and Directive (EU) 2019/771 of the European Parliament and of the Council on certain aspects of contracts for the sale of goods, amending Regulation (EU) 2017/2394 and Directive 2009/22/EC and repealing Directive 1999/44/EC ('Sales of Goods Directive').

582. Both the directives regulate similar aspects of the contracts: the period of performance, rights in the event of delay in performance, conformity of performance with the contract – either in objective or subjective terms, the claims arising from unsatisfactory performance, and the right of recourse between traders in the supply chain.

583. The subject matter of the Sales of Goods Directive largely overlaps with Consumer Sales and Guarantees Directive (Directive 1999/44/EC), which was repealed as of 1 January 2022. On the contrary, the Digital Content Directive deals with a completely new subject matter related to the use of digital assets (digital goods and services) in data economy and its scope is not limited to a particular type or types of contracts.

584. Both Directives represent the full harmonization and EU Member States are not permitted to implement or retain consumer protection requirements that differ from those set forth in the directives, including those that are more or less stringent. EU Member States were expected to adopt the transposition measures by 1 July 2021 and apply them from 1 January 2022.

774. *See* ss 420/2 and 1810/ff of the Civil Code.

585. The scope of the Sales of Goods Directive largely follows that of Directive 1999/44/EC. It applies to sales contracts concluded between consumers and sellers[775] and to contracts for the supply of goods to be yet manufactured or produced.[776] The Sale of Goods Directive applies to contracts under which ownership of a tangible movable thing, including goods yet to be manufactured or created, is transferred for consideration. According to Article 2(5)(b) of the Sale of Goods Directive as goods are also considered movable tangible objects that contain digital content or services so that the goods could not fulfil their functions without the embodiment of this digital content or services ('goods with digital elements'). Thus, if 'smart products' such as smart TVs or smartwatches have any defects that derived from the nature of digital elements incorporated, the consumer is entitled to pursue claims guaranteed by the non-conformity of the purchased good with the sale contract.

586. On the contrary, the Sales of Goods Directive does not apply to contracts for the delivering digital content or digital services covered by the second directive.[777] Digital Content Directive, according to its recital (19), covers the supply of (e.g., streaming) video, audio or other file sharing services, word processing, digital games or games offered in a cloud computing environment and social media. In order to meet consumer expectations and to provide a clear and simple legal framework for traders of digital content, the Digital Content directive should also apply to digital content provided on tangible media such as DVDs, CDs, USB sticks and memory cards, as well as to tangible media when used exclusively for the transmission of digital content.

587. The Digital Content Directive and the Sale of Goods Directive take a novel approach to contract compliance by explicitly differentiating subjective and objective standards for conformity of the digital services or digital content with the contract.[778] As a result, both are extensively covered in the directives' provisions, which include three fundamental principles (functionality, compatibility, and interoperability) as requirements for digital content, digital services, and digitally enhanced items. The distinction between subjective and objective requirements refers to aspects that arise directly from the consumer-trader interaction (subjective approach) and features that are only indirectly part of the contract since they are reasonably expected by the consumer (objective criteria).

588. One of the most important aspects of the Digital Content Directive is that it applies not only to contracts in which the provider provides digital content in exchange for a monetary payment, but also to agreements in which the counter-performance includes personal data or any other type of data.[779] Therefore, legal

775. *See* Art. 3(1) of the Sale of Goods Directive.
776. *See* Art. 3(2) of the Sale of Goods Directive.
777. *See* Directive (EU) 2019/770 of the European Parliament and of the Council of 20 May 2019 on certain aspects concerning contracts for the supply of digital content and digital services, OJ L 136, 22.5.2019.
778. *See* Arts 6 and 7 of the Digital Content Directive; Arts 6 and 7 of the Sale of Goods Directive.
779. *See* Art. 3(1) of the Digital Content Directive.

obligations in which the consumer provides personal data to the trader or agrees to provide such data are also covered. An exception applies in cases where the personal data provided by the consumer is processed by the trader solely for the purpose of providing digital content or digital services in accordance with the Directive or for the purpose of complying with legal requirements with which the trader must comply. Also excluded from the scope of the Directive are those contracts that have as their subject matter software offered by the trader under a free-and-open-source-license, provided that the consumer does not pay a price and the personal data provided by the consumer is processed by the trader solely for the purpose of improving the security, compatibility or interoperability of that particular software.[780]

589. None of these directives has been implemented in Czech law so far. The 2021 legislative proposal[781] envisaged that the general provisions on consumer protection in the sale of goods and services would be amended. Among other related issues, the concept of the 24-month statutory consumer guarantee[782] was to be changed to bring it into line with the requirements of the Sale of Goods Directive and to be replaced by a one-year presumption of non-conformity with the purchase contract[783] and the corresponding reverse burden of proof in favour of the consumer.

590. As regards the digital content and services supply, the proposal envisaged the creation of a separate section in the Civil Code,[784] placed behind the provisions regulating licence agreements, which ought to comprehensively transposed the requirements of the Digital Content Directive. We can assume that the directives will be transposed in a similar way in the new legislative proposal to be discussed by the newly elected Chamber of Deputies.

§2. Existing Provisions on the Sale of Goods or Services Online

591. Until both directives are implemented, the existing consumer protection provisions[785] will apply to the online sale of goods and services. EU law guarantees consumers that they can buy goods or services online from any country in the Union, and traders must not apply any geo-blocking measures in this context.[786]

780. *See* Art. 3(5)(f) of the Digital Content Directive.
781. Government Bill amending Act No. 89/2012 Sb., the Civil Code, as amended. Parliamentary Document No. 994 [online] https://www.psp.cz/sqw/text/tiskt.sqw?o=8&ct=994&ct1=0.
782. *See* s. 2165/1 of the Civil Code.
783. *See* Art. 11 of the Sale of Goods Directive.
784. *See* ss 2389a/ff of the Civil Code.
785. *See* s. 1811/ff of the Civil Code.
786. Regulation (EU) 2018/302 of the European Parliament and of the Council of 28 Feb. 2018 on addressing unjustified geo-blocking and other forms of discrimination based on customers' nationality, place of residence or place of establishment within the internal market and amending Regulations (EC) No 2006/2004 and (EU) 2017/2394 and Directive 2009/22/EC, OJ L 60I, 2.3.2018.

Under private law, a consumer is defined in section 419 of the Civil Code as a person who enters into a contract with an entrepreneur or otherwise deals with him or her outside the scope of their business activity or outside the scope of their independent professional activity.

592. In general, the legal regulation of consumer protection related to the conclusion of consumer contracts is regulated by sections 1810 et seq. of the Civil Code. The Civil Code provides that agreements which deviate from the law to the consumer's detriment shall be null.[787] Thus, arrangements that create a significant imbalance to the consumer's detriment are prohibited. In this respect, it is prescribed to interpret a contract in such a way that is most favourable to the consumer. Deviation from the law to the detriment of the consumer as the weaker party leads to relative nullity.[788]

593. The trader must also inform the consumer in a comprehensible manner of the facts that are decisive for the conclusion of the contract. Particularly, online sellers must disclose from the outset all costs associated with the purchase of goods.[789] Current law excludes the information for contracts for the supply of digital content on tangible media.[790] In contrast, information about the functionality of the digital content or interoperability must be provided.[791] The information communicated must be clear and understandable to the average consumer, and the communication must be readable in the language in which the contract is concluded.[792] Finally, all information must be preserved and retrievable.[793]

594. Distance contracts have specific requirements, as their conclusion brings certain disadvantages for the consumer. The purpose of the legislation is thus to compensate for the fact that the consumer does not have the opportunity to physically inspect the goods and find out more about their characteristics. It follows from the provisions of section 1820 of the Civil Code that distance contracts are contracts which can be concluded without the parties' physical presence and where a means of distance communication (Internet, telephone, e-mail) has been used in the contracting process. The provision on withdrawal from a distance contract also applies to the provision of services.

595. In distance contracts, the trader must inform the consumer of specific issues. The trader has to provide the consumer with the general information referred to in section 1811/2 of the Civil Code and the information defined in sections 1820/1 and 1826 of the Civil Code. This information must be provided before the conclusion of the contract or before the consumer makes a binding offer. The consumer

787. *See* s. 1812/2 of the Civil Code.
788. *See* Pavel Loutocký in *Právo informačních technologií*, p. 313 (Radim Polčák ed., Wolters Kluwer 2018).
789. *See* s. 1811/2/e of the Civil Code.
790. *See* s. 1811/3/b of the Civil Code.
791. *See* s. 1811/3/h/i of the Civil Code.
792. *See* s. 1811/1/b of the Civil Code.
793. *See* s. 1819 of the Civil Code.

must be informed about the binding nature of the contract, the possibility of withdrawing from the contract, and, where appropriate, out-of-court dispute resolution.[794] In addition, section 1826 requires that information on the technical processing of the contract, its storage, the different language versions and any codes of conduct by which the trader may be bound must also be provided. Breach of the information obligation may lead to the seller's obligation to compensate for damages. If the seller does not provide the consumer with information on the costs of delivery or return of the goods, the consumer is not obliged to pay those costs.[795] Failure to inform the consumer of his or her option to withdraw from the contract is sanctioned by extending the withdrawal period by one year.[796] In such a case, the consumer is also not liable for the damage to the goods or the decline of their quality from the time of receipt to the return to the trader.

596. A specific regulation applies in the case of the supply of unordered goods. If the trader delivers the goods to the consumer without the consumer having ordered them, there is a fiction of fair possession by the consumer. The consumer is then not obliged to return or pay for the delivered goods.[797] The purpose of the regulation is to protect the consumer from undesirable deliveries by the trader.

597. The consumer has fourteen days to withdraw from the contract, return the delivered goods for any reason and to obtain a refund.[798] There are, however, certain exceptions, such as train or air tickets, concert tickets or hotel reservations.

598. There is no form prescribed for consumer withdrawal. Therefore, to withdraw from a distance contract, either a withdrawal form can be used[799] or any other precise statement of withdrawal (typically an e-mail). If the consumer withdraws from the contract, the parties are required to reimburse each other. The consumer is thus obliged to send the goods to the trader within fourteen days of withdrawal. The seller is then obliged to refund the consumer the price of the original goods and to pay the original cost of sending the goods to the consumer.[800]

599. The withdrawal period in consumer sales of goods is calculated from the date of receipt of the goods, not from the conclusion of the contract itself.[801] The day after the consumer takes delivery of the goods is the first day of the fourteen-day period. If the end of the period falls on a Saturday, Sunday or public holiday, the period ends on the next following working day.[802] If the goods have not yet been delivered in their entirety, the withdrawal period will only run from the date of

794. *See* s. 1820/1/j of the Civil Code.
795. *See* s. 1832/3 of the Civil Code.
796. *See* s. 1829/2 of the Civil Code.
797. *See* s. 1838 of the Civil Code.
798. *See* s. 1829/1 of the Civil Code.
799. *See* s. 1830 of the Civil Code.
800. *See* s. 1832/2 of the Civil Code.
801. *See* s. 1829/1/a of the Civil Code.
802. *See* s. 607 of the Civil Code.

receipt of the last delivery.[803] It is also important that in order to withdraw from the contract, it is sufficient for the consumer to prove that he or she has sent the returned goods to the trader on the last day of the fourteen-day period.[804]

600. In the case of withdrawal from a contract for the provision of services, the withdrawal period runs from the time of conclusion of the contract.[805] The day after the consumer has concluded the contract shall be the first day of the fourteen-day period. If the end of the period falls on a Saturday, Sunday or public holiday, the period shall also end on the next following working day. When withdrawing from a distance contract for the provision of services, the seller is not obliged to refund the consumer the amount already paid.[806]

601. Withdrawal from a distance contract allows the consumer to become familiar with the goods' characteristics and test them. However, the law provides for exceptions in which the possibility of trying out the goods is excluded, and the contract cannot be withdrawn unless agreed otherwise.[807] The impossibility of withdrawal applies to multimedia or computer programs if they have been delivered on a tangible medium and the original packaging has been damaged. Under the current regulation, it is then also not possible to withdraw from a contract relating to the supply of digital content without a tangible medium.[808] This rule should change once the Digital Content Directive is implemented.

§3. Out-of-Court Settlement of Consumer Disputes

602. The amendment to the Consumer Protection Act[809] responding to the requirements of the Directive on Alternative Dispute Resolution (ADR)[810] has implemented into the Czech legal system a new out-of-court dispute resolution regime that consumers can use to resolve their consumer dispute with the trader. Disputes can be adjudicated by specialized bodies, such as the Financial Arbitrator [*Finanční arbitr*] in the field of financial services, the CTO [*Český telekomunikační úřad*] in the field of postal services and electronic communications and the Energy Regulatory Office [*Energetický regulační úřad*] in the field of electricity, heating and gas, and the Czech Trade Inspection Authority [*Česká obchodní inspekce*] for other contracts for the supply of goods or services. Other arbitration bodies are the Czech Bar Association [*Česká advokátní komora*] and the Association of Czech Consumer [*Sdružení českých spotřebitelů, z. ú.*].

803. *See* s. 1829/1/a of the Civil Code.
804. *See* s. 1831/1 of the Civil Code.
805. *See* s. 1829/1/second sentence of the Civil Code.
806. *See* s. 1831/1 of the Civil Code.
807. *See* s. 1837 of the Civil Code.
808. *See* s. 1837/l of the Civil Code.
809. *See* Act No. 634/1992 Sb., as amended.
810. *See* Directive 2013/11/EU of the European Parliament and of the Council of 21 May 2013 on alternative dispute resolution for consumer disputes and amending Regulation (EC) No. 2006/2004 and Directive 2009/22/EC, OJ L 165, 18.6.2013.

Chapter 7. Liability of Online Service Providers

§1. Introduction

603. The regulation of liability of information society services providers (ISSPs) is covered by EU legislation, namely Directive 2000/31/EC of the European Parliament and of the Council of 8 June 2000 on certain legal aspects of information society services, in particular electronic commerce, in the Internal Market (Directive on electronic commerce) ('E-commerce Directive').

604. Specific regulation regarding the online use of press publications and online content-sharing service providers comes from Directive (EU) 2019/790 of the European Parliament and of the Council of 17 April 2019 on copyright and related rights in the Digital Single Market (DSM). and amending Directives 96/9/EC and 2001/29/EC

605. Moreover, in the EU legislative process, there are two regulation proposals with significant implications for the liability of ISSPs. These are Regulation of the European Parliament and of the Council on a single market for digital services (Digital Services Act) and amending Directive 2000/31/EC and Regulation of the European Parliament and of the Council on contestable and fair markets in the digital sector (Digital Markets Act).

606. As can be seen from the above, currently the regulation relies on directives of the EU, which are transposed to national law of the Czech Republic. That will likely last until at least the Digital Services Act comes into force.

607. Relevant provisions of the E-commerce Directive (section 4) are transposed in Act No. 480/2004 Sb., on certain information society services and on amendments to some acts (ACISS).

608. Relevant provisions of DSM (Articles 15 and 17) are to be transposed into Act No. 121/2000 Sb., on copyright, rights related to copyright and on amendments to some acts (Copyright Act), as amended ('Copyright Act'). Despite the deadline for transposition (7 June 2021), the amendment of the Copyright Act is still in the legislative process.

§2. Liability According to ACISS (E-commerce Directive)

609. In general, the transposition of the E-commerce Directive into ACISS is somewhat brief and not entirely precise, although the overall impact is largely the same as can be expected from the wording of the directive.

I. Mere Conduit

610. According to the directive, in case of mere conduit (the transmission of information in a communication network), the ISSP is not liable for the information transmitted, if it does not (i) initiate the transmission, (ii) select the receiver of the transmission, and (iii) select or modify the information contained in the transmission.

611. The same is stipulated by ACISS, with the following additions. Mere conduit includes the provision of access to electronic communications networks for the purpose of transmitting information. The transmission of information and the provision of access also include the automatic short-term temporary storage of the information transmitted.

II. Caching

612. In case of caching (automatic, intermediate and temporary storage of information, performed for the sole purpose of making more efficient the information's onward transmission to other recipients of the service upon their request), the directive sets out that the ISSP is not liable for such if it (i) does not modify the information, (ii) complies with conditions on access to the information, (iii) complies with rules regarding the updating of the information, (iv) does not interfere with the lawful use of technology, and (v) acts expeditiously to remove or to disable access to the information it has stored upon obtaining actual knowledge of the fact that the information at the initial source of the transmission has been removed from the network, or access to it has been disabled, or that a court or an administrative authority has ordered such removal or disablement. These provisions were adopted in the ACISS using different wording, but with the same meaning as in the directive.

III. Hosting

613. While providing hosting (storage of information provided by the recipient of a service), according to the directive, the ISSP is not liable for the information stored at the request of a recipient of the service if it (i) does not have actual knowledge of illegal activity or information, or (ii) upon obtaining such knowledge, acts expeditiously to remove or to disable access to the information.

614. Similarly to the above, the wording in the ACISS is different, but in the case of (i) above, actually also conveys a slightly different meaning. According to the ACISS, the ISSP is responsible for the content of information stored at the request of a user, only if it could have known, in view of the subject matter of his or her activity and the circumstances and nature of the case, that the content of the stored information or the user's actions were unlawful.

615. If the ACISS was worded in the same way as the directive, a simple absence of knowledge would be enough for the ISSP to not be liable for the information. Pursuant to the ACISS, however, it needs to be examined whether the ISSP could have had knowledge.

IV. No General Obligation to Monitor

616. The directive stipulates that Member States shall not impose a general obligation on ISSPs, when providing the above-mentioned services, to monitor the information which they transmit or store, nor a general obligation actively to seek facts or circumstances indicating illegal activity. The absence of such obligation is stated in the ACISS in basically the same words as in the directive.

V. Conclusion

617. Aside from the slight, although notable, difference in liability of hosting service providers, the Czech regulation of ISSPs' liability is largely the same as in the E-commerce Directive.

618. The current proposal of the transposition of the DSM should be mentioned in this context as well. It is similar in the way that it mostly adopts the content of the directive without much ambition to change, detail, or specify it. However, some provisions from the directive are currently missing from the proposal, which is likely to be among the points of discussion during the legislative process. Due to the number of amendments to the proposal and the relatively early stage of the legislative process, the final form of the Czech transposition of the DSM is yet to be evaluated.

§3. Case Law

619. In regard to case law concerning liability of ISSPs, there is not much of such neither in quantity, nor in variety. The handful of decisions of higher courts relate to liability of hosting providers for content stored by recipients of the service (User-generated Content, (UGC)) or to liability of ISSPs for content affecting personality rights of individuals.

I. Liability of Hosting Providers

620. The Czech case law regarding liability of hosting providers consist of a few cases where rightsholders or collective rights managers sued hosting providers over UGC stored and shared via the providers' platforms. Such UGC consisted of works to which the plaintiffs held the rights, therefore the plaintiffs demanded the UGC to be taken down from the platform and the providers to take actions against the works' reappearance on the platform (essentially applying a 'notice and stay-down' mechanism). Some of the cases have been ongoing for a notable time; a final verdict has not been reached due to appeals.

621. One case concerned DILIA, divadelní, literární, audiovizuální agentura, z.s. (a collective rights manager) as a plaintiff against Uloz.to cloud a.s (a hosting provider) as a defendant. The subject matter of the dispute was mainly (i) to order the defendant to remove or make unavailable to the public the digital files containing the six specified audiovisual works and to refrain from making those works available to the public in the future, and (ii) to order the defendant to refrain from allowing public access to digital files with specified extensions containing six specified audiovisual works, provided that members of the public can search for those files by entering the title of the work in a search engine provided by the defendant for that purpose.

622. The Court of First Instance upheld the second plea and dismissed the action on the first plea. The court of Appeal upheld the dismissal of the action on the first plea and amended the judgment on the second plea by specifying the obligation to refraining from allowing downloading of the works and limiting the obligation by the duration of the proprietary rights in those works and for the period during which the plaintiff exercises those rights as a collective rights manager. The Court of Appeal based its decision regarding the first plea on the principle of safe harbour. Regarding the second plea, the Court of Appeal took into account not only the time limitation, but also the limitation to specific works which have been shown to be repeatedly and unlawfully present on the defendant's service and offered to the public for download. At the same time, the Court of Appeal clarified the obligation imposed on the defendant to refrain from allowing the downloading of digital files and not from making them publicly available, since the obligation thus imposed corresponds to the content of the service provided by the defendant and the mere uploading of files to the defendant's service may not in all cases be unlawful.

623. Both the plaintiff and the defendant appealed against the judgment of the Court of Appeal, but the Supreme Court, in the case 23 Cdo 1840/2021-II, rejected the plaintiff's appeal and dismissed the defendant's appeal.

624. Another case concerns Česká národní skupina Mezinárodní federace hudebního průmyslu, z. s. (or ČNS IFPI, a voluntary association of producers of sound and music sound-visual recordings) as a plaintiff against, *inter alia*, Hellspy SE (a hosting provider) as a defendant. The subject matter of the dispute was mainly (i) to refrain from providing remuneration to a user of the defendant's website for downloading files uploaded by him by a third party, unless that user has a consent thereto, (ii) to remove the option of a search engine from the defendant's website.

625. The Court of First Instance upheld the first plea and dismissed the action on the second plea. The Court of Appeal upheld the dismissal of the action on the second plea and dismissed the action on the first plea, as well. In regard to the second plea, according to the Court of Appeal, the defendants' conduct did not exceed the conditions for limiting the defendants' liability for illegal content on their websites (the safe harbour).

626. In regard to the first plea, the Court of Appeal concluded that there was a competitive relationship between the plaintiff and the defendants, but the defendants' conduct of providing remuneration to users when the user does not have consent to make files available to the public cannot constitute conduct that satisfies the conditions of the unfair competition general clause.

627. The Supreme Court, in the case 23 Cdo 2793/2020, overturned the Court of Appeal's decision, therefore the Court of Appeal will decide the case again. However, for the Court of Appeal (and the Court of First Instance, too), the legal opinion of the Supreme Court is binding.

628. The legal opinion of the Supreme Court in this case can be summarized thus: (i) the limitation of the hosting provider's liability does not apply to the assessment of unfair competition obligations that do not arise from the provider's liability for UGC; (ii) where a provider of a service that enables users to infringe or violate intellectual property rights to a competitively significant extent through UGC pays remuneration to those users, the amount of which is dependent on the number or extent of downloads of data files stored by them by other users, without reasonably verifying that such remuneration is not paid in connection with the infringement or violation of an intellectual property right, it is in principle engaging in unfair competition.

II. Liability of ISSPs for Content Affecting Personality Rights of Individuals

629. An interesting part of the Czech law related to liability of ISSPs concerns situations, in which personality rights of an individual are (negatively) affected by content on the ISSP's service, such as search engine or a website.

630. An older, but well-known case was about a thread on an online discussion forum of a finance-related website (operated by Internet Info, s. r. o., the defendant) where the forum users had some choice words about a reality broker (PROLUX Consulting Int., s. r. o., the plaintiff). The subject matter of the case was an obligation of the defendant to remove the aforementioned thread allegedly interfering with the plaintiff's reputation. Such was granted by the Court of First Instance.

631. However, the Court of Appeal amended the judgment of the Court of First Instance, holding that the defendant was only required to remove the defamatory adjective from the name of the thread, and otherwise the judgment of the Court of First Instance was overturned. Relying on the safe harbour principle, the Court of Appeal held that the defendant could be held liable for the content of the thread, if the information was unlawful, capable of damaging the plaintiff's reputation, and false. However, the court of appeal held that the information in question was not such and thus the defendant was not liable. The Supreme Court, in the case 23 Cdo 2623/2011, dismissed the plaintiff's appeal on more or less procedural grounds.

632. Another case concerned an Internet publisher (the defendant) and an individual (the plaintiff) who felt his personality rights were negatively affected by the defendant. The subject matter of the case was, *inter alia*, an obligation for the defendant to refrain from claiming that the plaintiff and his family are related to a former president of Czechoslovakia and (ii) to request from operators of certain websites a removal of articles concerning the defendant and his family in relation to the former president. The Court of First Instance dismissed the action. The Court of Appeal essentially upheld the judgment of the Court of First Instance.

633. An interesting part of the reasoning of the Court of Appeal is that, contrary to the Court of First Instance, the Court of Appeal concluded that the defendant was liable for the publication of false information and had passive standing in the case. If the defendant has acknowledged the falsity of its allegations, withdrawn them from its website, has not republished them and has declared that it will refrain from doing so in future, the plaintiff's claim for restraint was no longer justified. The plaintiff's request that the defendant be ordered to send a notice to the website operator requesting the removal of the articles containing the contested information was also unfounded – it was the plaintiff himself, not the defendant, who had the active right to make such a request. The Supreme Court, in the case 25 Cdo 27/2020, dismissed the plaintiff's appeal on more or less procedural grounds.

Part IV. Intellectual Rights

Chapter 1. Patent Law

§1. Patent Protection in the Czech Republic

634. Technical inventions can be protected in the Czech Republic in several ways. The first is national patent protection, the second is utility model protection[811] and finally the third is European patent protection. Although the Czech Republic has signed up to the enhanced cooperation under the European patent with unitary effect,[812] the Czech Parliament has not yet ratified the UPC Agreement (as of May 2022). This means that it will not yet be possible to apply for this form of unitary protection for the territory of the Czech Republic, but it is still possible to protect an invention in the form of a European patent granted by the European Patent Office under the European Patent Convention.

635. In the Czech Republic, patent protection is regulated by Act No. 527/1990 Sb., on Inventions and Improvements, as amended (hereinafter referred to as

811. A utility model is sometimes considered a more accessible version of patent protection. It can also protect technical solutions that are novel, industrially applicable, and that are beyond mere technical skill. With regard to the right to utility model protection and the requirements of a utility model application, similar principles apply as in the case of an application for patent protection. Nevertheless, utility model protection is quicker and less costly compared to patent protection. The procedure is based on the registration principle [Roman Horáček, Karel Čada, Petr Hajn, *Práva k průmyslovému vlastnictví*, p. 248 (C.H.Beck 3rd ed. 2017)]. A utility model application is subject to an examination of the registrability of the utility model. Thus, the Industrial Property Office enters the utility model in the Register without examining whether the subject matter of the application is eligible for protection in terms of novelty and being beyond mere technical skill. However, all methods of manufacture or work activities and biological reproductive materials are excluded from the possibility of protection by utility models [s. 3/c Utility Models Act]. The maximum duration of a utility model protection, subject to payment of renewal fees, is half that of a patent, i.e., 10 years [s. 15/2 Utility Models Act].

812. The regulatory framework for the European patent with unitary effect is based on two regulations adopted by the European Parliament and the Council in 2012 (Regulation (EU) No 1257/2012 of the European Parliament and of the Council of 17 Dec. 2012 implementing enhanced cooperation in the area of the creation of unitary patent protection; Council Regulation (EU) No 1260/2012 of 17 Dec. 2012 implementing enhanced cooperation in the area of the creation of unitary patent protection with regard to the applicable translation arrangements). The framework is complemented by the Agreement on the Unified Patent Court. Unlike the EU regulation, this is an international treaty establishing the Unified Patent Court as a common judicial body of the contracting parties for the adjudication of patent disputes. It also contains the Agreement on European Patent Litigation, which contains procedural rules.

'Patents Act'). The substantive patent law is fully harmonized with the European Patent Convention and the Directive 98/44/EC of the European Parliament and of the Council of 6 July 1998 on the legal protection of biotechnological inventions. The Czech Republic also provides additional protection for inventions in the pharmaceutical and phytosanitary industries. The Industrial Property Office [*Úřad průmyslového vlastnictví*] grants supplementary protection certificates for substances protected in the Czech Republic by a valid patent if they are active substances of products that are subject to registration before being placed on the market. The legal framework is contained in two EU Regulations. These are Regulation (EC) No 1610/96 of the European Parliament and of the Council of 23 July 1996 concerning the creation of supplementary protection certificates for plant protection products and Regulation (EC) No 469/2009 of the European Parliament and of the Council of 6 May 2009 concerning supplementary protection certificates for medicinal products (codified version).

§2. Conditions for Patentability

636. Patents are granted for inventions that are new, the result of inventive activity and capable of industrial application.[813] Not only new products and technologies can be patented, but also chemically produced substances, pharmaceuticals, industrial production micro-organisms, as well as biotechnological processes and products obtained by means thereof. In contrast, discoveries or scientific theories, computer programs, new plant varieties and animal breeds, and methods of treating humans and animals cannot be patented.[814] However, if these objects and processes become part of a technical solution, then the patentability of such an entity is not excluded.[815] Besides, the Patent Act also provides for what categories of technical results patents are not granted for.[816] Thus, patents are not granted for 'inventions the use of which would be contrary to public policy or good morals'.[817] Similarly, plant varieties and animal breeds, as well as biological methods of growing plants or breeding animals, cannot be patented.

637. With regard to novelty, the Patents Act provides that 'an invention is new if it is not part of the state of the art'.[818] The state of the art is every information that has been made available to the public in writing, orally, by use or in any other manner before the date from which the right of priority is due,[819] including the content of applications for inventions (at national, international or European level), provided that they are 'made public on or after the date from which the applicant has a priority right'.[820]

813. *See* s. 3/1 Patents Act.
814. *See* s. 3/2 Patents Act.
815. *See* s. 3/3 Patents Act.
816. *See* s. 4 Patents Act.
817. *See* s. 4/a Patents Act.
818. *See* s. 5/1 Patents Act.
819. *See* s. 5/1 Patents Act.
820. *See* s. 5/3 Patents Act.

638. In addition, the Patents Act contains a grace period,[821] which means that the state of the art 'shall not be such a disclosure of an invention which has not taken place earlier than six months before the filing of the application for the invention and which results, directly or indirectly, from an obvious misuse in relation to the applicant or his predecessor in title or from the fact that the applicant or his predecessor in title has exhibited the invention at an official or officially recognized exhibition pursuant to an international treaty'.[822] In the case of an international exhibition, it is necessary to state at the time of filing the application that the invention has been exhibited and to certify this fact to the Industrial Property Office within four months from the date of filing the application.

639. Furthermore, the invention must be the result of inventive activity, by which the Patents Act means that the invention 'does not arise in a manner obvious to a person skilled in the art'.[823] However, the content of applications which have not been published as of the priority date is not applicable for the assessment of this requirement. This condition's purpose is to ensure that the invention contributes to state of the art. The law provides for a presumption that the invention is not obvious to a person skilled in the art. Thus, if the Industrial Property Office takes a different view, it must prove in the patent proceedings that the invention was obvious to a person skilled in the art.

640. An expert is a fictitious person with knowledge appropriate to the field of technology who can make an informed determination that patentable inventions are not merely the result of ordinary handicrafts or routine work. An expert may also be a collective of persons according to their overlap in different fields of technology. The assessment of novelty and inventive activity differs in particular in that while assessing inventive activity, the state of the art does not include non-disclosed applications for inventions and allows for a combination of sources of information.

641. Industrial applicability means that the subject matter can be manufactured or otherwise used (at any time reproduced, produced or utilized) in industry and agriculture,[824] and can enhance the knowledge in that fields in some sense. In this regard, it is presumed, that the invention satisfies the utility requirement. However, in case of doubts, the Office may invite the applicant to submit the proof of invention's utility in the proceedings.[825] In respect of the utility requirement, the Patents Act further provides that 'methods of surgical or therapeutic treatment of the human or animal body and diagnostic methods used on the human or animal body'[826] are not considered industrially exploitable.

821. *See* Vojtěch Chloupek & Kateřina Hartvichová et al., *Patentový zákon. Komentář*, p. 39 (C.H. Beck 2016).
822. *See* s. 5/5 Patents Act.
823. *See* s. 6/1 Patents Act.
824. *See* s. 7 of the Patents Act.
825. *See* s. 26/3 Patents Act.
826. *See* s. 3/4 Patents Act.

§3. National Patent Proceedings

642. The procedure for the patents' granting is an administrative procedure with the deviations from the formal proceedings as provided for in the Patents Act.[827] Among the traditional administrative rules, the Patents Act explicitly provides different regulations for the waiving time limits,[828] an inspection of the file,[829] identification hearings[830] or appeal proceedings,[831] as well as the conditions for the legal representation on behalf of foreign nationals.[832]

643. The procedure for granting a patent starts with the filing of a patent application with the Industrial Property Office.[833] The application must indicate the inventor or that he or she wishes to remain anonymous.[834] An administrative fee is payable for the filing of the application.[835]

644. An application for an invention may relate to only 'one invention or a group of inventions linked together in such a way as to constitute a single general inventive idea'.[836] The application must explain the invention 'so clearly and completely that a person skilled in the art can carry it out'.[837]

645. Patent application proceedings may be suspended if litigation is initiated in respect of the right to the patent litigation.[838] If the applicant requests that the application procedure be maintained, he or she should continue in the proceedings within three months of the legal force of the court decision on the patent right. Then, the priority right shall be maintained.[839]

646. As regards the priority period, the filing of the application allows the patent applicant to apply for a priority right; however, if such a right already exists under an international treaty (Paris Union Convention or priority right derived from Agreement on Trade-Related Aspects of Intellectual Property Rights (TRIPS), the applicant must invoke it already in the application and prove it by a priority document, otherwise it disregarded.[840]

827. *See* s. 63 Patents Act.
828. *See* s. 65 Patents Act.
829. *See* s. 66 Patents Act.
830. *See* s. 67 Patents Act.
831. *See* s. 68 Patents Act.
832. *See* s. 70 Patents Act.
833. *See* s. 24 Patents Act.
834. *See* Art. 4ter Paris Union Convention; s. 25/2 Patents Act.
835. *See* s. 24/5 Patents Act.
836. *See* s. 24/5 Patents Act.
837. *See* s. 26/2 Patents Act.
838. *See* ss 28 et seq. Patents Act.
839. *See* s 28/3 Patents Act.
840. *See* s. 27 Patents Act.

647. After the expiry of eighteen months following the priority date, the invention application is published, although such publication can be made available also earlier at the applicant's request.[841]

648. Following the application filling, the Office carries out a preliminary examination of the invention application. In the course of this examination, the subsequent points are examined: whether the application does not contain subject matter which is manifestly contrary to the conditions of patentability,[842] whether the applicant has described the invention in a sufficiently clear and precise wat to enable a person skilled in the art to reproduce it,[843] whether the application does not contain subject matter which is not considered to be an invention[844] or excluded from patentability for reasons of public interest or morality,[845] whether the application is free from defects which prevent its publication, or whether the applicant has paid the corresponding administrative fees. Should the above grounds exist, the Office shall refuse the application; however, it shall allow the applicant to make revisions before doing so.[846]

649. The next part of the proceedings entails a full substantive examination of the invention application. At this point, upon the request of the applicant, another person or ex officio, it is verified whether all the conditions for patentability are fulfilled.[847] Additionally, after the publication of the application, 'anyone may submit observations to the Office on the patentability of its subject matter'. However, these persons do not become parties to the proceedings.[848] The proceedings may be dismissed at this point if no request for an examination is filed within the prescribed period (maximum thirty-six months from the filing of the invention application) and the Industrial Property Office does not carry out such an examination even ex officio.[849] The application is then rejected (after the opportunity to comment on the grounds) if the conditions for patentability are not satisfied.[850] Alternatively, if the conditions are met, the Office grants the patent to the applicant.[851] The applicant then becomes the owner of the patent. The patent owner shall be issued with a patent certificate containing the name of the inventor, the description of the invention, and the patent claims, the grant of which shall be announced in the Bulletin of the Industrial Property Office.

841. *See* s. 31 Patents Act.
842. *See* s. 3/1 Patents Act.
843. *See* s. 26/2 Patents Act.
844. *See* s. 3/2 Patents Act.
845. *See* s. 4 Patents Act.
846. *See* s. 30/3 and 4 Patents Act.
847. *See* s. 33 Patents Act.
848. *See* s. 32 Patents Act.
849. *See* s. 30/5 Patents Act.
850. *See* s. 34 Patents Act.
851. *See* s. 34/3 Patents Act.

§4. The Right to a Patent

650. An inventor is defined as someone who has completed an invention by his or her own creative work. He or she has the right to a patent on the invention,[852] as well as his or her successors in title.[853] Suppose more than one person has participated in the creation of the invention. In that case, all these co-inventors are entitled to a patent to the extent of their participation in a technical result. The right to a patent is a property right (the right to dispose of the rights in the invention and to file an application or to transfer the right to be granted the patent certificate). It should be distinguished from a personality-invention-right (the inventor's or co-inventors' right to be identified by names in the application and in the patent registry). Nevertheless, only the right to the patent, which is of a property nature, can be transferred.

§5. Enterprise Invention

651. An enterprise invention is not a special category of invention but is an invention that is created in an employment relationship. Even upon the termination of the employment relationship, the rights and obligations in connection with the enterprise invention remain unaffected.[854] Regarding enterprise inventions, the right to the patent passes to the employer upon the statutory assignment.[855] The employee is obliged to notify the employer in writing of the creation of the invention and to provide the employer with all supporting documents to enable the employer to assess whether or not to claim the right to the patent.[856] Since the statutory provision allows parties for contractual freedom, it may be agreed otherwise by contract. The employer must invoke the right to the patent within three months of the notice, otherwise the right reverts to the inventor. Moreover, both parties, the inventor and the employer, must maintain confidentiality.[857] When the employer claims the right to the patent, the employer is obliged to pay the inventor a reasonable remuneration according to the technical and economic importance of the invention while taking into account the proportion between his or her share in the creation of the invention and the extent of the inventor's contribution.[858] If the remuneration already paid is apparently disproportionate to the revenues obtained by the exploitation of the invention, the inventor is entitled to an additional settlement.

---

852. *See* Roman Horáček, Karel Čada & Petr Hajn, *Práva k průmyslovému vlastnictví*, p. 113 (C.H.Beck 3rd ed. 2017).
853. *See* s. 8 Patents Act.
854. *See* s. 10 Patents Act.
855. *See* s. 9 Patents Act.
856. *See* s. 9 Patents Act.
857. *See* s. 9/3 Patents Act.
858. *See* s. 9/4 Patents Act.

§6. Disposition with Patents

652. After the patent is granted, the patent owner has the exclusive right to 'exploit the invention, to give a consent to exploit the invention to third persons or to transfer the patent to them'.[859] However, the assignment of a patent must always be distinguished from the assignment of the right to a patent (the transfer of the right to being granted protection). The transfer of a patent is based on an innominate contract. Since a patent is a right registered in a patent register, the effects of the transfer of a patent against third parties do not take effect until it is entered into the patent register.

653. A patent may also be licensed on the basis of a licence agreement, the general elements of which are regulated in the Civil Code. The licensing agreement takes effect against third parties upon registration in the patent register.[860]

654. Besides licensing or transferring the patent, the patent may also be subject to a compulsory licence or an offer of license. A compulsory licence means the possibility to exploit the patent if 'the patent owner [does] not exploit the invention at all or does not exploit it sufficiently and has not accepted a proper offer to conclude a licence agreement within a reasonable period of time', and if there is a public interest in exploiting the patent.[861] With regard to the 'offer of a licence', if the applicant or the patent proprietor declares that he will 'grant to anyone the right to exploit the invention (offer of a licence), the right to exploit the invention shall be conferred on anyone who accepts the offer of a licence and notifies the applicant or the patent proprietor in writing'.[862]

655. Co-ownership of a patent means that the patent rights belong to several persons, co-owners, who exercise joint ownership of the patent. Unless otherwise agreed between the co-owners, the right to exploit the invention belongs to each of them.[863] The consent of all co-owners is then needed (unless otherwise agreed) when a patent is licensed or transferred. Each co-owner is entitled to transfer his or her co-ownership interest to one of the co-owners without the consent of the others. Besides, the transfer of the co-ownership interest to third parties is possible but is conditioned by the co-owner's pre-emptive right; the transfer offer must be made in writing and at least one month in advance.[864]

§7. Patents Rights and Its Limitations

656. The scope of patent protection is defined by the patent claims, which are usually supported with descriptions and drawings.[865] No person may manufacture,

859. *See* s. 11/1 Patents Act.
860. *See* s. 2358/3 Civil Code.
861. *See* s. 20 Patents Act.
862. *See* s. 19 Patents Act.
863. *See* s. 16/2 Patents Act.
864. *See* s. 16/4 Patents Act.
865. *See* s. 12 Patents Act.

offer or market the subject matter of a patent or use a process which would be the subject matter of a patent without the patent owner's consent.[866] These activities are referred to as direct exploitation of patent rights. In addition, the possibility of indirect exploitation exists, which protects, for example, supplying 'a person other than the person entitled to exploit the patented invention with means relating to an essential element of that invention'.[867]

657. The law also specifies situations where patent rights are not infringed. Exceptions and limitations include the use of the invention for non-commercial purposes.[868] Similarly, the rights of the patent owner are not infringed if the protected invention is used, for example, on 'ships of other countries which are members of the Paris Union Convention for the Protection of Industrial Property [...] when such ships enter the Czech Republic temporarily or incidentally if the products are used here only for the purposes of the ship or in the construction or operation of aircraft or vehicles of Union countries or parts of such aircraft or vehicles when they enter the Czech Republic temporarily or incidentally'[869] as well as in activities carried out with the subject matter of the invention for experimental purposes.[870]

658. Further, the patent does not operate against those who, prior to the priority right, exploited the invention independently of the inventor or patent owner. Such persons have what is known as a prior-user-right.[871] This right is proprietary and non-transferable.[872]

659. If a product containing an invention protected by a patent is put on the market within the States forming the EEA, the principle of exhaustion of rights applies. The patent proprietor then has no right to prohibit third parties from dealing with the product covered by the patent if the product has been placed on the market by or with the patent owner's consent.[873]

§8. Duration of Protection, Termination and Revocation of a Patent

660. The maximum term of patent protection is twenty years from filing the patent application.[874] A maintenance fee must be paid each year, failing which the patent protection is terminated.[875] In this regard, the law also provides a grace

866. *See* s. 13 Patents Act.
867. *See* s. 13a Patents Act.
868. *See* s. 18/d Patents Act.
869. *See* s. 18/a/b Patents Act.
870. *See* s. 18/e Patents Act.
871. *See* s. 17 Patents Act.
872. *See* Vojtěch Chloupek & Kateřina Hartvichová et al., *Patentový zákon. Komentář*, p. 150 (C.H.Beck 2016).
873. *See* s. 13b Patents Act.
874. *See* s. 21/1 Patents Act.
875. *See* s. 22/b Patents Act.

period of six months by which the maintenance fees must be paid, but with an additional 100% surcharge. If the patentee exceeds even this time limit, the patent will lapse.

661. Generally speaking, it is necessary to distinguish the termination of a patent from its revocation.[876] While the termination of a patent operates *ex nunc* and the patent is always cancelled in its entirety, the revocation operates *ex tunc* and may even concern only a part of the patent.[877] The Industrial Property Office may revoke a patent, in particular, if it is found that the invention did not meet the conditions of patentability, if the scope of protection under the patent has been extended beyond the contents of the original application for the invention, or if the patentee is not entitled to it under not being the inventor in relation to the invention in question.[878]

662. Finally, we must underline that a patent's termination and revocation are not interdependent in order. Besides the conditions for the termination described above, a patent is also terminated by expiry of the term or surrender by the proprietor.[879]

§9. Patent Protection for Computer-Implemented Inventions

663. Historically, computer programs have been protected under copyright law in Europe since the 1970s. The computer programs are protected as literary works within the meaning of Article 2 of the Berne Convention.[880] This approach is adopted by Directive 2009/24/EC of the European Parliament and of the Council of 23 April 2009 on the legal protection of computer programs (codified version). The Article 1(1) Software Directive, in line with the Article 10(1) TRIPS Agreement, provides that the object of protection is always the expression of a program in any form in particular in the form of source or object code, while explicitly excluding from protection the ideas and principles on which the program is based. The only criterion for the copyright protection of a program is its originality, i.e., the fact that the program is the author's own intellectual creation.[881] Similarly, the identical requirements for computer programs protection are set out in sections 2(2) and 65 of the Copyright Act.

664. The consequence of the copyright regime for software protection is, among other things, that the author of a computer program cannot claim copyright against the author of another quite identical program, which was created by the author's own intellectual activity and thus represents his or her own intellectual creation

876. *See* Roman Horáček, Karel Čada, Petr Hajn, *Práva k průmyslovému vlastnictví*, p. 189 (C.H.Beck 3rd ed. 2017).
877. *See* s. 23/3 Patents Act.
878. *See* s. 23/1 Patents Act.
879. *See* s. 22 Patents Act.
880. *See* Art. 4 WIPO Copyright Treaty; Art. 10(1) TRIPS Agreement.
881. *See* Art. 1(3) Software Directive.

within the meaning of the CJEU's case law. This means that copyright does not protect the functionality of the computer program[882] or any ideas or principles on which the computer program is based.[883]

665. Differently to copyright, patent law protects the technical idea underlying the invention. For computer programs, this would mean that they can be protected abstractly and independently of their specific formulation in a computer language. The owner of a software patent in the USA can enforce the rights under the patent not only against the unauthorized copying of the same program, but also against the producer of a program with a similar function.[884]

666. Under the Czech patent law, a patent holder can prohibit anyone from commercially manufacturing the protected products or commercially using the protected process.[885] However, according to section 3/2/c Patents Act, programs for data processing systems are excluded from patent protection. According to the express provision of the law, they do not constitute protectable inventions. Only inventions with a technical character that solve a technical task and have technical features can be protected. Nevertheless, according to section 3/3 Patents Act, the exclusion of computer programs applies only to programs as such, i.e., not to inventions which, in addition to other parts, also contain a program.

667. These provisions show that a standard computer program cannot receive patent protection without further technical contribution. Conversely, a product or process that is technical in nature may be patentable, even if the claimed subject matter includes a computer program. Moreover, a computer program independently, or captured in the medium or as a signal, may be considered an invention if, when run on a computer, it can produce a technical effect which goes beyond the regular physical interaction between the program and the computer. We speak then of computer-implemented inventions. Examples of technical effects may also include, for example, the control of an industrial process, the processing of data representing a physical entity, or the control of the internal functions of a computer.[886]

668. The concept of computer-implemented inventions is based on the decision-making practice of the Technical Boards of Appeal of the European Patent Office (T0208/84, T0158/88, T1173/97). This practice first allowed inventions involving a computer, a computer network or other programmable device to be patented even though one or more elements of such an invention were carried out by means of a computer program or programs. However, protection is conditional on the technical contribution of the invention to the state of the art.

---

882. *See* Case C-406/10 *SAS Institute Inc. v. World Programming Ltd.*, 2 May 2012, ECLI-:EU:C:2012:259, para. 39.
883. *See* Recital 11 of the Software Directive.
884. *See* Jan Tomíšek In *Právo informačních technologií*, p. 183 (Radim Polčák ed., Wolters Kluwer 2018).
885. *See* s. 13 Patents Act.
886. *See* Vojtěch Chloupek & Kateřina Hartvichová et al., *Patentový zákon. Komentář*, p. 12 (C.H.Beck 2016).

669. According to the judgment of the Municipal Court in Prague of 21 December 2017, for example, Patent No. 297879, entitled 'Method of collecting, recording and disclosing information on healthcare and its results and its use', could be protected by patent protection. The essence of the patent was in a system for exchanging healthcare information, in particular medical records. Although the court was critical of the novelty of the claimed invention, it found that the claimed invention was technical in nature and therefore not excluded from patentability.

670. The claims of the contested patent described a method of collecting, recording and disclosing healthcare information, its results, and its use, comprising a method of controlling a networked computer system comprising a central computer storage device, multiple computer storage devices of a healthcare professional and a healthcare facility, and multiple computer storage devices of a client, interconnected in a public communication network and/or communication links. According to the section 3 Patents Act, implementing a method according to the invention must require technical considerations. Such technical considerations must include the existence of a technical problem that the claimed invention solves and related patent claims. In the discussed case, the computer-implemented invention was vested with a demanded technical effect within the meaning of section 3/1/c Patents Act. Although the invention contained also non-technical features, such as collecting, recording and disclosing information about healthcare and its results, the invention was endowed with at least one feature having a technical character.

Chapter 2. Trademarks

§1. Designation Rights

671. Trademarks belong to the group of industrial property rights, namely to the rights which subject matter is signs. The main function of these intangible goods is the identification function, as they serve to mark products or services, to mark persons or enterprises.[887] Designation rights include trademarks, geographical indications/designations of origin, trade names, protection of the name of a natural person, the name of legal entities, domain names, logotypes, or identifications of copyrighted works.

672. Designation rights may relate to the designation of a specific object (product, service, commercial establishment, etc.) or a specific entity (natural person, legal entity). In this respect, we divide designations into (i) 'subject' and 'object' designations. Another criterion that divides sign rights is the legal classification of these rights. There can be either rights of (ii) absolute or relative nature, (iii) economic rights or rights attached to the person (moral rights).

673. From the point of view of this classification, trademarks are signs that are object-based (attached to goods or services). Nevertheless, trademark rights are also absolute in nature and belong to the group of property (economic) rights.

674. A particular sign may be the subject of multiple sign rights at any one time. For example, the name of a natural person as a subject sign (enjoying protection under sections 77 to 78 Civil Code) may also be subject to rights relating to object signs. Thus, the name may constitute a tradename, or a trademark.[888] Similar conclusions apply to the overlapping protection of absolute and relative property rights. Unauthorized use of a particular sign may result in infringement of the registered trademark and at the same time in unfair competition proceedings.[889]

675. Trademarks are protected at the national level by Act No. 441/2003 Sb., on Trademarks and on Amendments to Act No. 6/2002 on Judgments, Judges, Assessors and State Judgment Administration and on Amendments to Some Other Acts (hereinafter referred to as 'Trademarks Act').

676. A trademark may also be protected simultaneously by different industrial property regimes. For example, the icon as a graphic symbol[890] which is protected as a registered industrial design may be protected as a figurative mark. Although the

887. *See* Helena Pullmannová, *Ochrana obchodního jména a její projevy ve známkoprávní reformě EU*, p, 16 (Leges 2019); Pavel Koukal, *Zákon o ochranných známkách: komentář*, p. XXVIII (Pavel Koukal et al. Wolters Kluwer 2017).

888. *See, e.g.*, the word mark JAN BECHER, registration No. 262435.

889. *See* Judgements of the High Court in Prague, Case No. 3 Cmo 397/95, 3 Cmo 1446/94; the Judgement of the Supreme Court, Case No. 23 Cdo 1961/2004.

890. *See* s. 2/b Industrial Designs Act.

concurrence of protection is not expressly formulated in the Trademarks Act the admissibility of concurrent protections is established by both case law and legal doctrine.[891]

§2. Purpose of Trademark Rights and Its Function

677. The purpose of trademark law is to protect signs which serve in the course of trade to distinguish products or services of different producers. A trademark serves a number of functions, which play role in particular in (i) the assessment of distinctiveness, (ii) the absolute or relative grounds examination, (iii) the scope of protection in trademark litigations.

678. The primary function of any sign is the distinctive function. The trademark is intended to identify the producer and to ensure that goods of the same manufacturer are offered to the consumer under the same sign.[892] In order for a trademark to play its role in the system of competition, it must guarantee that all the goods or services it designates have been produced or provided under the control of a single entity to which responsibility for their quality can be attributed.[893] In addition to this main function, the trademark also has the function of 'guaranteeing the quality of the products/services' coming from a particular manufacturer;[894] a promotional and advertising function;[895] or the investment function.[896] The distinctive function is also linked to the competitive function, as the trademark is intended to help producers or service providers to establish themselves on the market, to maintain or strengthen their position in competition with competing producers.[897]

891. *See* Telec Ivo & Pavel Tůma Ivo, *Autorský Zákon: Komentář*, p. 1176 (C.H. Beck 2nd ed. 2019). Pavel Koukal et al., *Zákon o Ochranných Známkách: Komentář*, p. XXXIX (Wolters Kluwer 2017); Judgement of the Supreme Court of 23 Sep. 2011, Case No. 23 Cdo 2500/2010.

892. *See* Judgements of the Supreme Administrative Court, Case No. 6 A 39/2001, No. 6 A 61/2002.

893. *See* Case C 299/99, *Koninklijke Philips Electronics NV v. Remington Consumer Products Ltd*, 18 Jun. 2002, ECLI:EU:C:2002:377, para. 30; Case C-323/09, *Interflora Inc. Marks & Spencer plc, Flowers Direct Online Ltd*, 22 Sep. 2011, ECLI:EU:C:2011:604, para. 37; Case C-206/01, *Arsenal Football Club plc v. Matthew Reed*, 12 Nov. 2002, ECLI:EU:C:2002:651, para. 48.

894. *See* Case C-324/09, *L'Oréal SA v. eBay International AG*, 12 Jul. 2011, ECLI:EU:C:2011:474, paras 80–81; Case C-487/07, *L'Oréal SA v. Bellure NV*, 18 Jun. 2009, ECLI:EU:C:2009:378, para. 58; Case C-337/95, *Parfums Christian Dior SA and Parfums Christian Dior BV/Evora BV*, 4 Nov. 1997, ECLI:EU:C:1997:517, paras 54, 59.

895. *See* Case C-64/02 P, *Erpo Möbelwerke v. OHIM*, 21 Oct. 2004, ECLI:EU:C:2004:645, para. 35; Case C-323/09, *Interflora Inc. v. Marks & Spencer plc, Flowers Direct Online Ltd*, 22 Sep. 2011, ECLI:EU:C:2011:604, paras 40, 55.

896. *See* Joined Cases C-236/08 and C-238/08, *Google France and Google* [2010] ECLI-:EU:C:2010:159, para. 77; C-487/07, *L'Oréal SA v. Bellure NV*, C-487/07, 18 Jun. 2009, ECLI-:EU:C:2009:378, para. 58; Case C-323/09, *Interflora Inc. v. Marks & Spencer plc, Flowers Direct Online Ltd*, 22 Sep. 2011, ECLI:EU:C:2011:604, paras 60 to 63.

897. *See* the Judgement of the Supreme Administrative Court of 28 Nov. 2008, Case No. 4 As 1/2008.

§3. Notion of Trademark and Its Categories

679. A trademark may be any sign (words, names, colours, designs, letters, numerals, shapes, sounds, combinations of these elements) which is capable of being expressed in the trademark register in a manner which enables the competent authorities and the public to identify clearly and precisely the subject matter of the protection afforded to the proprietor of the trademark and which is capable of distinguishing the goods or services for which it is protected from identical goods or services on the market provided from other commercial entities.[898] Thus, a trademark cannot exist on its own, but only ever in connection with the specific products which it designates or the specific services which are provided under that mark (this concept is known as the speciality principle of the trademark protection).

680. In general, trademark protection is acquired by registering a sign as a trademark in the register operated by the Industrial Property Office in Prague [*Úřad průmyslového vlastnictví*].[899] However, trademarks can also come into existence by means of an international application within the meaning of the Madrid Agreement Concerning the International Registration of Marks or the Protocol to the Madrid Agreement. Moreover, EU-wide trademark protection may also be acquired by registration in a register kept by the EU Intellectual Property Office (EU Trademarks). The last type of trademark protection that a sign may obtain in the Czech Republic is the well-known trademarks within the meaning of Article 6bis of the Paris Union Convention (here, the registration is not required and protection in relation to all classes of goods and services is provided if the sign is well-known by the general public).

681. The proprietor of the trademark shall have the exclusive right to designate his or her goods or services by the trademark or to use it in connection with those goods or services.[900] Nobody else may use a sign identical or confusing with his trademark for identical or similar goods or services without the consent of the proprietor.[901]

§4. Trademarks Registration Procedure

682. Not every word, image or 3D object can be registered as a sign. The absolute grounds for refusal are regulated in section 4 Trademarks Act which specifies category of signs that cannot be protected as a trademark.[902] Of particular importance is the exclusion for trademarks which lack any distinctive character for the goods or services,[903] which consist exclusively of signs or indications which have

898. *See* s. 1a Trademarks Act.
899. *See* s. 2/a Trademarks Act.
900. *See* s. 8/1 Trademarks Act.
901. *See* s. 8/2 Trademarks Act.
902. *See also* the Judgement of the Supreme Administrative Court, Case No. 9A 62/2010; decision of the Industrial Property Office, Case No. 0-500282, 0-520313.
903. *See* s. 4/b Trademarks Act.

become customary in the current language to designate the goods or services,[904] or which consist exclusively of signs or indications which may serve in trade to designate the kind, quality, quantity, intended purpose, value, geographical origin, the time of production of the goods or of rendering of the service, or other characteristics of the goods or services.[905]

683. The purpose of the absolute grounds of trademark application refusal is not to monopolize selling of goods or services through trademark protection and leave it accessible for the use of other competitors. Both the issue of distinctiveness[906] and the necessity to keep a sign free for relevant reasons defined in section 4 Trademarks Act are ultimately assessed according to the public's perception, and they correlate only to the goods or services specified by the applicant in the trademark application.[907] Thus, words describing a specific product cannot be registered as trademarks for that product, but they can be registered as trademarks for other goods.

684. Nevertheless, a sign which is not distinctive in itself or for which there would generally exist the necessity to keep it free for other competitors can still be protected if it has acquired secondary meaning in the trade as a trademark.[908] This means that the generic sign, for example, must have acquired meaning as a trademark at least among the majority of the relevant public, i.e., among the majority of consumers or users of the goods it designates.[909]

685. A further requirement for registration is that the trademark must be designated for specific goods or services classes. Thus, in the consumer's mind, a connection must have been established between the sign and the business or origin of the source to which the trademark application relates. This requirement contrasts trademark protection from tradenames, which protects the name under which a commercial entity is registered in the commercial register.[910] While a tradename protects the sign as such,[911] a trademark protects the sign only in relation to the registered goods or services. These are systematically listed in different classes of goods or services known as the Nice Trademark Classification. For example, in the case of software production, a sign can be registered for a software application, related business materials or services connected. As a rule, we can probably speak

904. *See* s. 4/d Trademarks Act.
905. *See* s. 4/c Trademarks Act.
906. *See* s. 4/b Trademarks Act.
907. An example of a descriptive mark would be FAST AND EXTENT for the Internet searching services – classes 35 and 42 of the Nice Classification.
908. *See* s. 5 Trademarks Act.
909. *See* the Judgement of the Supreme Administrative Court of 18 Apr. 2012, Case No. 1 As 40/2012.
910. *See* s. 423/1 Civil Code.
911. *See* Jarmila Pokorná & Eva Večerková, *Firemní právo v České republice: Vývoj a srovnání s Německem a Slovenskem*, p. 62 (Masarykova univerzita 2013).

of goods when distributing standard computer programs,[912] whereas one must speak of services when producing individual software or offering software-as-service in the form of cloud services.[913]

686. An application for a national trademark is filed by the applicant with the Industrial Property Office.[914] By filing the application, the applicant obtains the right of priority to the sign against other competitors on the market.[915] After the application has been filed, the Office shall verify whether the application has all the necessary requirements. Suppose it finds defects that would prevent further proceedings (e.g., incorrect classification of the list of goods or services, missing power of attorney). In that case, the Office shall invite the applicant to remedy the imperfections within a specified period.

687. Should the applicant fail to respond to the Office's notice and fail to remedy the defects, the Office will refuse the trademark application by administrative decision.[916] However, if the application's defects concern only part of the list of goods or services, the Office shall refuse the application to that extent only. If the application does not have such defects or if the applicant has remedied them, the Office carries out a substantive examination of the trademark application based on the absolute grounds for refusal as provided by section 4 Trademarks Act.

688. If the sign applied for is eligible for registration, the trademark application is published electronically in the Office Bulletin. Within a period of three months from the date of the publication, persons whose previously acquired rights may be affected by the published sign may file an opposition to the trademark registration.[917] The filing of opposition to the registration of a trademark is based on the relative grounds of non-registrability of trademarks,[918] in particular on the fact that the sign is confusingly similar to an existing trademark, benefits from the reputation of the trademark or interferes with an earlier right from another industrial property rights. When filing an opposition, it is necessary to pay an administrative fee, describe the circumstances justifying the trademark application's refusal, and support the opposition with evidence.[919]

689. The likelihood of confusion, which is prohibited by section 7 Trademarks Act, must exist either that both the applied and already registered sign is visually, orally, and semantically similar or that the goods or services for which the mark is used are so close that there is a risk of confusion or association.[920] Thus, the risk of confusion depends not only on the similarity of signs, but also on the proximity of

912. *See* Class 9 of the Nice classification.
913. *See* Class 42 of the Nice classification.
914. *See* s. 19/1 Trademarks Act.
915. *See* s. 20/1 Trademarks Act; Art. 4 Paris Union Convention.
916. *See* s. 21/3 Trademarks Act.
917. *See* s. 25 Trademarks Act.
918. *See* s. 7 Trademarks Act.
919. *See* s. 25/2 Trademarks Act.
920. *See* s. 7/1/b Trademarks Act.

the goods or services concerned. How strong the likelihood of confusion must be also depending on the distinctive character of the marks. A very concise and distinctive mark enjoys greater protection than a mark which is not particularly distinctive in itself and has only just been declared registrable.

690. In the case of comments, no administrative fee is payable, and they may be submitted within the same time limit as opposition.[921] However, a person who files comments does not (unlike an opposition applicant) become a party to the administrative procedure to the sign applied for trademark registration. This means that he or she cannot, for example, appeal against the decision of the Industrial Property Office. However, that person will be informed about the outcome of the trademark application proceedings.

691. If opposition is filed after the deadline by an unauthorized person or is not filed properly, the Office shall reject them without examining their merits.[922] Otherwise, the Office shall send the opposition to the trademark applicant for replica, and thereafter, the Office will make a decision on merit. If it appears from the contents of the file and on the basis of the facts alleged and proved that the applied-for sign infringes the opponent's earlier rights protected by law, the Office shall refuse the application. If, on the other hand, the Office concludes that the sign applied for does not interfere with the opponent's earlier rights, it shall reject the opposition.[923]

692. Should the opponent justify his or her opposition on the grounds of interference with an earlier right to a trademark which has been valid for at least five years, he or she is obliged, at the request of the applicant to prove to the Office that he or she has duly used his or her rights to that earlier trademark during the five years preceding the date of filing of the application by the applicant.[924] If he or she fails to do so, the Office shall reject the opposition. The result of the opposition proceedings shall be published by the Office in the Bulletin.[925]

693. If no opposition is filed, or if the opposition submissions are settled in favour of the trademark applicant, the sign shall be entered in the Trademarks Registry. The applicant thus becomes the proprietor of the trademark, and the notice of registration is published in the Office Bulletin.[926] Otherwise, the Office shall reject the application; alternatively, it shall reject it in part and enter the partially applied for sign in the Trademarks Registry.

921. *See* s. 24/1 Trademarks Act.
922. *See* s. 26/1 Trademarks Act.
923. *See* s. 26/3 and 4 Trademarks Act.
924. *See* s. 26a and s. 13 Trademarks Act.
925. *See* s. 26/5 Trademarks Act.
926. *See* s. 28/2 Trademarks Act.

§5. Beginning, Duration and Scope of the Protection

694. Trademark protection arises on the registration date of the registered sign in the Trademarks Registry.[927] It establishes the trademark's owner the exclusive rights to use the trademark concerning the goods and services for which the sign is registered.[928]

695. The period for which the registered sign is protected is ten years from the time of filing the application.[929] Upon expiry of that period, the trademark protection shall lapse.[930] However, the protection can be extended indefinitely at the Office for (further) ten years against payment of the administrative fee.[931] In this regard, an extension may be requested no earlier than twelve months before the expiry date of the protection period and no later than six months after the expiry date (the post-expiration (grace) period).[932] Furthermore, the term of protection is extended with effect from the trademark protection date of termination.[933] If an extension of the term of protection is requested within the post-expiration period, the administrative fee shall be paid in double the amount.

696. A trademark does not confer on its owner the exclusive right to use the sign in all commercial use areas. Protection extends only to the form of the sign that is registered in the register and only in relation to the specified classes of goods and services.

697. The proprietor of the trademark has the bundle of exclusive rights defined in sections 8, 8a and 9 of the Trademarks Act. In particular, the owner has the exclusive right to mark the goods and services with the registered sign, to use the trademark on the products and in relation to the services for which it is registered, and the right to prohibit the use of an identical or similar sign in commerce in relation to identical or similar products and services, if there is a likelihood of confusion on the part of the public, including a likelihood of association between these signs.[934] The proprietor shall also have the right to prohibit the use of the trademark by his or her representative if he or she has registered the trademark in his name without the owner's consent, unless he or she has duly justified his or her action.[935] Should the reproduction of a trademark in a dictionary, encyclopaedia or similar work give the impression that it is a generic designation for goods or services, the proprietor has the right to demand from the publisher that the reproduced trademark be supplemented with the indication that it is a registered trademark.[936]

927. *See* s. 28/3 Trademarks Act.
928. *See* s. 8/1 Trademarks Act.
929. *See* s. 29/1 Trademarks Act.
930. *See* s. 29/1 Trademarks Act.
931. *See* s. 29/2 Trademarks Act.
932. *See* s. 29/2 and 3 Trademarks Act.
933. *See* s. 29/7 Trademarks Act.
934. *See* s. 8/2 Trademarks Act.
935. *See* s. 8/4 Trademarks Act.
936. *See* s. 9 Trademarks Act.

698. The law also provides certain exceptions to the exclusive protection.[937] The rights of a trademark apply only to its use in the course of trade. Even in the course of trade, however, the trademark owner is not entitled to prohibit others from using their name and surname, signs which are not distinctive per se, or signs which are necessary to achieve the purpose of the product or service in particular in connection with the sale of accessories or spare parts.[938]

699. In addition, the trademark owner is also limited by the right of the prior user[939] if the rights to the sign arose before the trademark application was filed and the use of the sign is in accordance with the Czech law. Furthermore, the law provides for a trademark limitation due to possible non-use of a trademark[940] or in cases where the owner of an earlier trademark knowingly tolerated the use of a subsequent trademark for five consecutive years.

700. The rights of the proprietor of the trademark are also limited by the exhaustion of rights to a trademark. The doctrine of exhaustion of rights is a consequence of the balance between the principle of free movement of goods and the protection of intellectual property, which is applied territorially. On this basis, the European Court of Justice has held in its case law[941] that the first placing a product on the market by or with the consent of the rightsholder exhausts certain intellectual property rights relating to the product. The proprietor of a trademark cannot, therefore, by utilizing trademark protection, prevent the free movement of products which he or she himself or herself has placed on the market or which have been placed on the market by someone else with his or her consent (e.g., a licensee). It also follows that exhaustion of rights does not, by its nature, apply to trademarks registered for services.

701. In order to prevent abuse of trademark protection by creating blocking trademarks (trademarks created only to prevent someone else from registering them), trademark law introduced the institution of the proper use of a trademark. If the trademark owner does not properly use the trademark for a continuous period of five years,[942] not only does the owner of the trademark lose the right to claim his or her rights against third parties who would interfere with his or her rights,[943] but he or she also runs the risk that the Office will revoke his or her trademark.[944] Similarly, suppose the owner of a trademark has tolerated for a continuous period of five years the unauthorized use of his or her registered sign by another person in a manner that resulted in the existence of a (later) trademark rights conflicting with his or her trademark. In that case, he or she cannot subsequently seek to prohibit the use

937. *See* s. 10 to 10b Trademarks Act.
938. *See* s. 10/1 Trademarks Act.
939. *See* s. 10/2 Trademarks Act.
940. *See* s. 10a Trademarks Act.
941. *See, e.g.*, Case C-16/74, *Centrafarm BV and Adriaan de Peijper v. Winthrop BV*, 31 Oct. 1974, ECLI:EU:C:1974:115.
942. *See* s. 13 Trademarks Act.
943. *See* ss 10a, 26a & s. 32c Trademarks Act.
944. *See* s. 13/1, s. 31/1/a Trademarks Act.

of the later trademark. However, the proprietor has this right if the application for the later trademark was filed in bad faith.[945]

§6. Trademark as an Object of Ownership

702. The right to a trademark is transferable on the basis of a written contract.[946] Accordingly, the effects of the transfer of the right to a trademark materialize with *erga omnes* effects only upon registration in the trademark register.[947] However, the *inter partes* effects arise already upon the effectiveness of the transfer contract.

703. Similarly, the right to a trademark is eligible for a succession of rights to another person. Likewise, with the contractual transfer, the acquisition of the trademark rights by the successor in title is materialized with the effects against third parties again only upon registration in the trademark register.[948]

704. The trademark owner may also grant a licence to the trademark.[949] A non-exclusive licence agreement may also be concluded orally. However, if it is an exclusive licence, the licence agreement must be in writing.[950] The *erga omnes* effects of the licence agreement take effect upon registration in the trademark register;[951] the *inter partes* effects already take effect upon the effectiveness of the licence agreement.

705. The trademark may be the subject of a pledge or other rights in rem (if the nature of the trademark right so permits), enforcement of a judgment or execution, and may also be included in the estate in insolvency proceedings.[952] The effects of the trademark-pledge take effect upon registration in the trademark register.[953]

706. The right to a trademark may also belong to several persons.[954] The legal relations between these persons are then governed by the general rules of sections 1115 et seq. Civil Code. Unless otherwise agreed between the trademark co-owners, each of them has the right to use the trademark; and each of them is likewise entitled to assert claims for infringement of the trademark right separately. However, the consent of all of them is required for the transfer of the trademark right or the grant

945. *See* s. 12/1 Trademarks Act.
946. *See* s. 15 Trademarks Act.
947. *See* s. 15/3 Trademarks Act; s. 1102 Civil Code.
948. *See* s. 15/4 Trademarks Act.
949. *See* s. 18 Trademarks Act.
950. *See* s. 2358/1 Civil Code.
951. *See* s. 18/4 Trademarks Act and s. 2358/3 Civil Code.
952. *See* s. 17/1 Trademarks Act.
953. *See* s. 17/5 Trademarks Act, s. 1316 Civil Code.
954. *See* s. 18a Trademarks Act.

of a licence. An exception is the transfer of the interest to another co-owner or transfer to a third party if none of the co-owners are interested in the transfer offer. The above also apply mutatis mutandis to a trademark application.[955]

§7. Lapse of the Protection

707. Trademark protection may lapse in whole or in part (i.e., in relation to certain classes of goods and services for which it is registered).[956] Termination may occur by (i) expiry of the term of protection,[957] (ii) surrender of the rights in the mark,[958] (iii) cancellation of the mark,[959] or (iv) invalidation of the mark.[960] All these events are always recorded in the Trademarks Register and published in the Bulletin of the Industrial Property Office.

708. A trademark may be cancelled if the relevant circumstances justifying the termination of trademark protection occurred after its creation, i.e., after the date of registration of the sign applied for in the Trade Marks Register. A trademark may be cancelled only upon the application filed with a third party (i.e., not on the initiative of the Office), for example, on the ground that it has not been used properly[961] in the five years preceding the date of the application for cancellation, and there was no circumstance justifying non-use. Another ground for cancellation is that the mark is confusing or deceptive. If the use of the trademark constitutes unfair business practice and there is a court decision confirming that issue, a petition for cancellation of the trademark may also be filed. The time limit for filing a petition for cancellation on this ground is six months from the date of entry into force of the court decision in question.[962] Where a trademark has been finally cancelled, it shall be regarded as having ceased to exist retrospectively to the date of the petition for cancellation.

709. A trademark may also be declared invalid even if it has been revoked, surrendered by its owner, or its protection has expired. Where a trademark has been declared invalid, it is treated as if it had never been registered.[963] A trademark is invalid if the circumstances justifying its invalidation occurred before the date of the trademark application. Similar to the cancellation of a trademark, invalidity proceedings can only be initiated upon the application of a third party. A trademark may be declared invalid if it has been registered in violation of the absolute[964] or relative

955. *See* ss 15/8, 17/6, 18/8, 18a/5 Trademarks Act.
956. *See* ss 29/6, 30, 31/4 and 32/7 Trademarks Act.
957. *See* s. 29/1 Trademarks Act.
958. *See* s. 30 Trademarks Act.
959. *See* s. 31 Trademarks Act.
960. *See* s. 32 Trademarks Act.
961. *See* s. 13 Trademarks Act.
962. *See* ss 31/1 and 2 Trademarks Act.
963. *See* s. 32/5 Trademarks Act.
964. *See* s. 4 Trademarks Act.

grounds of trademark non-registrability[965] or because the trademark application was filed in bad faith. An application for a declaration of invalidity of a trademark, which is based on the grounds set out in section 7 of the Trademarks Act, may be brought only by a person who has a right that justifies the grounds for invalidity.

§8. Collective and Certification Trademarks

710. A collective trademark is a sign distinguishing products or services originating from the members or associates of a legal entity established for the purpose of jointly marking the products or services from those of other legal entities. Unlike an individual trademark, a collective trademark can only be applied for by a legal person.[966]

711. The application for a collective trademark must, in addition to the details set out in section 19 Trademarks Act, also contain a list of the partners/members of the legal entity, who are entitled to use the collective trademark, and the legal entity must attach a 'contract of use' to the application for a collective trademark, containing at least a list of the partners/members of the applicant who are entitled to use the collective mark, the conditions of membership of the applicant and the conditions for use (including penalties) of the collective mark.[967]

712. The exclusive right to use the collective mark is vested in the members or partners of the legal entity or participants of the association registered in the trademark register, under the conditions set out in the primary document relating to the collective mark (the 'contract of use').

713. As opposed to an individual trademark, a collective trademark cannot be licensed.[968]

714. A certification trademark ensures that the recipient (consumer) of the products and services so marked can rely on a certain level of the production so presented. The certification mark distinguishes products and services that have been certified (by the owner of the certification mark) from those that have not been so certified.[969] Its legal regulation can be found in Section 40a–40d of the Trademarks Act. However, we also apply provisions on the individual trademarks in a number of aspects.[970]

965. *See* s. 7 Trademarks Act.
966. *See* s. 35/2 Trademarks Act.
967. *See* s. 36 Trademarks Act.
968. *See* s. 39 Trademarks Act.
969. *See* s. 40/1 Trademarks Act.
970. *See* s. 40a/3 Trademarks Act.

715. An application for a certification trademark may only be filed by a person who is authorized to certify the goods and services for which the certification trademark is to be registered, and at the same time, that person does not carry on a business activity involving the supply of the goods or services for which the mark is to be registered.[971]

716. The applicant is obliged to attach the rules for using the certification mark to the trademark application. As is applicable to a collective mark, the rules for using the certification mark are published in the Trademarks Register. A certification trademark may be subject to a license, unlike a collective trademark.

§9. Keywords and Trademarks on the Internet

717. Keywords are either single words or phrases that an advertiser chooses when, for example, creating their Google Ads or Skliks (under the responsibility of the Czech Internet provider *Seznam.cz*). These keywords are used to match the advertiser's ad with a term that the user has typed into an online search engine. This method of matching types allows the advertiser to restrict the ad to display only when the user's search term is identical to the advertiser's keyword or phrase, or conversely, it may allow the ad to display for phrases that are not literally identical to the keyword.

718. Since 2004, Google has enabled paid optimization through Google Ads, formerly known as AdWords, allowing advertisers to select key keywords that match competitors' trademarks. Google search engines (in the Czech environment also the above-mentioned Seznam.cz Internet searching provider), allow anyone to advertise keywords that match the trademarks, not only their own but also those of a competitor. This situation has been the subject of a number of lawsuits, as search engine customers and advertisers deliberately enter a keyword in Google Ads that is identical or similar to a competitor's trademark in an attempt to get users who search for terms that match a competitor's trademark.

719. The service works on the principle of an Internet database. For each keyword, it keeps a list of advertising messages and their position. Any natural or legal person can enter the selected keyword into the system according to which the advertisement will be displayed. When a search term is entered into the Google search engine, the Google AdWords matches the search term against the list of keywords held. If the term entered into the Google search engine is not included in the Google AdWords keyword list, no advertisement will appear next to the search links. However, if there is a match between the search term and the keyword, the ad that is currently at the top of the list for that keyword will be displayed.

720. The Court of Justice of the European Union (CJEU), in response to preliminary questions in the cases of *Louis Vuitton Malletier SA and others v. Google*

971. *See* s. 40a/2 Trademarks Act.

France SARL[972] held that although the operator of a search engine with online advertising can be considered a provider of information society services within the meaning of Article 2(b) of Directive 2000/31,[973] the safe harbour rules apply to search engines as well. Therefore, it could be held liable if the search engine operator knew about the content's illegality or controlled the information, or if, after becoming aware of the unlawful nature of the stored data or the advertiser's activities, it did not immediately remove or disable access to the data. Notably, according to the CJEU's decision, Google cannot be considered an active ISP, since the keyword system is fully automated and the provider does not play an active role in the service.

721. In the same decision, the Court also expressed its views on the issue of the use of the keyword and possible unauthorized interference with a trademark protection. The Court concluded that, although the applicants' trademarks were used in the course of trade, it was not the Google search engine that used those trademarks but the advertisers themselves who chose the keywords. The keywords, which consist of signs identical to the trademarks, were therefore used in the course of trade, without the consent of the proprietor and for products identical to those for which the trademarks were registered. The rationale of the decision was of whether the use of keywords identical to the trademarks for the purpose of displaying sponsored advertising links was capable of interfering with one of the functions of the trademark, which is a prerequisite for the trademark proprietor to be entitled to prevent the use of a sign identical to its trademark as a keyword.

722. The decisive criterion in this case, according to the CJEU, was the manner in which the sponsored advertising messages were presented. The Court first analysed the possibilities of interference with the investment function of a trademark and held that interference with the investment function occurs if the proprietor of the trademark is substantially prevented from using his trademark to acquire or maintain a reputation. According to the Court, it was clear that the objective of an advertiser who chose a keyword corresponding to a trademark with a reputation was to ensure that Internet users who entered that word as a search term would click not only on the displayed links which came from the proprietor of that trademark but also on the advertising link of that advertiser. This action took advantage of that trademark's distinctive character and reputation. On the other hand, the Court of Justice has held that advertising displayed on the Internet by means of a keyword corresponding to a trademark with a reputation, which promotes an alternative to the trademark proprietor's products or services without offering a mere imitation of the trademark proprietor's products or services falls within the limits of fair competition, even though that advertising may lead to dilution or tarnishment of the trademark's reputation. The Court has thus highlighted the interest in operative and free competition above the interests of trademark proprietors.

972. *See* Joined Cases are C-236/08 to C-238/08 and L'Oréal v. eBay (C-324/09).
973. In Czech law, this provision has been implemented into s. 2/d of the Act No. 484/2004 Sb., on Certain Information Society Services, as amended.

723. In the Czech case law, keywords were the subject of a dispute between Teco company and the searching operator Seznam.cz, which, like Google, runs a system of paid optimization known by the Sklik service. In its judgment of 6 October 2015, Case No. 21 Cm 8/2015, the Municipal Court in Prague dealt with the unlawful use of the word trademarks TECOMAT and FOXTROT, which were owned by the plaintiff and which were used illegally within the Sklik system by the advertiser Elko. In the present case, the defendant-paid-advertiser was demonstrably aware of the unlawful use of the trademarks, and failed to take action against such infringement, even after being notified by the applicant. For these reasons, the court rejected the safe harbour application, and given that the defendant could have reasonably assumed and was demonstrably notified about the infringement by the keywords used, the Municipal Court held that the advertising provider's position was identical to that of an active ISP. It, therefore, ordered the defendant to refrain from providing unlawful paid keyword optimization. The position of the advertiser was then resolved between the same parties by the Supreme Court in its judgment of 16 April 2018, case No. 23 Cdo 4931/2017. There, referring to the case law cited above, the Supreme Court held that the defendant had interfered with the investment function or the function of the designation of origin of the trademarks in question. For those reasons, it dismissed the appeal and upheld the judgments of the lower courts.

Chapter 3. Design Protection (Application to Digital Products)

724. Design protection in the digital context is significant in the areas of web design, Graphical User Interfaces (GUIs), and the use of data files in 3D printing.

§1. Different Types of Design Protection

725. Generally speaking, design protection can be guaranteed in several ways. Design can be protected both through the relative property rights provided by unfair competition protection[974] but also through absolute rights.

726. Such protection includes, for example, protection through three-dimensional trademarks. However, the most common forms of design protection are copyright protection, the protection afforded by registered industrial designs, and the protection afforded by unregistered Community designs.

727. Several international treaties provide for design protection. The Paris Union Convention provides that industrial designs are the subject of industrial property protection.[975] The Convention then obliges all Member States forming the Paris Union to protect industrial designs in their territory.[976] However, it does not specify the form of protection to be granted to industrial designs.

728. The Berne Convention distinguishes between works of applied art protected by copyright[977] and works of applied art protected by industrial designs.[978] The Berne Convention provides that States may provide for a shorter term of protection for photographic works and works of applied art than for other types of works.[979] However, this period may not be shorter than twenty-five years from creating the work. In the Czech Republic, this exception does not apply, and the term of protection is the same for all works of authorship.

729. The TRIPS Agreement goes further in particular regarding the conditions and duration of protection of industrial designs. The TRIPS Agreement provides for an obligation for the Member States to grant protection to independently created industrial designs that are 'original (original) or new'.[980] Further, protective criteria need not include features of technical predetermination. The duration of protection under the TRIPS Agreement is to be at least ten years.[981] The TRIPS Agreement does not oblige Contracting Parties to provide a specific form of protection for

974. *See, e.g.*, by the prohibition of the likelihood of confusion under s. 2981 Civil Code or parasitizing on reputation according to s. 2982 Civil Code.
975. *See* Art. 1(2) Paris Union Convention.
976. *See* Art. 5quinquies Paris Union Convention.
977. *See* Art. 2(1) Berne Convention.
978. *See* Art. 2(7) Berne Convention.
979. *See* Art. 7(4) Berne Convention.
980. *See* Art. 25 TRIPS Agreement.
981. *See* Art. 26(3) TRIPS Agreement.

industrial designs. Thus, Contracting Parties may choose all known forms of protection, including unfair competition protection. However, concerning the protection of fashion (textile) designs, it explicitly gives Contracting States the choice of whether to protect a special industrial design arrangement (sui generis) or through copyright protection.[982]

§2. The EU Framework for Design Protection

730. At the EU level, design protection is regulated by the Directive on the Legal Protection of Industrial Designs.[983] However, a second important piece of legislation is the Regulation on Community Designs, which guarantees a unified form of EU-wide protection and establishes a system of registered and unregistered Community designs which are protected uniformly in the territory of all EU Member States, similar to an EU trademark.

731. Taking into account the national focus of this publication, we will focus only on the domestic protection of national registered designs and leave aside the EU legislation.

§3. Design Protection at the National Level

732. In the Czech Republic, industrial designs protection is covered by the Industrial Designs Protection Act (hereinafter referred to as 'Industrial Designs Act'),[984] which is the result of the implementation of the Directive on the Legal Protection of Industrial Designs. The Directive obliges Member States to establish a sui generis protection regime in their national legal systems under which industrial designs will be registered.[985]

733. In the Czech Republic, the protection of registered industrial designs is based on the registration principle with a full substantive examination of registrability.[986] This approach is seen as a rarity in the international context (e.g., compared to France, Spain, Italy or the Benelux countries), where no substantive examination is carried out.[987] Therefore, the examiner of the Industrial Property Office [*Úřad průmyslového vlastnictví*] examines not only whether the design application has the prescribed requirements (formal examination), but in particular whether the subject matter applied for is an industrial design at all, whether it meets

982. *See* Art. 25(2) TRIPS Agreement.
983. *See* Directive No. 98/71/EC.
984. *See* Act No. 207/2000 Sb., Industrial Designs Protection Act, as amended.
985. *See* Art. 3 Directive on the Legal Protection of Industrial Designs.
986. *See* s. 37 Industrial Designs Act.
987. *See* Miroslav Černý in *Zákon o ochraně průmyslových vzorů: komentář*, p. 188 (Pavel Koukal et al. Wolters Kluwer 2015).

the criterion of novelty, individual character, whether it is consistent with good morals and public policy, or whether it does not conflict with prior rights.[988]

§4. Design

734. The industrial design is defined as 'the appearance of a product or a part thereof, consisting in particular of the lines, contours, colours, shape, structure or materials of the product itself, or of its decoration', the product being 'an industrially or crafted article, including components intended to be assembled into a single composite product, packaging, design, graphic symbol and typographical feature, except for computer programs'.[989] Graphic symbols such as icons of computer programs or mobile applications, including GUIs, are considered to be products.

§5. Eligibility Requirements

735. In order to be protected as a registered design, the design must be new and possess individual character. In assessing registrability, no account is taken of features which are 'predetermined by the technical function of the design' or which must 'necessarily be reproduced in precise form and dimensions so that the product in which the design is embodied or on which it is applied can be mechanically connected to another product or placed in, around or within another product so that both products can perform their function.'[990] According to the decision of the Municipal Court in Prague of 19 December 2012, Case No. 9 Ca 328/2009-126, '*a feature in the form of the shape of a structural element of a certain product is not predetermined by its technical function if the identical purpose (function) of this structural element can be achieved by means of solutions that differ in shape and thus in appearance*'.

736. Concerning novelty, the Industrial Designs Act provides that 'an industrial design shall be deemed to be new if, before the date of filing the application or before the date of priority right, an identical industrial design has not been made available to the public', which means any industrial design whose 'features differ only insignificantly from the industrial design in question'.[991]

737. Individual character, as a further requirement, means that the overall impression which the industrial design 'produces to the informed user differs from the overall impression produced to such user by an industrial design which was made available to the public before the date of filing of the application or before the date of priority right', and in assessing this requirement, 'the degree of freedom

988. *See* s. 37/6 Industrial Designs Act.
989. *See* s. 2/a and b Industrial Designs Act.
990. *See* s. 7 Industrial Designs Act.
991. *See* s. 4 Industrial Designs Act.

which the originator had in developing the design shall be taken into account'.[992] By informed user, we understand a person familiar with the designs in the respected field (e.g., Webdesign or graphical design) and, by giving the impression, he or she can compare these designs. Particularly, the informed user 'without being a designer or a technical expert, the user knows the various designs which exist in the sector concerned, possesses a certain degree of knowledge with regard to the features which those designs normally include, and, as a result of his interest in the products concerned, shows a relatively high degree of attention when he uses them'.[993]

738. For the assessment of novelty and individual character, the public disclosure is essential, which means disclosure by 'registration or display of the design, use in commerce or other publication', except where 'the disclosure could not have become known in professional circles active within the EC and specialized in the field in the normal course of business before the filing date of the application or before the date of priority right'.[994] With regard to the definition of public disclosure, the exception applicable here is illustrated by disclosure in the form of familiarity with the industrial design under the condition of confidentiality.[995] The Industrial Designs Act further exempts from disclosure to the public cases where the designer published the industrial design twelve months before the application's filing date or before the date of priority, or where the disclosure is made as a result of abuse of the relationship with the designer.[996]

739. The grace period is the twelve-month period within which the design was made available to the public. This concept means that the designer may use and publish the design. However, to obtain protection by a registered design, he or she must file a design application within twelve months of such publication. The other conditions for registrability include compliance with public policy, good morals, and absence of conflict with earlier rights. The Industrial Property Office will not enter in the register a design that is contrary to public policy and good morals or if an identical design with an earlier priority right is already registered in the register.[997]

§6. Industrial Designs Application Proceedings

740. The industrial design application procedure is an administrative procedure regulated by Act No. 500/2004 Sb., Administrative Code, as amended, with the exceptions provided for in the Industrial Designs Act.[998] The proceedings begin with filing the industrial design application with the Industrial Property Office.[999] A

992. *See* s. 5 Industrial Designs Act.
993. *See* Case C-281/10 P, *PepsiCo, Inc. v. Grupo Promer Mon Graphic SA,* 20 Oct. 2011, ECLI-:EU:C:2011:679.
994. *See* s. 6/1 Industrial Designs Act.
995. *See* s. 6/1 Industrial Designs Act.
996. *See* s. 6/2 and 3 Industrial Designs Act.
997. *See* s. 8 and 9 Industrial Designs Act.
998. *See* s. 40 Industrial Designs Act.
999. *See* s. 34 Industrial Designs Act.

fee is payable thereafter. The application filing gives rise to a right of priority for the applicant; however, if such a right exists under an international treaty (Paris Union Convention), the applicant must declare it in the application and prove it; otherwise, it is disregarded.[1000]

741. Following the filing of the application, the Office examines the design application in which it assesses, *inter alia*, the novelty and individual character of the design. This examination (qualitatively comparable to the substantive examination for patents) is unique among design proceedings in the EU since it covers the substantive examination of the novelty and individual character.

742. In the event of insufficiencies in the application that are not remedied even upon the Office's request, the Office shall suspend the design application proceedings.[1001] If the subject of the application is not an industrial design, the design does not meet the requirements under the Industrial Designs Act (i.e., it is not new or does not have an individual character), or there is a conflict with an earlier identical industrial design with effects in the Czech Republic, the Office shall refuse the application; however, it shall first allow the applicant to respond to the grounds for refusal.[1002]

743. If the proceedings are not suspended or the application is refused, the Office shall enter the design in the Register and issue a certificate of registration to the applicant.[1003] Unlike patents or trademarks, the application is not published during the registration procedure. The Office will publish the registered design only with the registration (however, there is a possibility to postpone publication for a maximum of thirty months from the date of filing of the application or the date of priority right). The Office will announce the registration (or postponement of publication) in the Official Bulletin.[1004]

§7. Scope and Duration of Protection

744. The scope of protection is relevant in particular to the prevention of third parties from using (producing, marketing, importing etc.) the design. It is determined by the very representation of the design in the register,[1005] with certain exceptions, such as features which are predetermined by the technical function of the design or features which must 'necessarily be reproduced in precise form and dimensions so that the product in which the design is embodied or on which it is

1000. *See* s. 36 Industrial Designs Act.
1001. *See* s. 37/4 Industrial Designs Act.
1002. *See* s. 37/6 Industrial Designs Act.
1003. *See* s. 38 Industrial Designs Act.
1004. *See* s. 38 Industrial Designs Act.
1005. *See* Pavel Koukal, *Zákon o ochraně průmyslových vzorů: komentář*, p. 59 (Pavel Koukal et al. Wolters Kluwer 2015).

applied can be mechanically connected to another product or placed in, around or against another product so that both products can perform their function.'[1006]

745. The term of protection of an industrial design is five years from the filing of the application and may be repeatedly extended in five-year cycles up to a total term of twenty-five years. The application for renewal is filed during the last year of the relevant period.[1007] If the renewal application period is missed, the Industrial Designs Act provides for the possibility of filing an application within six months of the date on which it should have been filed at the latest [the post-expiration period]; however, such a step is sanctioned by a double fee.[1008] If the application for renewal is not filed even within this time limit, the industrial design will then expire on the date on which it should have originally expired. If third parties have already begun 'to exploit the design or have made serious and effective preparations for such exploitation' within the six-month period, their rights are not affected by the renewal within that period.[1009]

§8. Design Right and Effects of a Registered Design

746. The right to the industrial design belongs to the designer or his/her successor in title, or to a co-inventor to the extent of his or her share; these are the persons who may file an application for an industrial design,[1010] unless they transfer the right to the industrial design to another person or the right passes to the employer. An 'employee industrial design' is an industrial design which the designer has created for the performance of a job task emerging during the course of the employment.[1011] In this case, the right to the industrial design passes to the employer who 'ordered the designer to create the industrial design'. The employee who created the industrial design (the originator) is obliged to notify the employer in writing of the creation of the industrial design and to provide him or her with all supporting documents. The employer then has three months to exercise the design right, otherwise the right passes back to the designer (during this period, both parties must maintain confidentiality).

747. A registered industrial design grants its owner the right to use the design and to prevent third parties from using it without his or her consent from the date of filing the application.[1012] Furthermore, the owner may grant a licence to the registered design, make it the subject of a pledge or transfer (e.g., sell) the right to the design to a transferee.

1006. *See* s. 10/1 Industrial Designs Act.
1007. *See* s. 11/1–3 Industrial Designs Act.
1008. *See* s. 11/4 Industrial Designs Act.
1009. *See* s. 11/5 Industrial Designs Act.
1010. *See* s. 12 Industrial Designs Act.
1011. *See* s. 13/1 Industrial Designs Act.
1012. *See* s. 19/2 Industrial Designs Act.

748. However, the rights from the registration do not apply, for example, to the actions of third parties for non-commercial or experimental purposes or in the application of other exceptions, nor do they apply, for example, to the importation of spare parts and accessories into the Czech Republic for the purpose of repairing a certain means of transport.[1013]

749. The rights of an industrial design are further limited by the exhaustion of the rights and rights of the previous user. Exhaustion of rights is the principle according to which the rights to a given registered industrial design do not apply to the disposal of the product in which the design is embodied or to which it is applied, if the product has been placed on the market in the EU or in a State forming the EEA by the design owner or with his or her consent.[1014] The right of prior user then means that the rights from the registered industrial design do not extend to third parties who, before the filing of the application or before the date of the priority right related to the territory of the Czech Republic, used the design or created it independently of the submitted design application.[1015]

§9. Extinction and Cancellation of the Registered Industrial Designs

750. The right in a registered design expires in two situations, namely, if the term of its protection expires or if the owner renounces it.[1016] A registered industrial design may also be cancelled from the register. Cancellation is carried out by the Industrial Property Office under the conditions laid down by the law[1017] upon a written application submitted by a third party. The grounds for cancellation include, for example, the lack of novelty or individual character, the absence of the owner's right to the design, conflict with copyright and others. The cancellation itself has the same effect as if the design had not been entered in the register.[1018] However, before the decision on cancellation is taken, the owner is given the opportunity to comment on the grounds for cancellation within a given time limit.

§10. Graphical User Interfaces

751. The industrial design can also protect GUIs, in class 14-04 of the Locarno Classification, which are 'captured on a product' in the form of a display on a computer screen, tablet, or a mobile phone. GUIs allow the user to select and manipulate graphical icons on the screen and operate application software by means of a control device (e.g., a mouse or a finger clicks). However, only five interfaces are protected by the Czech registered industrial design in this way so far (as of 30 May

1013. *See* s. 23 Industrial Designs Act.
1014. *See* s. 24 Industrial Designs Act.
1015. *See* s. 25 Industrial Designs Act.
1016. *See* s. 26 Industrial Designs Act.
1017. *See* s. 27 Industrial Designs Act.
1018. *See* s. 28 Industrial Designs Act.

2022), as the Czech Industrial Property Office has for a long time refused this form of fixation of the industrial design onto a product.

752. Nevertheless, GUIs can also benefit from copyright protection. According to a ruling of the European Court of Justice in *Bezpečnostní softwarová asociace – Svaz softwarové ochrany v. Ministerstvo kultury,*[1019] GUIs do not constitute a form of expression of a computer program and therefore do not enjoy copyright protection for computer programs. Yet, the ECJ clarified that a GUI might benefit from general copyright protection if there is a creative achievement, i.e., if the user interface is sufficiently original. This criterion is not met, for example, if the design of the user interface is dictated by its technical function.

753. Since patent protection is available only for technical inventions and thus computer programs are expressly excluded from patent protection,[1020] there has been disputed whether a GUI that is generated by a computer program is also excluded from the patent protection. The Technical Board of Appeal of the European Patent Office has answered this question in the affirmative. In the decision of 16 October 2003 (T643/00), the Board of Appeal noted that the arrangement of menu elements on a screen could indeed solve a technical problem. In particular, the problem could be to make it easier for a user to perform a technical task, such as searching for and downloading files. Therefore, a computer program for generating a GUI may be patentable if it simplifies or improves the operation of a computer, e.g., requires fewer steps or leads more quickly to the desired result.

§11. 3D Printing and Design Law

754. 3D printing is a flexible production method and is used in many industries. These include in particular medical technology (replacement knees), the automotive industry, but increasingly also the household goods industry, the glass industry or even the food industry (production of lollipops, chocolate figurines or cakes). 3D printing is penetrating all sectors of the economy where mass production is not applicable or where a customised product is required.

755. Since the shape of products is protected by an industrial design, manufacturing the protected objects on a 3D printer for commercial purposes is not permitted. In the same way as the product itself is protected, an industrial design provides protection for a part of the product that remains visible in normal use by the end consumer and itself meets the requirements of novelty and individual character.[1021] Normal use here means use by the end-user, excluding maintenance, servicing and repair work.[1022]

1019. *See* Case C-393/09, *Bezpečnostní softwarová asociace – Svaz softwarové ochrany v. Ministerstvo kultury,* 22 Dec. 2010, ECLI:EU:C:2010:816.
1020. *See* s. 3/2/c Patent Act; Art. 52(2)(c) European Patent Convention.
1021. *See* s. 3/2 Industrial Designs Act.
1022. *See* s. 3/3 Industrial Designs Act.

756. Thus, the commercial production of products or most of visible spare parts that are intended for service or repair is an infringement of design rights. This applies to both registered designs (national and registered Community designs) and unregistered Community designs, which are protected against copying for three years after publication. The exception is 3D printing of products or spare parts for personal use only, which is not covered by the rights of a registered or unregistered design.[1023] However, design protection only applies to the product as such. Therefore, the mere scanning of products and converting them into Computer-Aided Design (CAD) files which are then used to print the design on a 3D printer is not an infringement of the industrial design rights. However, offering such files on the Internet without the consent of the right holder, is already an infringement of design rights, as the Industrial Designs Act refers to 'offering' as one of the forms of use of a protected design.[1024]

757. Nevertheless, even stricter and more important is copyright law, which applies to original designs from the moment of their creation. Industrial design and copyright protection is cumulative,[1025] so that both types of protection can be applied simultaneously to the same subject matter. Protection under copyright law is permissible for works of applied art if it is the author's own personal intellectual creation reflecting his or her personality. Copyright, unlike design protection, applies to any reproduction of a work.[1026] Therefore, even scanning of copyrighted designs may constitute copyright infringement. The same applies to offering CAD files on the Internet.

758. Therefore, if one does not want to commit intellectual property infringement before a product or its part is commercially scanned, shared for printing on the Internet, or printed on a 3D printer, one must first make sure that none of these processes are subject to either design or copyright protection. The only exceptions are those acts that are carried out purely for personal use.[1027]

1023. *See* s. 23/1/a Industrial Designs Act; Art. 20(1)(a) Regulation 6/2002 EU.
1024. *See* s. 19/1 Industrial Designs Act.
1025. *See* s. 1/2 Industrial Designs Act.
1026. *See* s. 13/1 Copyright Act.
1027. *See* s. 23/1/a Industrial Designs Act; s. 30/1 Copyright Act.

Chapter 4. Copyright Protection in the Digital Context

§1. Introduction

759. This chapter introduces the Czech system of authors' rights protection with a focus on issues relevant to the digital context. Firstly, it sketches out the basic regulatory framework. Then, it focuses on the issue of protected and unprotected subject matter. Next, the rights granted, their scope, duration, and limitations are discussed. The explanation of licensing modes, both individual (including the public licenses) as well as collective, follows next. The chapter ends with a brief overview of the s' possibilities of how to protect and enforce their rights by preventive means, i.e., technological protection measures and reactive measures, i.e., legal remedies.

760. Despite the title of this chapter and terminology used even in the EU sources of copyright law, it must be noted that the term 'copyright' as understood in common law systems is not equivalent to the continental, or Czech for that matter, understanding of this regulatory institute – a proper denomination should be thus 'authors' rights'.[1028] However, in this chapter and the chapter concerning software protection, the terms 'copyright law' and 'copyright' are generally used when referring to this regime of protection, knowing this fundamental difference.

§2. The Regulatory Framework

761. The Czech Republic is a member of World Intellectual Property Organization (WIPO) and the WTO and has ratified not only all the major relevant international copyright and related rights conventions and treaties but also, for the digital context, most important, the Agreement on Trade-Related Aspects of Intellectual Property Agreement, the WIPO Copyright Treaty and the WIPO Performances and Phonograms Treaty.[1029] In 2004, the Czech Republic joined the EU. Therefore, not only is the Czech copyright law substantially shaped by the respective EU legislation, but it must be interpreted and applied in conformity therewith.[1030] The ever-increasing relevant case law of the CJEU must be necessarily also considered.

1028. *See* Radim Polčák, *§ 10 Obsah práva autorského, in Autorský zákon*, p. 102 (Radim Polčák et al., Leges 2020).

1029. *See* the status of the Czech Republic vis-à-vis WIPO-administred treaties at the World Intellectual Property Organization IP Portal at: https://wipolex.wipo.int/en/treaties/ShowResults?code=CZ. The Czech Ministry of Culture that is responsible for legislation in the area of copyright provides basic overview at https://www.mkcr.cz/copyright-15.html?lang=en.

1030. As concluded by the (then) European Court of Justice in the Case 14/83, *Sabine von Colson and Elisabeth Kamann v. Land Nordrhein-Westfalen*, 10 Apr. 1984, ECLI:EU:C:1984:153 and case C-106/89, *Marleasing SA v. La Comercial Internacional de Alimentacion SA*, 13 Nov. 1990, ECLI:EU:C:1990:395. The Czech Supreme Court confirmed this interpretation rule, e.g., in its judgment of 16 Sep. 2015, Case No. 30 Cdo 796/2015.

762. The substantial Czech copyright law is entailed in Act No. 121/2000 Sb. Act on Copyright, on Rights Related to Copyright and on Amendments to Certain Acts, as amended ('Copyright Act').[1031] Albeit being drafted and passed before the joining of the EU by the Czech Republic, the lawmaker aimed to reflect the main EU copyright law instrument at the time[1032] – the Information Society Directive.[1033] Nevertheless, the 'Euro-amendment' in 2006 was a complex update to fully align Czech law with the Information Society Directive.[1034] The Copyright Act was further amended substantially to incorporate international and EU copyright law developments. For example, the Orphan Works Directive[1035] was implemented in 2014,[1036] the Collective Management Directive[1037] in 2017,[1038] and the EU legislative acts implementing the Marrakesh Treaty[1039] in 2019.[1040] Further substantial updates of the Copyright Act are to be expected with the passing of the legislature transposing the Digital Single Market Directive.[1041]

1031. *See* Act No. 121/2000 Sb., o právu autorském, o právech souvisejících s právem autorským a o změně některých zákonů (autorský zákon), ve znění pozdějších předpisů.

1032. *See* PARLAMENT ČESKÉ REPUBLIKY Poslanecká sněmovna. Důvodová zpráva k vládnímu návrhu zákona o právu autorském, o právech souvisejících s právem autorským a o změně některých zákonů (autorský zákon). Poslanecká sněmovna, 3. volební období, 1998–2002, sněmovní tisk 443/0, 18 Nov. 1999, p. 57.

1033. *See* Directive 2001/29/EC of the European Parliament and of the Council of 22 May 2001 on the harmonization of certain aspects of copyright and related rights in the information society, OJ L 167, 22 Jun. 2001 ('Information Society Directive').

1034. *See* Act No. 216/2006 Sb., kterým se mění zákon č. 121/2000 Sb., o právu autorském, o právech souvisejících s právem autorským a o změně některých zákonů (autorský zákon), ve znění pozdějších předpisů, a některé další zákony.

1035. *See* Directive (EU) 2012/28 of the European Parliament and of the Council of 25 Oct. 2012 on certain permitted uses of orphan works, OJ L 299, 27 Oct. 2012.

1036. *See* Act No. 228/2014 Sb., amending Act No. 121/2000 Sb., on copyright, on rights related to ropyright and on amendments to certain acts (Copyright Act), as amended, and Act No. 151/1997 Sb., on Valuation of Property and on Amendments to Certain Acts (Act on Valuation of Property), as amended.

1037. *See* Directive (EU) 2014/26 of the European Parliament and of the Council of 26 Feb. 2014 on collective management of copyright and related rights and multi-territorial licensing of rights in musical works for online use in the internal market, OJ L 84, 20 Mar. 2014.

1038. *See* Act No. 102/2017 Sb., amending Act No 121/2000 Sb., on copyright, on rights related to copyright and on amendments to certain acts (Copyright Act), as amended.

1039. *See* Directive (EU) 2017/1564 of the European Parliament and of the Council of 13 Sep. 2017 on certain permitted uses of certain works and other subject matter protected by copyright and related rights for the benefit of persons who are blind, visually impaired or otherwise print-disabled and amending Directive 2001/29/EC on the harmonization of certain aspects of copyright and related rights in the information society, OJ L 242, 20 Sep. 2017; Regulation (EU) 2017/1563 of the European Parliament and of the Council of 13 Sep. 2017 on the cross-border exchange between the Union and third countries of accessible format copies of certain works and other subject matter protected by copyright and related rights for the benefit of persons who are blind, visually impaired or otherwise print-disabled, OJ L 242, 20 Sep. 2017.

1040. *See* Act No. 50/2019 Sb., amending Act No. 121/2000 Sb., on copyright, on rights related to copyright and on amendments to certain acts (Copyright Act), as amended.

1041. *See* Directive (EU) 2019/790 of the European Parliament and of the Council of 17 Apr. 2019 on copyright and related rights in the Digital Single Market and amending Directives 96/9/EC and 2001/29/EC, OJ L 130, 17 May 2019 ('DSM Directive') – to be transposed by the following Bill: PARLAMENT ČESKÉ REPUBLIKY Poslanecká sněmovna. Vládní návrh zákona, kterým se mění zákon č. 121/2000 Sb., o právu autorském, o právech souvisejících s právem autorským a o změně některých zákonů (autorský zákon), ve znění pozdějších předpisů, a další související

763. Apart from issues of the enforcement of the rights and licensing, the Copyright Act is an all-encompassing complex regulation that aims to cover all the relevant issues. Therefore, there is no other main copyright-relevant act, e.g., regulating the collective management of rights, as is the case in other states.[1042] Section 1 of the Copyright Act clearly lays out what is being regulated therein, namely the copyright, related rights, rights of the maker of the database,[1043] the protection of the rights granted as well as collective management of selected rights. The first chapter of the Copyright Act focusing on copyright regulates all the pertinent topics. The further chapters do not reiterate the common provisions but reference this first chapter in particular question via reference provision.[1044] For example, the limitations and exceptions to related rights are not explicitly regulated – the respective referencing provisions only lay down which limitations and exceptions set for copyrighted works are applicable *mutatis mutandis* to the rights related to copyright.

764. The Copyright Act is a *lex specialis* to the Civil Code,[1045] the primary civil law regulation. Therefore, the general issues, which are also applicable to copyright law, such as the fundamental principles of civil law, contract law, civil liability, and others, are regulated in the Civil Code. Specifically, the Civil Code regulates in detail the issue of licensing. It contains licence agreement general provisions[1046] and specific provisions applicable only to a licence agreement to a subject matter protected by the Copyright Act (including publishing contracts).[1047]

765. As will be elaborated later in this chapter, these two acts provide together for the standard claims and remedies to be sought in civil law enforcement of the exclusive rights. Procedurally, these claims and remedies are realized in civil proceedings, which are regulated in Civil Procedure Code.[1048]

---

zákony [Government Bill amending Act No. 121/2000 Sb., on Copyright, on Rights Related to Copyright and on Amendments to Certain Acts (Copyright Act), as amended, and other related Acts]. 11 Nov. 2021, 9. electoral term, Parliamentary print no. 31/0. Available in Czech from: htt ps://www.psp.cz/sqw/text/tiskt.sqw?O=9&CT=31&CT1=0 ('DSM Directive Amendment Act').

1042. As is the case, e.g., in Germany (Verwertungsgesellschaftengesetz vom 24. Mai 2016 (BGBl. I S. 1190), das zuletzt durch Artikel 2 des Gesetzes vom 31. Mai 2021 (BGBl. I S. 1204) geändert worden ist).

1043. Legal protection of databases remains out of scope of this chapter. *See* the Part IV, Chapter 6. Protection of databases (incl. 'data ownership').

1044. *See* s. 66/5 of the Copyright Act for computer programs; s. 74 of the Copyright Act for performers and their performances; s. 78 of the Copyright Act for producers of audio recordings and their recordings; s. 82 of the Copyright Act for producers of audiovisual recordings and to their recordings; s. 86 of the Copyright Act to broadcasters and to their broadcasting; and s. 94 of the Copyright Act to makers of the databases and their databases.

1045. *See* Act No. 89/2012 Sb., Civil Code, as amended ('Civil Code'). Official English translation available at: https://obcanskyzakonik.justice.cz/images/pdf/Civil-Code.pdf. This translation does not, however, reflect the subsequent amendments.

1046. *See* ss 2358 – 2370 of the Civil Code.

1047. *See* ss 2371 – 2384 of the Civil Code.

1048. *See* Act No. 99/1963 Sb., Civil Procedure Code, as amended. The English translations of Civil Procedure Code quoted (and if necessary adapted) below in the text stem from the Legal Information System ASPI, Wolters Kluwer ČR, 2022.

766. The rightsholder might also resort to enforcement by administrative and criminal means that, however, follow a different aim – namely, the protection of societal values and punishment of encroachments thereupon. The administrative branch of copyright enforcement aims at punishing less severe copyright infringements – petty (administrative) offences. Materially, the specific administrative offences, such as unlawful use of the protected subject matter, are regulated in the Copyright Act. The general issues of administrative liability, both substantial as well as procedural, are regulated in the Administrative Offences Act.[1049]

767. The *ultima ratio* for the punishment of most grievous copyright infringement cases is criminal enforcement.[1050] The backbone of this branch of copyright enforcement consists of Penal Code[1051] and Penal Procedure Code.[1052]

768. The Act 355/2014 Sb., on the Scope of the Customs Administration of the Czech Republic in Connection with the Enforcement of Intellectual Property Rights, grants the Customs the power to support the rightsholders in the enforcement of copyright, e.g., by granting specific customs measures.

769. Finally, copyright also enjoys constitutional protection. In the Czech Republic, the intangible (intellectual) property is protected by Articles 11 and 34 of the Charter of Fundamental Rights and Freedoms.[1053] As a result, the rightsholder may contest any action by a public authority that has allegedly infringed the constitutionally guaranteed fundamental rights and basic freedoms with a constitutional complaint.[1054] The Constitutional Court, however, does not act as a 'fourth instance' in the judiciary system deliberating upon the issues of 'simple law' but stands outside the system of common courts.[1055]

1049. *See* Act No. 250/2016 Sb., on Liability and Proceedings for Administrative Offences, as amended ('Administrative Offences Act').

1050. The principle of subsidiarity of criminal repression is also expressed in the s. 12 of the Act. No. 40/2009 Sb., Penal Code, as amended, that reads: *'The criminal liability of an offender and the criminal consequences associated with it may only be applied in socially harmful cases where application of liability under another legal regulation is insufficient.'* The English translations of Penal Code quoted (and if necessary adapted) below in the text stem from the Legal Information System ASPI, Wolters Kluwer ČR, 2022.

1051. *See* Act No. 40/2009 Sb., Penal Code, as amended.

1052. *See* Act No. 141/1961 Sb., Penal Procedure Code, as amended.

1053. *See* Constitutional Act No. 2/1993 Sb., RESOLUTION of the Presidium of the Czech National Council of 16 Dec. 1992 on the declaration of the CHARTER OF FUNDAMENTAL RIGHTS AND FREEDOMS as a part of the constitutional order of the Czech Republic, as amended. Official English translation available at: https://www.usoud.cz/fileadmin/user_upload/ustavni_soud_www/Pravni_uprava/AJ/Charter_of_Fundamental_Rights_and_Freedoms.pdf.

1054. *See* ss 72 et seq. Act No. 182/1993 Sb. on Constitutional Court, as amended. English version available at: https://www.usoud.cz/fileadmin/user_upload/ustavni_soud_www/Pravni_uprava/AJ/ConstitutionalCourtAct_1.pdf.

1055. *See* Art. 91/1 and Art. 83 of the Czech Constitution.

§3. PROTECTED SUBJECT MATTER

770. The issue of delimitation of the protected subject matter is fundamental to any further discussion. If the respective intangible asset does not fulfil the set requirements for granting of protection, there is, logically, no need to elaborate, e.g., what is the scope of exclusive rights granted thereto, what are their limits, how long do they last or how to enforce them.

771. The principal and central object of protection under the Copyright Act is the work of authorship.[1056] Section 2 of the Copyright Act regulates what is or is not to be qualified as such work. Firstly, the creation must be a literary work, work of art,[1057] or scientific work. As the literary work is also a work of art, basically, the artistic or scientific works are protected. Next, it must be objectively perceptible, i.e., materialized in such a way that others could perceive it.[1058] However, fixation on tangible media is not required – an ephemeral (temporary) expression of work, e.g., recitation or singing, is sufficient.[1059] Finally, the work must be a unique outcome of the author's creative activity. This criterion of the individuality of the author's work in the sense of the statistical probability of uniqueness of the work means that it is not possible to protect two identical (or highly similar) works.[1060] The personal traits of the author predetermine the creative activity[1061] – it is thus not present when the objectively perceivable result stems from mechanical (causal) activity, as there is no room for the author's creative choices.[1062] However, even the Czech Supreme Court ruled that the 'works of small coin', i.e., works with a lower level of the individuality of the author's work, might be protected.[1063] On the other hand, under section 2/1 of the Copyright Act of no importance for qualification as a unique outcome of the creative activity and thus the granting of the status as the copyrighted work are the criteria of scope, purpose, and meaning.

772. For computer programs, databases, and photographs section 2/2 of the Copyright Act requires the presence of only a lower standard, 'originality' (in Czech 'původnost'), to be protected. A later created 'original' work that is identical or substantially similar to a previous work might be well protected independently.[1064] However, there are no differences in the quality of protection granted – both

---

1056. *See* Radim Polčák, *§ 2 Autorské dílo, in Autorský zákon*, p. 42 (Radim Polčák et al., Leges 2020).
1057. The s. 2/1 of the Copyright Act also demonstratively lists typical forms of a work, such as *'verbal work expressed in speech or writing, musical work, dramatic work or musical-dramatic work, choreographic work or pantomimic work, photographic work or work expressed by a technique similar to a photograph, audiovisual work, such as cinematographic work, a work of visual arts, such as painting, graphic or sculptural work, architectonic work including an urbanistic work, work of applied arts or cartographic work'*.
1058. *See* s. 2/1 of the Copyright Act.
1059. *See* Ivo Telec & Pavel Tůma, *Autorský zákon. Komentář*, p. 22 (C.H.Beck 2019).
1060. *Ibid.*, p. 20.
1061. *Ibid.*, p. 18.
1062. *See* Radim Polčák, *§ 2 Autorské dílo, in Autorský zákon*, p. 49 (Radim Polčák et al., Leges 2020).
1063. *See* Judgement of the Supreme Court of 31. 8. 2016, Case No. 30 Cdo 733/2016 and Judgement of the Supreme Court of 24. 6. 2015, Case No. 30 Cdo 360/2015.
1064. *See* Radim Polčák, *§ 2 Autorské dílo, in Autorský zákon*, p. 54 (Radim Polčák et al., Leges 2020).

'unique' and 'original' works are treated similarly regarding the rights granted.[1065] The eventual specific disparities in regulation stem from other circumstances, such as the type of work – for example, the section 66 of the Copyright Act regulates a different set of limitations of the granted rights for computer programs.

773. The CJEU, however, stipulated that the *'concept of work ... must be given an autonomous and uniform interpretation throughout the European Union'*[1066] and elaborated on the conceptual features of the 'work' extensively.[1067] To classify an intangible subject matter as work, it must be original in the sense that it is the *'author's own intellectual creation'* and 'expression' thereof that is identifiable with *'sufficient precision and objectivity'*.[1068] The originality is then expressed by free and creative choices of the author that reflect her personality and give the work a 'personal touch'.[1069] On the other hand, the intellectual 'investment' (skill, labour, effort) is not relevant in assessing the fulfilment of these conceptual features.[1070] By the ongoing decision-making activity of the CJEU, the fundamental *'author's own intellectual creation'* criterion was expanded as regards its applicability from only specific works (computer programs, databases, and photographs) generally to all the works. In this context, the importance of the strict Czech national distinction between the criteria of uniqueness and originality seems to diminish – the notion of the individuality of the author's work needs to be reinterpreted following the conclusions of the CJEU as a middle ground between these two Czech criteria of 'uniqueness' and 'originality'.[1071] Nevertheless, the overall evaluation of whether an intangible result is a copyrighted work is ultimately a question of law, and it is to be decided by the court, not by an expert witness.[1072]

774. As stipulated by section 2/3 of the Copyright Act, the copyright protection extends to all development stages of the work and parts thereof, including the title

1065. *Ibid.*, p. 53.
1066. *See* Case C-310/17, *Levola Hengelo BV v. Smilde Foods BV*, 13 Nov. 2018, ECLI-:EU:C:2018:899, para. 33.
1067. Case C-05/08, *Infopaq International v. Danske Dagblades Forening*, 16 Jul. 2009, ECLI-:EU:C:2009:465); case C-310/17, *Levola Hengelo BV v. Smilde Foods BV*, 13 Nov. 2018, ECLI-:EU:C:2018:899; Case C-469/17, *Funke Medien NRW GmbH v. Bundesrepublik Deutschland*, 29 Jul. 2019, ECLI:EU:C:2019:623; Case C-683/17, *Cofemel – Sociedade de Vestuário SA v. G-Star Raw CV*, 12 Sep. 2019, ECLI:EU:C:2019:721 (Cofemel); Case C-833/18, *SI a Brompton Bicycle Ltd v. Chedech / Get2GetBrompton*, 11 Jun. 2020, ECLI:EU:C:2020:461.
1068. *See* Case C-310/17, *Levola Hengelo BV v. Smilde Foods BV*, 13 Nov. 2018, ECLI-:EU:C:2018:899, para. 40.
1069. *See* Case C-05/08, *Infopaq International v. Danske Dagblades Forening*, 16 Jul. 2009, ECLI-:EU:C:2009:465.
1070. P. Bernt Hugenholtz & João Pedro Quintais, *Copyright and Artificial Creation: Does EU Copyright Law Protect AI-Assisted Output?* 52 IIC – International Review of Intellectual Property and Competition Law, 1190, 1197 (2021). *See also* Case C-604/10, *Football Dataco Ltd and Others v. Yahoo! UK Ltd and Others*, 1 Mar. 2012, ECLI:EU:C:2012:115, para. 42; Case C-469/17, *Funke Medien NRW GmbH v. Bundesrepublik Deutschland*, 29 Jul. 2019, ECLI:EU:C:2019:623, para. 23.
1071. *See* Pavel Koukal, *Autorské právo, lidská práva a public domain*, pp. 87, 440 (Masarykova Univerzita 2019).
1072. *See* Ivo Telec & Pavel Tůma, *Autorský zákon. Komentář*, p. 23 (C.H.Beck 2019).

and name of the characters, provided that even these parts meet the qualification criteria discussed above. The same applies to a collection of independent works or other elements – the author's creative activity is then realized in the selection and arrangement of the content. Even a creative adaptation of an existing work may give rise to a new work; however, the rights of the author of the underlying (preexistent) work remain unaffected.[1073] An unauthorized adaptation might thus be an infringement of both moral (right to integrity) as well as economic rights (right to use the work, predominantly in the form of reproduction and communication to the public).

775. The section 2/6 of the Copyright Act also defines what is not to be considered a work of authorship. Namely, objectively unperceivable data (idea, procedure, principle, method, discovery, scientific theory), non-creative data (daily news or any other info-data), and data that are of mere technical character (mathematic or similar formula and a statistical graph).[1074]

776. The Copyright Act protects other intangible assets, including the performance of the performing artist, the audio recording (phonogram), audiovisual recording (videogram), and television or radio broadcast.[1075] Apart from the performance of the performing artist that must reflect her personality, there are no specific requirements as regards the emergence of protection.[1076] These remaining intangible assets are not 'creations' resulting from the creative activity of a human but the result of an economic (production) activity.[1077] The protection of press publications, as envisaged in the DSM Directive, is yet to be transposed into the Copyright Act by the DSM Directive Amendment Act.

§4. Authorship and Entitled Persons

777. The Czech copyright law follows the European continental natural law tradition that only a natural person can be an author – creator of a work of authorship.[1078] This concept of 'ontological unity' of the creation and its creator, therefore, binds the existence of the creation to the expression of the creative abilities of its creator.[1079] Consequently, any non-human entity (legal person, animal, artificial intelligence) must not be regarded as the creator. Only the natural person – the author is thus the original bearer of moral and economic rights. A peculiarity of the Czech copyright law is that the director of a theatre play is not regarded as an author

1073. *See* s. 2/4 of the Copyright Act.

1074. *See* Radim Polčák, *§ 2 Autorské dílo, in Autorský zákon*, p. 63 (Radim Polčák et al., Leges 2020).

1075. As a result of the transposition of the Database Directive, also a database in which its producer made a substantial investment, is protected by *sui generis* rights. *See* for details Part IV, Chapter 6. Protection of databases (incl. 'data ownership').

1076. *See* Martin Valoušek, *§ 67 Umělecký výkon a výkonný umělec, in Autorský zákon*, p. 543 (Radim Polčák et al., Leges 2020).

1077. *See* Ivo Telec & Pavel Tůma, *Autorský zákon. Komentář*, p. 781 (C.H.Beck 2019).

1078. *See* s. 5/1 of the Copyright Act.

1079. *See* Ivo Telec & Pavel Tůma, *Autorský zákon. Komentář*, p. 92 (C.H.Beck 2019).

but merely a performing artist.[1080] On the other hand, the director of the visual work is its author – the rights of the works utilized in the audiovisual work, however, remain unaffected.[1081]

778. However, it is possible that more persons have willingly expressed their creative abilities vis-à-vis one creation together. The individual results of the creative activity of the co-authors might be distinguishable but not capable of independent use, i.e., the use of the individual contribution would make no sense.[1082] The emerging exclusive rights belong to the co-authors jointly and severally.[1083] The co-authorship in Czech law is built on the principle of unanimity – no matter the size, qualitatively or quantitatively evaluated, of the contribution of the individual co-author, all the co-authors are equal as regards deciding about disposing of the work.[1084] On the other hand, the size of the contributions shall be proportional to the share of the proceeds if not agreed otherwise by the co-authors.[1085] In case of rights infringement, section 8/4 of the Copyright Act stipulates that any co-authors might take the necessary steps to protect them individually. As regulated in section 8/2 of the Copyright Act, involvement of another person in a non-creative way, such as 'providing of assistance or advice of a technical, administrative or professional nature or providing of documentary or technical material', does not give rise to the co-authorship. The same holds for mere initiation of the creative process, i.e., an instigator is not a co-author.[1086]

779. In specific cases, the Copyright Act either entitles other persons to directly exercise the author's economic rights or specifically curtails their exercise by the author. This modification of the status quo is justified by the non-creative involvement (primarily investment) of this other person in creating the work.[1087] The first of such cases is a work created by an employee to fulfil her obligations arising from the employment relationship. In exchange for bearing the related economic risks, the employer is entitled to exercise all the economic rights in his own name and on his own account, including the possibility to assign such entitlement to exercise the economic rights.[1088] The author's consent for such an assignment is needed;[1089] however, it is standardly part of the employment contract. As regards moral rights, under the section 58/4 of the Copyright Act, these are *ex lege* limited in such a way that the employer is entitled to decide about the divulgation of the work, may interfere with the integrity of the work (e.g., adapt it or modify it), and decide upon the indication of authorship. The employer is also entitled to complete the work.

1080. As confirmed by the judgments of the Supreme Court of 18. 5. 2021, Case No. 27 Cdo 159/2020 and Case No. 27 Cdo 940/2020.
1081. s. 63/1 of the Copyright Act.
1082. *See* Radim Polčák, *§ 2 Autorské dílo, in Autorský zákon*, p. 87 (Radim Polčák et al., Leges 2020).
1083. *See* s. 8/3 of the Copyright Act.
1084. *See* s. 8/4 of the Copyright Act.
1085. *See* s. 8/5 of the Copyright Act.
1086. *See* v. 8/2 of the Copyright Act.
1087. *See* Ivo Telec & Pavel Tůma, *Autorský zákon. Komentář*, p. 649 (C.H.Beck 2019).
1088. *See generally* s. 58 of the Copyright Act.
1089. *See* s. 58/1 of the Copyright Act.

According to the section 58/3 of the Copyright Act the employee is entitled to request a licence grant under usual conditions if the employee's work is not utilized sufficiently. Moreover, according to the section 58/6 of the Copyright Act, the employee, if not agreed otherwise, may claim reasonable additional remuneration against the employer if the remuneration paid to her is manifestly disproportionate to the gains from the exploitation thereof.[1090] Even if the legal relationship (employment) ceases, this regime remains unaffected.[1091] However, when the employer dies or ceases to exist without a legal successor, according to the section 58/2 of the Copyright Act, the right to exercise economic rights reverts to the author. As neither the moral nor the economic rights are assignable/transferable under section 26 of the Copyright Act, the assignment of the entitlement to exercise the economic rights to the work created in the employment relationship is, as to its effect, as closest as possible under the Czech law to the complete translative transfer/assignment of copyright as is known, e.g., in the USA. However, this specific regime can be overridden by the employer and employee's agreement.

780. Another situation where the economic rights are exercised *ex lege* by another person than the author is the collective work. The qualification of work as a collective work, as laid down in section 59/1 of the Copyright Act, presupposes a multiplicity of authors who participate in the creation of the work in such a way that their contributions are not capable of independent use. Furthermore, as stipulated by the section 59/1 of the Copyright Act, this work must be created at the initiative and under the direction of another natural or legal person, under whose name the work must be made available to the public. The Czech Supreme Court also explained what must be understood as the direction of the creative activity, namely *'constant supervision of the performance of the creative activity and its management, consisting in particular in determining the overall concept and the content, functional or economic character of the work and its final appearance'.*[1092] According to the section 59/2 of the Copyright Act, the collective works created to order are considered to be employee's work to which the above-described regime applies, where the customer (investor) is the fictive employer, the person entitled to exercise the economic rights.

781. In the case of work created to order, it is deemed that the author has granted the customer a licence to fulfil the purpose of the contract.[1093] Standardly, however, the licence specifications are agreed upon in detail in the contract that combines the contract for work and licence agreement. If not stipulated otherwise, according to the section 61 of the Copyright Act, the work may be used by the author herself and she can also grant a licence to another party if it does not conflict with the customer's legitimate interest.

1090. Pursuant to the s. 58/6 of the Copyright Act this additional remuneration cannot be claimed, however, does not apply to computer programs, databases, and cartographical works.
1091. *See* s. 58/8 of the Copyright Act.
1092. *See* Judgement of the Supreme Court of 29 Nov. 2012, Case No. 30 Cdo 725/2012.
1093. *See* s. 61/1 of the Copyright Act.

782. The possibility to dispose of the work might be merely curtailed by another natural or legal person. In the case of schoolwork, as regulated in sections 35 and 60 of the Copyright Act, i.e., work created by a pupil or student to fulfil her study obligations, the respective educational institution may require granting a licence under standard conditions. If not agreed upon otherwise, the author is free to utilize the schoolwork provided that the institution's legitimate interests are not jeopardized with such use.[1094] Finally, the institution might, according to the section 60/3 of the Copyright Act also request a financial contribution from the earnings gained from the utilization of the work for the costs incurred by the creation of the work.

783. Due to the economic (investment) nature that lacks the creative element, the originally entitled person in the cases of subject matter protected by related rights may also be a legal person such as a business corporation. The only exception to this rule is the rights granted to the performance of a performing artist – only the performer as a natural person may be the original holder of the moral and economic rights granted.[1095]

§5. Rights Granted

784. The Copyright Act regulates copyright (more precisely, authors' rights as elucidated above) and rights related to copyright. These differ mainly in the subject matter they protect, their nature, and their transferability. On the other hand, both copyright and related rights need no formalities to arise, not even the copyright notice. Therefore, the expression of the work in perceptible form suffices to enjoy complete protection.[1096] The same applies to the performer's right to her performance mutatis mutandis. The related rights also do not require fulfilling any formalities to come into effect. Here, merely the sole making of the respective recording or broadcasting of the respective broadcast (radio or television) suffices to give rise to the protection.

785. The author's rights include, according to the section 10 of the Copyright Act, exclusive moral rights, and economic rights. Both cannot be waived and are not transferable/assignable.[1097]

786. The moral rights are laid down in section 11 of the Copyright Act and include the right of divulgation (decision on publication of the work), right to claim authorship, and right of integrity, i.e., the right to control any alteration and interference with the work. As a general rule expressed in section 11/3 of the Copyright Act., any other person using the work must not do so in a manner tarnishing its value. No moral rights are granted to the subject matter protected by related rights,

1094. *See* s. 60/2 of the Copyright Act.
1095. *See* s. 69 of the Copyright Act.
1096. Apart from the fulfilment of the other legal preconditions, such as originality of such expression as discussed above.
1097. *See* s. 11/4 and s. 26/1 of the Copyright Act.

apart from the performance of the performer, who enjoys the right of divulgation and protection against any deformation, mutilation, or other change of her performance which would harm her reputation.[1098]

787. The economic rights include mainly the right to use the protected subject matter and the resale right for the benefit of the author of an original work of art and remuneration right for the statutory allowed private copying and rental. The right to use the work is, at its core, an exclusionary control right vis-à-vis the exploitation of the work itself in intangible form (any communication to the public)[1099] or tangible form (reproduction, distribution, rental, lending, and exhibition).[1100] The forms of use expressed in section 12 of the Copyright act are listed demonstratively. Furthermore, the Supreme Court noted that the term 'use of work' must be interpreted broadly.[1101] In the digital context, mainly the use in the form of reproduction and communication to the public are of importance and thus will be discussed in more detail.

788. The right of reproduction, as regulated in section 13 of the Copyright Act, covers any copy of the protected subject matter in any form, both permanent and temporary. The CJEU considers the regulation in the Information Society directive of this economic right as *'a measure of full harmonization of the corresponding substantive law'*.[1102] Therefore, when interpreting and applying the national law, all the relevant case law of the CJEU must be considered. Consequently, even 'incidental' copies without any self-standing economic value are relevant from the copyright point of view, albeit allowed to be done by the respective limitation of copyright regulated in section 38a of the Copyright Act.[1103] This right is also infringed when only parts of the protected subject matter are copied without authorization, provided these parts fulfil the legal requirements for protection.[1104] The right of reproduction is not subject to exhaustion.[1105] Digitalization, i.e., format shifting, is to be regarded as a reproduction of the protected subject matter; however, per se does not give rise to any new exclusionary and erga omnes effective right.[1106] Therefore, when an unprotected subject matter belonging to the public domain is digitized, the maker of the digital reproduction is not granted an exclusive absolute right to the digital copy.

1098. *See* s. 70/1 and 4 of the Copyright Act.
1099. The right of communication to the public, however, does not encompass only the online uses, including the making available of the protected subject matter on demand online (s. 18/2 of the Copyright Act), but also more traditional uses such as broadcasting (s. 21 of the Copyright Act).
1100. *See* Pavel Koukal, *§ 12 Majetková práva, in Autorský zákon*, p. 118 (Radim Polčák et al., Leges 2020).
1101. *See* Judgement of the Supreme Court of 11. 2. 2015, No. 30 Cdo 2789/2013.
1102. *See* Case C-476/17, *Pelham GmbH and Others v. Ralf Hütter and Florian Schneider-Esleben*, 29 Jul. 2019, ECLI:EU:C:2019:624, para. 86.
1103. As explained in detail in Case C-302/10, *Infopaq International A/S v. Danske Dagblades Forening*, 17 Jan. 2012, ECLI:EU:C:2012:16, paras 47–57.
1104. *See* s. 2/3 of the Copyright Act.
1105. *See* Pavel Koukal, *§ 12 Majetková práva, in Autorský zákon. Komentář*, p. 124 (Radim Polčák, et al., Leges 2020).
1106. *See* Ivo Telec, *Digitalizace filmů, Právní rozhledy*, 15–16, p. 526 (2015).

789. The prevalence of digital distribution of copyrighted subject matter renders the right of communication to the public gradually more relevant than the rights relating to tangible media. Taking into account the case law of the CJEU, this right is invoked when there is 'communication' by any technical means to the 'public', i.e., *'larger indeterminate number of potential recipients and implies, moreover, a fairly large number of persons'*.[1107] Communication via new technical means must always be authorized.[1108] Moreover, if there is a 'new public', i.e., a public not foreseen by the rightsholder when authorizing the first use (initial communication), this economic right might be infringed, even if the technical mean of communication remains the same.[1109]

790. Where a protected subject matter is made available to the public on-demand online, the reproduction thereof is a technical prerequisite and necessity within the whole process.[1110] The Czech Supreme Court thus already qualified various technical means of unauthorized utilization of a protected subject matter as infringing both economic rights. Examples include the uploading of the film works to a public file-hosting server and subsequent sharing of hyperlinks enabling the download of these works on a discussion forum;[1111] the 'sharing' of the protected subject matter on P2P networks (referred to by the Supreme Court also as *'internet exchange networks'*)[1112] or the presentation of the part of the work on a web site.[1113] Interestingly, in the cases concerning P2P networks, the Supreme Court noted that communication to the public of the protected subject matter via this technical means is notoriously known in the general public for its illegality.[1114]

791. The use of the protected subject matter in the form of a link was extensively evaluated by the Czech courts.[1115] The Constitutional Court aptly summarized the qualification thereof as communication to the public under the Copyright

1107. *See* Case C-306/05, *Sociedad General de Autores y Editores de España (SGAE) v. Rafael Hoteles SA*, 7 Dec. 2006, ECLI:EU:C:2006:764, para. 37.
1108. *See* Case C607/11, *ITV Broadcasting Ltd and Others v. TVCatchUp Ltd*, 7 Mar. 2013, ECLI-:EU:C:2013:147, para. 24.
1109. *See* Case C527/15, *Stichting Brein v. Jack Frederik Wullems*, 26 Apr. 2017, ECLI-:EU:C:2017:300, para. 33.
1110. *See* Irena Holcová, *§ 13 Rozmnožování, in Autorský zákon a předpisy související (včetně mezinárodních smluv a evropských předpisů): komentář*, p. 160 (Irena Holcová, et. al., Wolters Kluwer, 2019.
1111. *See* Judgement of the Supreme Court of 29 Mar. 2017, Case No. 5 Tdo 211/2017; Judgement of the Supreme Court of 21. Jul. 2021, Case No. 5 Tdo 636/2021.
1112. *See* Judgement of the Supreme Court of 23 Feb. 2011, Case No. 5 Tdo 164/2011; Judgement of the Supreme Court of 18 Oct. 2017, Case No. 5 Tdo 1167/2017.
1113. *See* Judgement of the Supreme Court of 31 Aug. 2016, Case No. 30 Cdo 733/2016.
1114. *See* Judgement of the Supreme Court of 18 Oct. 2017, Case No. 5 Tdo 1167/2017, para. 18.
1115. *See* Judgement of the Supreme Court of 27 Feb. 2013, Case No. 8 Tdo 137/2013 (examined by the Judgement of the Constitutional Court of 10 Sep. 2013, Case No. III. ÚS 1768/13 – confirmed); Judgement of the Supreme Court of 29 May 2013, Case No. 5 Tdo 271/2013; Judgement of the Supreme Court of 12 Nov. 2014, Case No. 5 Tdo 1136/2014-21 (examined also by the Judgement of the Constitutional Court of 25 Oct. 2017, Case No. I. ÚS 578/15 – confirmed); Judgement of the Supreme Court of 15 Aug. 2018, Case No. 5 Tdo 692/2018.

Act.[1116] Considering the relevant case law of the CJEU, the court identified four possible situations that may arise.[1117] The protected subject matter is not communicated to the public in the first three situations. This is the case where the link leads to either protected subject matter published lawfully or unlawfully on the website in question, but that is lawfully published elsewhere online for the same public. Finally, linking to protected subject matter 'that was published unlawfully on the target of the link and not lawfully published elsewhere, where the linking is not done for profit by a person who did not know or could not reasonably have known of the unlawful nature of the publication' is also not to be qualified as communication to the public.[1118] On the other hand, according to this Judgment, the situation where a link to the protected subject matter, which has not been lawfully published online elsewhere, is posted without authorization by a person who knows or could reasonably have known of the infringing nature of the publication thereof is to be qualified as an unauthorized communication to the public. The Constitutional Court the followed, that the for-profit nature of such linking causes the knowledge about the unlawful nature of the publication of the protected subject matter to be presumed. Due to the date of its issuance, this Constitutional Court judgment logically did not incorporate the temporally subsequent relevant case law of the CJEU. The further criteria elaborated by the CJEU, i.e., the existence of contractual restrictions enforced by technical protection measures,[1119] must also be evaluated when qualifying the respective link as communication to the public.

792. The exclusive rights (both moral and economic) granted are not perpetual but limited in time. The Czech Republic follows the EU legislation and limits the author's economic rights for the duration of life and seventy years *post mortem auctoris*.[1120] According to the section 28 of the Copyright act, after this term, the work enters the public domain and might be used by anyone. As stipulated in section 11/4 of the Copyright Act, the author's moral rights cease upon death. However, even after that, nobody can claim the authorship over the work and use it in a manner diminishing its value – this 'postmortal protection' might be invoked by the close person of the author, respective CMO, or societies associating authors.[1121] Where there are more co-authors, the seventy-year term shall be calculated since the death of the last co-author.[1122] In the case of a collective work, where the authors were not revealed to the public, the term of protection is seventy years *post publicationis*, i.e., since the lawful publication of the work.[1123] In case of the audiovisual work the

1116. *See* Judgement of the Constitutional Court of 25 Oct. 2017, Case No. I. ÚS 578/15.

1117. *Ibid.*, para. 17.

1118. *Ibid.*

1119. *See* C-392/19, *VG Bild-Kunst v. Stiftung Preußischer Kulturbesitz*, 9 Mar. 2021, ECLI-:EU:C:2021:181.

1120. *See generally* the Directive 2006/116/EC of the European Parliament and of the Council of 12 Dec. 2006 on the term of protection of copyright and certain related rights (codified version, i.e., with the amendments done by the Directive 2011/77/EU of the European Parliament and of the Council of 27 Sep. 2011 amending Directive 2006/116/EC on the term of protection of copyright and certain related rights), OJ L 372, 27 Dec. 2006.

1121. *See* s. 11/5 of the Copyright Act.

1122. *See* s. 27/2 of the Copyright Act.

1123. *See* s. 27/3 of the Copyright Act.

Section 27/5 of the Copyright Act identifies the start of the *seventy years term* is actually postponed up until the death of the last of the following persons: '*the director, the author of the script, the author of the dialogues and the composer of the music specially created for use in the audiovisual work*'.

793. The rights related to copyright last standardly for fifty years since the creation of the performance or making of the recording or the first broadcasting.[1124] However, Copyright Act foresees certain situations where the duration and/or decisive day for the start of the term of protection is different. If the performance is fixed in a recording, the rights shall, according to the section 73 of the Copyright Act, expire after fifty years (respectively seventy years in the case of a phonogram) from the first day of the lawful publication or communication to the public of such performance, whichever is earlier. According to the section 77 of the Copyright Act, the rights of the phonogram producer are prolonged to seventy years if the phonogram is lawfully published or, if it was not published, lawfully communicated to the public within the original term of protection (fifty years). If the audiovisual recording is published, the duration of rights of the producer shall be counted from the day of such publications.[1125] Next, according to the section 87a of the Copyright Act, the publisher of a not yet published work for which the term of protection lapsed is granted economic rights akin to the author's rights, however, only for twenty-five years. The publisher of a work has the right to remuneration for the legally allowed copying for personal purposes that, according to the section 87/2 of the Copyright Act lasts fifty years since publishing the work. As set in the DSM Directive Amendment Act, the to-be-introduced rights of the publisher of a press publication shall last two years from the publication.

§6. Limits of Protection

794. The copyright law aims to also fulfil and protect interests other than the private moral and economic interests of the rightsholders. These include, *inter alia*, the general interest in incentivizing the artistic and scientific activity of humans, the general interest in access to the resulting culture and knowledge as well as the private interest of the users in the possibility to realize themselves by getting inspired and building upon the existing art and knowledge.[1126]

795. The limits of protection granted by the Copyright Act are thus fundamental for the protection of these other interests by enabling the use of the protected subject matter even without consent by the rightsholder or even against her will. This principle, concerning exceptions and limitations, is enshrined in EU copyright

1124. *See* s. 77 of the Copyright Act for the right of the phonogram producer; s. 81 of the Copyright Act for the right of the producer of an audiovisual recording; s. 85 of the Copyright Act for the broadcaster's rights.

1125. *See* s. 81 of the Copyright Act.

1126. *See* Matěj Myška, *Výjimky a omezení autorského práva v prostředí digitálních sítí*, p. 30 (Wolters Kluwer ČR 2020).

law[1127] and has been repeatedly confirmed by the CJEU in its judgments[1128] and is thus generally applicable also in Czech copyright law. Moreover, the CJEU also noted that the national courts must interpret the exceptions and limitations so that their effectiveness and fundamental rights enshrined in the Charter of Fundamental Rights of the EU must be safeguarded.[1129]

796. The Czech copyright law recognizes general and specific intrasystem limits of the rights granted.[1130] The former category includes the above-discussed delimitation of what is being protected (protected subject matter) and for how long (term of protection).[1131] The principle of exhaustion of the right of distribution is also regarded as a general intrasystem limit.[1132] The latter limits include the specific exceptions and limitations regulated in Part IV of the Copyright Act.[1133]

797. The Czech lawmaker transposed all the exceptions and limitations to exclusive rights available in Article 5 of the Information Society Directive in the Copyright Act, apart from the 'pastiche' exception, which is to be transposed by the DSM Directive Amendment Act.

798. In the digital context, two of the exceptions and limitations (internal limits) are of particular interest – the one is allowing private copies, and the other is allowing temporary acts of reproduction. Namely, the first one concerns the most common legal title on which the users rely when making copies of the protected subject matter. The second one allows technically needed copies.

1127. *See, e.g.*, recital 31 of the Information Society Directive, recital 6 of the DSM Directive.
1128. *See* specifically in the cases related to application of exceptions and limitations: Case C-516/17, *Spiegel Online GmbH v. Volker Beck*, 29 Jul. 2019, ECLI:EU:C:2019:625, para. 3; Case C-469/17, *Funke Medien NRW GmbH v. Bundesrepublik Deutschland*, 29 Jul. 2019, ECLI:EU:C:2019:623, para. 3.
1129. *See* Case C-516/17, *Spiegel Online GmbH v. Volker Beck*, 29 Jul. 2019, ECLI:EU:C:2019:625, ruling para. 3; case C-469/17, *Funke Medien NRW GmbH v. Bundesrepublik Deutschland*, 29 Jul. 2019, ECLI:EU:C:2019:623, ruling para. 3.
1130. *See* Petr Prchal, *Limity autorskoprávní ochrany*, pp. 136–137 (Leges 2016). Extrasystemic limits include *inter alia* other fundamental rights (such as the freedom of speech), consumer protection and competition protection (Generally on this distinction, *see also* Petr Prchal, *O vyváženosti a vnějších omezeních autorskoprávní ochrany v digitálním prostředí, in Nové technológie, internet a duševné vlastníctvo*, pp. 40–73 (Zuzana Adamová ed., Typi Universitatis Tyrnaviensis 2019). For overview of the exceptions and limitations in Czech copyright law, *see* Matěj Myška, *Exceptions and Limitations: A Consideration of Copyright Theory and Practice In the Czech Republic, in Cambridge Handbook of Intellectual Property in Central and Eastern Europe*, pp. 165–194 (Mira T. Sundara Rajan ed., Cambridge University Press 2019).
1131. *See* Petr Prchal, *Limity autorskoprávní ochrany*, p. 37 (Leges 2016).
1132. *Ibid.*
1133. The s. 47b/1 of the Act No. 111/1998 Sb., on higher education institutions and on amendments and supplements to some other Acts (Higher Education Institutions Act), as amended also includes a specific limit on the rights of the author as it obliges the higher education institutions *'to provide public access to a on a non-profit basis, bachelor's, master's, dissertation and rigorous theses that have been defended, including the opinions of the opponents and the record of the course and result of the defense, through the database of qualifying theses that it manages'*. This provision is discussed in detail by Matěj Myška, *Providing public access to theses and copyright law*. 12 *Grey Journal*, 36 (2019).

799. The former limit of copyright, denominated in section 30 of the Copyright Act, somewhat confusingly as 'free uses', allows the copying of protected subject matter for the personal needs of a natural person if there is no direct or indirect economic or commercial advantage. The criterion of 'personal use' is to be understood as private use by the person making the copy or in the circle of her family, friends, or close persons.[1134] Interestingly, the use of protected subject matter in a store for the sole enjoyment of the salesman is also to be qualified as personal use if this use does not bring any direct or indirect economic or commercial advantage to the shop and does not influence consumers in any way, i.e., if the public is not perceptive to the respective use.[1135] Even though this condition is not set in the Copyright Act,[1136] due to the judicial activity of the CJEU,[1137] the source copy must be legal. The lawmaker accepted this conclusion in the explanatory memorandum to the amending act No. 50/2019 Sb., that implemented the EU legislative acts relating to the Marrakesh Treaty, where the requirement of a legal source was stipulated as a 'general rule' for the application of any exception or limitation.[1138]

800. The latter discussed limit of copyright enables the basic technical functioning of various activities and services in the digital context, such as browsing websites or caching data relayed via networks.[1139] According to the section 38a of the Copyright Act a transitory or subsidiary copy that forms an integral and necessary part of a technological process and does not have any independent economic significance does not infringe the exclusive rights. However, this copy's sole purpose must be either to enable the transmission of the protected subject matter via a network between third parties by an intermediary or the lawful use of the protected subject matter. The latter condition, together with the three-step test, excludes the application of this limitation to temporary copies necessarily created in 'streaming' of the protected subject matter published on third-party websites without rightsholders' authorization.[1140] Vis-à-vis computer programs, the limitation applies only to the transmission thereof and does not apply to databases.[1141]

1134. *See* Judgement of the Regional Court in Brno of 31 Oct. 2005, Case No. 23 C 34/2004-232, confirmed by the Judgement of the Constitutional Court of 1 Jan. 2010, Case No. II. ÚS 423/10.

1135. *See* Judgement of the Constitutional Court of 15 Apr. 2014, Case No. II. ÚS 3076/13.

1136. The Supreme Court previously even decided to the contrary, i.e., that a legal source is not needed (Judgement of the Supreme Court of 25 Mar. 2009, Case No. 5 Tdo 234/2009).

1137. *See* Judgement of the Court of Justice of the European Union of 10 Apr. 2014, Case No. C-435/12, para. 38; Judgement of the Court of Justice of the European Union of 12 Nov. 2015, Case No. C-572/13, para. 59.

1138. Důvodová zpráva k vládnímu návrhu zákona, kterým se mění zákon č. 121/2000 Sb., o právu autorském, o právech souvisejících s právem autorským a o změně některých zákonů (autorský zákon), ve znění pozdějších předpisů [online]. Poslanecká sněmovna, 8. volební období, 2017–, sněmovní tisk 175/0, 15 May 2018, to point 5 – to s. 39a, p. 15.

1139. Důvodová zpráva k vládnímu návrhu zákona, kterým se mění zákon č. 121/2000 Sb., o právu autorském, o právech souvisejících s právem autorským a o změně některých zákonů (autorský zákon), ve znění pozdějších předpisů [online]. Poslanecká sněmovna, 4. volební období, 2002–2006, Parliamentary print 1111/0, 7 Sep. 2005, to point 28 – to s. 38a, p. 51.

1140. *See* C527/15, *Stichting Brein v. Jack Frederik Wullems*, 26 Apr. 2017, ECLI:EU:C:2017:300, para. 70.

1141. *See* s. 66/7 and s. 94 of the Copyright Act.

801. Under the section 29/1 of the Copyright Act, every exception and limitation in Czech copyright law is subjected to the 'three-step test'. Consequently, it must be applied only in certain special cases without conflicting with the normal exploitation of the protected subject matter and the legitimate interests of the rightsholder must not be unreasonably prejudiced. This additional condition exposes the users trying to rely on the exceptions and limitations to a high degree of legal uncertainty. Not only must they fulfil the preconditions of the respective exception or limitation, but they must also pass this relatively vague test that is used as a justification for restrictive interpretation and application of the exception and limitation at hand.[1142] Furthermore, as regulated in section 29/2 of the Copyright Act, exceptions and limitations are applicable, apart from few exceptional cases, only to protect subject matter that has been already made public.

§7. Licensing

802. Granting a licence is a standard way to allow another person to use the protected subject matter. In cases of copyrighted works to which the absolute rights are not assignable/transferable under Czech law, also the only way to do so *inter vivos*.[1143] The Czech regulation of licence and licence agreement is contained in the Civil Code. It consists of a general part applicable to licenses to any intellectual property (sections 2358–2370 Civil Code) and a specific part applicable only to subject matter protected by copyright, related rights, and databases (sections 2371–2389 Civil Code).

803. The licence agreement is standardly regarded as a contract between the licensor and the licensee, by which the terms and conditions of use of the protected subject matter are stipulated. The minimum content of the contract (*essentialia negotii*) should include, apart from the parties, the specification of the licensed subject matter, the granting of the licence (i.e., authorization to use), and the arrangement of remuneration.[1144] The licence could also be granted as gratuitous. The scope of the license, however, is not an essential element. The Civil Code sets out subsidiarily in section 2376, that, if not agreed or if it is not apparent from the purpose of the contract otherwise, the territorial scope of a licence is limited to the territory of the Czech Republic, and the temporal scope of a licence is limited to the period usual for the given type of protected subject matter and manner of use (with the maximum of one year however), and the quantitative scope of a licence is limited to the amount which is customary for the given type of subject matter and manner of use. It is, however, not standard to rely on the subsidiary statutory regulation but

1142. *See, e.g.*, Judgement of the Supreme Court of 28 Mar. 2013, Case No. 30 Cdo 3093/2012; Judgement of the Supreme Court of 31 Jan. 2013, Case No. 30 Cdo 3056/2012.

1143. In case of death of the author the economic rights are transferred to the heir(s) *mortis causa* (*see* s. 26/2 of the Copyright Act).

1144. *See* Ivo Telec & Pavel Tůma, *Autorský zákon. Komentář*, p. 564 (C.H.Beck 2019).

to set out all the details in the contract individually. If not expressly agreed otherwise, the licence granted is presumed to be non-exclusive, as stipulated by the section 2362 of Civil Code, i.e., the same subject matter might also be licensed to another party. In the case of an exclusive license, even the rightsholder must refrain from exercising the licensed right to the protected subject matter, if not expressly agreed otherwise, as regulated in 2360/1 of the Civil Code. The second paragraph of this section of the Civil Code further stipulates that a licence granted during the duration of the exclusive licence shall not arise without the consent of the exclusive licensee. The DSM Directive Amendment Act introduces the specific measures aimed at achieving fair remuneration in exploitation contracts of authors and performers by amending the Copyright Act and Civil Code.[1145]

804. The 'public licenses' prevalent in the digital context are fully acknowledged by the Civil Code. In contrast with the standard contracting process described above, in this case, the offer to enter into a licensing agreement may be aimed at an indefinite number of persons (*offerta ad incertas personas*) as foreseen by the section 2373/1 of the Civil Code. The respective conditions of the licence agreement might be set according to the section 2373/2 of the Civil Code by reference to standardized licensing terms (e.g., Creative Commons terms and conditions or various software-related ones such as GNU GPL family of terms and conditions). Section 2373/2 of the Civil Code foresees that the contract is concluded as soon as the licensee-to-be performs a specific act without notifying the offeror by giving or accepting performance, standardly by using the protected subject matter.[1146] By definition, the 'public licenses' are non-exclusive licenses. However, the 'public licenses' have not yet been extensively tested before the Czech courts.

805. The Czech copyright law respects the autonomy of the rightsholders who *'are free to decide how to or not to exercise their private rights ... '*.[1147] Exceptionally, an exhaustively enumerated set of economic rights are legally entrusted to a Collective Management Organization (CMO) for collective exercise within the system of collective management of rights.[1148] This means complete management of the selected rights that is undertaken consistently, in the name and at the sole responsibility of the CMO and on the rightsholder's account.[1149] The collective management of certain rights to particular protected subject matter can be exercised only by one CMO, i.e., the Copyright Act construes in section 96a/2/c a legal monopoly in this regard that must not be misused.[1150] This means that the user cannot obtain a licence for the same use of the same protected subject matter from two different CMOs. The CMOs must, according to the section 96a of the Copyright Act, based on a public law authorization granted by the Ministry of Culture. However, not all the protected subject matter might be collectively managed, merely

1145. *See* Arts 18–23 of the DSM Directive.
1146. *See* s. 2373/2 of the Civil Code.
1147. *See* Ivo Telec & Pavel Tůmak, *Autorský zákon. Komentář*, p. 982 (C.H.Beck 2019).
1148. *Ibid.*
1149. *See* s. 97/3 of the Copyright Act.
1150. As *inter alia* discussed in C-351/12, *OSA – Ochranný svaz autorský pro práva k dílům hudebním o.s. v. Léčebné lázně Mariánské Lázně a.s.*, 27 Feb. 2014, ECLI:EU:C:2014:110, paras 72, 84, 86.

'works, published or offered for publication, performances, phonograms, and audiovisual recordings'.[1151] Most notably, the rights of broadcasters are not included. Also, according to the section 95/3 of the Copyright Act, only specific rightsholders may be represented by a CMO, namely, the original rightsholders or, where possible, the person to which the rights have been transferred; persons *ex lege* entitled to exercise the rights (e.g., the employer) and persons who have been granted an exclusive licence for the duration of that economic right and with a right to sublicense it (at least of the territory of Czech Republic).

806. The Copyright Act distinguishes three regimes of collective management of rights – mandatory,[1152] extended,[1153] and voluntary. The first two regimes are explicitly regulated in the Copyright Act, where the collectively managed types of rights are exhaustively enumerated. In the case of mandatory collective management, the rightsholders cannot exercise their economic rights by themselves, and there is no option to opt out or revoke this regime.[1154] The most notable right managed in this regime is the right to remuneration for the allowed copying for personal use ('private copying levies') regulated in section 25 of the Copyright Act. The extended collective management of rights is characterized by the all-encompassing ('extended') effect of the granted licenses. Such a licence then covers not only the whole repertoire of the CMO for the specific use but also other works of the same type for the same use, where the other rightsholders are represented *ex lege* automatically.[1155] The rightsholders might, with certain exceptions, generally opt-out of this regime. As an example, the use of out-of-commerce work is managed in this regime.[1156] The third regime (voluntary) is established by the rights management contract between the CMO and the rightsholder, and its scope is defined by the respective authorization of the Ministry of Culture.[1157] The rightsholders are thus under no obligation to enter into the contract, may revoke it, if they have already into it, or parts of it, or may modify the rights, categories of rights or works, or types of works managed under this contract.[1158] The most important rights for the use in the digital context, i.e., the right of communication to the public in the form of making the protected subject matter available on demand and reproduction, are generally collectively managed in this voluntary regime.

1151. *See* s. 95/1 of the Copyright Act. For the discussion of computer programs as an object of collective management of rights, *see* the discussion below.
1152. *See* s. 97d of the Copyright Act.
1153. *See* s. 97e of the Copyright Act.
1154. *See* Ivo Telec & Pavel Tůma, *Autorský zákon. Komentář*, p. 974 (C.H.Beck 2019).
1155. *See* s. 97e/1 of the Copyright Act.
1156. *See* s. 97e/4/i of the Copyright Act.
1157. *See* Jan Barták, *Kolektivní správa práv autorských a práv souvisejících, in Autorské právo a práva související Vysokoškolská učebnice. 2. Aktualizované Vydání*, p. 319 (Jiří Srstka et al., Leges 2019).
1158. *See* s. 97a/6 of the Copyrgiht Act.

807. There are currently six authorized CMOs operating in the Czech Republic, which differ in terms of the rightsholders they represent and the protected subject matter and rights to it they manage.[1159] These include the following:

(a) OSA – Ochranný svaz autorský pro práva k dílům hudebním, z. s., (OSA – Collective rights management society for musical works, registered association)[1160] that represents authors (composers, lyricists) and (musical) publishers (i.e., licensees in the sense of de facto rightsholders) and manages selected rights to musical works (with or without lyrics), but not dramatico-musical/stage works (opera, musical).
(b) DILIA – Divadelní, literární, audiovizuální agentura, z.s. (DILIA – theatre, literary, and audiovisual agency, registered association)[1161] that represents authors of literary, as well as dubbing directors (if adapting the script), film and other audiovisual directors, print publishers, licensees (in the sense of de facto rightsholders), and manages selected rights to literary, dramatic, dramatico-musical, choreographic works and entertainments in dumb show, audiovisual works (only licensed on behalf of directors).
(c) INTERGRAM – Nezávislá společnost výkonných umělců a výrobců zvukových a zvukově-obrazových záznamů, z. s. (INTERGRAM, an independent society of performers and producers of phonograms and audiovisual fixations)[1162] that represents performers and producers of a phonograms and audiovisual recordings, licensees (in the sense of de facto rightsholders) and manages selected rights to artistic performances, phonograms, audiovisual recordings (audiovisual fixations).
(d) OOA-S – Ochranná organizace autorská – sdružení autorů děl výtvarného umění, architektury a obrazové složky audiovizuálních děl, z.s. (OOA-S Organization for the protection of authors – Association of fine artists, architects and artists involved in audiovisual works) that represents authors of visual art, architects (including authors of the visual part of audiovisual works, i.e., directors of photography, architects, stage designers, and other authors of the visual part of audiovisual works), and their licensees (i.e., licensees in the sense of a de facto rightsholder) and manages selected rights to works of art, i.e., paintings, graphic works, sculptures, photographic works and works expressed by a process similar to photography, architectonic works, including works of urbanism; visual part of audiovisual works, i.e., works utilized in audiovisual works (photography, architecture, stage design and other parts of visual part of audiovisual works).
(e) GESTOR – ochranný svaz autorský z.s. (GESTOR – The Union for the Protection of Authorship, registered association)[1163] that represents authors of visual art and their licensees (i.e., licensees in the above-mentioned sense of a de facto

1159. The website of the Ministry of Culture offers a brief info about the CMOs and their activities on the FAQ webpage: https://www.mkcr.cz/frequently-asked-questions-953.html?lang=en.
1160. Web page: https://www.osa.cz/en/about-us/about/.
1161. Web page: http://www.dilia.eu/index.php/about-us.
1162. Web page: https://www.intergram.cz/?lang=en.
1163. Web page: http://www.gestor.cz/en/.

rightsholder) and manages rights to originals of the visual work of art (as defined in the section 24/3 of the Copyright Act).

(f) OAZA – Ochranná asociace zvukařů, z. s. (The Protective Association of Sound Engineers, registered association)[1164] that represents authors – sound engineers and their licensees (i.e., licensees in the above-mentioned sense of a de facto rightsholder) and manages selected rights to works of the sound engineers (sound design).

Due to the transposition of the Collective Management Directive, the independent management entities[1165] might also manage the rights in the voluntary regime management.[1166]

808. The system of collective licensing in practice, i.e., what types of use for what protected subject matter is managed by whom, is unfortunately too complicated to be described in the necessary depth in this limited space. Therefore, it is advisable to check the status of the use of the protected subject matter and the possibilities/necessities of licensing thereof by the respective CMO before the actual use if there is no exception or limitation of the copyright applicable. The CMOs have, according to the section 97c of the Copyright Act, duty to keep a list of rightsholders for whom they manage the respective rights; therefore, the information could be easily obtained, whether the rights need to be cleared with the CMO or directly with the rightsholder.

§8. Enforcement of Rights

809. The rightsholders might proactively protect their protected subject matter and rights by employing technical protection measures or *ex post* by retorting to various private and/or public law means.

810. The former *ex ante* measure, namely various technical methods of copy and access control, enjoys protection against circumvention. The section 43 of the Copyright Act regulates a specific copyright delict of circumvention of effective technical protection measures as well as commercial dealings in illicit devices enabling the circumvention thereof.[1167] Civil, administrative, and criminal liability may result from perpetrating these delicts.

811. The technological protection measures disrupt the sought-after balance of rights and interests of various parties in the copyright law system. Due to their binary nature and technological 'blindness', these measures cannot accommodate the uses allowed by law. Only in relation to selected exceptions and limitations, the

1164. Web page: https://www.oaza.eu/en/.
1165. *See* s. 104a of the Copyright Act – in Czech 'nezávislý správce práv'.
1166. *See* Ivo Telec & Pavel Tůma, *Autorský zákon. Komentář*, p. 982 (C.H.Beck 2019).
1167. The s. 43 of the Copyright Act is the transposition of the Art. 6 Information Society Directive that again reflects the Art. 11 of the WIPO Copyright Treaty.

rightsholder is obliged by the section 43/4 of the Copyright Act to make the protected subject matter accessible so that the purpose of the respective exception and limitation might be fulfilled by the user. The Copyright Act, however, does not regulate any practicalities of the procedure. Therefore, the actual realization of protecting the users' interests seems to be only theoretical. According to the section 43/4 of the Copyright Act, the rightsholder may completely disregard such request related to the application of the private copy limitation. In the case of measures protecting subject matter made available online under contractual terms, there is pursuant section 43/5 of the Copyright Act even no obligation to make the protected subject matter accessible at all. Moreover, the Czech law does not at all address the consequence of the rightsholder's non-compliance with such request, nor is there a public institution dealing with these issues. Therefore, the legal protection of technical protection measures could be qualified as considering the interests of the rightsholders only.

812. The latter, *ex post*, measure includes the enforcement by civil, administrative, and criminal law means.[1168] The civil law track of enforcement should be considered as a standard and primary means. The administrative and criminal law is to be applied in more grievous cases of copyright infringement. Moreover, criminal law enforcement must be applied scarcely as an *ultima ratio* to respect the principle of subsidiarity of criminal repression.[1169]

813. The civil law remedies and injunctions available to the rightsholder when the exclusive rights are infringed or exposed to infringement are stipulated in section 40 of the Copyright Act. According to this section, the rightsholder may request the following: recognition of authorship; prohibition of further infringement/of exposition to the danger of infringement; information related to copyright infringement; restitution of the consequences of infringement; adequate satisfaction for the immaterial damage (including pecuniary satisfaction, if the apology is not satisfactory); injunction – prohibition of the provision of the service used by third parties to infringe or to expose to danger of infringement.[1170] Moreover, the rightsholders may request the publicization of the judgment finding the copyright infringement.[1171]

1168. The enforcement mechanisms in Czech law reflect the TRIPS agreement and are also result of the transposition of the Directive 2004/48/EC of the European Parliament and of the Council of 29 Apr. 2004 on the enforcement of intellectual property rights, OJ L 157, 30 Mar. 2004 ('IPRED').

1169. As expressed in s. 12 of the Penal Code and observed not only by jurisprudence, but also Constitutional Court in its judgement of 1 Oct. 2006, Case No. I. ÚS 69/06.

1170. This last injunction is applicable against non-infringing providers (third parties acting as intermediaries) of services used by its users to infringe the rights protected by the Copyright Act. The s. 40/1/f of the Copyright Act is a transposition of Art. 8(3) of Information Society Directive and Art. 11 IPRED (*see* Ivo Telec & Pavel Tůma, *Autorský zákon. Komentář*, p. 592 (C.H.Beck 2019)).

1171. *See* s. 40/3 of the Copyright Act.

814. The claim for damages and unjust enrichment is materially regulated in the Civil Code.[1172] However, in section 40/4, the Copyright Act lays down specific rules for determining the amount claimed.[1173] Instead of the actually incurred damage or unjust enrichment, the rightsholder may claim a lump sum in the form of a 'licence analogy', i.e., request the amount that would be due if the user would have been authorized. In the case of unjust enrichment, the amount might be even double the standard licensing fee.

815. The list of legal means how to protect her rights stipulated in section 40 of the Copyright Act is only demonstrative, and the claims and remedies may be applied individually or cumulatively.[1174] The actively legitimated person to make use of the above-described claim is, according to the section 41 of the Copyright Act, not only the author but also the exclusive licensee, as well as the *ex lege* entitled person, such as the employer.

816. According to the section 74 of the Civil Procedure Code, the actively legitimated person may ask for an interim measure (preliminary measure, interlocutory injunction) that may '*be ordered by the presiding judge before proceedings are initiated, if necessary, to provisionally modify the relation of participants, or if feared the enforcement of the judicial decision could be jeopardized*'. According to the section 76/2 of the Civil Procedure Code, not only the direct infringers may be targeted with the interim measure, but also non-liable bystanders, however, '*only if this may justifiably be requested from such person*'.

817. In order to obtain the interim measure, the rightsholder must, pursuant to the section 75/2 of the Civil Procedure Code, describe and prove '*the facts that it is necessary to provisionally modify the relations of participants or if it is feared that the enforcement of the court decision could be jeopardized, a description of facts providing reasons for the interim measure, and it must clearly suggest which interim measure the plaintiff is enforcing*'.

818. As was already noted, less serious copyright infringements may also be classified as administrative offences. The liability is then based on the provisions of the section 105a, 105b of the Copyright Act, with section 105c Copyright Act serving as a common provision in this area. The respective offences consist of unlawful use of the protected subject matter[1175] and infringement of legal the protection of the technological protection measures.[1176] Furthermore, even CMOs not fulfilling their legal obligations might commit this type of offence that is regulated in section

1172. The claim for damages is regulated in ss 2894 et seq. of the Civil Code, the claim for unjust enrichment in ss 2991 et seq. of the Civil Code.

1173. *See* Ivo Telec & Pavel Tůma, *Autorský zákon. Komentář*, p. 512 (C.H.Beck 2019).

1174. *Ibid.*, p. 493.

1175. *See* s. 105a/1/a of the Copyright Act (for a natural person as an offender) and s. 105a/1/a (for a legal person or if a natural person-entrepreneur acts as an offender).

1176. *See* s. 43/1 or s. 43/2 of the Copyright Act, which are regulated in s. 105a/1/b) of the Copyright Act (for a natural person as an offender) and in s. 105b/1/b) of the Copyright Act (for a legal person or if a natural person-entrepreneur acts as an offender).

105ba of the Copyright Act. The Administrative Offences Act lays down general issues of administrative liability, both substantial as well as procedural.[1177] The administrative offences are handled in first instance by the municipal office of a municipality with extended competence ('obecní úřad obce s rozšířenou působností', i.e., an administrative body), in whose territory the administrative offence was committed,[1178] not by general courts.[1179] The regional office (in Czech 'krajský úřad') serves as an appellate body. Punishment for copyright-related administrative offences is a monetary fine.

819. The last resort of enforcement is the criminal law. The Penal Code regulates the general issues of criminal liability and sets out specifically in its section 270, that *'whoever interferes, substantially, with the legally protected rights to authorship works, artistic performance, audio or audiovisual recordings, radio or television broadcasts, or a database without authorization, shall be punished ... '*. This provision is qualified as a 'blanket norm' (norm with blanket disposition).[1180] Therefore, in assessing the criminal liability, a proper evaluation whether there has been a use of the protected subject matter or whether the exceptions and limitations from the Copyright Act point of view must be undertaken.[1181] As a result, it is observable, that, paradoxically, the criminal law senates of the Supreme Court have decided upon fundamental issues of copyright law.[1182] The punishment for criminal infringement varies, as regulated in the section 270 Penal Code, upon the circumstances such as the extent of infringement or amount of damage caused but may include imprisonment (up to eight years in cases of large-scale infringement) and other penalties – disqualification (i.e., prohibition of activity), forfeiture of items and monetary penalty.

1177. *See* Act No. 250/2016 Sb., on Liability and Proceedings for Administrative Offences, as amended.
1178. *See* s. 105c/1/a of the Copyright Act.
1179. According to the s. 105c/1/b of the Copyright Act, in cases of the offences committed by CMOs and offences related to collective management of rights, the respective body is, however, the Ministry of Culture.
1180. *See* Pavel Šámal, *§ 270 Porušení autorského práva, práv souvisejících s právem autorským a práv k databázi, in Trestní zákoník: komentář. II: § 140-421*, p. 2737 (Pavel Šámal & Vladimír Kratochvíl eds., C.H. Beck 2012); *see also* Judgement of the Constitutional of 1 Oct. 2006, Case No. I. ÚS 69/06.
1181. *See* Judgement of the Supreme Court of 24 May 2006, Case No. Tdo 542/2006.
1182. An example might be the decisions of the Supreme Court in assessing the linking as a copyrighted use of the protected subject matter in the form of communication to the public as discussed above.

Chapter 5. Legal Protection of Software

§1. Introduction

820. This chapter introduces the Czech system of copyright protection of computer programs.[1183] As the computer programs are, according to the section 2/2 of the Copyright Act, protected as literary works under Czech law, there is no need to reiterate the explanation of the generally applicable regulation discussed in the previous chapter. The most prominent examples thereof include the issues of licensing and enforcement of exclusive rights. In these areas, the above mentioned is entirely applicable. Furthermore, there is no specific need to introduce the regulatory framework in detail, as all the relevant international instruments (most notably the Article 10 of the TRIPS, Article 4 WIPO Copyright Treaty), as well as the EU Software Directive,[1184] are reflected in the Copyright Act.[1185] As the legal protection of computer programs is fully harmonized by the EU law, in describing the Czech regulation, attention necessarily must be paid to the fundamental decisions of the CJEU. This chapter focuses mainly on the description and explanation of the relevant specificities of the computer programs' legal regulation. First, the chapter focuses on the issue of protected and unprotected subject matter. Second, the issue of persons entitled to exercise the granted rights, including the various modes thereof based on the constellation how the computer program was created, is discussed. Finally, the specific limits of the exclusive rights are discussed.

§2. Protected Subject Matter

821. In Czech law, the terms 'software' and 'computer program' are both used without specific distinction. For example, in the Civil Code,[1186] the section 1811 thereof, regulating pre-contractual information duties of the trader in consumer contracts, obliges the entrepreneur to inform the consumer about the compatibility issues *'between the hardware and software'*. On the other hand, the Copyright Act follows the Software and regulates 'computer program' without providing an explicit definition thereof. The terminological debate seems to be, however, a bit futile, as, in practice, the terminology does not seem to generate any real problems, provided that the involved parties reach an understanding of what is meant thereby.[1187]

1183. The patent protection of computer-implemented inventions is discussed in Part IV, Chapter 1. Patent law (applied to software, etc.).

1184. Directive 2009/24/EC of the European Parliament and of the Council of 23 Apr. 2009 on the legal protection of computer programs (Codified version), OJ L 111, 5. May 2009, ('Software Directive').

1185. Due to the vertical harmonization of copyright protection of computer programs the case law of the CJEU has a profound impact on the interpretation of the national law.

1186. For details on the issues of consumer protection, *see* Part III, Chapter 6. Consumer protection (online sales and online services).

1187. *See* Radim Polčák, *§ 2 Autorské dílo, in Autorský zákon*, p. 58 (Radim Polčák et al., Leges 2020).

822. The Copyright Act follows the current regulatory approach consisting of protecting the computer program as literary work.[1188] Consequently, any objectively perceivable expression of the computer program is thus protected if it is original.[1189] The form of expression, be it in human or computer-only readable form or the programming language in which code is expressed, is irrelevant.[1190] As the CJEU noted, *'the object of the protection ... is the expression in any form of a computer program which permits reproduction in different computer languages, such as the source code and the object code'*.[1191] The originality requirement is fulfilled when the work – a computer program – is an author's own intellectual creation.[1192] An original, and therefore protectable, computer program might also be based on another program whose functionality has been reverse engineered, provided the new code is formally different.[1193] Due to Article 1(3) of the Software Directive, it is also the only criterion that can be used in assessing the eligibility of the computer program for protection.[1194] Any other criteria are to be disregarded. As the computer programs are ultimately 'written' and stored on a medium, there is no problem in making them identifiable with sufficient precision and objectivity as required by the CJEU.[1195]

823. Not only parts or the whole of the expression computer program are protected, but also the preparatory design materials that are original and lead to the creation, reproduction, or subsequent creation of the computer program are protected as a computer program.[1196]

824. On the other hand, various further elements cannot be protected as a computer program. Generally, ideas and principles upon which the computer program is based (or whereupon even the algorithms, logic, and programming languages are based), including the ones underlying its interfaces, are excluded from copyright protection.[1197]

1188. This 'traditional' view is, however, being criticized in the jurisprudence, as it misses the basic economic rationale. *See, e.g.*, Radim Polčák, *§ 2 Autorské dílo, in Autorský zákon*, p. 55 (Radim Polčák et al., Leges 2020).
1189. *See* s. 2/2 of the Copyright Act as well as the recital 13 and Art. 1(3) of the Software Directive.
1190. *See* s. 65/1 of the Copyright Act.
1191. *See* Case C-406/10, *SAS Institute Inc. v. World Programming Ltd,* 2 May 2015, ECLI:EU:C:2012:259, para. 35.
1192. *See* above for the discussion of details of this criterion and its understanding in the case law of the CJEU.
1193. Case C-406/10, *SAS Institute Inc. v. World Programming Ltd*, 2 May 2015, ECLI:EU:C:2012:259; *see* for details Radim Polčák, *§ 2 Autorské dílo, in Autorský zákon*, p. 55 (Radim Polčák et al., Leges 2020).
1194. *See* Marie-Christine Janssens, *The Software Directive, in European Copyright Law*, p. 84 (Irini Stamatoudi & Paul Torremans (eds.), Edward Elgar Publishing 2019).
1195. *See* Case C-310/17, *Levola Hengelo BV v. Smilde Foods BV*, 13 Nov. 2018, ECLI:EU:C:2018:899, para. 40; Case C-683/17, *Cofemel – Sociedade de Vestuário SA v. G-Star Raw CV*, 12 Sep. 2019, EU:C:2019:721, para. 32; Case C-833/18, *SI a Brompton Bicycle Ltd v. Chedech / Get2GetBrompton*, 11 Jun. 2020, ECLI:EU:C:2020:461, para. 25.
1196. *See* s. 65 of the Copyright Act and recital 7 and Art. 1(1) of the Software Directive.
1197. *See* s. 65 of the Copyright Act and art. 1(2) of the Software Directive.

825. Following the CJEU decision in *SAS Institute Inc. v. World Programming Ltd,*[1198] the computer program's functionality is not an expression of the computer program and is not protectable by copyright law.[1199] The opposite conclusion would lead to the monopolization of ideas and hinder progress in this area.[1200] As the CJEU noted, *'similar or even identical programs'* might be created by the author, provided that these are not copied.[1201] This conclusion is, however, regarded as paradoxical, as the function of the computer program is actually the only objectively perceivable expression for the user.[1202] Programming languages and data formats might be, however, protected as standard works under the Information Society Directive, if they are original (author's own intellectual creation).[1203]

826. Per the same CJEU decision, programming languages and data formats are not considered as expressions of the computer program and therefore not protected as such.[1204]

827. The GUI is also not protected as a computer program in the sense of section 65/1 of the Copyright Act as it is not an expression of the computer program enabling its copying but merely an 'interaction interface' allowing the user to enjoy the features thereof.[1205] However, the GUI might be protected by copyright law as a 'standard' work provided that, *inter alia*, the arrangement or configuration of the GUI's components are original, i.e., allow for the expression of the creativity of the author resulting in an original intellectual creation.[1206] This criterion is, however, not met in cases where the expression of the GUI's components is dictated by their technical function.[1207]

1198. *See* Case C-406/10, *SAS Institute Inc. v. World Programming Ltd*, 2 May 2015, ECLI:EU:C:2012:259.
1199. *See* for details Radim Polčák, *§ 2 Autorské dílo, in Autorský zákon*, p. 55 (Radim Polčák et al., Leges 2020). Specifically, also Dominika Galajdová & Jan Zibner, *Nedostatky autorskoprávní ochrany počítačového program*, Právní rozhledy, 22, pp. 784–789 (2018).
1200. *See* Opinion of the AG Bot in Case C-406/10, *SAS Institute Inc. v. World Programming Ltd*, 29 Nov. 2011, ECLI:EU:C:2011:787, para. 57.
1201. *See* Case C-406/10, *SAS Institute Inc. v. World Programming Ltd*, 2 May 2015, ECLI:EU:C:2012:259, para. 41.
1202. *See* Radim Polčák, *§ 2 Autorské dílo, in Autorský zákon*, pp. 56–57 (Radim Polčák et al., Leges 2020).
1203. *See* Case C-406/10, *SAS Institute Inc. v. World Programming Ltd*, 2 May 2015, ECLI:EU:C:2012:259, para. 45.
1204. *Ibid.*, para. 46.
1205. *See* Case C-393/09, *Bezpečnostní softwarová asociace – Svaz softwarové ochrany proti Ministerstvo kultury*, 22 Dec. 2010, ECLI:EU:C:2010:816, paras 40, 41 and the judgement of the Czech Supreme Administrative Court of 2. 2. 2011, Case No. 5 As 38/2008-288. *Cum grano salis,* this case referred from the Czech Supreme Administrative Court might be regarded as one of the most significant contributions in the form of a preliminary question to the EU copyright law stemming from Czech Republic.
1206. *See* Case C-393/09, *Bezpečnostní softwarová asociace – Svaz softwarové ochrany proti Ministerstvo kultury*, 22 Dec. 2010, ECLI:EU:C:2010:816, para. 48.
1207. *Ibid.*, para. 48.

828. The above-discussed unprotected elements, however, could be protected by other intellectual property rights (patent law), by unfair competition rules (tort of trade secret infringement), or contractually between the parties involved.[1208]

829. There is no specific regulation on videogames in the Copyright Act. According to the CJEU, these are to be treated as 'complex matter comprising not only a computer program but also graphic and sound elements, which, although encrypted in computer language, have a unique creative value which cannot be reduced to that encryption'.[1209] Therefore, both the computer program protection and its specificities, as well as protection for standard works discussed above, do apply simultaneously. However, no matter how unique and innovative the gameplay of the videogame is, it is not to be protected by rights granted by the Copyright Act.[1210] As in the case of other elements unprotected by copyright law, other protective regimes, such as unfair competition law, might apply.

§3. Rights Granted and Entitled Persons

830. Contrary to the Software Directive, the Copyright Act does not explicitly lay out the exclusive rights of the author pertaining to the computer program. Due to the protection of computer programs as literary works, 'standard' moral and economic rights are granted to the author. The moral rights are laid down in section 11 of the Copyright Act and include the right of divulgation, right to claim authorship, and right of integrity. The economic rights include mainly the right to use the computer program, as regulated in sections 12 et seq. of the Copyright Act, in its various forms (including the discussed rights of reproduction and communication to the public). As the private copying of computer programs is not allowed,[1211] logically the right to remuneration for the allowed copying for personal use ('private copying levies') regulated in section 25 of the Copyright Act.

831. In the aftermath of the *Bezpečnostní softwarová asociace – Svaz softwarové ochrany v. Ministerstvo kultury* case,[1212] the Czech Supreme Administrative Court specified the extent and scope of the rights granted vis-à-vis the GUI of a computer program – one of its elements, that is, however, not an expression thereof and thus not protected as such.[1213] Even if the GUI is protected by standard copyright, its broadcasting does not constitute communication to the public thereof as

1208. *See* Ivo Telec & Pavel Tůma, *Autorský zákon. Komentář*, p. 719 (C.H.Beck 2019).
1209. *See* Case C-355/12, *Nintendo Co. Ltd and Others v. PC Box Srl and 9Net Srl*, 23 Jan. 2014, ECLI:EU:C:2014:25 para. 25.
1210. *See* Pavel Koukal, *Autorská práva, lidská práva a public domain*, p. 67, 440 (Masarykova univerzita 2019).
1211. s. 30/3 of the Copyright Act.
1212. *See* Case C-393/09, *Bezpečnostní softwarová asociace – Svaz softwarové ochrany v. Ministerstvo kultury*, 22 Dec. 2010, ECLI:EU:C:2010:816.
1213. *See* the Judgement of the Supreme Administrative Court of 2 Feb. 2011, Case No. 5 As 38/2008.

the interactivity is not being communicated.[1214] On the other hand, this is the case when the guests of the Internet cafés use the GUI interactively.[1215]

832. With the new distribution models, these rights tend to lose their importance, as currently, allowing access to the functional results itself of the computer programs is predominant rather than any form of distribution of the code or its copying.[1216]

833. There is no specific regulation of the duration of the rights to the computer program; therefore, the general rules apply. For economic rights, this means the duration of protection in length of seventy years *post mortem auctoris*. Such an extent of protection makes practically no sense, as it is hard to imagine that a public domain software would be of any use after decades since its creation.[1217] The moral rights cease upon the author's death; however *post-mortem* protection also applies.

834. The Supreme Administrative Court collective management of rights to computer programs deemed as neither effective nor reasonable.[1218] On the other hand, because of the *Bezpečnostní softwarová asociace – Svaz softwarové ochrany v. Ministerstvo kultury* case, the outstanding issue was the collective management of rights to non-literal elements of computer programs – GUIs, that might be qualified as standard works. This issue was immediately put to the test, as after the judgment of the CJEU, the CMO OOA-S started to collect adequate remuneration for the rental of GUIs to the users. The reason and legal basis, therefore, was the entitlement of this CMO *'to enforce the right to adequate remuneration for the rental of the original piece of work or copies of works which are fixed in audiovisual recordings'*.[1219] In a legal dispute concerning the enforcement of payment of adequate remuneration, the Supreme Court ultimately upheld the legitimacy of such a claim.[1220] However, the practical relevance of this issue is becoming marginal because of the obsoleteness of the business model in question (Internet cafés).

835. The above-discussed regime of employee's work applies fully also to computer programs. Moreover, this regime also applies when the software is ordered

---

1214. *See* Case C-393/09, *Bezpečnostní softwarová asociace – Svaz softwarové ochrany proti Ministerstvo kultury*, 22 Dec. 2010, ECLI:EU:C:2010:816, para. 58 and Judgement of the Supreme Administrative Court of 2 Feb. 2011, Case No. 5 As 38/2008, para. 69.
1215. *See* Judgement of the Supreme Court of 25 Mar. 2015, Case No. 30 Cdo 5008/2014, confirmed later by Judgement of the Supreme Court of 25 Feb. 2020, Case No. 27 Cdo 4576/2018.
1216. *See* Radim Polčák, *§ 2 Autorské dílo, in Autorský zákon*, p. 59 (Radim Polčák et al., Leges 2020).
1217. *See* Dominika Galajdová & Jan Zibner, *Nedostatky autorskoprávní ochrany počítačového program*, Právní rozhledy, 22, pp. 784–789 (2018).
1218. *See* Judgement of the Supreme Administrative Court of 2 Feb. 2011, Case No. 5 As 38/2008, paras 75, 76.
1219. *See* s. 96/1b of the Copyright Act at that time.
1220. *See* Judgement of Supreme Court of 25 Mar. 2015, Case No. 30 Cdo 5008/2014. For detailed discussion of this judgment, *see* Pavel Koukal, *Collective Administration of Graphical User Interfaces (GUI) in the Light of the BSA Decision*, 10 Masaryk Journal of Law and Technology 128 (2016).

from a third party – a natural person.[1221] In this case, the created computer program is treated as an employee's work. This is, however, not true when the other party is a legal person, such as the software development company.

§4. Limits of the Protection

836. Apart from the general limits of protection regarding the subject matter, the Copyright Act transposes Articles 5 and 6 of the Software Directive and limits explicitly the exclusive rights of the rightsholder.[1222] Even without the rightsholder's authorization, the lawful user is entitled to perform the reserved acts to use the computer program normally in accordance with its intended purpose (including error correction), to make a back-up copy thereof, and to ensure its interoperability with another independently developed program. These limits of the granted protection are applicable only if they pass the three-step test[1223] and if the user of the computer program relying on these limits is a lawful one. As opposed to the Software Directive, the Copyright Act tries to define the lawful user of the computer program – it is, however, basically any person authorized to use a copy of a computer program.[1224] According to the Supreme Court, this might even be a person that obtained the computer program as a gift from an unknown person, provided that the right of distribution has been exhausted.[1225] The set limits of the exclusive rights must not be contracted out – the only exception being the allowed use of a computer program with its intended purpose.[1226] This conclusion must be, however, read in the context of the *Top System SA v. Belgian State* judgment of the CJEU, which stipulated that the way the lawful user may exercise the possibility to correct the errors of the computer program remains up to the agreement of the parties.[1227]

837. Firstly, the lawful user may reproduce, translate, adapt, arrange or alter the computer program if necessary to use of a copy of a program that has been lawfully acquired if done while loading and running of the computer program, correcting its errors, or if necessary for the use of the lawfully acquired copy of the program in accordance with its intended purpose.

838. The lawful user may also make a back-up copy of the computer program if it is necessary for the use thereof, e.g., for re-installing it after a hardware update.[1228] Due to the conclusions of the CJEU in the *Aleksandrs Ranks and Jurijs Vasiļevičs v. Finanšu un ekonomisko noziegumu izmeklēšanas prokoratūra and*

1221. *See* s. 58/7 of the Copyright Act.
1222. *See* s. 66 of the Copyright Act.
1223. *See* s. 29/1 of the Copyright Act.
1224. *See* s. 66/6 of the Copyright Act.
1225. *See* Judgement of the Supreme Court of 17 Jul. 2019, Case No. 5 Tdo 513/2019, para. 35.
1226. *See* s. 66/1/b of the Copyright Act.
1227. *See* Case C-13/20, *Top System SA v. Belgian State*, 6 Oct. 2021, ECLI:EU:C:2021:811 para. 74.
1228. *See* s. 66/1/c of the Copyright Act and Ivo Telec & Pavel Tůma, *Autorský zákon. Komentář*, p. 726 (C.H.Beck 2019).

Microsoft Corp. case, the back-up copy must not, however, be transferred to another person, even if the original material medium of the copy of the computer program would be destroyed.[1229]

839. To determine the ideas and principles underlying the computer program, the lawful user is, pursuant to the section 66/1/d of the Copyright Act, entitled to observe, study, or test the functioning of the program, however, only while performing any of the acts of loading, storing the computer program in the memory of the computer, displaying, running or transmitting program to which she is entitled.

840. The last enacted limit allows the lawful user to reproduce and translate the computer program to obtain the indispensable information necessary for achieving interoperability with another independently developed program as set in section 66/1/e of the Copyright Act. Beyond the requirement of the Software Directive, the Copyright act requires that these acts of the user must be done *'in the reproduction of the computer program or its translation or other adaptation, modification or other change'* to which the user must be authorized. The commentators conclude that this request is contrary to the EU copyright law.[1230] The other requirements for the allowed decompilation, however, follow the Software Directive. Thus, to be able to decompile, the indispensable interoperability information must not be readily available otherwise for the lawful user, e.g., provided by the rightsholder online. Also, only the relevant parts of the program containing the information might be decompiled. The acquired interoperability information has a specific protection regime. It must not be disclosed to other persons, apart from when essential for achieving interoperability. Furthermore, it must not be misused for the development, production, or commercial exploitation of a computer program that would be substantially similar in expression or for any other act which infringes copyright.

841. According to the section 66/3 of the Copyright Act, the lending right and rental right do not encompass the situations where the program itself is not an essential object of the lending or rental.

842. Following the Software Directive, the 'standard' exceptions and limitations applicable to other works are generally excluded from application to the computer programs.[1231] Consequently, the computer program must not be, *inter alia*, used for teaching, or a person must not quote from the computer program. However, the exception enacted for the purposes of use of the protected subject matter for public security reasons, judicial, administrative, parliamentary proceedings, or any other official purpose[1232] and the exception allowing the transmission in a network

---

1229. *See* Case C-166/15, *Aleksandrs Ranks and Jurijs Vasiļevičs v. Finanšu un ekonomisko noziegumu izmeklēšanas prokoratūra and Microsoft Corp.*, 12 Oct. 2016, ECLI:EU:C:2016:762, paras 43, 57.

1230. *See* Ivo Telec & Pavel Tůma, *Autorský zákon. Komentář*, p. 728 (C.H.Beck 2019); Dominika Collet, *§ 66 Omezení rozsahu práv autora k počítačovému program, in Autorský zákon*, p. 535 (Radim Polčák et al., Leges 2020).

1231. *See* s. 66/6 of the Copyright Act.

1232. *See* s. 34/1/a of the Copyright Act.

between third parties by an intermediary[1233] are applicable also to computer programs. These are regarded as not in conflict with the purposes of the Software Directive.[1234]

843. As the newly introduce mandatory exceptions and limitations in the DSM Directive, for digital and cross-border teaching activities, non-scientific research text and data mining, and preservation of cultural heritage, are also applicable to the rights pertaining to computer program,[1235] they are reflected accordingly in the DSM Directive Amendment Act. The computer programs might also be qualified as out-of-commerce work;[1236] therefore, the foreseen regime will also be applicable.

844. The standard regime of protection of the technological protection measures described in the previous chapter does not apply fully to these devices used on computer programs. Only dealings with illicit devices are considered illegal.[1237] To determine the underlying principles and ideas as well as decompilation, the rightsholder must make the computer program available without these technological protection measures.[1238] The rightsholder is obliged to mark the computer program that such measures are being used and provide the user with the contact information of the person that will make the computer program available without the devices for the above-mentioned purposes.[1239]

1233. *See* s. 38a/1/a of the Copyright Act.
1234. *See* Ivo Telec & Pavel Tůma, *Autorský zákon. Komentář*, pp. 733–734 (C.H.Beck 2019).
1235. *See* Arts 4(1), 5(1) and 6(1) of the DSM Directive.
1236. *See* Art. 8(2) of the DSM Directive.
1237. *See* s. 43/2 of the Copyright Act.
1238. *See* s. 66/8 of the Copyright Act.
1239. *Ibid.*

Chapter 6. Protection of Databases

845. On 11 March 1996, the European Parliament and the Council of the EU adopted Directive 96/9/EC on the legal protection of databases (hereinafter referred to as 'Database Directive'). This piece of EU regulation created new type of sui generis legal protection that protects substantial investments in databases by means of absolute rights provided under intellectual property law principles. The main objective of the directive was to provide a uniform legal framework for non-creative databases throughout Europe and to close existing protection gaps in individual EU Member States.

846. Although copyright law could also protect some (original) arrangements of data, it no longer sufficed for the increasing demand for non-original data selection and arrangement protection. Thus, by the dual-layer protection, the European Commission attempted to overcome the gap in the market and created a system where there may be different rightsholders of copyright and sui generis database right as well as different rightsholders of the database and its content.

§1. Categories of Database Protection

847. The protection of databases is mainly of two types: copyright protection based on section 1 Copyright Act (such databases are also referred to as original) and through sui generis protection provided for the database's producer based on sections 88a to 93 Copyright Act, which implements Article 7 ff. of the Database Directive. The overlap of both these two categories of protection is possible.[1240] Nevertheless, some databases are protected neither as a copyrighted work nor by means of sui generis protection but may be covered by innominate contractual obligations or under unfair competition protection.[1241]

§2. Copyright Protection of Databases

848. This category of database protection covers those databases that are the author's own intellectual creation and thus achieve a certain degree of originality.[1242] The demands on originality are not very high, however, every day, routine, or purely manual arrangement of database elements is not considered sufficient. For example, the alphabetical arrangement of the data in address and telephone directories, cannot represent enough creativity to be protected by the copyright regime.

1240. *See* Case C-604/10, *Football Dataco Ltd and Others v. Yahoo! UK Ltd and Others*, 1 Mar. 2012, ECLI:EU:C:2012:115, para. 45.
1241. *See* Pavel Koukal & Koščík Michal *Autorský zákon: komentář*, p. 576 (Radim Polčák et al. Leges 2020).
1242. *See* s. 2/1 and 2 Copyright Act.

849. Since there were no (electronic) databases in the traditional analogue environment, Article 2(5) of the Berne Convention only provides copyright protection for 'collections of works'. This includes, in particular, encyclopaedias and anthologies that represent own intellectual creations of authors due to the selection or arrangement of the material.[1243]

850. Copyrighted databases are subject to both economic rights which generally last for the lifetime of the author and for seventy years after his or her death[1244] and moral rights which lapse upon the death of the creator.[1245] Neither economic nor moral rights can be transferred by the full transfer of rights and can be licensed only.[1246]

§3. Sui-Generis Database Protection

851. Unlike copyright, sui generis database law serves to protect the producer for his or her professional and financial investment in the database. The object of protection of the database producer's right is not the data itself, but the substantial investment in the database.[1247]

852. Under the sui generis regime, the database is defined as a (i) collection of independent works, data or other elements (or materials), which is (ii) systematically or methodically arranged, and which is (iii) individually accessible by electronic or other means, regardless of the form of their expression.[1248]

§4. Independent Elements

853. As element, we understand both data and works. An element can be illustrated by text, sound files, images, numbers, musical works, audio or audiovisual recordings and, for example, football match schedules or satellite images. Database elements also cover elements necessary for searching or operating databases. Elements can be captured in both digital and analogue form. Directive 96/6/EC and sections 88 et seq. of the Copyright Act also apply to conventional analogue databases such as catalogues or card files, which are systematically or methodically organized and individually accessible.

854. Neither the Copyright Act nor Directive 96/9/EC specify how many elements a database must contain so that it is to be considered a database within the meaning of section 88 of the Copyright Act. However, the Recital 19 of Database Directive explains, that compilation of several recordings of musical performances

1243. *See also* ss 2/2 and 5 Copyright Act.
1244. *See* s. 26 Copyright Act.
1245. *See* s. 11/4 Copyright Act.
1246. *See* s. 12/1 Copyright Act.
1247. *See* s. 88a Copyright Act; Recitals 7 and 40, Art. 7 Database Directive.
1248. *See* s. 88 Copyright Act.

on a CD, does not come within the scope of this Directive, both because, as a compilation, it does not meet the conditions for copyright protection and because it does not represent a substantial enough investment to be eligible under the sui generis right.

855. The independence of elements means, in particular, their independence from other database elements, namely informational, semantic or contextual independence. A fictional independence test can be achieved by the removal of one database elements. Thus, if its removal does not change the informational value of another database element, it is an independent element. Independence requirement is also associated with the independence of the database as such (i.e., an element also has its meaning outside the database context, and the database retains its significance even after its removal).

856. According to the CJEU, the independence of the elements means that the element must have 'autonomous informative value'[1249] and that the elements can be separated from one another without it affecting their informational, literary, artistic, musical or other value.[1250] Thus, in accordance with section 88 of the Copyright Act and Article 1(2) of the Database Directive, a set of independent elements may be, for example, a topographic map, a telephone directory, a film database, a social network, a weather forecast dataset or a library catalogue.

§5. Arrangement of Elements

857. Finally, the independent and individually accessible elements must be arranged systematically or methodically. Principally, such an arrangement can subsist in a method or a system that can be used to search for an independent element in a database. Therefore, the decisive factor of the arrangement is the connection of the database itself with a query tool that enables targeted searches for individual elements. Only by that, a database achieves its function of information processing. In addition, the requirement that the arranged elements can be found again using query methods distinguishes a database from a mere collection of elements, which does indeed provide information but requires a separate means for processing the individual elements.

858. In this context, it is neither necessary that all the database elements are incorporated in one type of medium nor that the producer (or maker) of the database has direct control over them. According to Recital 21 to Database Directive, the individual elements need not be stored in a specific form and, according to the

1249. *See* Case C-490/14, *Freistaat Bayern v. Verlag Esterbauer GmbH,* 29 Oct. 2015, ECLI-:EU:C:2015:735, para. 22.

1250. *See* Case C-444/02, *Fixtures Marketing Ltd. v. Organismos prognostikon agonon podosfairou AE,* 9 Nov. 2004, ECLI:EU:C:2004:697, para. 29; Case C-490/14, *Freistaat Bayern v. Verlag Esterbauer GmbH,* 29 Oct. 2015, ECLI:EU:C:2015:735, para. 17.

CJEU, any system which makes it possible to search each of the elements constituting the database falls within the definition of a database.[1251] There are no enhanced requirements for specific systematic structuring. Rather, only such collections of elements should be excluded from database protection where probability plays a role. Thus, for example, electronic databases based on mere full-text research, which allow queries only at the expression level, meet the sui generis database protection requirements.

859. We can conclude that if the individual elements of the database are systematically or methodically arranged for the very purpose of being individually accessible,[1252] they meet the arrangement requirements.

§6. Individual Accessibility

860. Individual accessibility is a consequence of the previous two sui generis database protection requirements. Every single element of the database must be accessed independently and utilized independently of the other elements of the database. This criterion is intended to distinguish the database from works of authorship. Nowadays, in the context of digital and interactive media (where basically any element or part of a digital reproduction can be accessed individually), this criterion seems to be to some extent redundant, but it makes sense in the context of the first half of the 1990s, when analogue media were used to disseminate data.

861. In traditional analogue databases, the individual accessibility of the elements was made possible, for example, by opening a book or a paper-sheet. As far as electronic databases are concerned, the user is given individual access to independent elements via searching tools in CD-ROM or an online database.

§7. Substantial Investment

862. Sui generis protection requires an investment that is 'significant in nature and scope'. This includes the costs for acquiring the database content as well as for the data preparation. Nevertheless, also investments in the structuring and re-analysing of the database content are qualified. The database investments also include the expenses of procuring the computer programs required to set up and operate the database. Monetary and technical means, as well as time, labour and energy expended, must be taken into account as well.

1251. *See* Case C-444/02, *Fixtures Marketing Ltd. v. Organismos prognostikon agonon podosfairou AE*, 9 Nov. 2004, ECLI:EU:C:2004:697, para. 32.

1252. *See* Case C-444/02, *Fixtures Marketing Ltd. v. Organismos prognostikon agonon podosfairou AE*, 9 Nov. 2004, ECLI:EU:C:2004:697, para. 30.

863. However, the sui generis protection is subject to a significant restrictions through the case law of the CJEU, which rigorously separates the expenses for generating the data from the costs of obtaining the database content itself.[1253] Accordingly, costs for generating new data cannot be considered investments in supplying the database content.

§8. Characteristics of the Sui Generis Right and Its Duration

864. The sui generis right is fully transferable and licensable absolute right of a proprietary nature, which is also inheritable.[1254] Unlike copyright, it has no moral (personality) component and lasts for a much shorter period of time.

865. The sui generis right lasts for fifteen years from the acquisition of the database. However, if the database is made available to the public within that period, the database right expires fifteen years from the first of January of the year following the date when the database was first made available to the public.[1255] However, this period can be extended if the database producer makes new investments/contributions.[1256] Each new substantial investment extends the term again by fifteen years. Protection starts from the first day of the following year, and the updated database is protected thereafter.

§9. Database Producer

866. Unlike the author of a copyrighted work, which can only be a natural person,[1257] the database producer can be both natural and legal persons.[1258] Furthermore, unlike the copyright creation principle, the owner of the sui generis right is not the person who actually designed the database but the person 'who takes the initiative and bears the investment risk'.[1259] Therefore, ownership of the database producer's right and equivalent copyright protection of original databases can diverge. Determining producer attributes is not always easy. Still, of practical importance is that the database expressly excludes contractors or subcontractors, so that is to say that subcontractors who only act within the sphere of responsibility of the client are not to be regarded as database producers. Employees also do not fall under the producer definition.

1253. *See* Case C-338/02, *The British Horseracing Board Ltd. v. William Hill Organization Ltd.*, 9 Nov. 2004, ECLI:EU:C:2004:696; Case C-338/02, *Fixtures Marketing Ltd v. Svenska Spel AB*, 9 Nov. 2004, ECLI:EU:C:2004:696; Case C-444/02, *Fixtures Marketing Ltd v. Organismos prognostikon agonon podosfairou AE*, 9 Nov. 2004, ECLI:EU:C:2004:697.
1254. *See* s. 90/6 Copyright Act.
1255. *See* s. 93 Copyright Act.
1256. *See* s. 88a/1 Copyright Act.
1257. *See* s. 5/1 Copyright Act.
1258. *See* s. 89 Copyright Act.
1259. *See* Recital 41 of the Database Directive.

867. We may conclude that the database producer is not the purchaser of the dataset according to section 88 of the Copyright Act, but the investor who has made the substantial investment. Therefore, he or she bears the benefits and risks associated with the investment.[1260] The term does not apply to indirect investors such as shareholders, banks, or grant providers. Also, the producer is not, for example, the employee who had the idea to create the database, but the person who employed them. By investing monetary and other resources at their own expense and risk, the employer has created the conditions for the employee to design the database.

§10. Database Rights

868. According to section 90/1 of the Copyright Act, the producer has the right to extract or re-utilize the content of the database or a substantial part of it. The producer can also fully transfer his or her right to another legal subject or pro provide a license. These rights are independent of the possible protection of individual elements as well as of the copyright protection of original databases.

869. According to Article 7(2) of the Database Directive[1261] extraction means 'the permanent or temporary transfer of all or a substantial part of the contents of a database to another medium by any means or in any form'. The extraction rights correspond to the author's economic rights and include reproduction, distribution, public reproduction, and the right to communicate the database to the public. Besides, the extraction right means that the database or its part has been duplicated on a data carrier that is separate from the original database.[1262] In this regard, it is irrelevant whether the duplication emerges by automatic technical means or through a manual process, such as manual copying of analogue databases. It follows from the CJEU judgments that it is in principle irrelevant which technology is used to extract a substantial part of the database. A digital database can be extracted by manual transcription and keyboard tapping, an analogue database can be extracted using digital technologies. In all cases, this is an activity for which the consent (license) of the database producer is required. The fact that the database is freely available to the public does not constitute a licence to extract the database. In assessing the question of whether the extraction occurs, it is irrelevant whether the record is permanent or temporary,[1263] nor does it matter what the motives and objectives of the person who made the record are.[1264]

870. Re-utilization is defined as 'any form of making available to the public all or a substantial part of the contents of a database by the distribution of copies, by

---

1260. *See* Ivo Telec & Pavel Tůma, *Autorský zákon. Komentář*, p. 849 (C.H.Beck 2019); Pavel Koukal & Michal Koščík. *Autorský zákon: komentář*, p. 592 (Radim Polčák et al., Leges 2020).
1261. And corresponding s. 90/2 Copyright Act.
1262. *See* Case C-604/07, *Directmedia Publishing GmbH v. Albert-Ludwigs-Universität Freiburg*, para. 29.
1263. *See* s. 90/2 Copyright Act.
1264. *See* Case C-545/07, *Apis-Hristovič EOOD v. Lakorda AD*, 5 Mar. 2009, ECLI:EU:C:2009:132, para. 46.

renting, by on-line or other forms of transmission.'[1265] The notion of 're-utilization' has also been interpreted broadly by the CJEU.[1266] The purpose of the exclusive right of re-utilization is to protect the person who created the database against 'activities of the user which go beyond his legitimate rights and thus cause damage to the deposits of that person.'[1267] The CJEU's case law also includes, for example 'a series of successive acts, beginning with the publication of the data in question and ending with the transmission of that data to the interested public.'[1268]

871. Where the database has not been made available to the public without the consent of the person who invested in its creation, the notion of re-utilization includes cases where the database has been made available to the public, depriving the person of incomes which should have enabled him or her to repay the costs of that input.[1269] Re-utilization of a database thus covers any unauthorized conduct which constitutes a public dissemination of the content of a protected database or a substantial part of such content.[1270]

872. The notion of re-utilization of a database also includes the operation of metasearch engines which enable the entire content of the database, or any element of the database, to be searched and displayed on the basis of a search query entered directly into the search engine of that database. We draw this conclusion from the fact that the entire database is made available to end-users through the metasearch engines.[1271]

§11. Limitations

873. The limitations of the sui generis right are regulated in sections 91 and 92 of the Copyright Act, and its purpose is to ensure a balance between the rights of the database producer and the lawful user of the database. On the one hand, it is necessary to avoid too strong protection for the database producer, who could prevent users of the database or its part from searching for information and data

1265. *See* s. 90/3 Copyright Act.
1266. *See* Case C-202/12, *Innoweb BV v. Wegener ICT Media BV and Wegener Mediaventions BV*, 19 Dec. 2013, ECLI:EU:C:2013:850, para. 38.
1267. *See* Case C-203/02, *The British Horseracing Board Ltd and Others v. William Hill Organisation Ltd*, 9 Nov. 2004, ECLI:EU:C:2004:695, para. 45.
1268. *See* Case C-604/10, *Football Dataco Ltd and Others .v Yahoo UK Limited and Others*, 1 Mar. 2012, ECLI:EU:C:2012:115, para. 34.
1269. *See* Case C-203/02, *The British Horseracing Board Ltd and Others v. William Hill Organisation Ltd*, 9 Nov. 2004, ECLI:EU:C:2004:695, para. 51.
1270. *See* Case C-203/02, *The British Horseracing Board Ltd and Others v. William Hill Organisation Ltd*, 9 Nov. 2004, ECLI:EU:C:2004:695, para. 67; Case C-545/07, *Apis-Hristovic EOOD v. Lakorda AD*, 5 Mar. 2009, ECLI:EU:C:2009:132, para. 49.
1271. The content of the database can be consulted in real time by the user via the website of the dedicated metasearch engine; Case C-202/12, *Innoweb BV v. Wegener ICT Media BV and Wegener Mediaventions BV*, 19 Dec. 2013, ECLI:EU:C:2013:850, paras 40 and 53.

through the abusive enforcement of exclusive rights. On the other hand, the sui generis database producer needs to be protected from users abusing their rights to the detriment of the legitimate interests of the subject who provided substantive investment.

874. The restrictions under section 91 of the Copyright Act include the exploitation or re-utilization of an (qualitatively or quantitatively) insignificant part of the database that has been made available to the public by a lawful user. Extraction and re-utilization may serve any purpose, and they should be carried out in a routine and proper manner, not repetitively and systematically (as, for example, would be the operation of metasearch engines). It also cannot cause harm to the rightsholder.

875. The notion of a lawful user is not precisely defined, but it is assumed that it includes at least the licensee and the user who utilizes the database or its part under statutory exemptions. It is also deduced that the concept of lawful user should represent an end user who has accessed the database in a way that do not contravenes the law or a contractual obligation.

876. Other limitations to the sui generis database right are covered by the gratuitous statutory licenses provided by section 92 of the Copyright Act. The authorized user may exploit even a substantial part of the database content, but under the conditions that he or she does so for his personal use, for scientific, educational or quotation purposes, or if he or she uses the content for the purposes of public security, administrative or judicial proceedings.

§12. 'Data Ownership'

877. The civil codes in the Central Europe (ABGB, BGB, ZGB, KC) define the 'things in the legal sense' (legal assets) differently. While the German[1272] and Polish[1273] Civil Codes consider only tangible objects as legal asset, the Czech Civil Code, like the Austrian ABGB, is based on a broad concept of a thing in the legal sense,[1274] which includes both tangible and intangible assets.[1275] A thing in the legal sense is everything that is distinct from a person and serves the needs of people.[1276] 'Intangible things' are intangible objects distinct from a person in the legal sense (natural person, legal person), and private rights whose nature enables it, such as obligations or intellectual property rights (patents, trademarks, copyright etc.).

878. 'Intangible things' (intangible assets) can be subject to both absolute and relative property rights, through which a particular form of legal dominion is created. As far as relative property rights are concerned, intangible things involve the

1272. *See* Art. 90 BGB.
1273. *See* Art. 45 Kodeks cywilny.
1274. *See* Petr Tégl in *Občanský Zákoník: velký komentář. Svazek III: § 419-654 a související společná a přechodná ustanovení*, p. 199 (Filip Melzer & Petr Tégl, Leges 2014).
1275. *See* s. 496 Civil Code.
1276. *See* s. 489 Civil Code.

subject matter of obligations.[1277] Thus, for example, intangible assets would include employee's labour results,[1278] objects of intellectual property rights that are licensed,[1279] or works of intangible nature created and used in the course of performance contract.[1280]

879. Besides, intangible things (assets) may also be the subject of absolute property rights, such as intellectual property rights.[1281]

880. In general, however, intangible things are not subject to ownership in the narrow sense.[1282] The right of ownership in the subjective (narrow) sense traditionally refers only to tangible assets the nature of which is excludable and rivalrous.[1283] The interpretation which would permit unlimited legal dominion over any intangible asset, would not correspond to the enumerative principle (*numerus clausus*) that governs rights over intangible goods.[1284]

881. The characteristic of an object that is distinct from a person, useful for human needs,[1285] and is of an intangible nature, also fits for simple non-personal data. In contrast to the conclusions drawn by the German[1286] or Swiss[1287] doctrine, which are based on the pandectist conception of the 'thing in legal sense',[1288] non-personal data, can be subsumed under Czech concept of things in the legal sense.[1289] However, this conclusion does not determine that data is an object of ownership within the meaning of sections 1012 et seq. of the Civil Code. On the contrary, data are public goods by their very nature and can be subject to absolute property rights only if the law explicitly grants such protection.

882. In contrast, information that includes data about the existing objects, their characteristics and processes, is dynamic in nature and cannot be qualified as the legal assets.[1290] Thus, information expresses its properties or the effect of its use.

1277. *See* s. 1722 Civil Code.
1278. *See* s. 2401 Civil Code; ss 33 et seq. Labour Code.
1279. *See* s. 2358 Civil Code.
1280. *See* s. 2631 Civil Code.
1281. Patent rights (s. 11 Patents Act); trademark rights (s. 8 Trademark Act); industrial design rights (s. 19 Industrial Designs Act).
1282. *See* s. 1012 Civil Code.
1283. *See* Pavel Koukal, *Občanský zákoník: komentář. I, Obecná část, (§ 303-654)* p. 1529 (Petr Lavický (ed.), C.H. Beck 2nd ed. 2022); Petr Tégl *Občanský Zákoník: Velký Komentář. Svazek III: § 419-654 a související, společná a přechodná ustanovení*, p. 199 (Filip Melzer & Petr Tégl Leges, 2014).
1284. *See* s. 977 Civil Code.
1285. *See* s. 489 Civil Code.
1286. *See* Herbert Zech, *Information als Schutzgegenstand*, p. 146 (Mohr Siebeck, 2012).
1287. *See* Gianni Fröhlich-Bleuler, 'Eigentum an Daten?', Jusletter, No. 883, 2017, p. 4 https://jusletter.weblaw.ch/fr/dam/publicationsystem/articles/jusletter/2017/883/eigentum-an-daten-_8ba966db21/Jusletter_eigentum-an-daten-_8ba966db21_fr.pdf, accessed 10 Aug. 2022.
1288. *See* s. 90 BGB, Art. 641 and 713 ZGB.
1289. *See* s. 489 Civil Code.
1290. *See* Michal Koščík et al., *Výzkumná data a výzkumné databáze: právní rámec zpracování a sdílení vědeckých poznatků*, p. 26 (Wolters Kluwer, 2017).

However, it makes no sense to consider information to be a legal asset, just as it makes no sense to classify under 'things in the legal sense' attributes of the objects such as greenness, yellowness, speed, efficiency, etc.

883. If the law does not expressly grant absolute property rights, data can only be protected by contract, unfair competition[1291] or by means of already existing institutes such as the sui generis right of the database provider within the meaning of section 88 ff. Copyright Act. However, ownership in the narrower sense[1292] cannot apply to data as such.

1291. *See* ss 2976/ff. Civil Code.
1292. *See* s. 1012 Civil Code.

Chapter 7. Chips Protection

§1. Introduction

884. The protection of topographies of semiconductor products became part of the Czech law as a result of the Agreement on Trade Relations between the Government of the United States of America and the Government of the Czech and Slovak Federal Republic of 12 April 1990.[1293] The legal regulation[1294] was devised according to the Council Directive 87/54/EEC of 16 December 1986 on the legal protection of topographies of semiconductor products. It must be stated from the beginning that the regulation is obsolete and irrelevant, as it is simply not being used in practice.[1295] Historically, there were only seven (7) topographies registered in the national registry and currently, there is no valid national registration for the territory of the Czech Republic.[1296] This chapter is thus only a brief overview of the regulatory landscape.

§2. Protected Subject Matter and Entitled Persons

885. Section 2 of the Topographies Act contains the basic definitions. The semiconductor product is to be understood as 'the final or an intermediate form of microelectronic product, intended to perform an electronic function and that consist of a basic body of material which includes a layer of semiconducting material having at least one layer composed of conducting, insulating or semiconducting material arranged in accordance with a predetermined pattern'.[1297] The topography of semiconductor product is defined as 'a series of related images, however fixed or encoded, representing the three-dimensional permanent pattern of the layers of which a semiconductor product is composed, in which each image has the pattern or part of the pattern of a surface of the semiconductor product or the surface or parts thereof of the semiconductor product any stage of its manufacture'.[1298]

1293. *See* Karel Čada, *Topografie polovodičových výrobků, in Práva k průmyslovému vlastnictví. 3. Vydání,* p. 255 (Roman Horáček, Karel Čada & Petr Hajn, C. H. Beck 2017) and Sdělení federálního ministerstva zahraničních věcí č. 158/1991 Sb., o sjednání Dohody o obchodních vztazích mezi vládou Československé federativní republiky a vládou Spojených států amerických.

1294. *See* Act No. 529/1991 Sb., on the protection of topographies of semiconductor products ('Topographies Act').

1295. Even the jurisprudence does not pay much attention to this protective institute (*see, e.g.*, Roman Horáček, Karel Čada & Petr Hajn, *Práva k průmyslovému vlastnictví. 3., doplněné a přepracované vydání,* p. 255 (C.H. Beck 2017). The little significance for practice is mentioned by Annette Kur & Thomas Dreier. *European intellectual property law: text, cases and materials,* p. 374 (Edward Elgar 2013). In the second edition of this seminal book on intellectual property, the part describing the protection of topographies was omitted altogether.

1296. The whole registry (sic!) could be downloaded from https://upv.gov.cz/files/uploads/PDF_Dokumenty/vynalezy/rejstrik_topografii_polovodicovych_vyrobku.pdf. It is a single PDF file consisting of three A4 pages.

1297. *See* s. 2/2 of the Topographies Act.

1298. *See* s. 2/1 of the Topographies Act.

886. To be granted protection, the topography must be a result of its creator's own intellectual effort and must not be commonplace in the semiconductor industry.[1299] A topography that consists of a combination of elements that are commonplace in the industry might also be protected, provided that the combination thereof is the creator's own intellectual effort and is not commonplace in the semiconductor industry.[1300]

887. The originally entitled person to file the application and consequently obtain the protection is the creator of the topography or her successor.[1301] The interests of the person carrying the business risk are also protected inasmuch that the right for protection of a topography created as a fulfilment of an employee's task (or under a similar contractual obligation) shall belong to the employer if not agreed upon otherwise.[1302] According to section 4 of the Topographies Act the economic right for protection is also fully transferable; therefore, it might be contractually ceded to any other person, both natural as well as legal.

§3. Registration Procedure

888. The right for protection, i.e., the right to file the application and request the registration of the topography, is limited in time as the entitled person must register the topography within fifteen years since its creation unless it is used overtly for commercial purposes.[1303] In this case, pursuant to the section 9/1/a of the Topographies Act the protection arises from the day of such use, provided that the creator of the topography registers it within two years at the Industrial Property Office.

889. The written application for registration must, apart from the registration request, contain the documents enabling the identification of the topography and evidence of entitlement.[1304] As stipulated in the section 7/2/c of the Topographies Act, if the registration shall protect the topography retroactively since its first overt commercial use, the date of such use must also be documented.

890. The registration procedure is only a formal one, i.e., there is no examination of the material requirements of creativity or the non-commonness in the industry, and therefore no related comparison with state of the art is undertaken.[1305]

1299. *See* s. 1/1 of the Topographies Act.
1300. *See* s. 1/2 of the Topographies Act.
1301. *See* s. 3/1 of the Topographies Act.
1302. *Ibid.*
1303. *See* s. 5 of the Topographies Act.
1304. *See* s. 7/2 of the Topographies Act.
1305. *See* Karel Čada, *Topografie polovodičových výrobků, in Práva k průmyslovému vlastnictví. 3. Vydání,* p. 256 (Roman Horáček, Karel Čada & Petr Hajn, C. H. Beck 2017).

891. Provided all the needed requirements are met, the topography shall be registered.[1306] The owner is, pursuant to the section 8/1 of the Topographies Act issued a certificate of registration, and the registration is announced in the Bulletin of the Intellectual Property Office.

§4. Rights Granted and Their Limits

892. Since the registration, the owner is entitled to prohibit or license: '(a) the reproduction of the topography or its separately usable parts and the making of representations of the topography for production purposes; (b) the manufacturing of a semiconductor product in which the protected topography is incorporated; (c) the commercial exploitation or importation of a topography or a semiconductor product containing a protected topography or separately usable parts thereof, or a representation of a topography used for its manufacturing'.[1307] This protection might be invoked vis-à-vis third parties after the topography has been registered.[1308] Nevertheless, the owner may seek appropriate compensation against the person that fraudulently reproduced, commercially exploited, or imported the topography before the effective date of protection.[1309]

893. As is the case in other intellectual property rights, the protection granted to topographies is limited to balance the various conflicting interests. The protection thus does covers not cover activities conducted for non-commercial purposes.[1310] Furthermore, reproduction of the topography for purposes of analysis, research, development, and education is also out of the scope of the protection granted.[1311] If a new topography, itself a result of creative activity that is not commonplace in the industry, is developed as a result of such analysis, research, and development, the commercial use thereof is not prohibited.[1312] Finally, after the authorized introduction of the topography or the semiconductor product onto the market, the subsequent commercial use of the topography or a semiconductor product containing this topography does not fall within the ambit of protection, i.e., the rights are exhausted.[1313]

§5. Duration of Protection, Its Termination and Withdrawal

894. The rights from the registered topography last for ten years since the day of filing of the application or since its first overt use for commercial purposes.[1314]

1306. *See* s. 8/1 of the Topographies Act.
1307. *See* s. 10/1 of the Topographies Act.
1308. *See* s. 10/2 of the Topographies Act.
1309. *Ibid.*
1310. *See* s. 11/1/a of the Topographies Act.
1311. *See* s. 11/1/b of the Topographies Act.
1312. *See* s. 11/1/c of the Topographies Act.
1313. *See* s. 11/1/d of the Topographies Act.
1314. *See* s. 9 of the Topographies Act. However, the ten-year term is to be counted since the end of the year when the protection started to exist (*see* s. 9/2 of the Topographies Act).

In the latter case, as was already mentioned, the application for registration must be filed within two years since such use to obtain protection.[1315]

895. Anyone may submit a written substantiated application for deletion of the topography from the Register.[1316] Such application must contain evidence proving at least one of the reasons for deletion, i.e., that the topography was not eligible for registration; the application was not submitted within the two-year timespan in the case of retroactive registration of the overtly commercially used topography or the right for protection expired; the applicant was not eligible to obtain protection based on its domicile or non-reciprocity.[1317] According to the section 14 of the Topographies Act, the owner of the topography is entitled to comment on such an application and thus defend her registration. According to section 13/2 of the Topographies Act, the deletion is effective *ex tunc*, i.e., as if the topography had not been registered at all.

896. If it is later shown from the decision of the court that the alleged owner is not entitled to for protection within the meaning of the section 3 of the Topographies Act, the Industrial Property Office shall withdraw such registration.[1318] Such an application for withdrawal might be filed only by the person entitled for protection (or her successor) according to the decision of the court.[1319] On the basis of an application submitted within one month since the final decision of the court the Industrial Property Office shall register the entitled person as the owner of the topography.[1320]

1315. *See* s. 9/1/a of the Topographies Act.
1316. *See* s. 13/1 of the Topographies Act.
1317. *Ibid.*
1318. *See* s. 15/2 of the Topographies Act.
1319. *Ibid.*
1320. *See* s. 15/3 of the Topographies Act.

Chapter 8. Protection of Internet Domain Names

§1. Notion of Internet Domain Names

897. Internet domain names are characters that can be used to reach a specific web page in a computer network. They are essential because they carry a meaning that the average Internet user can understand. In contrast, the factual technical (internet protocol - IP) addresses used on the Internet are a combination of alphanumeric characters without any meaning that is intelligible to average users.

898. Computers communicate within computer networks using unique numeric or alphanumeric addresses called IP protocol. Thus, to make it easier for users to access the Internet webpages, meaningful signs (domain names) were invented long time ago to replace these alphanumeric character combinations in the user interface. From a technical point of view, a domain name is purely a communication parameter. Entering a domain name into a user's search engine allows the user to contact a specific computer connected to the Internet by automatically converting the domain name into the corresponding IP address.

899. The respective domain name holders themselves choose the significant components of domain names. Most providers use their own tradenames or trademarks to identify their homepages where they present their company, products or services. These designations, which are smoothly understandable by everyday users, were assigned to specific organizations (registrars) on the network, which manages most of the domain names in use today.

900. Internet addresses (domains) are exempted in the Czech law from the public administration of addresses performed by the CTO, pursuant to section 28(1) of Act No. 127/2005 Sb., on Electronic Communications, as amended, and therefore domain names are not subject to state regulation.[1321]

901. Suppose an entity wants to make its presentation available to other Internet users under a specific domain name in the national domain '.cz'. In that case, it must apply for such a domain name from the entity that manages the national domain '.cz', enter into a contract with it, and follow its rules. For the national domain '.cz', this registrar is the association of legal entities Czech National Domain Authority for.cz domain registry (CZ.NIC, z. s. s. p. o.)[1322] Thus, the allocation of a domain name to a particular user is based on the contract concluded between the applicant and CZ.NIC and the *Rules for the Registration of Domain Names in the Country-Code Top Level Domain (ccTLD) .cz* and the *Rules for ADR.*[1323]

1321. *See* Petr Hostaš, *Právo informačních technologií*, p. 276 (Radim Polčák at al., Wolters Kluwer 2018).
1322. Web https://www.nic.cz/.
1323. https://www.nic.cz/files/nic/doc/Pravidla_registrace_CZ_20160515_po_novele_ZOS.pdf.

§2. Domain Names as Legal Objects

902. Domain names are intangible legal assets (things in the legal sense),[1324] to which, however, only relative property rights (obligations) apply.[1325] Domain names become disposable legal objects as obligations arising from the domain registration contract. This contract is concluded by the user and the national domain name registrar (CZ.NIC legal entity).

903. Although a sign constituting the future domain name may theoretically constitute the subject matter of a trade secret protection[1326] or be protected under pre-contractual information,[1327] only the moment of registration constitutes a domain name as a thing in the legal sense, and only from that moment does a particular sequence of characters fulfil its identification function. Thus, exclusively the registration constitutes a private-law act, whereby the domain is granted protection against further appropriation.[1328]

904. However, the registration does not confer absolute protection,[1329] such as trademark or tradenames protection, but only relative (unfair competition) protection. Of course, a domain name may be protected in other ways; it may be protected by registration in the trademark register maintained by the Industrial Property Office[1330] or by registration in the commercial register maintained by the regional courts (*see* below).

905. From a legal point of view, it is essential for the creation of a national domain name that a domain registration contract is concluded, whereby the registrar of the national top-level domain obliges to register the second-level domain for the applicant and the applicant (future domain name holder) undertakes to pay a registration fee. Upon conclusion of the domain name registration agreement and succeeding registration of the domain in the registry, the domain name holder is entitled to hold a domain name and to use it. The domain registration contract is not specifically regulated, and thus it is simply an innominate contract[1331] usually concluded for a fixed term. As far as the duration of the contract is concerned, the domain registration duration is automatically extended by payment of the registration fee for the next registration period.[1332]

1324. *See* s. 496/2 Civil Code.
1325. *See* Pavel Koukal, *Občanský zákoník: komentář. I, Obecná část (§ 303-654),* p. 1530 (Petr Lavický ed., C.H. Beck 2nd ed 2022).
1326. *See* s. 504 Civil Code.
1327. *See* s. 1730/2 Civil Code.
1328. *See* Petr Hostaš, *Právo informačních technologií*, p. 276 (Radim Polčák at al., Wolters Kluwer 2018).
1329. *See* the Judgement of the Supreme Court of 19 Apr. 2012, Case No. 23 Cdo 3407/2010.
1330. *See* Simona Hejdová & Radim Charvát, *Zákon o ochranných známkách: komentář*, p. 169 (Pavel Koukal et al., Wolters Kluwer 2017).
1331. *See* s. 1746/2 Civil Code.
1332. *See* Rules for the Registration of Domain Names in the ccTLD .cz, Art. 5.

§3. Domain Name Functions

906. As far as designation rights principles are concerned, it is not the technical function of a domain name that is critical but its meaning to the users. From a technical point of view, domain names do not identify either a person (corporate entity, public institution, non-profit organization) or a specific product or service. However, for a user contacting a particular web page, the technical aspect of identifying a particular computer server on the Internet network is of little importance. Thus, legally speaking, the domain name identifies the website (a virtual space having a specific semantic meaning) and not the computer on which the presentation is located.[1333] Therefore, from the user's point of view, the semantic, phonetic, and visual aspects are crucial. If properly designed, a domain name identifies the person, goods, or services behind it. In this respect, an Internet domain name serves an identification function[1334] comparable to that of a trademark, the protection of the names of natural persons, the protection of corporate names, or the protection of a tradename. The identification function is performed by the domain name from the moment of registration.

§4. Domain Name Termination

907. A domain name can only last as long as it is registered in the domain list. The duration of a domain name registration is conditional upon the duration of the domain registration agreement. It is also affected by technical conditions (e.g., some top-level domains require that each registered domain be associated with available Domain Name System (DNS) servers).

908. The domain name holder is entitled to cancel the domain registration within the scope of his or her dispositive power, either by forgetting to pay the price for the next registration period or by directly instructing the cancellation of the registration.[1335] However, the termination of a domain name is not absolute since a domain name with identical content may be re-registered at any time, either by the original holder or by a third party.

909. Terminating a domain name registration should also suspend the holder's rights in the domain name. However, it follows from the decision of the High Court in Prague in the CAD.CZ domain name[1336] that the termination of a domain name registration for non-payment of the fee does not deprive the original holder of the right to prevent a third party from registering such a vacant domain name, provided that the original holder still holds the absolute right to the sign contained in the domain name (e.g., the right to a tradename).

1333. *See* Judgment of the High Court in Prague of 10 Aug. 2004, Case No. 3 Cmo 293/2003.
1334. *See* Judgment of the Municipal Court in Prague of 23 Nov. 2006, Case No. 15 Cm 46/2004.
1335. *See* Petr Hostaš, *Právo informačních technologií*, p. 277 (Radim Polčák at al., Wolters Kluwer 2018); Rules for the Registration of Domain Names in the ccTLD .cz, Art. 8.
1336. *See* Judgment of the Constitutional Court of 13 Sep. 2006, Case No. 3 Cmo 114/2006.

§5. Domain Name Transfer and Its Pledge

910. The transfer of a domain name is legally executed by assigning a claim,[1337] or the entire contractual position.[1338] As far as the assignment of a contractual position is concerned, not only rights but also obligations are transferred (e.g., the obligation of the domain name Registrar to maintain a record in the registry).

911. The transfer of the domain name is, in principle, completed by the effectiveness of the domain transfer agreement[1339] and the entry of the change in the register is not constitutive.

912. According to section 1335/1 Civil Code, a contractual claim can also be provided as a pledge that can be used as a security in a credit transaction. Therefore, a claim from a domain registration contract may also be pledged. As far as claims under a domain registration agreement are concerned, the pledge institutes from the moment of pledge agreement effectiveness. However, the parties may, following section 1335/2 Civil Code, arrange for the registration of the pledge in the register of pledges maintained by the Notary Chamber of the Czech Republic [*Notářská komora České republiky*].

§6. Protection of Domain Names

913. CZ.NIC protects rights to the signs registered as domain names based on the provisions of its Rules for the Registration of Domain Names in the ccTLD .cz. Here it is prescribed that the Registrar is entitled to cancel the registration or transfer the domain name to another person on the basis of a final and enforceable court decision or arbitral award.[1340] The Registrar is also entitled to suspend the transferring of the domain name to another person if the beneficiary proves that he or she has already filed a petition against the current holder to initiate the relevant proceedings.

914. In the past, by agreeing to the Domain Name Registration Rules and the ADR Rules, the applicant agreed to resolve the dispute regarding the domain name before the Arbitration Court of the Chamber of Commerce of the Czech Republic and the Agrarian Chamber of the Czech Republic [*Rozhodčí soud při Hospodářské komoře České republiky a Agrární komoře České republiky*].[1341] According to that arbitration offer, a third party who challenged any domain name of that holder in the .cz domain could bring a dispute before the Arbitration Court against the domain name holder. Nevertheless, the Supreme Court of the Czech Republic, in its decision of 17 December 2013, Case No. 23 Cdo 3895/2011, questioned the possibility

1337. *See* s. 1879 Civil Code.
1338. *See* s. 1895 Civil Code.
1339. *See* Rules for the Registration of Domain Names in the ccTLD .cz, Art. 7.
1340. *Ibid.*, Art. 20.
1341. Version of the Rules for the Registration of Domain Names in the ccTLD .cz in force until 1 Mar. 2015.

of concluding an arbitration agreement in the manner described above and thus the possibility of resolving domain name disputes before the Arbitration Court. Since 1 March 2015, in connection with the launch of the new ADR system, it has not been possible to arbitrate domain name disputes before the Arbitration Court.

915. As of 1 March 2015, the Rules for the Registration of Domain Names in the ccTLD .cz include a completely new document, the Rules for ADR.[1342] The dispute resolution system under these Rules of ADR is not an arbitration procedure under the law; the domain name holder undertakes to submit to it if the complainant chooses this resolution method. Dispute resolution, in this case, is also carried out on the platform administered by the Arbitration Court, according to the Rules for Dispute Resolution for .cz domains. This method of dispute resolution is based on a contractual basis, it is not an arbitration under Act No. 216/1994 Sb., on Arbitration and Enforcement of Arbitral Awards, and it is not possible to claim anything other than a cancellation of the domain name registration or its transfer. Therefore, no other claims can be awarded, in particular costs or damages. Furthermore, the decision issued is not a writ of execution for the enforcement of the decision, the dispute resolution under these Rules of ADR does not constitute an objection of *lis pedens* or *res iudicata.*[1343] Therefore, the same claims may be brought before the general court during or after the dispute resolution process. This dispute resolution system is binding on domain name holders who registered or renewed their domain names on or after 1 March 2015.

§7. Unfair Competition Protection

916. The protection of an unregistered sign that constitutes the ground of a particular domain name is most often based on unfair competition claims, particularly concerning the likelihood of confusion[1344] or unjust appropriation of the reputation.[1345] Not only are direct competitors providing similar services in a competitive relationship, but all other entities, including non-business entities operating in similar industries.

917. Under the general clause,[1346] unfair competition is an act in the course of trade which is contrary to the honest practices (good morals) of competition and is likely to cause injury to other competitors or customers. In the context of unfair competition, there is no need to distinguish between a registered domain name and a word sign used in the course of trade that forms the significant element of a particular domain name. In particular, the registration of a domain name that conflicts with the name of a competing product or business name may be considered unfair

1342. *See* Annex 3 to the Rules.
1343. *See* Rules for Alternative Dispute Resolution, Art. 7.
1344. *See* s. 2981 Civil Code.
1345. *See* s. 2982 Civil Code.
1346. *See* s. 2976 /1 Civil Code.

competition. Thus, a sign holder may obtain informal protection against *cybersquatting*[1347] or *typosquatting*[1348] through unfair competition protection. Similarly, a domain name holder can protect its domain name against a competitor who has unjustly registered a similar sign as a domain name that could create a likelihood of confusion among users.

§8. Collision with Tradenames and Names of Legal Entities

918. A domain name may also interfere with the rights to a tradename, especially if the domain name is identical or similar to the tradename. A business name can be understood in the context of section 423/1 Civil Code as the name under which the entrepreneur is registered in the Commercial Register. A trade name serves primarily as a distinctive sign in competition (similarly to trademarks). Therefore, the registration of a domain name identical or similar may fall under the category of unauthorized use of a tradename pursuant to section 423/2 Civil Code.

919. In addition to the protection of a tradename, which applies only to entrepreneurs who are registered in the Commercial Register, the Civil Code also protects the name of a legal entity. Section 135/1 Civil Code provides that a legal entity which has been affected by the unauthorized use of its name or which has suffered or is threatened with damage as a result of unauthorized interference may demand that the unauthorized interference be refrained from by the infringer or that the infringement is eliminated. Thus, if the name of a legal person is used in registered domain name, the right holder may seek a claim for cancellation from the register and a claim for injunctive relief.

920. On the contrary, in contrast to the protection of a tradename, the protection of the name of a legal entity does not in itself confer a right to satisfaction.[1349]

§9. Domain Names and Trademark Protection

921. A trademark-domain conflict typically relates to a word or combined trademarks.[1350] According to the Trademarks Act,[1351] the trademark owner has the exclusive right to designate goods or services with signs corresponding to the registered trademark.[1352]

1347. *See* Judgment of the Municipal Court in Prague of 31 Mar. 2006, Case No. 41 Cm 195/2004.
1348. *See* Judgment of the High Court in Prague of 24 Oct. 2011, Case No. 3 Cmo 167/2011.
1349. *See* Judgment of the Supreme Court of 30 Nov. 2021, Case No. 23 Cdo 327/2021.
1350. *See* Simona Hejdová & Radim Charvát in *Zákon o ochranných známkách: komentář*, p. 169 (Pavel Koukal et al., Wolters Kluwer 2017).
1351. *See* Act. No. 441/2003 Sb., Trademarks Act, as amended.
1352. *See* s. 8 Trademarks Act.

922. Domain names containing elements of publicly known signs may often also conflict with well-known trademark rights in the Czech Republic.[1353] The advantage of well-known trademarks is that they are not governed by the principle of specialty and that they cover all classes of goods and services.

923. According to the settled decision-making practice of the administrative courts, similarity must be assessed in terms of visual, phonetic, and semantic resemblance based on the overall impression they give to the average consumer.[1354]

924. Where the registration of an identical or confusing domain name results in an unjustified interference with trademark rights, or where, on the contrary, the rights of the domain name holder are infringed as a result of such a clash, the owner of the trademark may claim, in particular, that the interferer refrains from the unauthorized use and that the infringement is remedied.[1355] Damages, as well as the payment of unjust enrichment, may also be claimed if they have been caused as a result of the infringement. Other claims include the publication of the judgment.

§10. Domain Name Conflicts with a Natural Person's Name

925. According to section 77 Civil Code, a natural person has the right to protection of his or her personal name and surname, or a pseudonym.[1356] Under section 82/2 Civil Code, the exercise of the right to protection of personality after the death of the natural person concerned is reserved to persons close to the person concerned, such as parents or children, siblings and spouses or partners, persons who are married, persons who live together permanently or other persons in a family or similar relationship, if the harm suffered by one of them would reasonably be perceived by the other as harm to himself or herself.

1353. *See* s. 2/d Trademarks Act.
1354. *See* Judgment of the Supreme Administrative Court of 28 Feb. 2013, Case No. 8 As 41/2012; Judgment of the Supreme Administrative Court of 24 Oct. 2008, Case No. 4 As 31/2008.
1355. *See* s. 4 of the Act. No. 221/2006, Sb., on the Enforcement of Industrial Property Rights and the Protection of Trade Secrets, as amended.
1356. *See* s. 79/2 Civil Code.

Part V. Cybersecurity Law

Chapter 1. Institutional Framework

§1. Factors Defining Institutional Framework of Cybersecurity

926. The institutional framework of cybersecurity is in the Czech Republic partly shaped by the post-communist history of the country. Relatively recent experience of all security institutions being practically concentrated under one politically determined rule is still strong enough to induce higher sensitivity regarding distinction and balancing of competences of various security authorities. Yet there is not any statutorily laid down 'balancing of powers' between intelligence, security, law enforcement and other institutions, these institutions are highly vigilant in respect of any of them getting new competences or powers. Consequently, an introduction of a relatively new security agenda triggered a strong debate regarding its institutional backing.[1357]

927. Second major factor in the development of the Czech institutional framework for cybersecurity was the fact that the Czech Republic was the first EU member, and one of the first democratic rule-of-law nations worldwide, that introduced a complex cybersecurity legislation in 2014.[1358] Thus, the need for an institutional framework in this field was relatively original and there were no examples to learn from.

928. The Cybersecurity Act originally entrusted competences in the developing security agenda of cybersecurity into the hands of the National Security Authority (Národní Bezpečnostní Uřad – NBU) that was until then mostly responsible for protecting classified information. Although cybersecurity represented quite different agenda in a comparison with security clearances or tempest protection, there were several reasons for which making this authority the central Czech public institution in cybersecurity made pragmatic sense.

929. At first, the NBU was always standing a bit apart from other Czech security and intelligence institutions, as it was independently assessing fitness of their

1357. The historical and political background of the development of the Czech Cybersecurity Act is explained in detail in Radim Polčák, *Kybernetická bezpečnost jako aktuální fenomén českého práva*, Revue pro právo a technologie, vol. 6, No 11, pp. 95–151 (Masarykova univerzita 2015).
1358. *See* the Cybersecurity Act No. 181/2014 Sb.

staff, equipment, and processes to process classified information. It was also, thanks to its highly sensitive agenda of personal security clearances,[1359] well legally and institutionally shielded from politics. The NBU also had already some experience with compliance agenda in cybersecurity of information systems and networks, including administrative approvals, certifications, etc., although it was limited only to systems that were processing classified information.

930. With growing importance of cybersecurity regulatory agenda and corresponding growth of respective part of NBU, a decision was made by the government to separate cybersecurity, certification of information systems for processing of classified information and Galileo PRS[1360] to the National Cyber and Information Security Agency – NCISA (Národní úřad pro kybernetickou a informační bezpečnost – NÚKIB). The NCISA has the position of a supreme state authority, has its seat in Brno and its director is appointed by the government. Is serves as the competent authority according to Article 8 of the NIS Directive[1361] and national cybersecurity certification authority under the EU Cybersecurity Act.[1362]

§2. Institutions in Cybersecurity and Cyber-Defence

931. While NCISA acts as the general cybersecurity authority, the Military Intelligence was entrusted with competences in cyber-defence.[1363] Development of laws laying down roles and responsibilities in cyber-defence took significant time, also because of mostly unclear distinction between the domains of security and defence in cyberspace.[1364]

932. Traditional legal understanding of the distinction between defence and security assumes that defence agenda covers incidents that are aimed at or able to threaten sovereignty of the country, while security is about protecting individual rights and public order. That distinction may become problematic in the light of ongoing discussions as to whether cyberattacks are to be regarded just as security

1359. These procedures may include, depending on the level of security clearance, throughout investigations into private lives of respective individuals incl. highly sensitive personal details. NBU is in that respect a controller of personal files that are not available to any other public institutions, incl. intelligence or law enforcement.

1360. The Galileo Public Regulated Service (PRS) is an encrypted navigation service for governmental authorized users and sensitive applications, *see* https://www.euspa.europa.eu/european-space/galileo/services/prs.

1361. *See* Directive No. (EU) 2016/1148 concerning measures for a high common level of security of network and information systems across the Union.

1362. *See* Regulation (EU) 2019/881 on ENISA and on information and communications technology cybersecurity certification and repealing Regulation (EU) No 526/2013 (Cybersecurity Act).

1363. *See* s. 16a of the Military Intelligence Act No. 289/2005 Sb.

1364. For more detailed analysis, *see* Radim Polčák, Jakub Harašta & Václav Stupka, *Právní problémy kybernetické bezpečnosti,* p. 89 (Masarykova univerzita 2016).

incidents or should be rather considered as the use of force (or acts of war) according to public international law. In addition to this uncertainty, there is the understanding of cyber-defence which is common in computer science and refers to defensive measures as generally active in comparison with security measures that are passive by the definition.

933. The specification of competences of the Military Intelligence in cyber-defence is relatively vague which reflects on the above definitional uncertainties. Yet the scope of competences of the Military Intelligence in conducting cyber operations is limited only to matters of 'defence,' there is no specification as to how the mere term 'defence' translates to cyberspace. In any case, the Military Intelligence Act clearly states that the Military Intelligence has competences in gathering and processing data about security situation in the Czech cyberspace and that it is also entitled to develop and use offensive measures.[1365]

934. Both main competences of the Military Intelligence, i.e., gathering and analysing data regarding security situation in the Czech cyberspace and, most of all, development and use of offensive capabilities, are highly sensitive with regards to protection of fundamental rights as well as to the above inter-institutional balance. The Military Intelligence is generally under supervision of a permanent parliamentary committee, but cyber operations may be highly specific, and their understanding may require specialist knowledge and experience. Thus, the Military Intelligence Act introduced the function of an 'inspector for cyber-defence'.[1366]

935. The inspector for cyber-defence shall be a member of the Army or the Military Intelligence and it is assumed that is should be a person with excellent knowledge and experience from cyber-defence operations. That should provide him with the necessary knowledge, skills and abilities of the inspector to efficiently observe and review cyber-defence operations, while the direct subordination to the Minister of Defence should shield the inspector from undue influence from the inside of the Military Intelligence.

§3. CSIRTs and CERTs

936. The Czech Cybersecurity Act preceded by nearly two years the NIS Directive and, despite being built upon the same regulatory architecture, its terminology is sometimes a bit diverse from the Directive. One of such cases is the indication for the unit that is responsible for receiving and processing reports on cybersecurity incidents and reacting to these incidents. The NIS Directive speaks about (Computer Security Incident Response Team (CSIRT)), while the Czech Cybersecurity Act uses the term Computer Emergency Response Team (CERT).

1365. *See* s. 16g of the Military Intelligence Act No. 289/2005 Sb.
1366. *See* s. 16k and 16l of the Military Intelligence Act No. 289/2005 Sb.

937. The Cybersecurity Act is, compared to the NIS Directive, a bit more creative as to the structure of CSIRTs. The NIS Directive lays down a duty for the Member States to designate one CSIRT as a national point of contact and as a member of the EU CSIRTs network,[1367] while the Cybersecurity Act counts with two CSIRTs – the 'governmental' CSIRT and the 'national' CSIRT.

938. The purpose of this dichotomy is to cater the need for a dedicated public body that would have competences, technical and regulatory, to evaluate security situation of most important part of the Czech cyberspace, react to security incidents and communicate with similar public bodies in other EU member-states. At the same time, the duality of CSIRTs should respond to natural demand for state-backed cybersecurity service for those information systems and networks that do not fall within the scope of interest of the government.

939. The first purpose is met by the governmental CERT that is established as a unit within NCISA. It receives and processes incident reports and reacts, administratively and technically, to incidents and threats in critical information infrastructure, essential services, and important systems. It also collaborates with other Czech public authorities in security, intelligence, law enforcement or defence, and it is regarded as the national CSIRT according to the NIS Directive.

940. The national CERT is run by a private entity, the CZ.NIC, upon a public-law contract[1368] made with NCISA. The national CERT has no regulatory powers or administrative competences, and, from the scope of the Cybersecurity Act, it only receives and processes incident reports from important network providers[1369] and reports on 'incidents having a substantial impact'[1370] on digital services.[1371] However, the main role of the national CERT is to act as officially designated response team for the (rather massive) constituency outside the scope of the Cybersecurity Act.

941. The idea of legislating a privately run CERT for non-compulsory collaboration in cybersecurity assumes that private entities will be more willing to collaborate by sharing cybersecurity incident data and working with recommendations and guidance with another private entity rather than with a public authority. Another reason for establishing the national CERT arose from pragmatic assessment of the scope of possible operations of the government CERT.

942. NBU and later NCISA that run the govCERT are both public authorities which means that they can engage only in activities explicitly ordered or permitted by the statutory law. If govCERT was to be given full competences to creatively act

1367. *See* Art. 12 of the NIS Directive.

1368. Public-law contracts are instruments of administrative law that are used in specific cases for public authorities to entrust other public bodies or even private entities with some administrative or other public tasks.

1369. *See* s. 2/h of the Cybersecurity Act.

1370. S*ee* Art. 16(3) of the NIS Directive.

1371. *See* Art. 4(5) of the NIS Directive and s. 2/l of the Cybersecurity Act.

in preventing or responding to cybersecurity incidents, these competences would have had to be legislated so broadly that it would never pass the constitutional threshold for permissible risk of arbitrability in exercise of regulatory or administrative powers. In other words, it was not legislatively possible to give truly free hands for govCERT to creatively protect the Czech cyberspace while staying within the limits of the rule of law.

943. National CERT, to the contrary is run by a private entity that is allowed to act in any manner that is not contradictory to the applicable law. That allows the national CERT to develop and deploy even highly creative security solutions, as long, as these solutions do not violate any laws. A good example is a wholesale router with enhanced cybersecurity capabilities that was developed and later very successfully marketed by CZ.NIC.[1372] While it would be extremely difficult to legislate a way for such activity for NCISA or any other public authority (not speaking about the potential motivation of individuals or families to buy a router from a state security authority), it could have been done by CZ.NIC with no legal concerns.

1372. *See* https://www.nic.cz/page/4153/stribrna-verze-routeru-turris-omnia-a-novy-system-sentinel-zvysi-bezpecnost-internetu/.

Chapter 2. General Obligations

§1. Scope of Application

944. The Czech Cybersecurity Act uses relatively complicated classification of regulated subjects which is resulting namely from gradually developing pragmatic experience combined with the need to harmonize the NIS Directive. The main logic of this classification is object-based which means that the Act defines primary objects of interest and then subsequently assigns duties to respective subjects. In that sense, the Act distinguishes between:

(a) critical information infrastructure (information systems and networks);
(b) essential services;
(c) important information systems;
(d) important networks;
(e) digital services;
(d) electronic communications services.

945. The above classification is hierarchical. Critical information infrastructure consists of critically important information systems and networks that are designated as a specific part of the national critical infrastructure.[1373] Besides information systems and networks that are as such considered critically important, critical information infrastructure also includes those information systems and networks that are essential for the functioning of other elements of the national critical infrastructure.

946. Essential services were added as a specific category during harmonization of the Cybersecurity Act with the NIS Directive. Despite the NIS Directive used practically the same regulatory logic as the Cybersecurity Act, it was not chosen to merge the original critical information infrastructure according to the Cybersecurity Act with essential services according to the NIS Directive. The reason is that some essential services in health,[1374] gas transportation or chemistry are still not considered elements of the Czech national critical infrastructure. Despite these facilities are often truly essential, there has been steadily strong political resistance against including them into the general scope of the Crisis Act and so they were only included, for the sake of harmonization of the NIS Directive, into the scope of the Cybersecurity Act within the newly established category 'essential services' while being still neglected, for mostly dubious reasons, as elements of the national critical

1373. The process of designation of elements of critical infrastructure is laid down the Crisis Act No. 240/2000 Sb. The Act universally covers all sorts of critical infrastructure and subsequent duties in crisis planning and crisis management.

1374. Health facilities are formally within the scope of the definitions of the Czech Crisis Act. However, particular criteria, namely regarding sizing, are defined in a way that none of existing civic health facilities (incl. large hospitals) are considered a part of the national critical infrastructure.

infrastructure according to the Crisis Act.[1375] In any case, the importance of 'critical information infrastructure' and 'essential services' is considered comparable in the Cybersecurity Act and both categories are treated with similar duties (*see* below).

947. Important systems are information systems controlled by public bodies that are not considered critical from the national perspective but whose functioning is important for some significant group, region, or interest. The Cybersecurity Act and subsequent bylaw[1376] provide for criteria for designating information systems as 'important' that include namely functions (e.g., filing systems, document delivery, public procurement etc.) and risks (e.g., public procedures, rights of individuals, public interest etc.). Important systems include, for example, information systems of ministries and other supreme public authorities, systems of regional administrations and systems whose functioning is important for private life of more than 50,000 persons, including information systems of large universities. Explicitly exempt are only information systems controlled by municipalities.

948. Important networks are defined in a bit different manner compared to important information systems. The original intent of this category was to cover backbone networks that are not critical enough to form a part of the critical infrastructure, yet important enough to fall under the scope of the Cybersecurity Act to give their providers some duties in adopting security measures and reporting cybersecurity incidents. In result, the definition of the Act covers electronic communication networks[1377] that have either a direct connection either to a public communication network abroad or to an element of the national critical infrastructure.[1378]

949. Digital services are a category that was directly transposed from the NIS Directive, including its definition[1379] and duties (*see* below). It covers cloud services, online marketplaces, and search engines and, unlike in other EU members, it applies also to a national search engine, seznam.cz.

950. Electronic communications services are not a native term of the Cybersecurity Act or the NIS Directive, but it originates in the law of electronic communications.[1380] The Cybersecurity Act covers all providers of these services but gives them very basic duties that consist under normal circumstances of mere reporting of their contact addresses (*see* below).

1375. *See also* Radim Polčák, Jakub Harašta & Václav Stupka, *Právní problémy kybernetické bezpečnosti*, p. 95 (Masarykova univerzita 2016).
1376. *See* Decree on Important Information Systems No. 317/2016 Sb.
1377. As defined in Art. 2(1) of the Directive (EU) 2018/1972 establishing the European Electronic Communications Code.
1378. *See* s. 2/h of the Cybersecurity Act.
1379. *See* Art. 4(5) of the NIS Directive and s. 2/i of the Cybersecurity Act.
1380. *See* Art. 2(4) of the Directive (EU) 2018/1972 establishing the European Electronic Communications Code.

951. It is a special feature of the Cybersecurity Act that covers not only controllers (owners) of the above systems and networks but also to entities that are technically running them upon subcontracts. The logic of the dichotomy of a 'controller' and a 'provider' is like the one of the GDPR that distinguishes between a 'controller' and a 'processor'.

952. The reason for including contractors under the scope of the Cybersecurity Act was mostly the experience with enforcement of compliance obligations (*see* below).[1381] Initially, when the Act covered only controllers of respective systems, the authorities (NBU and later NCISA) often stated gaps and omissions in security measures, but recovery was not practically possible, because the systems in question were completely outsourced. In relatively common situations when respective contracts were poorly made (*see* Introduction, Chapter 4), the controllers often found themselves with practically no other options than to repeatedly pay fines and only try to negotiate painful compromises with their contractors. After including these contractors under the scope of the Cybersecurity Act, it is possible for the NCISA to directly order them to recover faults, defects etc.

§2. Security Measures

953. The NIS Directive is not overly detailed about obligations that Member States should impose onto essential service operators and that shall include risk management,[1382] incident prevention,[1383] reporting[1384] and handling.[1385] The Czech Cybersecurity Act makes in that regard a basic distinction between *ex ante* (compliance) security measures that are to be autonomously developed and deployed by regulated subjects and measures that are to be taken by them in response to some regulatory action.

954. Compliance obligations laid down in the Cybersecurity Act are performance-based which means that the law only defines fields of interest and basic standards, while it is a duty of each regulated subject to develop and deploy its own particular rules and measures that suit the nature and specifics of a respective system or network. This regulatory model, which is similar to the one used in the GDPR, reflects on the sheer variety of information systems that fall within the scope of the Cybersecurity Act. Also, there is nobody better positioned to define,

---

1381. *See also* Radim Polčák, Jakub Harašta & Václav Stupka, *Právní problémy kybernetické bezpečnosti*, p. 70 (Masarykova univerzita 2016).

1382. Art. 14(1) of the NIS Directive only states that '[m]ember States shall ensure that operators of essential services take appropriate and proportionate technical and organisational measures to manage the risks posed to the security of network and information systems which they use in their operations.'

1383. *See* Art. 14(2) of the NIS Directive.

1384. *See* Art. 14(3) of the NIS Directive.

1385. *See* Art. 14(2) of the NIS Directive.

develop and deploy particular technical, organizational and other measures for these systems or networks than their controllers or providers.[1386]

955. The advantage of performance-based compliance obligations is that they provide for enough flexibility for regulated subjects to autonomously choose most efficient security measures for their information systems and networks. The disadvantage is lack of certainty that arises from relative vagueness of legal obligations and generates a natural demand for *ex ante* assurance of regulatory compliance.

956. The Cybersecurity Act fundamentally distinguishes between organizational and technical security measures. Organizational measures are listed in section 5/2 of the Cybersecurity Act as follows (informal translation by DeepL):

(a) information security management system,
(b) risk management,
(c) security policy,
(d) organizational security,
(e) setting security requirements for suppliers,
(f) asset management,
(g) human resources security,
(h) traffic and communications management,
(i) access control,
(j) acquisition, development and maintenance,
(k) cyber security event and cyber security incident management,
(l) business continuity management; and
(m) control and audit.

957. Technical measures are listed in section 5(3) of the Cybersecurity Act as follows (informal translation by DeepL):

(a) Physical security,
(b) a tool to protect the integrity of communication networks,
(c) a tool for authenticating the identity of users,
(d) an access authorization management tool,
(e) malicious code protection tool,
(f) a tool for recording the activities of the information or communication system, its users and administrators,
(g) a tool for detecting cyber security events,
(h) a tool for collecting and evaluating cyber security events,
(i) application security,
(j) cryptographic resources,
(k) a tool for ensuring the level of availability of information and
(l) industrial and control systems security.'

1386. *See also* Pavel Loutocký & Kamil Malinka, *Bezpečnost ICT ve vnitřních předpisech a školení zaměstnanců*, Revue pro právo a technologie, vol. 7, No. 14, pp. 45–64 (Masarykova univerzita 2016).

958. More particular specification of the above categories is legislated in the Cybersecurity Decree No. 82/2018 Sb. However, even the Decree follows the performance-based nature of these obligations and provides for flexibility for regulated subjects to choose their own ways of fulfilling the legal requirements. Given the problems that the Czech public sector is experiencing with public procurement and outsourcing of public information systems (*see* Chapter 1), it is no wonder that the Cybersecurity Act and the Cybersecurity Decree are relatively detailed regarding necessary content of outsourcing contracts.[1387]

§3. Incident Reporting

959. The Cybersecurity Act distinguishes between security events and security incidents. Events are defined in section 7/1 of the Cybersecurity Act as potentially harmful irregularities, while incidents are regarded by section 7/2 of the Cybersecurity Act, in line with the definition of the NIS Directive,[1388] those events that turn out actually harmful or dangerous. Security measures that regulated subjects are obliged to develop and deploy are aimed at detecting all events, while reactive and reporting obligations follow only the appearance of incidents.

960. Incident reporting is obligatory for all networks and systems listed in the Cybersecurity Act (*see* above §1) except electronic communications services provided that they do not fall into any other category. Critical information infrastructure, essential services and important information systems report incidents to the governmental CERT, while important networks and digital services report incidents to the national CERT.[1389]

961. Incident reports may be highly sensitive from many perspectives. They may show that respective system or network is a frequent target of hackers, may reveal weak spots in its security, reveal defensive practices etc. Thus, the Cybersecurity Act specifically regulates filing and processing of incident reports,[1390] including secrecy duties for NCISA employees that have access to the incident database.

962. Processing of data from the database of cybersecurity incidents still represents a vibrant issue in inter-institutional relations described in Chapter 1. It was not completely resolved before the adoption of the Cybersecurity Act, so the Act only states in section 20/f that the governmental CERT (informal translation by DeepL): 'provide the operator of the national CERT, authorities exercising cybersecurity responsibilities abroad and other persons active in the field of cybersecurity with data from the incident register pursuant to Sec. 9/4.'

1387. *See* for example s. 6a, 4/5 of the Cybersecurity Act.
1388. *See* Art. 4(7) of the NIS directive.
1389. Digital service providers have a duty to report only serious incidents that have substantial impact to their services pursuant to Art. 16(3) of the NIS Directive.
1390. *See* ss 9, 10, 10a of the Cybersecurity Act.

963. Namely intelligence and law enforcement institutions have been steadily interested in accessing the database, but NBU and later NCISA still keep the practice of providing data from the database only upon particular reasoned demand. To facilitate the process of other security and law enforcement institutions accessing the incident database while keeping all necessary safeguards, there have been appointed liaison officers from these institutions to the governmental CERT.

§4. Administrative Orders

964. The NCISA has available the following standard administrative tools to order various general or specific cybersecurity measures:

(1) Warnings.
(2) Reactive orders.
(3) Protective orders.
(4) Orders to migrate data.
(5) Recovery orders.

965. Warnings are issued in cases when a security risk arises, and it is not enough to only inform regulated subjects about it using general channels like the website of NCISA or public media. A warning is directly communicated through contacts that regulated subjects are obliged to file with NCISA and that should provide for official assurance that regulated subjects were made aware of respective threat or risk. Warnings do not contain orders or any other regulatory elements which means it is always upon autonomous consideration of regulated subjects whether and how the risks stated therein are relevant and how should they be covered.

966. Despite no ordering or sanctioning is a part of warnings, there is subsequent potential liability that arises from general preventive obligations arising from private, administrative, and criminal law. Neglecting officially served warning may thus lead to damage or even administrative or criminal sanctions. Thus, regulated subjects may not leave warnings without attention, but should always assess and eventually cover respective risks.[1391]

967. The instrument of warning proved to be quite useful when NCISA obtained information about security risks arising from the use of network products manufactured by Huawei and ZTE in critical infrastructure. The warning that was consequently issued by NCISA gained broad international attention[1392] and led to

1391. For detailed explanation, *see* Jakub Klodwig, *Varování NÚKIB v systematice zákona o kybernetické bezpečnosti a možnosti jeho zohlednění v zadávacím řízení*, Revue pro právo a technologie, vol. 12, No 23, pp. 49–75 (Masarykova univerzita 2021).

1392. *See* Marc Santora, *Czech Cyber Security Agency Warns Against Use of Huawei* (New York Times 8 Feb. 2019).

reconsideration of some Czech public tenders for critical infrastructure.[1393] The warning is still valid despite the Chinese Government and said companies threatening the Czech government and attempting to take it down by legal and other means.[1394]

968. Reactive orders are standard administrative orders that can be addressed either to particular regulated subjects[1395] or to a specific group of regulated subjects[1396] (e.g., users of certain technology) and are issued in direct reaction to a cybersecurity incident or risk. The Cybersecurity Act is not specific as to what can be ordered, so possible duties can range from applying patches to refraining from using certain insecure technologies to even shutting down flawed or harmful systems.

969. Protective orders are issued by the NCISA in cases when there is a general need to enhance the protection of information systems or networks that fall within the scope of the Cybersecurity Act. These orders do not react to any particular incidents or risks, but provide for a possibility for NCISA to rapidly reflect the introduction of new security technologies, standards etc. Protective orders are thus as to their nature and purpose relatively close to security measures described above in §2 – only with the difference of being issued as administrative orders (public measures)[1397] and thus being more flexible.

970. Orders to migrate data were introduced later by an amendment to the Cybersecurity Act upon practical experience especially with problematic outsourcing contracts for public information systems that often led to serious lock-ins (*see* Chapter 1). The Cybersecurity Act thus gave the NCISA the power to order and directly enforce immediate migration of data of critical infrastructure or an important system[1398] provided that the controller of that system unsuccessfully claimed migration pursuant to contractual obligations of the provider or obligations laid down in section 6a of the Cybersecurity Act.

971. Recovery orders represent a standard tool of the Czech Administrative law and are issued to recover faults and defects detected during controls. NCISA is

1393. *See* Jason Hovet & Robert Muller, *China's Huawei Excluded from Czech Tax Tender after Security Warning* (Reuters 30 Jan. 2019).

1394. *See* Jason Hovet, *Huawei Seeks Solution to Czech Security Warning, Readies Legal Means* (Reuters 25 Feb. 2019). Despite the director of the NCISA Dusan Navratil being removed from office a year after the warning was issued, the warning was neither taken down by NCISA nor legally challenged.

1395. These have the form of a standard administrative decision.

1396. These have the form of a public measure which is an instrument of administrative law that is used by public authorities to order obligations to a generally defined group of subjects – *see* ss 171 to 174 of the Code of Administrative Procedure No. 500/2004 Sb.

1397. *See* ss 171 to 174 of the Code of Administrative Procedure No. 500/2004 Sb.

1398. *See* s. 15a of the Cybersecurity Act.

entitled to conduct controls of regulated subject regarding fulfilling of obligations established in the Cybersecurity Act[1399] and to subsequently order recovery of any found issues.[1400]

§5. CYBER-EMERGENCY

972. The Czech Law recognizes two security-related special regimes, the state of emergency and the state of national emergency.[1401] The Cybersecurity Act adds another regime indicated as 'the state of cyber-emergency' ('stav kybernetického nebezpečí') that may be declared by the director of NCISA when 'the security of information in information systems or the security of electronic communications services or the security and integrity of electronic communications networks is threatened on a large scale, which could violate or endanger the interests of the Czech Republic within the meaning of the law governing the protection of classified information'.[1402]

973. The Cybersecurity Act stipulates that the state of cyber-emergency may be declared only under the condition that respective threat or incident cannot be covered by regular activities of the NCISA.[1403] That should reserve this extraordinary tool for security incidents that go beyond the control of NCISA and prevent the director of NCISA from declaring the state of cyber-emergency just to e.g., facilitate responding to regular incidents.

974. Systematically, the state of cyber-emergency should serve for major cybersecurity incidents whose adversary effects to information systems and network within the scope of the Cybersecurity Act effects cannot be efficiently mitigated by standard tools and procedures described in previous chapter. However, if such incident causes a major systemic disruption that cannot be treated by NCISA using special competences (*see* below), the Cybersecurity Act lays down a procedure for the director of NCISA to propose to the government a declaration of the state of emergency under the Security Act.

975. Special competences of NCISA that follow the declaration of the state of cyber-emergency include an extension of the scope of subjects under the jurisdiction of administrative orders (*see* above, §4) also to all electronic communications service providers and providers of important networks. NCISA can also get direct access to contact data gathered by national CERT.

1399. *See* s. 23 of the Cybersecurity Act. Controls are conducted according to the general Control Act No. 255/2012 Sb.
1400. *See* s. 24 of the Cybersecurity Act.
1401. *See* ss 5 to 7 of the Security Act No. 110/1998 Sb.
1402. *See* s. 21/1 of the Cybersecurity Act.
1403. *See* s. 21/5 of the Cybersecurity Act.

Chapter 3. Sector-Specific Obligations

976. The legal framework of cybersecurity in the Czech Republic was not built on a sectoral basis. Instead, the leading regulatory agency, National Cyber and Information Security Authority [*Národní úřad pro kybernetickou a informační bezpečnost*] ('NCISA') was established as a specialized regulatory agency on cyber security of all sectors. The legal framework consists of Act No. 181/2014 Sb., on cybersecurity ('Cybersecurity Act'). It was in part established by lawmakers on the national level and partially contains the national implementation of the Directive (EU) 2016/1148 of the European Parliament and of the Council of 6 July 2016 concerning measures for a high common level of security network and information systems across the Union ('NIS Directive'). As a result, the Cybersecurity Act is a comprehensive legislation and virtually all cybersecurity obligations stem from it (*see* Part V, Chapter 2). Hence there is very little legislation available regarding sectoral cybersecurity framework with special requirements, which would have been similar to the, e.g., US cybersecurity or data protection regulation.

977. However, within the existing legal framework, NCISA addresses some of the issues typical for some sectors in their general activity. As a result, some of the regulatory activity aims at specific sectors, providing targeted requirements under the general umbrella of the Cybersecurity Act. In addition, NCISA is authorized to issue public measures, which might introduce specific obligations on top of the existing performative rules. As a result, sector-specific requirements may exist within the general cybersecurity legal framework.

978. In this chapter, NCISA's activity targeting the health sector and energy sector will be described. Additionally, the Czech government intended to establish obligations to report cyber incidents and to share incident information within the financial sector.

§1. Proposal of 2017 Targeting the Financial Sector

979. In 2017, the Czech government proposed sector-specific cybersecurity legislation. The proposal was to amend Act No. 21/1992 Sb., on banks ('Banking Act'), to establish an obligation to report cyber incidents within the financial sector and to submit information on these incidents into a dedicated database allowing more efficient sharing of incident data. Despite the proposal providing some interesting points, it never became law. In 2017, the cybersecurity framework was changing as the NIS Directive was being implemented. Therefore, the proposal was unsystematic regarding the then effective Cybersecurity Act and the incoming implementation of the NIS Directive.

980. The critical point of the proposal was the requirement for banks and foreign bank branches to report cybersecurity incidents occurring within their information and communication systems. Information about incidents, including attack vectors and other technical information, was to be submitted to a dedicated database operated by the [*Česká národní banka*] (CNB). Information about incidents was to be shared without delay after detecting the incident. Measures to mitigate the impact were to be reported within thirty days of their implementation. Additionally, the proposal would have added not reporting an incident and not filing the measures undertaken to mitigate its impact into the database as new administrative offences.

981. Furthermore, this sector-specific cybersecurity package contained a proposal for a decree on information sharing. The proposed decree contained details as to what incidents were to be reported. Additionally, in the form of Annexes, this proposal contained forms to be used when reporting a cyber incident, including its impact assessment and information about affected systems. The explanatory memorandum specifically noted that the package was not an implementation of the NIS Directive,[1404] which was in time also underway in terms of amendments to the Cybersecurity Act.

982. On 31 May 2017, the Parliamentary Committee for Security recommended accepting the proposal. However, the committee suggested changes regarding the regulatory scope of the proposal. Instead of focusing on banks' information systems or communication networks, the proposal was to be changed to contain references to the regulatory scope of the Cybersecurity Act. The original scope of the proposal was to be much larger – banks would have been required to report incidents that impact virtually all their systems – while the changes were to bring it closer to the terminology of the Cybersecurity Act, which does not focus on regulated subjects (companies, public offices), but focuses on regulated systems operated by these subjects.

983. In the end, the proposal did not become law. The Parliament did not approve it before the end of its term in 2017.[1405] It was not proposed again to the new Parliament. As a result, the effort to introduce sector-specific cybersecurity legislation by amending the Banking Act failed. Further examples of sector-specific requirements are within the scope of the general cybersecurity legislation (Cybersecurity Act) and under NCISA's auspices.

§2. Health Sector

984. The health sector is one of the critical services the Czech government provides to its citizens. It is widely diverse, with health service providers spanning many types and categories, starting with highly specialized facilities focusing, e.g., on oncology, followed up by large hospitals providing general services within large campuses, all the way to general practitioners. All of these require storage of health data and access to it. General practitioners are often considered a weak link to the

1404. *See Explanatory memorandum of the proposal to amend Banking Act*, special part, p. 61, available at https://www.psp.cz/sqw/text/tiskt.sqw?O=7&CT=1061.

1405. Parliamentary elections were held on 20 and 21 Oct. 2017.

cybersecurity of the health sector due to their lack of preparedness and age structure, which makes them less susceptible to the deployment and proper use of technology.[1406] Sector-specific requirements regarding the deployment of eHealth in the Czech Republic are analysed in detail elsewhere (*see* Part II, Chapter 2). Under Act No. 325/2021, on eHealth ('eHealth Act'), the Ministry of Health will be required to issue eHealth standards, which will define security measures to be implemented to maintain the high level of security of the eHealth infrastructure.[1407] Starting 1 January 2026, all health service providers will have to observe these standards.[1408] Non-compliance will be subjected to administrative sanctions.[1409]

985. However, the sector requires significant cybersecurity efforts in terms of the value of available data and the impact of their potential unavailability or lack of integrity. NCISA dedicates significant attention to this sector, even under the general cybersecurity legislation. However, not all health service providers fall within the scope of the Cybersecurity Act. As a result, the sector-specific efforts of NCISA do not impact the whole healthcare sector. However, the scope of the Cybersecurity Act evolved to include a more significant portion of the health sector. One of the bylaws of the Cybersecurity Act, Decree No. 317/2014 Sb., on important information systems and their defining criteria, was amended to broaden its scope. As a result, starting 1 January 2021, Cybersecurity Act regulates not only the 16 largest hospitals but also an additional twenty-eight regionally significant hospitals. The amendment brought the total number of regulated subjects in the health sector to forty-four.

986. Under the Cybersecurity Act, NCISA is authorized to issue three types of public measures to either inform (warning),[1410] to impose an obligation to act to mitigate the impact of an ongoing incident (responsive measures)[1411] or to undertake measures to prevent the incident from occurring in the first place (protective measure).[1412] One of the warnings that NCISA issued focused on the health sector and, as a result, imposed sector-specific obligations.[1413]

987. On 16 April 2020, NCISA issued the warning against the threat of a major campaign of cyberattacks on information and communication systems in the Czech Republic, specifically on information and communication systems of health service providers. The warning stated that the campaign might severely impact information availability, confidentiality, or integrity in health-related information and communication systems. At the same time, NCISA stated that the threat is urgent and may

1406. *See* Vladimíra Těšitelová et al., *Elektronizace zdravotnictví řečí paragrafů,* p. 256 (Ústav zdravotnických informací a statistiky ČR 2021).
1407. *See* s. 2/6 of eHealth Act.
1408. *See* s. 4/a of eHealth Act.
1409. *See* s. 40 of eHealth Act.
1410. *See* s. 12 of Cybersecurity Act.
1411. *See* s. 13 of Cybersecurity Act.
1412. *See* s. 14 of Cybersecurity Act.
1413. *See* warning of NCISA from 16 Apr. 2020, file no. 350-231/2020, available at https://www.nukib.cz/download/uredni_deska/Varovani_NUKIB_2020-04-16.pdf.

materialize within days. Furthermore, it informed that the preparatory phase for the campaign (spear-phishing attacks) was already on the way.

988. NCISA recommended that health service providers alert users about spear-phishing threats and encourage them to come forward if they have recently opened suspicious attachments. Additionally, health service providers were to:

(1) alert users to the possibility of masked executable files in phishing activities;
(2) use the central setting to prevent any active content and macros from running; and
(3) block the remote access to the infrastructure and allow the services to remain open to the public network only when necessary;
(4) Finally, providers were encouraged to create offline backups and check the consistency of the already created backups.

989. The warning remained in effect until 20 May 2020.[1414] NCISA concluded that the acute threat has subsided. At the same time, NCISA stated that the termination of the warning should be in no way interpreted the threat being over.

990. Besides the public measures, NCISA has targeted the health sector with non-binding recommendations prepared in cooperation with the Ministry of Health. Issued on 25 February 2022, the recommendation aimed to address the threats associated with the Russian invasion of Ukraine.[1415] The recommendation focused on two types of threats: (1) the distributed denial of service attacks and (2) the ransomware attacks. Regarding both threats, the recommendation contained specific preventive steps to mitigate the threat and the steps to mitigate the consequences of an ongoing incident.

§3. Energy Sector

991. The energy sector was also subjected to additional sector-specific requirements within the regulatory scope of the Cybersecurity Act. On 30 May 2022, NCISA issued the warning against the threat of deploying technical solutions or software from countries outside of the EU, Organisation for Economic Cooperation and Development (OECD), and NATO Member States. The warning is related to the deployment of smart meters (technologies enabling the direct measurement of consumption).[1416]

1414. *See* termination of warning of NCISA from 20 May 2020, file no. 350-231/2020, available at https://www.nukib.cz/download/uredni_deska/Ukonceni_varovani_NUKIB_2020-05-20.pdf.

1415. *See* NCISA/Ministry of Health, Recommendation to reduce cyber threats associated with the current armed conflict between the Russian Federation and Ukraine from 25 Feb. 2022, available at https://www.nukib.cz/download/aktuality/2022-02-25_doporuceni-poskytovatele-zdravotnich-sluzeb-UkrajinaA.pdf.

1416. *See* warning of NCISA from 30 May 2022, file no. 350-747/2022, available at https://www.nukib.cz/download/uredni_deska/2022-05-30_varovani-smartmetering_final_1.0_podepsno.pdf.

992. The warning aims at the intersection of two groups:

(1) energy companies falling within the regulatory scope of the Cybersecurity Act; and
(2) the companies falling within the scope of the Directive (EU) 2019/944 of the European Parliament and of the Council of 5 June 2019 on common rules for the internal market for electricity.

993. The directive was implemented into Czech law by Act No. 458/2000 Sb., on the business conditions and the exercise of state power in energy sectors ('Energy Act') and required operators of electricity distribution systems to deploy smart metering technology. Since these companies are required to deploy smart metering technology but also fall within the regulatory scope of the Cybersecurity Act, they must include the technology in their cybersecurity policies. Furthermore, smart meters have to be often obtained through the public procurement procedure, and following the procurement, it will be difficult to change the supplier. As a result, the issue was deemed by NCISA to be both time-sensitive and challenging to implement correctly.

994. Overall, NCISA states that the impact of the security incident within the smart metering technology would be more significant than that of the incident within today's technology. Additionally, causing such an incident by the provider of smart metering technology is easier compared to providers of the previous generation of meters. NCISA pointed out three main issues resulting in incidents:

- manipulation with data and delivery of incorrect data to a central system;
- disconnecting specific subscription points from electricity; and
- mass disconnection of thousands of subscription points resulting in instability of electricity distribution and, potentially, a blackout.[1417]

995. The warning contains guidelines for assessing non-technical risks (such as procurement of technology from countries with untrustworthy environments) related to the purchase of specific smart metering technology. NCISA specifically mentions that countries with trustworthy legal environments generally fulfil the following conditions:[1418]

- Their government has been elected democratically. The country has an independent opposition and functioning checks and balances.
- An independent judicial system exists within the country. It is not subjected to direct political interference and observes basic principles (such as the right to a fair trial, a presumption of innocence and others).
- Legal acts and policies issued by the state follow the rule of law principles.
- The government respects intellectual property.

1417. *See* s. 8 of warning of NCISA from 30 May 2022.
1418. *See* s. 14 of warning of NCISA from 30 May 2022.

- There is no long-term or systematic violation of international law. The country is not subjected to official criticism from the Czech Republic or organizations and alliances of which the Czech Republic is a member.
- The country maintains partnerships with the Czech Republic and does not conduct activities in conflict with the vital interests of the Czech Republic or its allies.
- The country does not consider the Czech Republic an enemy state.

996. As a result, these requirements[1419] are mandatory for the energy sector to consider when procuring the technology. As a result, this may lead to potentially discriminating conditions, as companies from states not fulfilling the conditions outlined in the warning may be excluded from public procurement. The exact nature of these warnings, and their impact on the procurement procedure, is still being discussed[1420] and might eventually be subjected to judicial review. However, similarly to the health sector, NCISA's warning introduced sector-specific requirements that companies within the energy sector required to deploy smart meters must comply with.

1419. These requirements can stem either from sector-specific or general warnings. Comp. warning of NCISA from 17 Dec. 2018, file no. 110-536/2018, available at https://nukib.cz/download/uredni_deska/Varovani_NUKIB_2018-122-17.pdf.

1420. *See, e.g.*, Jakub Klodwig, *Varování NÚKIB v systematice zákona o kybernetické bezpečnosti a možnosti jeho zohlednění v zadávacím řízení*, Revue pro právo a technologie, vol. 12, no. 23, pp. 49–75 (2021).

Chapter 4. Liability and Remedies

997. It is a part of fundamental regulatory philosophy of the Cybersecurity Act that it does not aim at sanctioning the perpetrators of cybersecurity incidents, but rather defines duties to controllers and providers of information systems and networks to prevent the emergence of cybersecurity incidents and provide for efficient reactions in cases when some incidents appear. This basic philosophy of the Cybersecurity Act, like the one of the NIS Directive, is to lay down sanctions only for non-compliance with statutory duties regarding security measures or administrative orders (*see* Chapter 2).

998. When the Cybersecurity Act was adopted, administrative fines were set at maximum CZK 100.000 (approx. EUR 4,000). That was rather symbolic considering that most of regulated subjects were either public bodies or large private establishments in essential sectors like energy, utilities etc. The purpose for initially setting fines that low was mostly to declare that the primary concern of the Act was to positively motivate regulated subjects to develop and deploy security measures upon performance-based statutory requirements. As the Czech Cybersecurity Act was rather a pioneering piece of legislation (*see* Chapter 1), it was not even the initial intention of the NBU and later the NCISA to impose fines in cases of non-compliance with relatively new type of legal obligations that neither regulated subjects nor respective authorities had any experience with.

999. Currently, fines for regulated subjects are laid down in section 25 of the Cybersecurity Act and they amount to maximum 5 million CZK (approx. EUR 200.000) for serious conducts, maximum 1 million CZK (approx. EUR 40.000) for less serious breaches of legal obligations and maximum CZK 10.000 (approx. EUR 400) for administrative omissions. In addition, the Cybersecurity Act defines a fine of up to CZK 50.000 (approx. EUR 2000) for employees of state for breaching secrecy obligations regarding incident reports (*see* Chapter 2).

1000. Sanctioning perpetrators who cause cybersecurity incidents is thus a matter of general criminal law liability and of institutional activity of law enforcement institutions, namely the Police and the Public Prosecution. Civil law remedies also fall entirely outside the scope of the Cybersecurity Act and are considered mostly upon general liability rules of the Civil Code and of the Labour Code in cases of liability of employees.

Part VI. Cybercrime

Chapter 1. Application of International and Regional Agreements

1001. The Czech Criminal Code contains neither a separate heading, nor a separate article regarding 'cybercrime'. However, the Criminal Code that has been adopted in 2009 sought to ensure that a new socially harmful phenomena associated with the development of modern technology (such as cybercrime or crimes committed via the Internet) would be addressed adequately.

1002. Its manifestations can also be found in the sphere of protection against cybercrime, where obligations to criminalize acts listed in Articles 2–10 of the Convention on Cybercrime[1421] were taken into account. At the same time, obligations to criminalize acts according to EU Council Framework Decision 2005/222/JHA of 24 February 2005, on attacks against information systems, were implemented.

1003. The Criminal Code matches the Directive 2013/40/EU of the European Parliament and of the Council of 12 August 2013 on attacks against information systems and replacing Council Framework Decision 2005/222/JHA, which was also acknowledged by the report of European Commission,[1422] which did not bring up any substantial remarks towards the Czech Republic. The liability of artificial persons for the above-mentioned criminal activities has been introduced by the Act. No. 418/2011 Sb. (it came into force 1 January 2012).

1004. The Czech Republic signed and ratified also the Additional Protocol to the Convention on Cybercrime (Strasbourg, 2003).[1423]

1005. International treaties on cybercrime and EU law have had only a limited impact on criminal procedure. In this context, the Criminal Procedure Code has only been amended by a provision on data freezing (in 2018).

1421. The Convention was signed (9 Feb. 2005) and ratified (22 Aug. 2013) by the Czech Republic.

1422. Report from the Commission to the European Parliament and the Council assessing the extent to which the Member States have taken the necessary measures in order to comply with Directive 2013/40/EU on attacks against information systems and replacing Council Framework Decision 2005/222/JHA; COM(2017) 474 of 13 Sep. 2017.

1423. The Additional Protocol was signed (17 May 2013) and ratified (7 Aug. 2014) by the Czech Republic.

1006. In the following chapters it will be shown how the obligations of the Cybercrime Convention have been transposed into the provisions of criminal codes.

1007. The Czech Republic, or its predecessor, the Czech and Slovak Federal Republic, signed and ratified both major Conventions concerning legal assistance in criminal matters and most of[1424] their additional protocols. These include, particularly, the following documents:

1008. European Convention on Extradition, opened for signature in Paris on 13 December 1957 (CETS No.: 024); the Czech and Slovak Federal Republic signed the Convention on 13 February 1992, ratified it on 15 April 1992 and it entered into force for the Czech Republic on 1 January 1993.

1009. Additional Protocol to the European Convention on Extradition opened for signature in Strasbourg on 15 October 1975 (CETS No. 086); the Czech Republic signed the Protocol on 18 December 1995, ratified it on 19 November 1996 and it entered into force for the Czech Republic on 17 February 1997.

1010. Second Additional Protocol to the European Convention on Extradition opened for signature in Strasbourg on 17 March 1978 (CETS No. 098); the Czech Republic signed the Protocol on 18 December 1995, ratified it on 19 November 1996 and it entered into force for the Czech Republic on 17 February 1997.

1011. Third Additional Protocol to European Convention on Extradition, opened for ratifying in Strasbourg on 10th of November 2010 (ETS č. 209); The Czech Republic signed the Convention on 4th of April 2012, ratified it on 17th of January 2013, and it became effective for the Czech Republic on 1st of May 2013.

1012. European Convention on Mutual Assistance in Criminal Matters opened for signature in Strasbourg on 20 March 1959 (CETS No. 030); the Czech and Slovak Federal Republic signed the Convention on 13 February 1992, ratified it on 15 April 1992 and it entered into force for the Czech Republic on 1 January 1993.

1013. Additional Protocol to the European Convention on Mutual Assistance in Criminal Matters opened for signature in Strasbourg on 17 March 1978 (CETS No. 099); the Czech and Slovak Federal Republic signed the Protocol on 18 December 1995, ratified it on 19 November 1996 and it entered into force for the Czech Republic on 17 February 1997.

1014. In matters not regulated by international conventions, regardless of whether these are the universal ones mentioned above or bilateral or multilateral agreements, the provisions of the Act No. 104/2013 Sb., on international judicial

1424. The Czech Republic did not yet sign the Fourth Additional Protocol to European Convention on, opened for signatures in Vienna on 20th of Sep. 2012 (ETS č. 212).

cooperation in criminal matters apply subsequently. Section 3/2 reads as follows: 'The provisions of this act shall apply only if an international agreement does not stipulate otherwise.'

1015. If legal relationships between the Czech Republic and another country are not regulated by an international agreement, the prosecuting bodies should accommodate a request made by a foreign State, but only if reciprocity is ensured, that is, if the State submitting such a request gives a guarantee that it will accommodate a similar request from an authority in the Czech Republic in future (section 4).

1016. Besides international agreements, framework decisions of the Council of the EU have been implemented in the Act on international judicial cooperation in criminal matters, particularly Council Framework Decision 2002/584/JHA on the European Arrest Warrant (sections 190 et seq. of the Act on International Judicial Cooperation in Criminal Matters), Council Framework Decision 2003/577/JHA on the execution in the EU of orders freezing property or evidence and many others.

Chapter 2. Specific Computer Crimes

§1. Introduction

1017. It should be noted that the Criminal Code left the former material concept of crime. The former Czech criminal law defined a crime as an act dangerous to society, the characteristics of which are listed in the Criminal Code. It was also stipulated that an act of a negligible degree of danger to society does not constitute a crime – even though it might encompass the characteristics of a crime.

1018. After broad debate regarding the new Criminal Code, there have been explicitly implemented two relative new general concepts, that is, the formal general definition of a crime followed by material corrective (as a replacement of the former material definition of a crime) and the principle of the use of criminal sanctions only as *ultima ratio*.

1019. According to section 12/2 of the Criminal Code, criminal liability and criminal consequences associated with it may only apply in such socially harmful cases where it will not be enough to apply liability under any other legislation. Recent experience shows that the practice tends to use the principle of *ultima ratio* of criminal sanctions (subsidiarity of criminal repression) quite in the same way as the earlier material corrective.

1020. In many cases, there will be the possibility of liability under other laws, particularly under the Civil Code, as well the provisions on liability for damages or liability for infringement of personal rights. Criminal liability will, therefore, take place only in cases where there is an act so socially harmful that the application of civil liability (or responsibility for the administrative offence) is not sufficient.

1021. The Criminal Code provides protection to the confidentiality, integrity and availability of computer data and systems, mainly in the provisions of section 182 (breach of mail secrets), section 183 (breach of confidentiality of documents and other privately kept documents), section 230 (unauthorized access to a computer system and unauthorized interference with a computer system or data carrier), section 231 (procurement and holding of an access device and a computer system password and other similar data) and section 232 (tampering with a computer system or data carrier by negligence). The vast majority of offences against confidentiality, integrity and availability of computer data and computer systems fall within Chapter V (Property Crimes). The so-called interception of data is governed by section 182 and section 183 among offences against protection of personal rights, privacy and mail secrets. An unauthorized disposal of personal data is punished under section 180.

1022. The term 'computer system' is defined in section 136a as a device or group of interconnected or interrelated devices, one or more of which performs automatic data processing on the basis of a program. Computer system also means data stored, processed, retrieved or transmitted by that device or group of devices for the purpose of its or their operation, use, protection and maintenance.

1023. According to the Czech Criminal Code, not only completed crimes are held punishable. The offender's act imminently directed towards achievement of a crime can be criminalized under the Criminal Code section 21 as the attempt of a crime, even though the crime itself was not completed. An attempt is punishable in the same way as a crime itself. Intentional conduct which is directed towards completion of a crime, but not imminently, may be inflicted under section 20 of the Criminal Code as a preparation for a crime. However, preparation is only punishable when directed towards commissions of particularly serious crimes, that is, where the Criminal Code expressly provides. Thus, none of the computer-related crimes listed in this chapter are punishable in the stage of preparation.

1024. Besides perpetrators and accomplices of a crime, an organizer, instigator or helper is liable as well.[1425] For the criminalization of participation, it is required that the perpetrator of the crime has at least attempted committing the crime. If so, then participation shall be basically criminalized in the same way as committing.

1025. It should also be mentioned in the preface that for every crime in the special part of the Criminal Code, a sentence of imprisonment is given as a universal punishment. However, alongside or instead of imprisonment, other types of punishment can also be imposed regardless of the fact whether they are explicitly mentioned for the particular offence or not. It is sufficient that the conditions as set out in the general article of the Criminal Code are met. Such punishments include house arrest, community service, expulsions and so forth.[1426]

1026. All crimes are prosecuted ex officio which means that there is no private prosecution or enforcement. Prosecution of an offender violating the confidentiality of documents and documents held in private according to section 183 is possible only with the consent of the victim, provided that the offender is a person closely related to the victim (*see* section 163 of Code of Criminal Procedure).

§2. Unlawful Access and Illegal Interception

I. Unlawful Access

1027. From 1 January 2010, mere unauthorized access to a computer system or its parts has become punishable.[1427] The requirement for violation thereof, though, is that the perpetrator has overcome safety measures. The basic physical elements mentioned in section 230/1 neither provide for the element of intention to cause damage, other detriment or to acquire benefit, nor does it require that such effects

1425. *See* s. 24 of the Criminal Code.
1426. *See* ss 52 et seq.
1427. *See* s. 230 of the Criminal Code.

occur. The intention to cause damage or other detriment or to acquire an unjust enrichment for oneself or another person is an especially aggravating circumstance under section 230/3, and to bring about such effects is an especially aggravating circumstance under section 230/4. The specificity of unauthorized access lies in the fact that it can be an objective in itself. The reason for this might be a hacker's desire to prove he/she is smarter than others – and the desire to overcome security measures designed specifically to avoid intrusion. Still, his/her conduct mostly pursues a different objective and breaking into a system is merely the preparation to commit another serious attack (e.g., data corruption) or it is directly included in it. From the criminal and political point of view, it is highly questionable whether every unauthorized access should be considered as a crime itself, or if criminalization should rather be limited only to access enabling the perpetrator to commit a crime or an access which is directly part of the crime. The second issue is whether the degree of computer system security, into which the offender has penetrated, should have an impact on criminalization, for it often happens that the computer system is not secured at all or the security system is very simple.

1028. A hacking with the intention to cause a serious harm, although in some cases only in the form of crime preparation, should be considered as a separate prematurely accomplished crime. Social harm is determined here by a variety of circumstances. It is necessary to consider the method of performing the act, as the offender when undermining the privacy of users often uses his/her specific knowledge or specific uncommon tools and resources which he/she needs to obtain. On the other hand, a breakage into an unsecured system where the perpetrator does not need to overcome any safety measures is to be treated differently. In that respect, it is possible to apply the analogy of unauthorized intrusion into another person's dwelling that is to be found in foreign literature.

1029. Although in the last case mentioned it is domiciliary freedom that is protected (i.e., the inviolability of the home), inviolability of the home is meant, primarily, to protect the privacy of the people who live in it. The same goes for penetration into a computer system, for the user's privacy is violated in the very same way. In a computer, there is information stored of a private and often of very intimate content. It can be objected that a victim acted recklessly by not sufficiently securing the access to his/her computer system, still, the fact remains that a person entering a system without the user's consent violates his/her privacy. After all, it is of a particular significance what the user's computer is like, for example, whether it is a personal or a business one. Also, the way of how the offence was committed matters, that is, whether it was a computer freely accessible at work as well as turned on – or whether the offender used a computer network to access it. Finally, the principle of '*ultima ratio*' cannot be omitted. Criminalizing, therefore, starts only when the offender has accessed a computer system unlawfully by overcoming a security measure (e.g., passwords).

1030. A security measure is such a measure that is aimed at preventing free access to a computer system or media (e.g., password or firewall application). The level and extension of the security does not matter. It is sufficient that the offender must overcome some technical obstacles. The mere existence of a security system clearly indicates that the user does not wish anyone unauthorized to enter the system, yet there must be an offender's enhanced effort to access it.

1031. Access means conduct enabling the offender to dispose freely of a computer system or its components as well as to use its informational content. The access must be unauthorized. An authorized access is not a crime in itself even if overcoming the security measures is in the above sense.

II. Illegal Interception

1032. The Criminal Code distinguishes between transmitted computed data[1428] and stored computer data.[1429] Moreover, there is a special distinction for information kept in private.[1430] Under section 182/1, the offence of breach of mail secrets is committed (among others) by any person who knowingly compromises the secret nature of:

(1) a data, text, voice, sound or picture message, which is sent via an electronic communications network and can be matched with an identified participant or user accepting such message; or
(2) non-public transmission of data into a computer system, from it or within it, including electromagnetic emissions from the computer system transmitting such data.

1033. It should be noted that in letter (c) of the same article, secret non-public transmission of computer data is protected as well. What is important is the nature of the transmission rather than the nature of the information. Transmission ought to be of a non-public nature of the transfer, and it does not really matter whether the transmitted information is private or public. Eavesdropping of the information is prosecutable, be it from the computer system, to or within it. Even the capture of a computer systems' electromagnetic emissions is considered a crime, as information can be reconstructed from them.

1034. In the same way, by a term of imprisonment up to two years or prohibition of undertaking the activity is punishable, when anyone with the intention to cause damage or other detriment to another or to acquire unjust enrichment for himself or for another person:

- discloses a secret, which the perpetrator gathered from a document, telegram, telephone call or by means of a network of electronic communications not addressed to him/her;
- or makes use of such a secret.

1428. *See* s. 182 of the Criminal Code.
1429. *Ibid.*, ss 183 & 230.
1430. *Ibid.*, s. 183.

1035. A stricter punishment (a term of imprisonment from one up to five years, a monetary penalty or a prohibition of undertaking the activity) can be imposed on an employee of a postal services operator, telecommunications or computer systems operator, or anyone else engaged in communications, even if they amend or suppress a report made by non-public transmission or other similar means of computer data.

1036. Provided that computer data has already been received and stored in private, an unauthorized violation of its confidentiality committed by publishing it, making it available to third parties or using it in any other way constitutes a crime punishable in accordance with section 183 as a violation of secret documents and other documents held in private. For committing this crime, a term of one-year imprisonment, prohibition from undertaking activity or forfeiture of a thing can be imposed. In cases of completing some particularly aggravating circumstances such as a large extent of damage, a stricter punishment is set (imprisonment for two to eight years).

§3. Data Interference and System Interference

1037. The provisions of section 230 are constructed in a complex way. While the first paragraph affects unauthorized access to computer systems, the second paragraph goes on to cover cases of unauthorized interference with data storage media or computer systems. Other paragraphs (3–5) contain particularly aggravating circumstances applying to both.

1038. According to section 230/2, the offence of unauthorized access to a computer system and unauthorized interference with a computer system or data carrier is committed by a person, who interferes with a computer system or a data carrier by:

- illegally uses data stored in the computer system or on the data carrier;
- illegally deletes or otherwise destroys, damages, alters, suppresses, deteriorates the quality of, or makes inapplicable, the data stored in the computer system;
- forges or modifies data stored in the computer system or on the data carrier so that they are deemed authentic, or that they are acted upon as if they were authentic, regardless of whether they are directly readable and intelligible data; or
- illegally inputs or transfer data into the computer system or on the data carrier, or otherwise interferes with the software or hardware of the computer or other data processing device.

1039. The objective elements of a crime are met when an offender interfere with a computer system or data carrier by at least one of the following ways listed alternatively under the letters (a)–(d). The merit referred to in section 230/2 neither includes the sign of deliberately caused damage, another detriment or acquisition of unjust enrichment, nor does it require such an effect to occur. Access to a computer system or data carrier might be acquired in an unauthorized as well as in an authorized way. The offence does not require access as such, intervention is sufficient.

1040. For the interference malicious software (the so-called malware) is widely used. These programs, however, require installation on the target computer. It is possible to install it either directly to a specific computer provided that the offender has at least a moment to access the computer system, or various fraudulent practices are used in order to make the user install the program himself. Both these ways of committing are covered by the above cited provision.

1041. The merit contained in the letter (a) includes a conduct which might be described as an e-espionage, whereas the merit in letter (b) goes for e-sabotage. The letter (c) relates to computer-related forgery.

1042. The Criminal Code exceeds the obligations following from international treaties and EU law, and criminalizes some kinds of negligent interferences with data or computer equipment (other technical devices for data processing). This is provided for in section 232 (tampering with a computer system or data carrier by negligence). The provision concerns persons, whose duties are connected with their employment, profession, position, or office or duties imposed by law or assumed by a contract. A person violates his/her duties if he/she:

(a) destroys, damages, alters or makes inapplicable data stored in a computer system or on a data carrier; or
(b) interferes with the hardware or software of a computer or other technical device for data processing and, thus, causes considerable damage to the property of another.

1043. Criminalization of negligent fault is disputable in this case. On one hand, immense damage can result from improper manipulation with a computer; on the other hand, it is possible to bring about relatively serious damage by one click of a mouse. Consequently, the legislature limited criminal liability to cases of gross negligence (where the perpetrator's approach to the requirement of due care proves his/her apparent recklessness as regards interests protected by criminal law – section 16/2_ and when causing considerable damage (at least CZK 1.000,000). The punishment imposed in such a case is not especially high, that is, a term of imprisonment of up to six months, prohibition from undertaking activity or forfeiture of a thing. When having caused damage to a large extent, a term of imprisonment of up to two years, prohibition from undertaking activity or forfeiture of a thing may be imposed.

§4. Misuse of Devices

1044. The crime under section 231 (procurement and holding of an access device and a computer system password and other similar data) reflects the international obligation issuing from the Convention on Cybercrime (section 6).

Otherwise, the conduct described as physical elements would not be punishable, since it would constitute just the preparatory stage of a crime, which can only be punished in cases of extremely serious offences.

1045. It is punitive if a person produces, distributes, imports, exports, smuggles, offers, procures, sells or otherwise makes available, provides for himself/herself or another person or possesses any of these devices:

(a) a device or its part, procedure, tool or any other means, including a computer program, designed or adapted to enable (1) unauthorized access to a network of electronic communications, or to a computer system or its part, or (2) unauthorized interference with a computer system or data carrier;
(b) a computer password, access code, data, procedure or any other similar means by which it is possible to acquire access to a computer system or its parts.

1046. For an act to be punishable, it is required that there be the intention to commit an offence of breach of mail secrets under section 182/1/b & c, or an offence of unauthorized access to a computer system and unauthorized interference with a computer system or a data carrier under section 230/1 & 2. If the perpetrator produces, distributes, holds and so forth such devices because of a different intention – punishability from the act does not arise.

1047. In this way, non-punishable cases are distinguished when someone acquires or retains access to facilities for other purposes (e.g., an expert witness for the purpose of expert activity, a security expert to test the security of computer systems, another person for a legitimate purpose) or when he/she acquires such access without a particular purpose.

1048. A person committing this offence can be punished by a term of imprisonment of up to two years, forfeiture of a thing or prohibition to undertake activity. A stricter punishment will be imposed upon an individual provided that he/she commits the offence as a member of an organized group, or acquires considerable benefit for himself/herself or for another person by such act (sentence to a term of imprisonment for up to three years, prohibition from undertaking activity or forfeiture of a thing). Yet stricter punishment (a term of imprisonment from six months up to five years) will be imposed on a perpetrator, who acquires unjust enrichment for himself/herself or for another person.

§5. Computer-Related Forgery

1049. Conduct often referred to as computer-related forgery is hidden in the provision of section 230. According to paragraph 2 letter (c) of this provision, the crime of unauthorized access to a computer system and unauthorized interference with a computer system or data carrier is committed by a person, who interferes with a computer system or to a data carrier and forges or modifies data stored in that computer system or on a data carrier so that they are deemed authentic, or that they are acted upon as if they were authentic, regardless of whether they are directly readable and intelligible data.

1050. Genuineness (authenticity) might relate to the data's author or to the data content, that is, the accuracy. Falsification of data relating to the author might be considered when a perpetrator conceals his/her identity by an identity of someone else. As an example of the change of data regarding the authenticity of the content, a case of judicial practice[1431] might be brought forward. There, the offender encroached on a database information system from a computer located in a computer lab, and he changed the point value of the admission tests results dropping the amount of achieved points below the level required for admission in four cases – and rising the points to a level necessary to secure admission in one case.

§6. Computer-Related Fraud

1051. The Convention on Cybercrime in its Article 8 determines a computer-related fraud as a perpetrator's conduct committed intentionally and without right, causing a loss of property to another person by:

(a) any input, alteration, deletion or suppression of computer data;
(b) any interference with the functioning of a computer system;
(c) with the fraudulent or dishonest intent of acquiring an unjust enrichment for himself/herself or for another person.

1052. The Czech Republic has implemented the requirements of the Convention in somewhat problematic way.

1053. As listed above, the Convention requires (in simple terms) the punishment for intentional damages to a property (damages), by inserting, uploading, changing, deleting or suppressing the original computer data, or (alternatively) and interference with the proper function of the computer system,[1432] with the fraudulent/malicious intent to acquire monetary gain for self or other person.

1054. Opposing is the crime listed under section 230 of the Czech Criminal Code, punishing the unlawful acquisition of an access itself.[1433] More severe punishment is then given for unlawful interference with the computer data.[1434] And even more severe punishment is imposed, if such unlawful access (under paragraph

1431. *See* District Court's in Ostrava Judgment Ref. No. 111/2005 of 74 T 27 5, 2005.
1432. Highlighting here that the interference with the proper function it viewed upon more as a means of committing a crime.
1433. *See* s. 230/1 of the Criminal Code.
1434. *See* s. 230/2/a-d of the Criminal Code, except other inserting, uploading, tampering with, or suppressing, but also other ways – *see* the very casuistic factual basis.

1), or interference with the data (under paragraph 2) accompanied by an intent to (a) cause harm or damages to other person or to acquire an unlawful gain for self or other person,[1435] or (alternatively) (b) unlawfully restrict the operation and function of a computer system or other technical instrument for data processing.[1436]

1055. The difference lies therefore, that unlike the Convention, the Czech Criminal Code does not require the damages to happen (an intent to cause such damage is enough, causing of a larger damage is then punished even more grievously), and that this intent is punished since the qualified factual basis (i.e., it is not a part of the basic factual basis). The other difference can be noted at restriction the operation or function of the computer system. While the Convention includes such restriction or interference as a means of committing a crime, the Czech Criminal Code considers a crime, in the frame of a qualified factual basis, the intent to restrict the operation of the computer system.

1056. Another troublesome aspect can lie in the lone basis of the crime mentioned. The Convention calls it Computer Fraud, while the fraudulent behaviour is seen especially in the fraudulent or malicious intent to acquire some gain. In the context of the Czech law the 'fraud' is connected especially in misleading someone, exploiting someone else's mistake, or obscuring certain facts.

1057. Even with these differences, it can be in our best opinion concluded, that the requirements of the Convention for criminalization of behaviour listed in its Article 8, was, in the end, fulfilled by the Czech legislature.

1435. *See* s. 230/3/a of the Criminal Code.
1436. *See* s. 230/3/b of the Criminal Code.

Chapter 3. Traditional Crimes in a Digital Context

§1. General Introduction

1058. The Criminal Code 2009 brought a number of changes which should make it easier to prosecute some traditional crimes committed by means of a computer system or computer network. These changes have resulted partly from the needs of practice as well as partly from international obligations. At this point, it is appropriate to mention the complex provision of section 230, which, in section 230/2/c, acknowledges the obligation to criminalize certain acts under Article 7 of the Convention (computer-related forgery), as well as section 230/3/a, which reflects Article 8 of the Convention on Cybercrime (computer-related fraud).

1059. The general rules defining crimes and their circumstances have also been amended by a new specific aggravating circumstance relating to the use of ICT, that is, that the crime was committed by a publicly available computer network. It was disputed whether sending an e-mail with harmful content (e.g., child pornography) is to be regarded as disseminating it through publicly accessible computer networks. After a few different decisions of the Supreme Court, the Supreme Court adopted a unifying opinion.[1437] According to this opinion, sending pornographic materials by e-mail to the e-mail mailboxes accessible through a password could not be regarded as dissemination through a 'publicly accessible computer network'. In the case of sending pornographic materials to multiple e-mail addresses, it depends whether the effect of this form of dissemination (namely with regards to the number of recipients) is comparable to committing the crime by other public means like press, film, radio, television or publicly accessible computer networks. If so it fulfils the conditions for the application of another aggravating circumstance consisting in 'other similarly effective manner'. As it was already ruled by the Czech criminal courts, the sending of pornographic materials to 163 recipients fulfils this condition and so the aggravating circumstance consisting in 'other similarly effective manner' applies.

1060. As far as content-related offences are concerned, dissemination and possession of child pornography is held liable in the Criminal Code. Similar to many other countries, it is also questionable in the Czech Republic whether the spreading of or even a simple holding of so-called virtual child pornography is punishable. The acts of a racist and of a xenophobic nature committed through computer systems might be classified among content-related offences as well.

1061. Protection of copyright is provided by the provisions of section 270 (infringements of copyright, related rights and database rights).

1437. *See* the Judgement of the Supreme Court of 30 Jan. 2013, Case No. Tpjn 300/2012.

1062. Misrepresentation acts as an element of some criminal offences. For instance, the crime of fraud is committed by a perpetrator who by misrepresentation, by taking advantage of someone's mistake or by hiding substantial facts enriches himself/herself or another person to the detriment of the property of another and, thus, causes not insignificant damage (not less than CZK 10,000). Therefore, a question has arisen that whether a computer can be subject to misrepresentation – as only people can be mistaken and not technical devices. To remove all doubts, Article 120 determines:

> It is possible to misrepresent or to take advantage of someone's mistake by means of interfering with datastored in a computer system or on an information carrier, interfering with software or hardware of a computer system or by performing another computer operation, interference with electronic or other technical device, including interference with objects designed for controlling such devices, or by means of making use of such operation or such interference performed by another person.

1063. In other words, technical devices are just a means of how to make use of a mistake or cause a mistake by a natural person. If, however, the processing is completely automatic, such as in cases of Internet banking, no natural person can be misrepresented through the technical device and section 209 (fraud) is inapplicable. The provision regulating the possibility to misrepresent a computer was taken from the previous Criminal Code, having just a minor change in wording.

1064. The current Criminal Code took the provision defining a thing for the purposes of criminal law from the previous Criminal Code, putting it into its provision of section 134. It originally came from the Civil Code of 1964 that defined a thing in a relatively narrow manner. The concept of a thing did not include money on a bank account or securities. That would mean, that Criminal Code provisions where a thing was the element could not have been applied (such as the crime of theft or concealment of a thing of another). If a perpetrator managed to acquire monies in an account of another person by some way other than misrepresentation or making use of a mistake, such act could not be qualified as fraud, or as theft or concealment of a thing. The original wording of section 134 of the new Criminal Code reacted by expanding the definition of a thing for the purposes of the criminal law, when it stated, that provisions regarding things also cover money on a bank account and securities. In addition, former conception of a thing also broadened the physical elements of some crimes, where it was appropriate, so that the target of an attack can be, besides a thing, another proprietary value.[1438] Since 1 January 2014, the new Civil Code is effective (statute No. 89/2012 Sb.). In its provision of section 489, a thing is listed much broader, as everything that is different from a person and serves the needs of people. The expanding interpretation of a thing in the Criminal Code

1438. For example, the crime of embezzlement under s. 206 of the Criminal Code, participation under ss 214, 215, legalization of proceeds of crime under s. 216 of the Criminal Code. Even these provisions had omitted the reference to other proprietary value as a reaction on the new Civil Code, bringing wide concept of a thing.

regarding money on a bank account is therefore not necessary and was omitted from the provision of section 134. It is also not necessary to make difference between a thing and other proprietary value.

1065. Besides the above-mentioned, we can cite other provisions. Under section 234 of the Criminal Code (unlawful acquiring, counterfeiting and altering means of payment), a person who, for himself/herself or for another person and without approval of the lawful holder, procures, makes available, accepts or possesses means of payment of another, namely non-transferable cash cards identifiable by name or number, electronic money, a balance order, travellers' checks or a check guarantee card, will be punishable. It is obvious from the citation that the conditions for criminal liability have been significantly extended in comparison to section 249/b of the previous Criminal Code, which applied only to unlawful procurement of a non-transferable cash card of another, identifiable by name or number, or a thing capable to perform its function. We can highlight that the law will punish not only possession of non-transferable cash cards identifiable by name or number, but also of other means of payment. Electronic money, such as the PayPal system, is expressly mentioned. Under section 4 of Act No. 370/2017 Sb., Payment System Act, electronic money is defined as a financial value, which:

(1) represents a claim against the issuer;
(2) is stored electronically;
(3) is issued against the acceptance of financial means for the purpose of money transactions; and
(4) is accepted by persons other than their issuer.

1066. The term 'publicly', which constitutes a statutory element of some offences, now expressly includes a publicly accessible computer network (section 117). The fact that an offence was committed by means of a publicly accessible computer network represents a circumstance justifying a higher severity of sentence in a number of offences.

§2. Content-Related Offences

1067. Dissemination of illegal content can be qualified as a number of criminal offences. Unlike in cases of attacks against confidentiality, integrity and accessibility of computer data and systems, the focus here is on the content of information, or the message itself. Society needs to protect itself against certain types of content, or rather to protect certain groups of people against it. There is a conflict between freedom of expression and the freedom to impart information guaranteed by Article 17 of the Charter[1439] on one hand, and other fundamental rights and freedoms or justified interests of society on the other hand. However, none of these rights are absolute. It is, therefore, necessary to apply the principle of proportionality so that none

1439. *See* Art. 19 of the International Covenant on Civil and Political Rights, Art. 10 of the Convention for the Protection of Human Rights and Fundamental Freedoms.

of these rights is unjustifiably preferred to another. This conclusion can be found in judicial decisions of the Constitutional Court of the Czech Republic.[1440] The Constitutional Court's findings are based on the premise that there are content limits on the freedom of expression consisting in the rights of others 'regardless whether such rights arise as constitutionally guaranteed rights from the Constitutional Order of the Republic or from other obstructions given by law and protecting interests or values of the society as a whole'. The right to express one's opinions can be deprived of constitutional protection not only because of these content limits, 'as also the form in which opinions are expressed outwardly is closely connected to the constitutionally guaranteed right to which it attaches. If a published opinion exceeds the rules of decent conduct generally recognized in a democratic society, it loses the character of a correct judgment (report, commentary) and, as such, it is usually outside the scope of constitutional protection'.[1441] It is obvious from the citation that society protects itself against information:

(1) which encroaches upon individual rights of other persons; or
(2) which is contrary to the interests and values of society as a whole.

1068. At present, the dissemination of pornography, racial hatred and extremism on the Internet are considered to be the most serious problems. This is why we attend to them specifically at this time.

I. Dissemination of Pornography

1069. In the Czech Republic, dissemination of some types of pornography has been traditionally prosecuted. The current Criminal Code, similarly to the previous one, distinguishes three types of pornography:

(a) so-called hard pornography (pornographic production depicting or otherwise exhibiting sexual intercourse with an animal, or depicting violence or disrespect for a person);
(b) so-called child pornography (pornographic production depicting or otherwise making use of a child);
(c) so-called simple pornography (other pornographic productions).

1070. The offence of dissemination of pornography[1442] applies not only to the dissemination of so-called hard pornography, but also to the dissemination of so-called simple pornography. Simple pornography is subject to punishment only in two cases, that is, when it becomes (or can become) available to children. In the case

1440. *Compare*, for instance, the Judgments of the Constitutional Court, Cases No. IV. ÚS 154/97, II. ÚS 357/96, II. ÚS 94/05.
1441. *See* the Judgment of the Constitutional Court of 10 Jul. 1997, Case No. III ÚS 359/96.
1442. *See* s. 191 of the Criminal Code.

of simple pornography, the law punishes: (a) offering, surrendering or making pornography available to a child; or (b) exhibiting or making pornography otherwise available in places which are open to children. The term child is defined as a person under 18 years of age.[1443]

1071. Under section 192 (production and other disposition of child pornography), not only dissemination of child pornography is punishable, but also its possession and it is furthermore punishable even when access to child pornography is acquired through information or communication technology. The provision of section 192 reads as follows:

(1) A person who possesses a pornographic product in the form of photographs, films, electronic or other form, depicting or making other use of a child or a person, who appears to be a child, shall be punished by a sentence of imprisonment up to two years.
(2) A person, who acquires access to child pornography through information of communication technology will be punished equally.
(3) A person who produces, imports, exports, smuggles, offers, makes available to the public, procures, distributes, sells or provides in any other way a pornographic product in the form of photographs, films, electronic or other form, depicting or making other use of a child or a person, who appears to be a child, or a person who profits from such pornographic product, shall be punished by a term of imprisonment from six months up to three years, prohibition from undertaking activity or forfeiture of a thing.

1072. The amendment of Criminal Code (Act No. 141/2014 Sb.) added two more crimes: participation on a pornographic performance, in which a child is included[1444] and establishing prohibited contacts with a child.[1445] According to section 193b punished will be a person, who will propose meeting to a child younger than 15 years of age with the intention to commit a crime according to section 187/1 (sexual abuse), section 192 (manufacturing and other dealing with child pornography), section 193 (abusing to child to manufacture pornography), section 202/3 (seduction towards sexual intercourse) or other sexually motivated crime, will be punished by imprisonment for up to two years.

1073. The Criminal Code does not provide a definition of a pornographic product or child pornographic product. Certain criteria were created by theory and judicial decisions. Pornography can be described as a product which obtrusively arouses a sexual urge; the prevailing opinion is that it exceeds the generally recognized limits of decent sexual behaviour, and unacceptably offends the sense of decent sexual behaviour. Thus, the test of the pornographic nature of a product consists in evaluation of whether the overall impression from it causes moral indignation in a reasonably sensitive person. Child pornography can be defined as a pornographic

1443. *See* s. 126 of the Criminal Code.
1444. *See* s. 193a of the Criminal Code.
1445. *See* s. 193b of the Criminal Code.

product depicting or making other use of a child. Pornography depicting a child can be, for instance, snaps of naked children exposing genitals in provocative positions for sexual satisfaction, snaps of children showing the positions of actual or pretended sexual intercourse with them or other similar sexually arousing pictures of children. If the pictures do not fit this description, then the conclusion whether the product is of a pornographic nature or not cannot be deduced just from the fact that such pictures are made available with the aim to satisfy people suffering from a sexual deviation (i.e., persons who are sexually attracted to minors), by means which such people utilize.[1446]

1074. Several problems are being discussed within the context of punishability of child pornography possession. First, what is meant by 'possession'? We can assume that possession means any type of holding of child pornography. The length of duration of possession is immaterial. The offender need not hold child pornography directly (in a bag, in a desk, at home, at the place of work, in a computer); rather, it suffices to have control over it (e.g., it is stored in an e-mail box placed on a server of an Internet provider). Another problem concerns so-called virtual child pornography, which is a pornographic material that was not created by child abuse (such as literary works, drawings or animated cartoons). The vast majority of experts[1447] inclined to believe that, unlike dissemination of virtual child pornography, its holding is not punishable. The Act No. 330/2011 Sb. that amended section 192/1 & 2 of the Criminal Code then added words 'or person who appears to be a child' to existing word 'child'. This opened the way to punish the production, distribution and so forth of a pornographic piece that shows also a person older than 18 years or even a non-existing child (i.e., an artificially created picture) if the shown figure appears to be a child.

1075. Since the production of child pornography does not necessarily imply child abuse (e.g., copying of an existing piece of work is production), lawmakers prosecute independently the abuse of a child for the production of pornography.[1448]

II. Racist and Xenophobic Expression

1076. The Czech Republic, rather consistently prosecuting racist and xenophobic expression, is an epitome of the European doctrine of active intolerance. The Czech Constitutional Court confirmed this position in 1992, when it decided that:

(a) movements provably aimed at the suppression of civil rights or preaching of a defined hatred, regardless of their name or the ideal or goal underlying their existence, are movements which endanger the democratic State, its security and

1446. *See* Act No. 35/2005 Sb., Collection of Criminal Decisions.
1447. *See* Jiří Herczeg, *Virtuální dětská pornografie: Zločin bez oběti?*, in *Pocta Otovi Novotnému k 80. narozeninám*, 42 (Marie Vanduchová & Tomáš Gřivna ed., Wolters Kluwer, 2008).
1448. *See* s. 193 of the Criminal Code.

the security of its citizens; therefore, their statutory prohibition is an indispensable measure to limit the freedom of expression and freedom of assembly according to section 17/4 and section 20/3 of the charter of Fundamental Rights and Freedoms;

(b) criminal prohibition of the support and promotion of certain ideologies which, both by their doctrine and practical steps, have excluded the dissemination of other ideologies, helps to enhance the plurality of views, ideologies, political and other movements and actual possibility of their dissemination; such restriction protects not only human rights, but also democratic foundations of the State.[1449]

1077. There are several offences specified in the Criminal Code, which protect society against extremist expression. They are, namely, the following crimes: violence against a group of persons and against an individual,[1450] dangerous threatening,[1451] defamation of nation, race, ethnic or other group,[1452] inciting hatred against a group of persons or restriction of their rights and freedoms,[1453] establishing, supporting and promoting movements aimed at the suppression of rights and freedoms of persons,[1454] expressing sympathy with movements aimed at the suppression of rights and freedoms of persons,[1455] and denying, challenging, approving or justifying genocide.[1456] In several crimes,[1457] the circumstance conditioning the imposition of a harsher punishment is the commission of an offence by the means of a publicly accessible computer network. Prosecuting this type of crime appears to be a very serious problem in practice under sections 403–405, if offences are committed via the Internet.

1078. Racist and other hate speeches are most frequently published on the websites of servers of Internet providers in the United States where it is virtually impossible to discover who the website operator is. Requests for legal assistance are regularly turned down by the United States on the grounds that such activity does not constitute a crime there, since the First Amendment to the Constitution guarantees the freedom of expression.[1458]

1449. *See* the Judgment of the Constitutional Court of the Czech and Slovak Federative Republic (CSFR) of 4 Sep. 1992, Case No. Pl. ÚS 5/92, *Sb. nál. a usnesení ÚS ČSFR 1992 [Collection of Findings and Resolutions of the Constitutional Court of the CSFR]*, 25.
1450. *See* s. 352 of the Criminal Code.
1451. *Ibid.*, s. 353.
1452. *Ibid.*, s. 355.
1453. *Ibid.*, s. 356.
1454. *Ibid.*, s. 403.
1455. *Ibid.*, s. 404.
1456. *Ibid.*, s. 405.
1457. *Ibid.*, ss 355, 356 & 403.
1458. Compare Jiří Herczeg, *Trestné činy z nenávisti*, pp. 90 et seq. (Wolters Kluwer, 2007). *See also* Jan Hart, *Svoboda projevu v USA a v Evropě* (Právní rozhledy, 2002).

§3. Offences Related to Infringements of Copyright and Related Rights

1079. The Criminal Code provides for the infringement of copyright in section 270, as did the previous code in section 152. Section 270/1 reads as follows:

> A person who unlawfully and not insignificantly interferes with the legally protected copyright, rights in artistic performance, sound or sound-picture recording, radio or television broadcasting or database, shall be punished by a term of imprisonment up to two years, prohibition from undertaking activity or forfeiture of a thing.

1080. Criminal protection is very wide-ranging and it is not limited to infringements in the commercial environment or to infringements committed through computer systems. Only insignificant infringements of copyright are not covered. Thus, Czech legislation exceeds the requirements laid down by the Convention on Cybercrime. The provision of section 270/1 of the Criminal Code is the rule with a blanket disposition referring to the regulation of copyright and related rights. The basic regulation of copyright law is provided in Act No. 121/2000 Sb., *on Copyright, Related Rights and on changes in some other acts (Copyright Act)*. This statutory enactment conforms to the Paris Act of 24 July 1971, which amended the Berne Convention for the Protection of Literary and Artistic Works, the International Convention for the Protection of Performers, Producers of Phonograms and Broadcasting Organizations made in Rome on 26 October 1961, and the Agreement on Trade-Related Aspects of IP Rights concluded within the framework of the World Trade Organization Agreements. It also conforms to other WIPO treaties, made at the diplomatic conference in 1996, which are generally designated as Internet treaties. These are, namely, the WIPO Copyright Treaty and the WIPO Performances and Phonograms Treaty. Finally, it also incorporates the relevant legislation of the EC.

1081. When considering the condition that the interference in the aforementioned legally protected rights must not be negligible, it is necessary to consider the circumstances of the individual case, especially the intensity of such an intervention, the way of how the act was committed, its consequences, especially in the form and severity of the interference in the personal and property rights of respective individuals and in case of repeated intervention or intervention of a longer duration, and also the number of such cases, the duration of the violation of the particular protected right and so forth. Additionally, the personality of the offender, the degree of his/her culpability, his/her motives and so forth are of a particular importance, including the fact whether it is the perpetrator's first disruption of the such legally protected rights or it is a recurrence. Slight interference could be considered as sporadic or marginally significant interference with a protected right such as, for example, sporadic provision of free copies of film pieces or provision of a computer game to a friend without permission of the copyright and associated right holders, taking into consideration the circumstances of the particular case.

1082. The Supreme Court of the Czech Republic has dealt with a case of a minor, who using a hosting service, placed links in space reserved for his website that allowed access to illegal copies of television and movie artwork on external servers. The Supreme Court ruled, that as unauthorized breach into rights protected by law as in section 270/1 of Criminal Code can also be considered such conduct of the perpetrator, who places embedded links in space reserved for his website, that allowed access to illegal copies of artwork (e.g., television and movies) on external servers in such a way, that anyone can access these through this Internet site, even though he does not have the consent of the rightful owners of such artwork. In this case, by placing the embedded link, the perpetrator enabled access to a copy of an artwork, being a person different from owner of the copy, or other authorized person. Such an activity must be considered a breach of author rights to individual artworks, and breach of the rights to relaying the artwork towards the public as in section 18/1 & 2 Author Code.[1459]

1083. In different case, the Supreme Court commented on the matter of determining the damages in case of a perpetrator, who, through the Internet, without the consent of rightful bearers of the author rights, inserted 372 audiovisual artworks or video recordings, and copies of 33 musical artworks on two public file-hosting servers, knowing that these artworks are protected by author rights, and that he wasn't given consent to spread these artworks by the rightful owner. The Supreme Court commented, that the damages caused to the rightful owners of these artworks has the nature of loss of profits. Determining its amount will depend on the amount that its rightful owner would receive, if they had legally made accessible, in a comparable way and to the same extent copies of the artwork in the given time. The amount of damages cannot be derived from the usual cost of legally sold medium (e.g., CD or DVD) with copy of such a piece of artwork in common distribution network.[1460]

1459. *See* Decision No. 7/2014 of Collection of Judicial Decisions and Opinions, Criminal Section.
1460. *See* Decision No. 39/2015 of Collection of Judicial Decisions and Opinions, Criminal Section.

Chapter 4. Criminal Procedural Aspects

§1. Introduction

1084. Considering the positive development of substantive criminal material law on one hand, it seems that the criminal procedural law is lagging behind. In the Czech Republic, the Code of Criminal Procedure of 1961 is still in force. It has already been amended more than one hundred times and even the Constitutional Court has in numerous cases quashed some of its provisions. The Act No. 141/1961 Sb., *Code of Criminal Procedure, as amended*, with a few exceptions, lacks provisions concerning specific computer data. For this reason, the existing institutes of the Code of Criminal Procedure are being utilized, for example, the duty to surrender an item,[1461] seizure of an item,[1462] seizure, opening and tracking of consignments,[1463] monitoring and recording of telecommunications operations,[1464] surveillance of persons and items.[1465] These, however, are not always suitable with regard to the specifics of computer data.

§2. Search and Seizure of Stored Computer Data

1085. The Czech Code of Criminal Procedure does not include, with one exception, any special provision specifically concerning computer data. This is clearly due to the fact that criminal law experts do not devote great attention to these problems. Some aspects are regulated under Act No. 127/2005 Sb., on Electronic Communications ('Electronic Communications Act'). However, the Code of Criminal Procedure (Act No. 141/1961 Sb.) itself lacks provisions concerning specific computer data. For this reason, the existing institutes of the Code of Criminal Procedure are being utilized, for example, the duty to surrender an item,[1466] seizure of an item,[1467] seizure, opening and tracking of consignments,[1468] monitoring and recording of telecommunications operations,[1469] surveillance of persons and items,[1470] which are, however, not always suitable with regard to the specifics of computer data. The only exception is the data freeze order according to Article 7b (amendment to the Code of Criminal Procedure implemented by Act No. 287/2018 Sb., coming into force 1 February 2019). The order may be made by the President of the Senate in the judicial phase of the proceedings and, in pre-trial proceedings, by a public prosecutor or a police authority. According to Article 7b, where it is necessary to prevent the loss, destruction or alteration of data relevant to criminal proceedings which are

1461. *See* s. 78 of the Code of the Criminal Procedure.
1462. *Ibid.*, s. 79.
1463. *Ibid.*, ss 86–87c.
1464. *Ibid.*, s. 88 and 88a.
1465. *Ibid.*, s. 158d.
1466. *See* s. 78 of the Code of the Criminal Procedure.
1467. *Ibid.*, s. 79.
1468. *Ibid.*, ss 86–87c.
1469. *Ibid.*, s. 88–88a.
1470. *Ibid.*, s. 158d.

stored in a computer system or on an information medium, the person who holds or has under his or her control the data may be ordered to preserve such data in an unaltered form for a period of time specified in the order and to take the necessary measures to prevent disclosure of the fact that the data have been ordered to be preserved. Where necessary to prevent the continuation or repetition of criminal activity, a person who holds or has under his control data which is stored in a computer system or on a medium may be ordered to prevent other persons from accessing such data. The provisions of section 97/3 of the Electronic Communications Act stipulate that a legal or natural person, which is a public network operator or a provider of public electronic communications services, is obligated to retain for the period of six months operating and localization data and is also obligated, upon request, to provide such data to the authorities competent to request them according to a special law. This special law consists, particularly, in the Code of Criminal Procedure (mainly section 88a). However, this also includes Act No. 154/1994 Sb., on the Security Intelligence Service (section 8a), Act No. 289/2005 Sb., on Military Intelligence (section 9), Act. No. 273/2008 Sb., on the Police of the Czech Republic (section 66), Act. No. 137/2001 Sb., on the special protection of witness and other persons in connection with criminal proceedings (section 10a), Act. No. 15/1998 Sb., on the supervision of the capital market (section 8). Pursuant to section 97/5 of the Electronic Communications Act, a legal or natural person that is a public telephone operator is obligated, at the expense of the applicant, to provide the Police of the Czech Republic, upon request, with information from the database of all users of its public telephone network services in the form and to the extent as stipulated under the implementing regulation.

1086. The Code of Criminal Procedure regulates security acts under Title Four, Part One[1471] and also in some other provisions.[1472] The provisions on the obligation to surrender an item[1473] and seizure of an item[1474] can be used to acquire media or a computer system with computer data. Pursuant to section 78, any person who is in possession of an item that can serve for evidence purposes is obligated to submit it to the court, public prosecutor or police authority at their request; if it is necessary to secure such an item for clarification of matters significant for criminal proceedings, he/she is obligated to surrender it to these authorities upon request. If an item that can serve for evidence purposes is not surrendered upon request, it may be seized from the person that has it in his/her possession, based on an order by the presiding judge and, in preliminary proceedings, on an order by the public prosecutor or police authority. A police authority requires the consent of the public prosecutor to issue such an order. The police may issue such an order without the prior consent of the public prosecutor only in a case where it is not possible to obtain such prior consent – and the matter is urgent. Opinions exist in literature and practice that, after printing on a printer, an e-mail message must be treated as a consignment within the meaning of section 87c of the Code of Criminal Procedure. According to

1471. *See* ss 67–118 of the Code of Criminal Procedure.
1472. *Ibid.*, ss 158 et seq.
1473. *Ibid.*, s. 78.
1474. *Ibid.*, s. 79.

other opinions,[1475] such a message is an item that is important for criminal proceedings and, as such, can be requested or seized pursuant to sections 78 and 79 of the Code of Criminal Procedure. The provisions of sections 86–87c of the Code of Criminal Procedure on seizure and opening of consignments, their exchange and monitoring relate to transported consignments and undelivered consignments in transit.

1087. Items that can serve for evidence purposes (computer systems and media) may be secured within the framework of a house search,[1476] which may be ordered only by the presiding judge and, in preliminary proceedings, by a judge on the application of a public prosecutor.

1088. To reveal the contents of an e-mail account, the provision of Article 158d of the Code of Criminal Procedure is used, falling under the institute of surveillance of persons and things. Such practice is endorsed by the Supreme Public Prosecutor's Office in its official viewpoint.[1477]

§3. Interception

1089. It is necessary to differentiate between current telecommunications operations[1478] and completed telecommunications operations.[1479] Pursuant to section 88 of the Code of Criminal Procedure, the presiding judge and, in preliminary proceedings, a judge on application of a public prosecutor may order the monitoring and recording of telecommunications operations, provided that the criminal proceedings are concerned with an intentional crime, on which the Criminal Code infers a penalty of imprisonment with the upper limit of the penalty of imprisonment of at least eight years, or when criminal proceedings are conducted for a crime expressly listed, no matter the penalty for such crime, or other intentional crime, which must be prosecuted under an international agreement and where it can be reasonably assumed that they will yield significant facts for criminal proceedings. Amendment of 2008[1480] introduced into the Code a special type of proceeding, that is, a proceeding for reviewing an order for eavesdropping and recording of telecommunications.[1481] This was a response to the eavesdropping of politicians, journalists and others. The prosecutor who orders the end of the investigation or the presiding judge in the proceedings before the Court of First Instance after the final end of a case have a duty to inform the person about the ordered eavesdropping and recording of the telecommunication. At the request of the person concerned, the

1475. *See* Pavel Šámal et al., *Trestní řád. Komentář. I. díl*, 6th Issue, 727 (C.H. Beck, 2008).
1476. *See* ss 82, 83, 85 et seq. of the Code of Criminal Procedure.
1477. *See* Official Viewpoint No. 1/2015 of the Collection of Interpretation Viewpoints of the Supreme State Prosecutor's Office.
1478. *See* s. 88 of the Code of Criminal Procedure.
1479. *Ibid.*, s. 158d (content data), 88a (location and process data).
1480. *See* Act No. 177/2008 Sb.
1481. *See* ss 314l–314n of the Code of Criminal Procedure.

Supreme Court of the Czech Republic (NS) will review the legality of the order in a closed session. In its resolution, it will then express whether or not the law was violated.

1090. Where it is necessary to ascertain data of a completed telecommunications operation[1482] that is the subject of telecommunications secrecy or is subject to the protection of personal and mediation data, the presiding judge and, in preliminary proceedings, a judge on the application of a public prosecutor, may order legal or natural persons that are telecommunications operators to provide such data, either to this judge or, in preliminary proceedings, to the public prosecutor or police authority. Pursuant to section 88a of the Code of Criminal Procedure, the presiding judge and, in preliminary proceedings, a judge on application of a public prosecutor may order to provide such data only if the criminal proceedings are concerned with a crime for which the maximum limit of punishment is at least three years or it is one of the crimes explicitly listed in the section 88a or some other intentional crime, which must be prosecuted under an international agreement and where it can be reasonably assumed that they will yield significant facts for the criminal proceedings. An order is not required, if the user of the telecommunications facility to which the data is assumed to relate gives his/her consent to the provision of such data about the realized telecommunications operations. In this way, it is possible to obtain so-called operating and localization data.

1091. Recently, the issue of monitoring has become highly topical. An amendment to the Code of Criminal Procedure has introduced, among other things, proceedings on subsequent review of an order for monitoring and recording of telecommunications operations by the NS. In connection with monitoring, the monitoring of Internet telephony is also being discussed. Peer-to-peer networks appear to pose a problem in this respect (e.g., calls using Skype).[1483]

1092. It is not without importance that user information may be requested by the prosecuting bodies pursuant to section 8 of the Code of Criminal Procedure (cooperation of governmental authorities, natural and artificial persons), according to which governmental authorities, legal and natural persons are obligated to accommodate requests of prosecuting bodies made in the course of fulfilment of their tasks without any undue delay and, unless stipulated otherwise by a special law, also without consideration. The duty to accommodate requests may be refused with reference to the duty to observe secrecy of confidential information protected under a special law or to a confidentiality duty imposed or acknowledged by the State. According to the Code of Criminal Procedure, a confidentiality duty acknowledged by the State should not be a duty whose scope is not defined by a law, but rather results from a legal act performed under a law. If the conditions, under which information that is kept confidential pursuant to a special law may be divulged for the

1482. *See* ss 158d or 88a of the Code of Criminal Procedure.

1483. *See* Petr Klement, *Možnosti odposlechu tzv. Internetové telefonie*, 37–44, (Státní zastupitelství 2008).

purposes of criminal proceedings, are not defined by this law, this information may be requested for criminal proceedings after prior consent of a judge.

§4. Electronic Evidence

1093. Identically as in the previous point, it can be stated, as a preliminary remark, that the Czech Code of Criminal Procedure does not include any special provision on receipt of evidence that would specifically concern computer data. Expert opinions, witness testimonies, substantive and documentary evidence are mainly used in practice. Expert opinions, especially, have substantial weight in court litigations. Experts, who are appointed by the Ministry of Justice of the Czech Republic, enjoy substantial authority and must act independently and impartially in proceedings. Apart from them, expert institutions also exist, among which the Criminal Institute has an eminently unique status. Mostly, it is just the experts who confirm the authenticity, integrity of secured data and its treatment. Experts also express their opinions on whether seized data has not been illegally tampered with. However, it is necessary to emphasize that, already during the securing of data in preliminary proceedings, the prosecuting bodies must act in a manner that will not raise any uncertainty about the way in which the data was obtained, how it was stored and whether it has been interfered with. For this reason, all acts are usually documented. It is common that the expert has already participated in these early stages of the proceedings. However, there are no rules stipulated by law. For this reason, it is necessary, in each individual case, mainly on the basis of a plea raised by the defendant's counsel, to examine the procedural applicability of secured evidence. The absence of legal rules is not considered a problem either by the professional public or in practice.

1094. Unlike the legislature, the Czech legal theory deals with the electronic evidence and its specifics.[1484] Electronical evidence is usually defined as 'means of evidence, whose transition into a form comprehensible to a human requires some electronic device'. Their sources include computers, data storages, computer networks or clouds. Specifics of such means of evidence can, in practice, present advantages and disadvantages. The experts point out the possible existence of technical obstructions in presenting the electronic evidence (presented namely by poor technical equipment of the courts) and the necessity of an assistance of an expert (e.g., when a source code is an evidence). On the other hand, the advantage of such evidence can be for example, the possibility of making unlimited copies of them. Widely discussed is also the issue of acquiring data from i-cloud storage spaces.[1485] We assume, that the specifics of electronic means of evidence will require some reaction in the legislature.

1484. *See,* e.g., Radim Polčák, František Púry & Jakub Harašta. *Elektronické důkazy v trestním řízení,* 83–114 (Masarykova univerzita 2015).

1485. *See, e.g.*, Jaroslav Karmášek & Lenka Suchánková, *Domovní prohlídka v cloudovém úložišti – otázka rozsahu situací, v nichž mají orgány činné v trestním řízení povinnost použít postup podle § 85b trestního řádu, in Bulletin advokacie* 11, p. 39 (2014); *see also* Vladimír Smejkal. *Ochrana dat advokátů v elektronických úložištích, in Bulletin advokacie* 3, p. 15 (2015).

Selected Bibliography

Books

Josef Donát, Martin Maisner, Robert Piffl, Nařízení eIDAS: Komentář (C.H. Beck 2017).

Jiří Herczeg, Trestné činy z nenávisti (Wolters Kluver, 2007).

Roman Horáček, Karel Čada & Petr Hajn, Práva k průmyslovému vlastnictví (C.H.Beck 3rd ed. 2017).

Helena Chaloupková, Petr Holý & Jiří Urbánek, Mediální právo. Komentář (C. H. Beck 1st ed. 2019).

Vojtěch Chloupek & Kateřina Hartvichová et al., Patentový zákon. Komentář (C.H.Beck 2016).

Komentář (C. H. Beck 2021).

Zuzana Chudomelová et. al., Zákon o elektronických komunikacích. Komentář (Wolters Kluwer ČR 2016).

Pavel Koukal et al., Zákon o ochranných známkách: Komentář (Wolters Kluwer 2017).

Tereza Kyselovská, Pavel Koukal, Mezinárodní právo soukromé a právo duševního vlastnictví – kolizní otázky (Masarykova univerzita, 2019).

Petr Lavický et al., Občanský zákoník: komentář. I, Obecná část (§ 303-654) (C.H. Beck, 2022).

Matěj Myška, Výjimky a omezení autorského práva v prostředí digitálních sítí (Wolters Kluwer ČR 2020).

Radim Polčák et al., Autorský zákon (Leges 2020).

Radim Polčák et al., Právo informačních technologií (Wolters Kluwer ČR 2018).

Radim Polčák, František Púry & Jakub Harašta, Elektronické důkazy v trestním rˇízení (Masarykova univerzita 2015).

Radim Polčák, Jakub Harašta & Václav Stupka, Právní problémy kybernetické bezpečnosti (Masarykova univerzita 2016).

Helena Pullmannová, Ochrana obchodního jména a její projevy ve známkoprávní reformě EU (Leges 2019).

Aleš Rozehnal, Zákon o provozování rozhlasového a televizního vysílání Komentář (Wolters Kluwer ČR, 2008).

Naděžda Rozehnalová, Instituty českého mezinárodního práva soukromého (Wolters Kluwer 2017).

Naděžda Rozehnalová, Jiří Valdhans, Klára Drličková, Tereza Kyselovská, Úvod do mezinárodního práva soukromého (Wolters Kluwer 2017).

Selected Bibliography

Karel Svoboda, Petr Smolík, Jiří Levý & Jiří Doležílek et al., Občanský soudní řád. Komentář (C. H. Beck 2021).
Pavel Šámal et al., Trestní řád. Komentář (C.H. Beck, 2013).
Pavel Šámal et al., Trestní zákoník. Komentář (C.H. Beck, 2012).
Ivo Telec & Pavel Tůma, Autorský Zákon: Komentář (C.H. Beck 2nd ed. 2019).
Vladimíra Těšitelová et al., Elektronizace zdravotnictví řečí paragrafů (Ústav zdravotnických informací a statistiky ČR 2021).
Miroslav Uřičař, Vladan Rámiš et al., Obecné nařízení o ochraně osobních údajů. Komentář (C. H. Beck 2021).
Zdeněk Zajíček, František Korbel, Dalibor Kovář et al., Zákon o právu na digitální služby.

Articles

Dominika Galajdová & Jan Zibner, Nedostatky autorskoprávní ochrany počítačového program, in Právní rozhledy, 22 (2018).
Jaroslav Karmášek & Lenka Suchánková, Domovní prohlídka v cloudovém úložišti – otázka rozsahu situací, v nichž mají orgány činné v trestním řízení povinnost použít postup podle §85b trestního řádu, in Bulletin advokacie 11 (2014).
Jakub Klodwig, Varování NÚKIB v systematice zákona o kybernetické bezpečnosti a možnosti jeho zohlednění v zadávacím řízení, in Revue pro právo a technologie, vol. 12, No. 23 (2021).
František Korbel & Filip Melzer, Písemnost, elektronický a biometrický podpis v elektronickém právním jednání, Bulletin advokacie, n. 12 (2014).
Jan Hart, Svoboda projevu v USA a v Evropě, in Právní rozhledy (2002).
Jiří Herczeg, Virtuální dětská pornografie: Zločin bez oběti?, in Pocta Otovi Novotnému k 80. narozeninám, 42 (2008).
Petr Klement, Možnosti odposlechu tzv. Internetové telefonie, in Státní zastupitelství (2008).
Pavel Loutocký & František Kasl, Potenciál a úskalí identifikačních služeb bankovní identity, Právník, vol. 160(12) (2021).
Pavel Loutocký & Kamil Malinka, Bezpečnost ICT ve vnitřních předpisech a školení zaměstnanců, in Revue pro právo a technologie, vol. 7, No. 14 (2016).
Pavel Mates, Právo na digitální služby, in Revue pro právo a technologie, vol. 11, No. 21 (2020).
Radim Polčák, Elektronické právní jednání – změny, problémy a nové možnosti v zákoně č. 89/2012 Sb, in Bulletin advokacie, n. 10 (2013).
Radim Polčák, Kybernetická bezpečnost jako aktuální fenomén českého práva, in Revue pro právo a technologie, vol. 6, No 11 (2015).
Vladimír Smejkal. Ochrana dat advokátů v elektronických úložištích, in Bulletin advokacie 3 (2015).

Index

The numbers here refer to paragraph numbers.

Index

www.ingramcontent.com/pod-product-compliance
Lightning Source LLC
Chambersburg PA
CBHW071422230926
51846CB00001B/104
* 9 7 8 9 4 0 3 5 0 8 1 7 7 *